Y0-EBL-773

UPROOTING AND AFTER...

Acknowledgments

We express our sincere appreciation to all those who made this book a reality: the authors, the publishers, the translators and the printers. For many of us this undertaking was a valuable and rewarding experience despite the numerous complications and delays caused by correspondence; ideologic, political and professional differences between the undersigned; revisions, and technical difficulties inherent in an intercontinental bookproduction.

In particular we are grateful for the courtesy of the following publishers and editors: Verlag Hans Huber, Bern, Switzerland; International Universities Press, New York, U.S.A.; Mildred K. Kaufmann/Kantor (editor) Clayton, Missouri, U.S.A.; Charles C. Thomas, Springfield, Illinois, U.S.A.; Universitets Forlaget, Norwegian Universities Press, Oslo, Norway; and the World Federation for Mental Health, then Edinburgh, U.K.

We extend our thanks to the following translators: Mrs. Daphne Dorell, Eastbury, U.K.; Dr. Robert Goldsmith, München, BRD; Dr. James Hull, Zürich, Switzerland; and Dr. H. Modinger, Bern, Switzerland.

We are also indebted to Professor Boris Lebedev, M.D., Leningrad, former director of the Mental Health Unit, World Health Organization, Geneva, Switzerland; for valuable advice given, Dr. Ernest Schmatolla M.D. Max-Planck-Institute for Brain research, Frankfurt, BRD, and Professor Erich Wulff M.D., University Hospital Giessen, BRD, for their critical reading of the work on "The nostalgic phenomenon and its exploitation", and to Dr. Nikola Jović and Mrs. Sally Ann Angermeier for their preparation of the author and subject index of this book, and to the Editors-in-Chief of the following journals: The Indian Journal of Psychiatry; Israel Journal of Medical Sciences; Psychopathologie africaine, Dahar, Senegal.

Charles Zwingmann
Maria-Pfister-Ammende

Acknowledgments

The photographs appearing on the book jacket are reprinted by kind permission of the United Nations High Commissioner for Refugees, for photograph No. 5713A-20 "African Refugees on the Move"; of the Swiss Red Cross, for photograph No. 80917 "Tibetan Refugees Leaving their Older Children in a Home in India"; and of the Swiss Red Cross and Jan Boon, Kitzbühel/Den Haag, for the photograph "Tibetans in Flight."

All rights reserved.

No part of this book may be translated or reproduced in any form without written permission from Springer-Verlag.

© 1973 by Springer-Verlag New York Inc.
Library of Congress Catalog Card Number 70-165795.

Printed in the United States of America.

ISBN 0-387-05516-9 Springer-Verlag   New York · Heidelberg · Berlin
ISBN 3-540-05516-9 Springer-Verlag   Berlin · Heidelberg · New York

UPROOTING AND AFTER...

Charles Zwingmann
and
Maria Pfister-Ammende

Springer-Verlag   New York · Heidelberg · Berlin
1973

Preface

The unifying theme in this book is the suffering of millions of people, and the attempts of many others to ameliorate such sufferings. A host of world-renowned medical and social science specialists describe their experiences with people who have been beaten, battered, tortured, displaced and uprooted, but have somehow survived those ordeals.

From these experiences arose new insights into the problems of uprooting, a new appreciation of the concept of "cultural relativism", and a new terrifying glimpse of the limits of "man's inhumanity to man".

The relevance of this book lies in the fact that such ordeals are by no means absent in our world today. In this sense then, the experiences presented and evaluated here serve to bring to focus for us as individuals concerns of all mankind. Through its explicit treatment of diagnoses, prognoses and therapeutic measures the book, however, offers hope, a hope which is much needed in our conflict-torn world of today.

W. F. Angermeier
Professor of Psychology

Heidelberg, 1973

Table of Contents

Preface v
Acknowledgements vii
Uprooting and After .... – General Review 1
    Ch. Zwingmann and M. Pfister-Ammende

Part I Basic Theoretical Construct

The Problem of Uprooting 7
    M. Pfister-Ammende
The Nostalgic Phenomenon and its Exploitation 19
    Ch. Zwingmann

Part II Socio-psychological and Psychiatric Investigations

Psychogenic Disturbances in a Linguistically Strange Environment 51
    R. Allers
Aliens' Paranoid Reaction 60
    F. Kino
Reactions to Evacuation 67
    A. Freud and D. Burlingham
Displaced Soviet Citizens in Switzerland 73
    M. Pfister-Ammende
Human Uprooting 103
    D. Müller-Hegemann
Mental Health Aspects of Voluntary Migration 110
    A. Weinberg
African Workers in France and Problems of Adaptation 121
    S. Diarra
Difficulties of Adjustment in Immigrant Children in Geneva 134
    R. Rodriguez
Nostalgic Behavior – A Study of Foreign Workers in West Germany 142
    Ch. Zwingmann

Part III Epidemiological Research

Emigration and Mental Health 155
   Ø. Ødegaard
Norwegian Emigration, Re-emigration and Internal Migration 161
   Ø. Ødegaard
Concentration Camp Survivors in Norway and Israel 178
   L. Eitinger
Mental Diseases among Refugees in Norway after World War II 193
   L. Eitinger
Migration and the Major Mental Disorders – A Reappraisal 204
   H. B. M. Murphy
The Low Rate of Hospitalization shown by Immigrants to Canada 221
   H. B. M. Murphy

Part IV Readjustment and New Growth

Transitional Communities and Social Reconnection 235
   A. Curle
Mental Hygiene in Refugee Camps 241
   M. Pfister-Ammende
Immigration to Australia – Mental Health Aspects 252
   A. Stoller and J. Krupinski
Migration and Mental Ill-Health in Industry 269
   K. Bhaskaran, R. C. Seth and S. N. Yadav
Mental Health Aspects of Camp Clearance (The Activities of the Mental
   Health Advisor to the U.N. High Commissioner for Refugees
   1959/1960) 282
   H. Strotzka
The Analysis of a Young Concentration Camp Victim 291
   E. Ludowyk Gyomroi
Uprooting and Resettlement as a Sociological Problem 312
   M. Pfister-Ammende

Annex – The Problem of Uprooting 323
   M. Pfister-Ammende

Origin of the Contributions and References 329

Author Index 347

Subject Index 350

UPROOTING AND AFTER...

UPROOTING AND AFTER...

Ch. Zwingmann and M. Pfister-Ammende

General Review

During the first half of the 20th century more than 100 million people of the Northern hemisphere left their homeland or were forcefully separated from it; they migrated, they were displaced or deported, they fled from persecution. The question has been raised whether there should be a distinction between voluntary and involuntary migration since emigration is mostly the result of an involuntary situation, i.e. a conflict. Such a conflict may be caused by external circumstances and pressure or by inner psychological factors resulting from the personality structure of the individual.

The motivations for the move or for the basis of the conflict situation have been classified as follows: *physical*: e.g. war or natural calamities like earthquakes, droughts, famine, floods, climate, etc.; *economic*: e.g. underemployment, low material living standards, absence of social security, move ordered by government (flooding of areas related to dam construction) — industrialization and urbanization, advanced social security benefits; *social*: family trouble, housing and occupational difficulties — future of children, attraction by relatives or friends already moved; *psychological:* personal conflict, escapism, restlessness, difficulties of adjustment to existing society, fear of persecution or war — transcultural interest, sense of adventure; *religious:* religious intolerance — religious freedom; *political*: discrimination, persecution — political ambition; *professional*: e.g. inadequate pay, inadequate research facilities, etc.

The ability to resolve these conflicts by moving depends among other things on the individual's personal stability; his age; the stability of his family life, his material resources and the information available to him at the time of the move; the kind and duration of migratory experience; and the possibilities of resettlement in the new environment for the individual and his family.

Psychiatrists, psychologists and social scientists have attempted to study and record the consequences of migration movements in their demographic, epidemiological, medical and socio-psychological significance. As early as 1921 Kraepelin (Kraepelin, 1921) recognized uprooting as a social-psychological problem when he said:

Particularly questions connected with uprooting are, together with other problems, suitable for giving us prospects on the future development of a science which today we more foreshadow than really know, that is social psychiatry.

Since then social psychiatry has indeed found its shape and place. However, it has also become evident that even this new type of psychiatry can only *contribute* to fighting against the uprooting of human beings. For, a whole range of measures is needed, and they are of a social, economical, psychological and ideological nature.

Later, Malzberg (1936, 1956), Ødegaard (1932) and others concerned themselves with migration and mental disease. The last world war caused the appearance of an increased amount of literature on the subject and some years ago particular attention was paid to the migration of intellectuals — the so-called brain-drain.

Repatriates present a special problem about which there exists little information as yet. Some of them return to their home country because, although they found what they were seeking in the way of better material facilities in the new country, they could not establish satisfactory social, psychological and affective links. Upon returning to their home country, difficulties may arise for the repatriates in connection with their readaptation.

It seems timely to review the literature in order to clarify the issue, and to determine which direction future action and research in this field should take. Such formulations are urgently needed in view of the acute, sometimes even explosive, worldwide processes of displacement and uprooting: numerous European nations face themselves with the task of receiving, and to a certain degree assimilating, hundreds of thousands of foreign workers; the African countries and the People's Republic of China experience large rural-urban migratory movements and transplantation of large sections of the population due to rapid industrialization; Australia and Canada find themselves amidst a significant phase of immigration; Israel is confronted with the assimilation of new immigrants with widely different cultural backgrounds; masses of Arabs were forced to flee from their occupied lands; France, the Netherlands, the United Kingdom and other countries recently had to cope with substantial repatriation problems, the United States are experiencing increased migratory movement; indeed, there are few nations today where population movements do not occur, and there are many regions of the world where they are made to occur. We think here especially of the hundreds of thousands of refugees as a result of aggression in the Middle East and Asia. Whereas this situation in the cases of open aggression as in Palestine and Vietnam is known today, it is much less known that there are regions where enormous numbers of refugees are "produced" by clandestine wars. In Laos alone, some 700,000 people lost their homes because of the terrorist activities of a certain agency; that is one-fourth of the population of that nation! (A.F.S.C. 1971)

This topic is not only of world-wide importance, but fraught with issues of vital political, economic and social concern, since understanding and active sympathy are not too frequently shown to the migrating individual or group by the receiving society. Few countries accept immigrants or foreign workers for humanitarian reasons. Mostly there is a demand that they should help to increase the national wealth and economy and sometimes also the defense potential. Foreign (seasonal) workers especially are often objects of exploitation and little, if anything, is done for their welfare. Although the immigrant is allowed to settle down and establish a home, adjustment may be impossible because of prejudice or bureaucratic measures. In certain areas there exists a paradox between pressure upon the newcomer toward assimilation and his rejection by society if he proves unsuccessful or too successful in it. He may be expected to conform to the host culture but not be allowed to become an integral member of it. Immigrants might then form their own closed group and, thus, become rather hostile, even aggressive minorities.

Uprooting is a phenomenon found among migrants, refugees and members of stable societies. Measures geared to the prevention of its adverse effect on mental health are, as mentioned earlier, of a social, psychological and economic nature. It has become clear over the last twenty years that these measures are the concern of the society as a whole and not only of specialists such as pyschiatrists, social scientists, administrators or others.

Progress in the direction of the practical implication of what has long been scientifically recognized has been very slow. Funds allocated for large-scale research in this area are in no proportion with the enormous scope of the problem.*

This volume includes theoretical works and significant research papers, descriptions of systematized socio-psychological preventive work for migrants and refugees, and of socio-psychiatric rehabilitation and individual psychotherapy. An attempt has been made to provide a certain cohesion in the field which, by its very nature, asks for a multi-disciplinary and transcultural approach. Most of the republished articles were revised.

We did not always agree on the choice of papers to be included (see especially the article of Ludowyk-Gyomroi). This disagreement is due to professional and ideologic differences. Although we attempted to give an international view on the uprooting problem, we were successful only within the limits set by the availability of studies.

We hope that our effort shows the significance of this neglected problem, and this significance is also defined by the gaps.

Geneva, 1972

References: See Page 329

---

*We want to call attention to two on-going research projects. The first is a long-term research project of the World Health Organization (WHO, 1970) on 'Social and mental adaptation of Serer (Senegal) migrants to urban life', on 'Social and physical adaptation of Tokelau Islands migrants to settlements in New Zealand' and one on 'Health effects on urbanization of rural migrants to urban conditions in Iran.' The second is the research-series on 'Personality and Uprooting' carried on by J. C. Brengelmann and D. Revenstorff (1970) at the Max-Planck-Institute for Psychiatric Research in Munich, (Initiated by Ch. Zwingmann and supported by the Werner-Reimers Research Foundation.)

PART I

Basic Theoretical Construct

THE PROBLEM OF UPROOTING

Maria Pfister-Ammende
Switzerland

In 1944 the Swiss Academy of Medical Sciences made a substantial sum available for research into the psychological aspects of the refugee problem in Switzerland. What follows is a summary of some of the findings of this survey for which I was responsible. They are based on the records of psychological interviews of 300 "normal" refugees, 700 case histories of refugees and Swiss repatriates suffering from mental disturbances as well as on socio-psychological observations among about 2000 Soviet-Russian refugees. Regarding the interviews of the 300 "normal" individuals an interview-schedule was designed, in which I was aided by collaborating refugees, physicians and psychologists. It is included in this Volume as an Annex on page 320. This schedule was followed freely by the interviewer according to his own judgment.

The material is grouped under three headings: flight; the refugee camp; and psychopathology of uprootal.

I. Flight

Four situational reactions were found common to persons uprooted from their social milieu and compelled to flee.

1. Fear of the persecutor with subsequent tendency to develop anxiety when the real danger is over, coupled with projection on to neutral persons of the new environment.

2. Hypertrophy of the instinct of self-preservation with deterioration of moral values. The main sphere affected appears to be that of moral behavior based on super-ego control of the drives. The ego-ideal, the 'personal ethos' (Binder, 1951) tends to remain unaffected.

3. Clinging to values that have remained intact or to the lost homeland amounting in some cases to fixation.

4. Overevaluation of the country of asylum or of persons in authority, a projection of savior phantasies which have remained in a mental vacuum without object-cathexis owing to the frustration inherent in expulsion from their own country.

These four flight reactions belong to the group of 'instinct formulas' (Kretschmer, 1947). They are 'semi-reflector processes' in the field of a 'vital main focus' ('vitaler Hauptbrennpunkt', Kretschmer), i.e. that of protection against danger. When life is threatened the reaction is physical; it is mental where total loss of love is involved. Persons reacting in this manner are in a mental borderline state. Their behavior cannot be assessed in terms of the norms of an ordered, intact society.

II. The Refugee Camp

The refugee camps in Switzerland, Germany and Austria gave plenty of scope for first-hand observation. My findings coincide in some respects with those of Vischer (1918) who coined the phrase "barbed-wire illness" for prisoners of war. I was also reminded of the reactive detention psychosis of prisoners of war. Though this does not imply the Ganser's syndrome of nonsense production, but rather corresponds to penitentiary explosions and prison stupor. For this reason "internment psychosis" seemed appropriate to cover the reactions of refugees to internment, this being analogous to the detention psychosis of prisoners of war. The symptoms of this traumatic neurosis are first to be traced to the undeniable fact of internment and secondly to the personality structure of the refugee as revealed in the anamnesis. I define the refugee as a mentally healthy person who, as a consequence of external force, has been deprived of his familiar surroundings and goods and chattels, for which reason the contours of his personality have become blurred, softened-up as it were, and his mental balance unstable. This internment psychosis can be traced at the physiological level to the enormous 'excitation-inhibition conflict' (Pavlov) which varies in accordance with the personality of the individual affected.

There are two phases: First, the aggressive, expressed in restlessness, projections of hate onto persons and objects distorted as negative illusions. This phase is sometimes preceeded by an initial period of depression. Should the aggressiveness not find discharge in explosive reactions, either as a result of restrictive measures or of anxiety against the drives, we encounter regressive avoidance reactions such as mass psychoses of flight or mass anxiety with projection onto related chance contents and persons. In such cases there result in accordance with the individual character and its modes of reaction, anxiety states, drug dependence, psychogenic ideas of persecution, active asociality, psychosomatic illness, deracination neglect and other reactions familiar to the psychiatrist.

The second phase, that of apathy, can be described as a dessication of the ego which is not only tonic immobility but a type of self-destruction. The 'movement storm' (Bewegungssturm-Kretschmer) has given way to a 'breakdown of the nervous system which tends to inhibition' (Ivanow-Smolensky, 1928). Brun (1946) quotes this author's remark on the phenomenon in the animal world: 'Several months of rest and care are often necessary before it is possible to do anything at all with such animals.' With regard to human beings overcome by this condition during internment, it was very difficult indeed to achieve any therapeutic results whatsoever; they form the core of camp inhabitants who have suffered the most serious damage.

III. Psychopathology of Uprootal

1. Firmly rooted individuals

The overwhelming majority of the persons interviewed retained a sense of inner security and appeared to be rooted. They were held by: Natural, tangible *ties to their real, still existing country of origin* and to the relatives that remained there. These people regarded themselves as being away from home only temporarily. Their country was still a living reality, a social area of activity and spiritual shelter. Although the ties to their world had been cut outwardly, they were unimpaired within.

Alsatians, crossing the Swiss border as if for a short visit only, illustrated this point clearly.

Yet not all those geographically separated from home for a time actually possessed roots in their country. Certain individuals had no ties or roots at home (see 2 below). On the other hand there were many refugees whose sole purpose in life was the reality of their home-country — although there was hardly a chance that they would ever return to it. Their roots were there and their country remained a living reality in the spiritual sense and in their memories. Consumed by great nostalgia they were in danger of fixation, like all those suffering from homesickness, a tragedy befalling those who, while clinging to the illusion of return, block their way to a new life in a new country.[1]

A relatedness to a new and again real *home-country* to which ties had already been established in anticipation of a new life in a new society that would be personally rewarding.

To many Zionists, for instance, Israel was a reality, not merely a vague hope. They were secure in the knowledge that they were wanted there by the entire people and by relatives. This was not the case, however, with many returning Swiss; they had literally come home, but their expectations were often disappointed because they were lacking close relationships and on account of cultural differences.

A spiritual bond born of a deep *commitment to an idea of religious, political or humanitarian nature*. Such individuals were able to find a deep meaning even in their present transitory existence; they were sustained by a genuine feeling of commitment; they found sense and meaning *everywhere* by working and living for the realization of their idea. Even camp-life held meaning for them. Rarely a general

[1] See Ch. Zwingmann, THE NOSTALGIC PHENOMENON AND ITS EXPLOITATION, Pp. 19-47.

humanitarian attitude proved a solid basis, particularly among middle-class women who, when confronted with real human suffering for the first time, spontaneously lent a hand, without, however, being motivated by a deep and true sense of human compassion.

A *tie to a coexistent national or ideological group.*

I saw groups of Italians or Russian women who lived a quiet, inwardly sustained life, as long as they received appropriate human assistance. Politically oriented unions of those electing to fight proved equally strong.

They gained strength from a vital comradeship which left no room for loneliness and isolation.

An *intimate relationship with others present,* whether friends or relatives, did not constitute as firm a hold as one would expect because the free flow of affection and the feeling of security in such ties suffered from the mental and emotional strain due to circumstances and the uncertain future.

In spite of the pathogenic situation about ¾ of those interviewed were held by one or several of these stabilizing factors (the Zionist preparing for his return to Israel, the socialist in the "political group"). Why then did other refugees questioned possess no such ties?

In the course of our interrogation I came to differentiate among various types and causes of uprootal. I would like to point out, however, that we are not dealing with the refugee, but only a small fraction of them. As has been described, most of the refugees possessed and maintained a measure of inner stability and security and some of them found new roots.

2. The uprooted

They can be classified as follows:

Isolated individuals from groups in need of leadership. In discussing the possibilities for stability and inner security I mentioned the relationship to an existing national or ideological group, particularly in those individuals who had the chance to live in camps conducted by competent leaders. If the leadership failed, however, because a good leader was replaced by an incapable one, dramatic anxiety and flight psychoses of the entire group occurred. The individual in such a group needs "his world" in the same way as the animals described by Hediger as "Biotop" and "Archetop" (Hediger, 1946). If the emigrant lives alone in hostile or unfamiliar surroundings and without sympathetic relationships, certain reactions occur which are of either a more active or passive type. These two types of reactions are found also in uprooted people who are not dependent on a particular group. The passively reacting individual freezes: either he will become ill and wither away like a wounded animal, or he remains outwardly adjusted to his environment, hiding his total inner upset ("Innere Totalirritation") behind a perfect front. The inner chaos of such people is often masked by a semblance of indifference or amiability – their dreams or a Rorschach-test will reveal their true mental and emotional state. The actively reacting person may show frank antisocial tendencies.

Withdrawn from his social environment through lack of libidinous ties, he lives in a state of irritation, disarray and alienation. It is difficult to establish real contact with these people and to restore their inner calm.

Deeply traumatized individuals, not dependent on a group. There are people who have roots, but whose suffering has been so great that they cannot go on despite good will and great effort. Some keep everything bottled up inside and die in every way except physically.

> I have known Jewish people who wanted very much to embark upon voluntary social work in order to be useful and to get over the past they had been through (it is not the personal blows which are the hardest, but those that felled the children), but they were unable to elicit a response in those whom they wanted to help. They told me that they had stopped dreaming: "I could not bear my dreams, I know what they are about, and what keeps coming back" said one Jewish woman who had lost all her children in a concentration camp.

The very sensitive have considerable difficulty in bearing up to the makeshift existence of typical camp life with its protracted isolation and lack of occupation; the more so if the surroundings are hostile or if the atmosphere in the camp is tense because of incompetent leadership. Such people frequently do not react at all and continue to exist in a state of living death like the isolated individual who is unable to live outside his group. They were not in a state of inner upset but rather in one of silent hopeless surrender. (See also Eitinger, page 175 and Müller-Hegemann, page 101.)

The active types often become embittered, they would like to change but cannot be different. Their reactions, though socially quite unpleasant, are less damaging to themselves than the silent suffering of the passive.

Thus far I have described people who have lost their roots through the force of events, but there were others who have never had roots for psychological reasons. They include those who *identified themselves with their social class or profession* which had come to mean everything to them. They had become identified with it because of a need or inclination: the "Professional Officer," the "Noble Lady," the "Herr Professor," the "Herr Präsident," "My Lady," the Postman, the "Herr Inspektor." For many a middle-class woman in her forties, the man was fighter and protector according to the standards of her class, while the place for a woman's great emotional resources was within the family as wife and mother. Not infrequently this type is unable to change or adjust, not for lacking activity but rather the ability for individual development and the creation of a life of her own. I have seen such women inaudibly break down after loss of home and husband. However they did continue to keep up appearances and the front they presented to the outside world appeared intact. They adjusted and even clung to their given environment, the camp, for instance. Although possessing strong feelings they were passive by nature; the vitality deriving from their environment had vanished and they had succumbed to the forces sweeping away their social milieu;

security and stability were gone along with their social environment. We are here dealing with a pseudo-rootedness ("Pseudoverwurzelung") because identification with and adherence to a social level have nothing in common with real security springing from a maternal soil, or with the vitality of those sustained by a universal idea for the common good. – There is a second variant: the demanding individual. His profound bitterness blinds him to the fact that his present social vacuum brought about by emigration is shared by a great number of people who have never enjoyed financial security. His discontent is not sublimated into a sense of compassion or a desire to be of help; instead regression into aloof embitterment sets in. He seeks the company of those who share his feelings and together they form a league who live in the past forever. His present surroundings may also serve as an outlet for his bitterness. Actual psychological short-comings in these surroundings aggravate his discontent. This may lead to real tragedy if, for instance, the person on whom he projects happens to react differently to the common misfortune. Then disappointment and aggressiveness become rampant magnifying the difficulty of a situation that might otherwise have been bearable. I have seen quite a few married individuals who filled the emptiness of their lives with such aggressions and projections on their partners.

Thus we have observed various forms of rootlessness of old and new origin such as: isolated individuals from groups needing, but lacking leadership; persons with roots but suffering from severe trauma; those identifying with a social or professional class. All these people lost, through the force of events, what they needed most: the feeling of belonging ("Geborgenheit") to the real, concrete world, a world they need because they are of it and live and breathe in it. They need it either because no separation has occured in them between subject and object, i.e. they had, so to speak, been living in a "participation mystique" with their environment, or because they cannot live without a relatedness to and a feeling of "home" derived from the immediate environment.

Drifting individuals and escapists are quite different. These people have been drifting all their lives and have never entered into a genuine relationship. They avoid difficulties, and if they cannot avoid them, they adjust to an extent, outwardly and smoothly, but always without real emotional ties. Some of them live in a world of their own in which they feel themselves well protected and all powerful. Such forms of infantile behavior may be called escapism. These escapists generally get along well in life, also as emigrants. They do not suffer from the lack of true relatedness.

Next I take up certain *psycho-neurotics*. It is well known that the experience of sudden shock can temporarily free a neurotic from his overt conflict and symptoms. However, with prolonged emigration, I have seen neurotics whose libido remained fixed to the old conflict; merely the object of their projections had changed along with their new surroundings. The scene of the drama had changed, but it was still the same drama. – Strikingly few of these people were capable of real sympathetic involvement with the political tragedy. Most of them were unable to sublimate their energies into active dedication to a social cause without prior analytical resolution of their conflicts; despite considerable effort to substitute this necessary process of inner clarification and maturation through community work, this work did not come naturally because they had not been able to free themselves of their neuroses.

Self-centered, exclusively egotistical individuals are found in all walks of life, among vagrants and among the educated. They have been and will remain rootless because in the give-and-take of human relationships they can only take. Although able to enjoy pleasure they cannot give love or accept responsibility. They take and then move on. They keep within the boundaries of respectability. Many build themselves a nest for practical reasons. Loss of social environment through emigration sometimes meant new freedom from old demands and obligations which had become burdensome. Such emigrants tend to look for an easy, convenient job. If they do not find one and are called upon to conform to rules and regulations of a group they rebel and protest fiercely against demands which they consider unjustified.

Problematiker. Certain people do not live "in this world," i.e. within a society. They are forever driven to deep and serious thinking about problematical questions. They keep searching for answers to these questions and if, after great effort, they have succeeded at least to formulate the question more clearly, then they are plunged into new chaos and new urgent questions demanding an answer. These people are rare. Among thousands of refugees, I have found only three. They were not neurotic individuals but genuinely engaged in problematical thinking. Although able to experience and love the other person and human society they are primarily concerned with their inner problem. Social surroundings not infrequently mean shelter from their inner loneliness and restlessness. They are as little rooted in their social environment as they are dedicated to a clear-cut spiritual idea. Rootless individuals of this type also need the world, but in a different way. Their vitality does not spring from an inner relatedness to the world, since they do not give themselves away to it; instead they take what the world offers them. They are not deeply attached to the world as a whole or to any of its individual manifestations. They are not object-directed, nor do they have a binding commitment and unshakable superpersonal hold. They are homeless because they are incapable of close, personal relationships.

Thus we have seen *three different aspects of rootlessness* in adults:
I. Individuals, dependent on their immediate environment, who *become uprooted* through outside forces.
   1. Loss of object by the object-directed.
   2. Loss of the possibility of building his life and of human relationships by the individuated, sensitive person.
II. Loss of identification with and clinging to the previous social level.

The type of reaction in a state of rootlessness depends on the personality of each individual. The sensitive, according to Kretschmer's interpretation, break

down; the active react violently and aggressively.
III. *Being rootless* due to inherited traits or faulty childhood development.
   1. Insufficient development of the ego-ideal, insufficient ability to give of oneself, certain forms of psycho-neurosis.
   2. Pronounced egocentricity, behavior regulated by the pleasure-principle: individuals who take but do not give.
   3. Incomplete formation of an ego-ideal and no inner relationship to the actual environment.

Individuals out of these three groups are rootless regardless of emigration. Some of them chose emigration unconsciously because they preferred this form of life to the demands and obligations of an organized society.

We can *summarize* as follows: Having roots is not a question of an individual's value but rather of his relatedness. There are two aspects of the problem, i.e. an individually psychological and a social one. The first is dependent on mental and emotional development, the latter on the relationship with a social environment. Human beings have roots in their "Heimat" or in a commitment to a spiritual ideal, preferably in both. The family is the intimate sphere of the child, the earth for his roots and protection. This, however, is insufficient for the adult. Home originally means the intimate group in the sense of Hediger's Biotop and Archetop, a truly maternal soil for roots. This can change to 'Heimat' in a larger sense, and frequently this has to take place, since certain forms of society and ideologies are vanishing, or are being destroyed, and instinctively formed groups and entities dissolved by the force of historical events. The human being caught up in these events is confronted with the necessity of changing and growing new roots elsewhere.

The emigrant is a special example of such general development. Absence from home, legally and psychologically, as well as legal statelessness are not identical with psychological uprootal. Most emigrants do not lose their roots because they are sustained by ideological ties, or because they find new relationships and occupations which — together with a degree of security — permit economic and psychological restoration and "transplantation" to a new environment. If the individual is unable to change his way of living and outlook on life, however, for reasons partly described, then he is away from a "home" in the sense of Biotop and living ideal. His inner balance is seriously threatened and he is in danger of becoming rootless.

A person who cannot develop an inner relationship either to a biotop as 'Heimat' or to an ideal, is completely uprooted.

Having roots is not the same as being adjusted. On the contrary: a good adjustment may conceal a lack of roots. Good adjustment can serve as a protective front towards the world outside and conceal the lack of inner relatedness.

The age at which people emigrate is important. The young and those in certain life-periods of change tolerate emigration better and strike roots in a new environment more rapidly. In states of mental stagnation emigration can in fact lead to an inner transformation and a reaffirmation of life. The second half of life is the more delicate because at this time a certain repose and security are needed for inner development and rounding off. In old age the capacity for responding to new impressions is restricted. With the loss of his milieu the old person often loses the ability to establish contact with a new environment. If abruptly bereft of his homeland, his place in the family and of his world rich in memories of the past, he often creates the impression of having suffered an organic brain lesion as a consequence of the mental shock of the trauma of uprooting. The stock of his memories is so negative that they can no longer be rendered dynamic. This condition can lead to stuporous depressions characterized by a peculiar void, a mental metamorphosis which has led to the emptying of the entire psychic apparatus ('Seelengefüge').

Thus we have followed many people on their journey through life: There were group-dependent individuals and those who − though no longer engaged in a "participation mystique" in the world − felt at home in it; others again, firmly rooted in the universal, regarded this world as a place for loving dedication and responsible activity. We have accompanied them on the most painful part of their journey through life. How many must travel this road can hardly be guessed. The driving force within us is always the same, whether finding expression in outer destiny or inner spiritual experience, or in both; the yearning for home and tranquility so that we may fulfill our destiny in peace and security and take our place as loving and active participants in the course of this world.

Conclusions

Refugee and country of asylum. My investigations lead to certain conclusions regarding refugee care through government. A responsible refugee policy, in addition to providing food and shelter, takes measures that will prevent additional traumata and assist the refugee in overcoming the injuries sustained. Concretely this means:

− Help in the return to the homeland or resettlement in a new country for a fresh start in life. Retraining, if indicated.

− A generous settlement policy, based on a positive attitude towards the refugee. Necessary administrative measures must make allowances for the special mental condition of the refugee; unnecessary directives that may impress him as senseless red-tape chicanery should be avoided. The question of strict confinement in each case must be carefully examined.

− Work which is reasonably acceptable to the refugee. However, the social conditions of the country of asylum may be such that this postulate remains illusory.

− The possibility to live in an atmosphere of intimacy, to cultivate contacts and to continue hitherto existing ties. Billeting refugees in prisons or forced labor-camps for an indeterminate time or separating families over periods of years is against humanitarian and mental health principles.

− Establishment of a tolerable camp atmosphere, if refugees have to be gathered in camps. Since this problem has been discussed by me in detail elsewhere[2] in this volume, I confine myself to one essential point only: A humanitarian refugee policy avoids a police-like approach on the part of the authorities and does not tolerate incompetent camp-leaders. In the care of a great number of people a smoothly functioning organizational and administrative apparatus is a fundamental requirement. Any temporary and improvised task, such as the care of refugees, will meet with difficulties due to lack of experienced and trained personnel. It is not enough, however, to overcome administrative difficulties. Satisfactory accomplishment of the task requires also a sufficient knowledge of the refugee's psychological make-up, his personal and social needs, and an awareness of the psychological stress inherent in his present situation.

Fundamental Comments. Is it possible to draw certain general conclusions from our material applicable to the inner and environmental situation of man? I am aware of the difficulties of such an attempt because we are dealing here with individuals in very particular circumstances with regard to their reasons for emigration, their situation in Switzerland and their prospects for the future. Therefore we cannot speak of "man" or "the refugee", but must evaluate the reactions we have recorded in relation to time and environment. Bearing this in mind I shall now attempt to arrive at certain conclusions.

We have seen two basic factors in the life of the individual: the growing of his inner self toward maturity and the acceptance of certain environmental factors.

The inner development. It is of vital importance that the individual develops a capacity for love and a sense of responsibility for his life and actions. This includes responsibility towards the super-personal, dedication to another human being, and a binding commitment to society. The latter should transcend nationality and become a kind of consciousness of humanity ("Menschheitsbewusstsein"), sustained, if possible, by a close relationship to a smaller group. This sense of fellowship with humanity at large imparts a conscious desire to give, i.e. a sense of responsibility as well as a feeling of belonging, thus enabling the person also to receive. The result is a deep feeling of security and protection in the human community. Historical development, present day patterns of society, and the present state of technological development, urgently call for an all-embracing social conscience. Very many have not yet succeeded in merging inner maturity with a feeling of social relatedness, a discrepancy which constitutes a basic cause for the alienation of many people in our time. Alone and isolated they stand vis-a-vis to the outer world instead of *living with it* in a mutual give-and-take. Although there is an urgent drive in many towards inner maturation and self-knowledge, the contact with the larger world outside has been lost. Like the group-linked in his group, the individuated personality can be firmly rooted, provided the sense of unity of all men is alive within him; if so, this will unite him with his fellow human beings everywhere, in contrast to those group-linked who can live within their group only.

---

[2] M. Pfister-Ammende, MENTAL HYGIENE IN REFUGEE CAMPS, p. 24

He who is wrapped up in his own self, as a unique problem and task worthy of his concentrated attention, forfeits the bonds of reciprocal human and social commitment. To him who is firmly united with common humanity the world and society become a source of sustaining strength and obligation. This does, of course, not preclude the necessity of developing the inner self whereby the individual learns to give and take within the confines of a close personal relationship. For the individuated personality mere group membership and instinctive ties suffice no longer; there is no way back; he must be or become a conscious and *active member* of the human community. He is neither bound to his environment by the ties of group membership, rendering him vitally dependent on it, nor does he exist in isolation against the world; he is *I and We at the same time.* That means that he is rooted in his world through a feeling of confidence and unity with it.

Environmental factors. The development of the inner self, however, is not everything. One cannot even speak of it without considering certain indispensable offerings from the environment, as follows:

The opportunity for establishing a personal sphere. By that I mean that the individual must have a chance to create and cultivate his own intimate circle for eros and sexual expression. There are the privacy of one's "own four walls," the family, the "little things" which, objectively small, represent emotional values of importance. If this chance to create "Heimat" in the sense of an intimate personal sphere is given, a feeling of belonging and contentment can develop.

Work, if possible, of free choice. In this respect conclusions concerning fundamental human needs should be drawn from my material only with caution. The exceptional circumstances of the refugee in Switzerland must be regarded as an important determining factor. Yet I have seen so much suffering through forced labor, senseless to the refugee, and psychic trauma caused by work prohibition, that I conclude that a degree of freedom of choice in one's occupation and an affinity for it constitute a minimum requirement for a fairly meaningful and satisfactory existence.

The opportunity for material and spiritual ties with a community. It is imperative, for the maturation of the individual as he develops a sense of fellowship with the community at large, that the community in turn must reciprocate by offering him a home in the wider sense. This relationship is mutual: security and a sense of belonging cannot develop if the external world appears dangerous and even destructive. There will be no individual security if society preys on the individual, or one people on another.

Only when the individual can approach his fellow humans in trust and confidence, and in the spirit of fellowship, a true sense of security and freedom will develop. Then the individual will be liberated from fear and material distress and will be able to savor the joys of life and building his future. In this connection we must again refer to the partnership between the community at large and the individual which is based on equal rights and obligations. As we are shaped by our intimate personal environment, and as the personal sphere means "Heimat" on a small scale, we can strike genuine roots in this world only if we feel at home in human society at large.

Annex: See Page 324.

THE NOSTALGIC PHENOMENON AND ITS EXPLOITATION

Charles Zwingmann
Switzerland

The crisis in man's existence provoked by separation constitutes one of the salient problems in the social, psychological and behavioral sciences. Separation frequently results in marked changes of behavior. While the consequences of separation from affective reference objects, primarily as applying to individuals separated from their homeland, and children separated from their parents, have been investigated (the latter mostly by psychoanalysts), the reaction to separation in its superordinate aspect of change and fear of change, which I designate as nostalgic, has so far received no adequate attention.[1]

I. Historical Survey of the Classical Concept

The phenomenon called "Heimweh" and "Nostalgia" first acquired prominence in organic medicine, and later in psychiatry, only to be more or less forgotten towards the end of the last century. Nostalgia "died," so to speak, as a pathological concept, and survived merely as a linguistic artefact.

"Heimweh" (Homesickness) appeared first in the Swiss literature of the sixteenth century in connection with the Greek concept of melancholia. It was described as a serious disease of epidemic proportions to which – in its typical form – Swiss mercenaries in the pay of European potentates succumbed. It competed with the plague, was often believed to be incurable. In 1678 it was for the first time treated systematically as a category of medical pathology under the name "nostalgia" derived from the Greek, by the Swiss physician J. Hoferus (1678). Although he attributed the disease partly to "the addiction to morning soup and the agalectia of this tribe" (the Swiss), and based his theory on two cases of which he claimed to have heard from "reliable" sources, his insight into the psychosomatic background of this phenomenon at that time nevertheless deserves high recognition.

---

[1]That the interest in this phenomenon is considerable, was shown not only by the large number of scientific reviews and requests for reprints that resulted from my first works, but by the reaction of American and German news media (a. o. KRISTAL, 1961, 2, and DER SPIEGEL, 1964, 18) often with distorted, sensational emphasis.

Shortly after this first description the concept "nostalgia" — known also as the "terrible Swiss disease" and as "pathopatridalgia" — became current throughout Europe, and the strange melody of the "ranz-des-vaches" was considered a dangerous trigger-factor for the ailment. J. J. Rousseau (Klemm, 1911) confirmed that a decree of the King of France even forbade the playing of this melody to Swiss mercenaries on pain of punishment because of causing nostalgia epidemics and mass desertions, H. de Balzac (Larouse, n.d.) mentioned nostalgia as sort of marasm caused by the desire return to the homecountry. Scheuchzer's theory (Jaspers, 1909), according to which nostalgia was provoked by changes in atmospheric pressure to which Swiss citizens were exposed on coming down from high mountains to the plains, also, had wide currency. Scheuchzer maintained that even whales fell sick of "Heimweh" on moving from northern into southern waters (this assumption may have been based on the as yet apparently unexplained cases of mass suicide among whales).

Hectic fever, constipation or diarrhoea, delusions and even convulsions are often cited as symptoms of nostalgia. Treatment consisted, among other things, in administering hypnotic emulsions, compressed air to ensure equalization of pressure, emetics, laxatives, blood-letting, interrupted sleep, swivel-chair treatment and confinement in a high tower. Nostalgia was a recognized nosological category in the eighteenth century, and well-known physicians such as A. von Haller resigned their chairs abroad for fear of succumbing to this physiological "homesickness."

In his second dissertation in 1780, "An Investigation between the Animal and Spiritual Nature of Man," the well-known German dramatist and poet Friedrich von Schiller dealt with the appalling nostalgia "which could wither a man to a skeleton." At about this time this curious disease became known in England under the name of "homesickness."

What had been considered to be a typical soldier's disease in the seventeenth century remained so — at least in France — throughout the nineteenth century. It was, moreover, found that the Swiss were not its only victims. Napoleon's physicians Percy and Laurent (1809), as well as Larry (Jaspers, 1909), mentioned the devastating nostalgia suffered by French troops in Russia and Africa. The army surgeon Haspel (1873) received the French Academy award in 1873 for his work, based on wartime experiences, in which he included among his seven organic forms of nostalgia a "stomach and intestinal" as well as a "pulmonary" form. Hapsel quotes even Napoleon as saying: "the Frenchman is practically nowhere outside his homeland; nevertheless, whatever tendency toward nostalgia there should exist, it is to be recognized that this natural disposition is efficiently counteracted by the mobility of the French character" (1873). The deaths which Percy, Laurent, and Larrey attributed to nostalgia were probably due to diseases unknown at that time, such as spotted fever or as cerebrospinal meningitis. The symptoms, deliria in which longings for the home and the loved ones were expressed, were held to be the cause, namely nostalgia).

In America, also cases of nostalgia were reported and "Homesickness" for the first time in 1863 as a "mild form of insanity" on the battlefield of the Civil War (Peters, 1863). And while, particularly in France, the dispute centered on the question whether nostalgia was a symptom of diarrhoea and fever, or whether diarrhoea and fever were symptoms of nostalgia, "Heimweh" made its appearance in Germany at the psychiatric-forensic level, in connection, for instance, with pyromania. That is to say, homesickness was regarded as a motivation for serious and otherwise inexplicable crimes, such as arson and murder committed by young servant girls at puberty.

The attention formerly devoted to homesickness as a disease is understandable when we consider the separation that lasted often for years and even for decades, the lack of hygiene, social amenities and medical treatment, the inferior status of people outside their own country; and the inability of troops to keep in touch with their relatives and home. It is conceivable that homesickness was indeed a serious ailment at the time.

In the literature of the 20th century, homesickness has received scant attention (see attached references). In 1909 the well-known psychiatrist and philosopher Karl Jaspers once again raised the question of homesickness in relation to crime in his dissertation. Even in Switzerland, the "birthplace" of "Heimweh," the problem has hardly been investigated. In 1957 the Swiss psychiatrist C.G. Jung wrote to me:

"I cannot say very much about nostalgia although the "Swiss homesickness" is so to speak a national disease. In this case nostalgia is an expression of the degree of rooting in the native ground. In this sense it may be considered an unavoidable psychic deficiency symptom. In certain cases it may, however, have a different significance depending upon a degree of individual complex attributes, as for instance familiar connections of the neurotic kind, absence of an intellectual reference, resistance against the conditions of the new life space in general, and in particular. I avoid general theories as much as possible and prefer to be taught by individual experiences. The psychic phenomenon is of such magnitude, that so far each theory turned into a Procrustean bed." (letter dated February 26, 1957)

My own work on the phenomenon was completed in 1959 under the title: 'Heimweh or Nostalgic reaction": a conceptual analysis and interpretation of a medico-psychological phenomenon" (Zwingmann, 1959)[2].

II. Theoretical Introduction

The concept "Heimweh" or "nostalgia" as a medico-psychological category is inadequate, as this notion is a remnant of an erroneous disease interpretation which does not fit into the framework of modern psychiatric and psychological personality theory. It is not possible to speak of nostalgia as an organic disease, nor

---

[2]Consult this work for a basic treatment and exhaustive literature on the subject.

is the phenomenon commensurate with the psychodynamic occurrences formerly ascribed to it. The concept "Heimweh" (homesickness) is inappropriate because it is misleading, and a definition of "home" is often difficult or impossible. Frequently this means the parental home, or the homeland, and sometimes the place of work. Not infrequently a mother living at home feels "homesick" for an absent child. The phrase "to feel homesick" is sometimes also used in the sense of longing for unknown regions. I propose instead the use of the concept "nostalgic" (reaction, behavior, etc.) to indicate the psychological process-nature of this phenomenon.

The nostalgic phenomenon must be seen in a broader aspect, i.e. not only as a reaction to spatial separation from reference objects, but as a reaction to change in a multi-dimensional sense, to change not only as an abrupt event, but to change as an anticipated event of negative personal significance. — In terms of the subjective timetable, gratification can be derived from all psycho-temporal activities, i.e. from projection (into the future), from participation (in the present), and from retrojection (into the past). In which dimension gratification is primarily sought, and the distance over which a temporal involvement has operational significance, is a matter of cultural, ideological and other kinds of conditionings, and of personal factors. Children and undifferentiated adults tend to seek immediate gratification — they live psychologically in the present. As will be shown there are systems which condition their population to behave like children.

Retrojection, i.e. the nostalgic reaction occurs, when participation in the present (reality) becomes uncomfortable or painful and/or projection offers no adequate gratification, because an obstacle (real or imagined) blocs the progression toward the goal. — Threat orientation which is also learned in some societies, plays an important role in nostalgic behavior.

As an experience nostalgic involvement consists of pictorial and other sensory representations of the personal past, and/or of the past which has been internalized by the rituals and teachings of a particular culture.

Dynamically, the nostalgic reaction can be shown as follows:

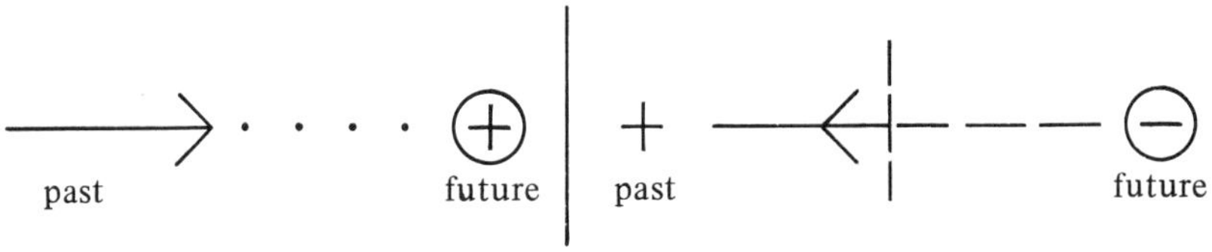

Fig. 1
Projective Activity

Fig. 2
Nostalgic Reaction

Fig. 1. Psychological progression towards gratifying activities and goals.

Fig. 2. Disruption of this progression by unaccustomed change (e.g. separation) which is experienced as upsetting the gratificational structure. The unfamiliarity of the new situation causes a gratificational reversal, i.e. gratification is no more sought in the present and in the future, but in the past (for instance, familiar objects, persons and institutions towards which the individuals attitude was, prior to separation, ambivalent become in the post-separation phase frequently "loved." Features of conditions which prior to separation remained unnoticed merge into the foreground of perception.)

Nostalgic involvement is determined by, and its intensity dependent upon various external and internal factors. Among the external factors can be mentioned: prevailing social, cultural and political conditions, contrast between pre- and post conditions of change, abruptness of change, voluntary or forced change, reversibility or irreversibility of change, communicational aspects etc. To the external personality factors belong: physical and health status, age, ideological frame of reference (philosophy of life, religious or areligious attitudes) intellectual status, educational background, level of aspiration – motivation (type and structure of goals), social and contact ability, relation to property etc.

The content of the nostalgic wish-image is known by the individual and can be described. This theory differs therewith from orthodox psychoanalytic interpretations which characterize as nostalgic the unconscious desire to return to the intra-uterine past (Fodor, 1950), to the mother's breast (Sterba, 1940) or (of a girl) to the father's penis (Nikolini, 1936). According to Fenichel (1945), the oral type has a particular propensity to nostalgia.

The nostalgic phenomenon can be defined as *a symbolic return to, or psychological reinstitution of, those events of the personal (real) past, and/or an impersonal (abstract, imagined, suggested) past which affords optimal gratification.*

III. Nostalgic Disposition and Reaction Potentials as Products of Conditioning

How man interprets and reacts to change (e.g. separation), and on which temporal dimension he places gratificational emphasis, is to a large degree dependent on factors inherent in a particular culture, i.e. in its socio-economic, political system and ideological structure.

At the basis of differences of temporal behavior lies the quality of human interaction. What role these differences play in the causation of nostalgic behavior can be made meaningful by using the notions "open" and "closed" system (or "microcosmos"), and by apposing them.

In the *open system*, social humanism is the guiding ideology with positive (equalitarian) trustful and affective communication among men, and the application of rational, objective methods to make this system accessible to all men (beyond national borders). The orientation in this system is essentially projective and futuristic because the goal (maximal welfare for all men) is unlimited;

postponement of gratification becomes in this ideology a gratification itself, whereas the past is perceived as relatively insignificant in the progression toward this goal. The nostalgic plays in this system therefore a negligent, or no role.

The *closed system*, from hereon called the *microcosmos*, is defined by egocentricity (and ethnocentricity); instead of man, some abstraction in form of a divine authority stand in the center of attention and acts as a compensation for proper human communication. — The longrange future has little or no attraction value because it is limited by egocentric preoccupations with its inevitable finality aspects (e.g. progressive economic uselessness, social isolation, death). Since progression into the future causes in this system more threat-perception than comfort the gratificational emphasis lies in the present, and in the past as a refuge to which one retires when oppressed, or in which one psychologically "lives" (in a situation of chronic stress). — In this system, defined by threat, fear and anxiety, the nostalgic serves an important affective continuity function. Such a closed system is the Christian-bourgeois microcosmos, which henceforth shall be the object of closer examination.

Perhaps no religious infrastructure of a microcosmos in recorded history has been equally efficient in torturing, manipulating, supressing and destroying directly and indirectly human relations over as long a time and on such a (global) scale as the Christian system.[3] In no other system there is so much talk about god, and peace and love, and so much murder and mass murder committed at the same time. The antihuman feature and threat aspect which is so decisive in nostalgic behavior and other symbolic flight activities can be followed through the history of Christianity without interruption from the times of the Crusades to the Inquisition, which brought hitherto unknown forms of torture and sadism and painful death to millions of men, the cruel conquests of the Americas, the religious wars among Christians themselves, colonial massacres, suppression and exploitation of peoples all over the world. In more recent history, the clerical fascistic terror has shifted to more subtle and insidious forms of activities with which men are manipulated, destroyed and prevented from attaining a critical consciousness, no compromise is too humiliating for the Christian clerus to achieve their end, even the simulation of sympathy for social revolutions, and the "association" with their arch enemy — the deeply hated communists. Now as then the executors of the "devine" message are the Christian-democratic governments. In the climate of the homicidal ethics of Christianity that what is called "technocracy" could develop, in the course of which inhuman practices were perfected and which found its climax in the testing of systems of mass destruction, by which Christians decimated each other successfully (World War I and II) and by the wayside also a few millions of non-Christians. As long as this microcosmos is in existence the periods between hot

---

[3]When Marx (1927) calls religion "opium for the people" then does this mean that no open system, as I use this notion here, can develop on the basis of religion. (cp. also Lenin, 1965, and the depth-psychological analysis of religious endeavors by S. Freud, 1955).

wars were filled with cold wars, by provocations, the reign of secret services like the CIA and other gangster organizations like the Mafia. More recently the homicidal course expanded into a suicidal one, in that man of the Western world has learned to kill himself in ever increasing proportions on the highways (because he is made to want more and more powerful automobiles, and because the safety of cars and the road net have been criminally neglected), and by poisoning his surroundings and himself in ever greater efficiency.

The inhumane, aggressive, imperialistic and hypocritical Christian practices which can be directly traced to the word of the Christian god, and the methods of manipulating and controlling man with threats and promises, and keeping him ignorant and superstitious so as to make him dependent, serve as models for the political conceptions of today's Christian-bourgeois (frequently called "Christian-Democratic") rulers.

In the Christian-bourgeois, capitalist class societies (the so-called "Western World") the nostalgic plays a unique role in that it is conditioned to function as a preserving element of the system (maintenance of the *status quo*). In order to preserve traditional bonds and moral values, the principal objectives of Christian-bourgeois strategists consists of turning the clock back by evoking the "good" old times (which have never existed but for privileged a few) and at the same time by evoking fear of change. The past (or aspects thereof) is manipulated positively, the future negatively.

In the future lies threat, in the abstractions of the past and in heaven lies promise. The cold war cliché "Free World" which Christian-bourgeois manipulators opposed to the Communist or unfree world, is a graft-product of the paradisical and heroic national past. According to the Christian-bourgeois threat scheme the future will be "unfree" that is, Communistic if ones does not blindly believe in the superior judgement of the clerical and political chiefs. The maintenance and reenforcement of ignorance and credulity (frequently achieved by a great quantity of education), play an important part in the exploitation of the nostalgic, because they render the individual suggestible and therefore dependent. The stability of the microcosmos is determined by the cognitive and affective dependence of the subjects. I call this dependence which is achieved with the means described (with emphasis on drawing the subjects into a world of wishful thinking and to condition them to behave biblically, namely like sheep or little children who uncritically follow their omnipotent political or divine shepherds), *"nostalgization."* Nostalgization is in the Christian-bourgeois microcosmos an institutionalized method of control.

The unconsciousness of the Christian-bourgeois, and his dependence on his unhuman microcosmos are so remarkable and so significant in the nostalgization process, that a brief observation on the development of these factors is necessary.

The Christian-bourgeois is made a member of his microcosmos without being aware of his initiation, by the act of baptizing. This first violation of his freedom is the prelude to further massive violations in the course of which his human relations are systematically poisoned. He learns to fear and hate others, even within his immediate surroundings; he learns that the Christian Catholic is different from the Christian Protestant, that for the Catholic Christian it is a deadly sin to marry a Christian of another confession (and especially to rear his children in another confession) that even in his own confession he is distinctly different from others by denomination, that a Protestant Lutheran is different from a Protestant Methodist, Baptist, and so on. He learns that women are inferior to men, and conceived as their servants, that he is essentially bad, sinful, unclean (especially with respect to his sexuality) already at birth, and what is significant for the development of the nostalgic disposition, that he is essentially worthless, incapable of proper reasoning and of shaping his own destiny — god does all this for him. Therefore only by utter reliance on god, his son, and the holy ghost, can he become "good," be "saved," and receive the "Kingdom of Heaven." He learns the theory of "loving" the neighbor, and the practice of killing him on the battlefield whenever holy or earthly fathers (usually in conjunction) give the signal, or of killing him on the front of the "free economy" (by "cut-throat" competition). That the "love thy neighbor" and other "divine" pronouncements are nothing but diversion clichés for a message of threat, discrimination, and hatred is openly demonstrated even today by the bloody feuds in Ireland, and the brutal colonial repression exercised by Catholic governments (especially Spain and Portugal) in Africa. What the respect for life and well-being means to many Christians in these nations, is shown by the torturing and killing of animals for amusement purposes (bullfights, and cockfights).

The development of a positive attitude towards the human collective during childhood is further made difficult or impossible by the authoritarian and exclusive affect ties of the individual with two persons only — the parents. During the most formative years, he is their property, has no legal rights and is kept dependent often until his twenty-first year. But even then he is not supposed to be free and independent, he must find another exclusive affect property and become such property himself by a monogamous union which binds him to last until death. What a Christian-bourgeois calles "love" and "happiness", namely egocentric pleasure, becomes now institutionalized. Hitherto forbidden sexual relations become acts of duty, and since altruistic communication, satisfaction derived from the well-being of others and the human collective as such, was not part of his curriculum vitae, this union is condemned to the nonsensical, monotonous existence which defines this microcosmos and which frequently leads into the nostalgic wish-world as a substitute for actual ego-gratification.

The absolutistic and monopolistic affect-constellation, or simpler, the early constriction of "love" communication to one or two persons only, together with the essentially negative conditionings to humans outside this exclusive "mini-circle" tends to render change by separation from the supply source of affect a traumatic nostalgic experience. This is especially obvious in children (Schwab, 1925; Vernon, 1940; Isaaks, 1941; Peiper, 1942; Freud and Burlingham, 1943; Lippert, 1950; a.o) and adolescents (Hall, 1920; MacCann, 1940; Rose, 1948; Moser, 1955; a.o) and in the large number of infantile adults even during short periods of separation. It is also very evident in case of separation by death of a member of the innermost circle of the microcosmos; mourning which frequently assumes pathologic proportions, is a form of nostalgic reaction.

The parental and clerical constriction and deformation of the affective moral and "spiritual" horizon of the child is followed by the massive efforts of other specialized institutions of the microcosmos to provide the cognitive superstructure for the individual to shape his personality in conformance with the microcosmic imperatives. This local-patriotic, ethnocentric training is achieved intentionally and unintentionally by means of both qualitative and quantitative geographical and historical misrepresentations (see von Friedeburg, Hübner, 1964). History is frequently taught in terms of a personality cult, whereby leaders who excelled in the destruction of men (by victorious battles) are heroized, while those who excelled in constructive efforts are often hardly mentioned. —In geography, the world is frequently pictured as an extension of the homeland which is given a disproportionate significance through a distortion of proportional and dimensional reality. It is, for instance, possible to prevent children from acquiring a proper and proportionate geographical perception by placing a map of the homecountry alongside the map — of the same size — of a much larger country, or even of the world, and by omitting to point out differences of the scale (cf. Schwind, 1946). In many schools geography is either grossly distorted or, as in some areas of the U.S.A., it is not systematically taught at all. J. Kennedy (1943) reported that nearly 80 percent of a batallion fighting in Africa were unable to identify their location on a map of the world. I myself ascertained — as a visiting professor to the University of California in the Far East (1953) — that, of those American troops in Korea with whom I came in contact, almost 80% had no notion about the location of the country for whose "freedom" they were fighting, and more than 90% were ignorant about its social structure.

The school is seldom concerned with human relationships as such; rather it helps to complicate such relationships by a negative approach to other systems and nations. Other countries are frequently classified in terms of what they have and have not, whether their governments are "for us" or "against us," whether they are communist or "free," developed or "undeveloped" (or "developing"), whether they believe in the same god, another god or no god; nations are liked (not the people), if they have something to be exploited and let themselves be exploited (especially oil and metals), if they have a high industrial production, if they are willing to accept military bases and bombers on their territory, a so-called "peace-corps," or at least have a favorable strategic position (which they submit to occasional aerial control) — but little or nothing about the problems and hopes of people in these countries. The goal is the inculcation of the famous "right or wrong, my country." Also, to turn the minds back, and to divert from urgent human issues, many institutions of learning still focus on the teaching of the Classics, the "golden rule," classical (dead) languages, classical philosophies, and cultures, the study of fossils, and the search for some holy spirit. Mythologization, the feeding with clichés, and what W. Johnson (1946) calls "semantic thumb sucking" belong to the daily menu of young and old.

The Christian-bourgeois microcosm or any other similar microcosm gives a feeling of safety and security as long as there is no change in the status quo. As soon as the individual is separated from the physical confines of his microcosm, or the gratifications he has learned to enjoy, he will notice that his microcosm is merely an illusory world which does not help him to understand, order and meet the demands of his new environment. Confrontation with a new milieu results in a threat experience in proportion to the degree in which communication with the microcosm is severed. Cognitively and affectively crippled, the individual is incapable of meeting the "world as it is."

Of importance in the framework of human relationships are the negative interplay and side-effects of nostalgic behavior. The fear of, and negative attitudes towards the new environment by the nostalgic individual are likely to provoke a negative attitude on the part of the people who constitute the new milieu, which in turn strengthens the nostalgic behavior because the negative attitude shown towards the nostalgic individual serves as legitimation for his own rejection of others. The nostalgic individual is not aware of these negative reenforcements. The affect-escalation may result in open acts of aggression.

IV. Separation: "spatial" (external)

Spatial separation as one of the exogenous criteria of the nostalgic reaction means the physical interruption of contact with primary (family), secondary (close friends) and tertiary (community institutions) objects of reference. These reference objects constitute together with other factors like geographic, topographic and climatic factors (Helpach, 1950), the content of the nostalgia imagery.

In review and expansion of the factors already mentioned in section II, the following factors influence the intensity of nostalgia reaction to spatial separation:

1. Circumstances of separation: voluntary or enforced?
2. Type of separation: from whom and from what is the individual in question separated? (Separation from the primary group is in general more traumatic than separation from the secondary group. —In a capitalistic society separation from personal possessions is also of nostalgic importance, as personal property acquires an affective value not infrequently equal to or greater than that of attachment to members of the primary group.)
3. Degree of contrast between pre- and post-separation situations.
4. Is the structure of the individual's goal affected by separation (e.g. his professional aims, his aim in life); if so, to what extent?
5. What are the actual possibilities of communication?
    a) with familiar persons and objects abandoned by the individual;
    b) with his new environment (e.g., are there language difficulties?).

The Nostalgic Phenomenon and its Exploitation 29

6. What is the attitude of the new environment towards the individual in question, and what is that of his former environment (for instance, does the reference group grieve over his absence, transmit bad news, etc.?)
7. Is the situation reversible, i.e., is there any hope of returning to the pre-change situation?

In view of these criteria, individuals like prisoners for life, exiles, soldiers in combat, and old people, seriously and chronically sick individuals, invalids and otherwise helpless people in foreign surroundings would be most subject to intense nostalgic involvement.

The intensity of the desire to return is most often not, as it may seem, due to the attraction of the "native soil", the familiar surroundings, or the persons whom the nostalgic individual "loves" — but the inability to cope with the new conditions (McCann, 1940; Rose, 1948). People who have been conditioned to be dependent and insecure are unable to structure the new field. What appears to be an affective bond is frequently a condition of pseudo-love, which exists in a situation of loss of support or fear of such loss and the inability to endure unstructured situations.

The strength of the nostalgic wish which to the outsider appears to be intense love of the native soil is evidenced by the return of survivors of cities which had been destroyed by earthquakes (e.g. Agadir) or by atom bombs (applied by Christians on Hiroshima and Nagasaki) although the survivors had been offered better living conditions elsewhere. The desire to return to familiar surroundings even for short periods of time assumes in some individuals compulsive, life endangering proportions: Göring, chief of Nazi Germany's airforce, complained about this compulsion of German pilots during the Second World War by saying: "We suffer these heavy losses because the German pilot is possessed by an incurable mania — the desire to sleep in his own bed", (i.e., instead of bringing his damaged aircraft down at the first available German airstrip, the pilot attempts to fly it back to his unit, often crashing as a result) (Varney, 1950).

Spatial separation from the place of work, where an individual feels sheltered and needed after long years of habit — for instance at retirement — may provoke intensive nostalgic behavior. In this connection attention is called to the extreme reluctance of many old people to leave their homes and the familiar objects contained therein.

With respect to family moves to foreign countries (e.g. for employment reasons), it should be mentioned that generally speaking, wives suffer more acutely from nostalgic involvement, than do husbands. The husbands usually find themselves back in their accustomed working surroundings, with many opportunities for varied and new contacts, whereas their wives are often socially isolated.

A philosophical contribution to spatial separation comes from Martin Heideger (1957); his existential interpretation is presented as follows: Those living abroad are denied a domiciliary relationship with the homeland. The connection formed by living in the homeland is lacking. But in this very absence we discern an intimate condition peculiar to that relationship, namely, homesickness. The very lack of the relationship thus gives it its existence."

V. Separation: temporal

The temporal dimension of the nostalgic phenomenon has hitherto received practically no scientific consideration. Yet this dimension is of marked social and political significance (a.o. because of the manipulation aspect as mentioned in section III).

Nostalgic behavior of this type is not occasioned by the abrupt interruption of human contacts as is the case in spatial separation, but by a gradual decisive change and an anticipated change of grave personal consequence. This is the case especially during the approach of old age, triggered by such events as graying hair, the gaining of weight, inability to pursue a favored sport activity, impotence, serious disease and other real or induced threat aspects. These events have unproportional significance because of the already mentioned (conditioned) characteristics of the Christian-bourgeois microcosmos, particularily the egocentric orientation. The preoccupation, with the self brings into sharp relief personal finality (which has been learned to be perceived as horrible) and the hardships that precede death (affective and social isolation, loss of prestige, etc.). The future becomes repulsive with progressive age, and the past, i.e. nostalgic involvement the only emotional crutch.

This nostalgic regret in old age is well expressed in Goethe's Faust: "Then bring me back the days of dreaming, when I myself was yet unformed . . . the force of hate, and love's disquiet — Ah, give me back my youth again!"

In view of the stipulated criteria the separation from the nostalgic wish object is aggravated because it is enforced and irreversible. Aggravating are also the, for the Christian belief so typical, feelings of sin and guilt in the sense that the nostalgic person suffers of self-reproaches and frequently perceives normal — and in this microcosmos to be expected — happenings, as punishment for something he has done wrong. Common are thoughts about what one would do differently if one had to relive his life again. In the same connection should be mentioned the frequent feelings, and delusions of persecution of old people in Christian-bourgeois societies. Temporal progression is one of the great threat factors in this microcosmos.

The (in youth mostly unconscious) fear of time-lapse, the distorted, negative and commercial attitude toward temporal progression and concretization of time is evidenced by innumerable expressions: "time works against us", "time is on our side," we "waste" time, we have "time enough," and we notice that time "creeps," Occasionally we risk our lives to "save" time, and we "kill" time. Far Eastern civilizations do not have this distorted attitude toward time and the passing of time.

A distinctly pathological conception of time and of the pattern of existence is expressed in the saying: "time is money," The equation of time with the real God of the Christian-bourgeois microcosmos namely money characterizes better than almost any other concept the thinking of a sick society in which frenetic greed of "making money" leaves no time for the making of friendly human relations. —In the Christian-bourgeois capitalistic society man fears the passing of time — because time devaluates him. He usually becomes aware of this only at the stage of life at which his appearance and his productive capacity are decreasing. As a result his social and affective value also depreciate. He becomes isolated and lonely. From every point of view aging represents a situation of loss — especially for those who belong to the underprivileged class.[4] Personal-value crisis with nostalgic consequence and depressions caused by a feeling of loss, are therefore to be expected in old people in the Christian-bourgeois microcosmos. These crises occur in different phases of life in the sexes. In women, they occur primarily during the phase of physiological change (climateric). The menopause signifies a psychological crisis of the woman in a society which glorifies appearance and youthful beauty. Women therefore are forced to retain their youthful appearance for as long as possible, and the mirror thus becomes an indicator of their moods. The exceedingly profitable cosmetics, textile and plastic industries (and surgery) do everything possible — and indeed impossible — to accentuate the fear of aging and to preserve or simulate the freshness of youth. With their costly "aides" homely girls become pretty and "sexy," old ladies young, and dead bodies "alive" and "healthy" in looks (cp. the custom of making up and padding corpses).

A man's appearance is considerably less important, his loss of vitality is not so obvious. Nostalgic problems tend to become pronounced for the male when he retires — that is to say, at the point at which he is eliminated as a member of the productive community. It is well known that the male mortality curve rises steeply immediately following retirement.

Nostalgic involvement during this phase of life is exacerbated by the necessity to keep this longing (e.g. for youth, beauty, power, etc...) to himself because expressing it is considered an additional symptom of old age.

The fact that aging does not need to be accompanied by crisis of self-doubt, depressions and severe nostalgic episodes is demonstrated by some of the socialistic societies. In these societies aging is no threat because of the realistic attitude toward life, and because there is no depreciation or isolation, with other words the system does not punish man for becoming old — old people remain fully integrated members of the community. Moreover, since members of these societies identify their existence with the existence of the people and their future with that of a liberated mankind personal death is not feared. Also, the funeral rites are neither elaborate nor unduly saddening events. (cp. by contrast the early conditioning of Christian-bourgeois children to fear death as a pathogenic, gruesome event, as an enormous loss, with morbid ceremonies, display of possessions, and grief reactions, etc.).

---

[4]The privileged classes can compensate these losses by "buying" social and affective relations (in a pseudo-sense).

Finally it should be pointed out that language factors influence temporal experience (cp. Delacroix [Israeli, 1936] Gross, 1958), and that certain structural characteristics of language prevent proper conceptualizations of the process- nature of realtiy (e.g. relativity). Western civilizations are predominantly oriented toward the past. Bally (Spielrein, 1923) pointed out that Indo-European languages possessed more symbols for the past, than either for the present or the future.

In spite of chronometry and the objectification of time, subjective perception of time-progression is erratically oriented, i.e. psychological experience of time is influenced by contingencies of expectation. Temporal points of reference are officially and ritually (e.g. by historical, political, and religious events) or personally determined. The former include "Independence Days," Easter, Christmas, etc. The latter include birthdays, vacations, anniversaries, etc. High-days and holidays speed up time perception, in that they are impatiently awaited. Anniversaries have a particular nostalgic significance, as they bring sharply in focus the personal and irrevocable cycle of life. The anticipation of a holiday is of accelerative significance, whereas the actual holiday — especially as it draws to a close — is frequently attended by anticlimax phenomena[5] with nostalgic involvement. After the holiday, time again passes "slowly."[6]

The subjective experience of time is masterfully analyzed in Marcel Proust's "Search for the lost" and "The refound time" (1919). Schopenhauer (1813) comments that youth is characterized by the search of happiness, old age by fear of unhappiness, and that seen from the viewpoint of youth, life is limitless future, from the viewpoint of old age, a brief past.

VI. The Nostalgic "Illusion"

By nostalgic "illusion" are meant modifications of retrospective experience. I refer here to the subjective changes in space and time perception already mentioned, and to the phenomena such as synchroneous disturbances, dimensional foreshortening or prolongation. The distance from the reference objects and the period of separation appear longer and larger respectively, the reference objects themselves are perceived as more important and more beautiful than ever before; even unpleasant incidences of the past may be exalted. Well known in the microcosmos under scrutiny are the many cases of veterans who in their monotonous, unconscious and irresponsible existence long for the battlefield, i.e. while they do not "remember" their inhuman (killing) behavior, and the hardships they were exposed to, they vividly remember and revel about the human events, the beautiful comradeship, merry events, sexual exploits and so on. The greater the discomfort and feeling of menace experienced, the more serene the nostalgic wish-image.

---

[5] cf. The notion "Sunday Neurosis"

[6] In connection with subjective time-perception, attention should be drawn to the ultra-rapid recapitulation of past experiences at a moment of catastrophe (flashback).

Retrospective distortion and idealization of the reference-objects, so typical of nostalgic reaction, may have very negative consequences, and as I will show later, this phenomenon constitutes the basis for ample manipulation. It is even probable that the nostalgic illusion is one of the determinants of the inability of Christian-bourgeois politicians to learn from the tragic events of history and is therewith co-responsible for the disastrous actuality of war.

The inflation of feeling during separation and the joy of being reunited with the reference object is often succeeded by a displacement or withdrawal of emotion: if for instance one has said "good-bye" to someone one loves but the separation does not take place as planned (for instance, due to cancellation of a scheduled flight), a sudden sensation of emptiness and dysphoria is experienced; there is nothing left to say to each other — because psychological separation has already occurred, i.e. the affect has been displaced from actual and direct contact (optical and physical) to the past symbolic level, the "love" has been temporarily withdrawn from the object.

In this connection, attention should also be drawn to feelings of unreality (alienation) quite often experienced by nostalgic individuals. R. Lemke (1957) states that in his refugee patients suffering from "nostalgia," conditions resembling schizophrenic reactions were observed; the characteristic split pertained to nostalgia, that is to say, they believed they lived in their former house, while, at the same time, they fitted in completely with the new surroundings.

In individuals who have been separated from their society, the subjective overestimation of their loss may cause a further deterioration of their human relationships because of the heightened contrast-effect (see the affect-escalation mentioned earlier in relation with aggressive behavior). Many people only become fervent patriots during their stay in a foreign country, i.e., as a result of the nostalgic illusion. They are victims of the glorious halo of nostalgic contemplations. These nostalgic illusions are, moreover, often the reason for the hostility and hatred felt by the Christian-bourgeois towards protest by young people who rebel against the nostalgic appeal, e.g. against the imposition of glorified conditions of the past with its by-products of political tutelage, hypocrisy and repression.

The nostalgic illusion is also operative in another way. The Heimweh literature postulates a painful experience. This is, however, not entirely correct. There is a fluctuation of feeling tone which I call "nostalgic paradox." Nostalgic retrospection is in itself pleasurable and gratifying. The feeling of discomfort arises in the phase of comparison between the overestimated past (nostalgic illusion), the uncomfortable present and a future which is perceived as threatening. With other words, the negative feeling quality arises in a sort of figure-ground vaccillation between the wish-image and reality.

VII. Release Factors and Manipulations of the Nostalgic Phenomenon

Certain events or objects act as trigger factors or as intensifiers of nostalgic involvement. Among those to be mentioned are traditional events, spontaneously occurring events, material objects, and produced (manipulated) factors. Social and traditional conditioned nostalgic release factors include events of significant general and individual nature, such as Christmas, Easter, birthday, anniversaries, etc. They tend to trigger nostalgic episodes or intensify an already existing nostalgic engagement because they constitute affective reference situations (pleasant and joyful childhood experiences, times during which one was the center of parental love and attention), while, at the same time they may bring into relief certain elements of threat in the present and future.

To the spontaneously occurring individual release factors belong pleasant stimuli of the sensory repertoire, but also events threatening life and well-being, such as serious illness, physical disability, death of a parent or spouse. To a lesser degree, certain time of the day (twilight), weather conditions (persistant rain or fog), certain seasons (for instance autumn), or the end of the year, etc., may intensify nostalgic involvement.

Material triggers of nostalgic episodes include such objects as photographs of loved persons, and mascots. The Christian-bourgeois custom of ensuring that he is the object of enduring nostalgic remembrance after death by his relatives, by means of a costly tomb, is to be mentioned here as evidence for the personality cult, egocentricity and the property consciousness of the Christian-bourgeois.

The production and manipulation of nostalgic involvement has been introduced in section III. It was stated that the Christian-bourgeois microcosm is characterized by a nostalgic disposition. This disposition is constantly nourished by the "guardians" of the culture, because it helps maintain the *status quo* and assure their authoritarian control. What I have called "nostalgization" has a stupefying effect in that it hinders the bourgeois from emancipation and from developing a critical consciousness. The production of retrospective needs and phantasies on a large scale is effective because of the idealistic superstitious substratum of the microcosmos which renders the individual highly suggestible. He is being made nostalgic not for what objectively *was* but for what is *induced as having been* — as a compensation for an unsatisfactory present and a threatening future.

The practice of dominating men by rendering them nostalgic is deeply rooted in the Christian tradition. Already the alleged founder of Christianity has recognized that for the absolute rule of God men must be reduced to the affective and cognitive niveau of little children: "Verily I say unto you except you be converted, and become as little children ye shall not enter the kingdom of heaven" (Matthew, 18.3).[7] The feudalistically symbolized heaven is presented as the only true home for the soul of the believer; the more nostalgic he can be made for heaven, the better he is supposed to support his earthly misery and repression.

What nostalgization in a pseudo-sense of suggested gratification may mean is evident in the Christmas cult. During Christmas, the bourgeois retrojects himself

---

[7] This "divine" model serves as legitimization for other rulers of the Christian-bourgeois microcosmos to lead their followers back into the paradise of their own making.

into the scenery of the stable, populated with the virgins Mary and Joseph, a donkey, sheep, floating angels, a peaceful smiling white baby in a fodderbox, and kings and camels transporting gifts to him. The microcosmos is saturated with pledges of neighborly love, charity, and goodness expressed with colorful, glittering Christmas trees, angelic songs, moving stories from the Bible, and other fairy tales from the past, peace addresses by the Pope and other Christian dictators, and gifts. And because of the gifts everybody (who is able to afford them) is happy in the microcosmos, especially the producers of gifts. Consumption must reach its peak during this time — also the consumption of delusions. And since Christmas is the time of peace, love, and goodness, even the ongoing mass-slaughter of communists is interrupted — at least on paper.

Examples for political exploitation of the nostalgic disposition by fairy-tales for adults and parochial mythology with exalted themes of the former "greatness of the fatherland" (usually in terms of victorious wars) could be given abundantly. Some of the nostalgic stimuli have achieved significance beyond national borders. Especially Europe is flooded with movies that make people nostalgic for the "heroic" past of the American shooting democracy, which consists of shooting farmers, shooting sheriffs, and shooting cowboys, even shooting women, who in Christian-Puritan fashion "cleaned" the North American lands from the "barbaric" Indians and other "bad" elements. It can be assumed that on personalities already conditioned by inhuman beliefs this nostalgization toward heroization of murder has played a part in the steady increase of inhuman behavior in the Christian-bourgeois hemisphere in the USA and after World War II in Europe. The playworld of boys is entirely dominated by shooting and killing games (Only recently US producers surprised the world with a new game for the children — torture toys!). How effective these conditionings are is actually shown by the enormous rise of murder and the endless chain of legalized mass murder by the US troops in Southeast Asia. Pertinent here is a tie-in to the previous section with the example of the veteran who is nostalgic for war-experiences, because this longing (which is partly a reaction to the communicational stress and the immanent threat of the microcosmos) is subject to exploitation of professional warmongers and power groups who constantly appeal to the aggressive and (conditioned) sadistic impulses of man. This exploitation of the nostalgic illusion by war literature and other mass media is often achieved by detour, i.e. over some "positive" aspects of war, aspects that are lacking in the microcosmos not in war namely those that go under the label "comradeship." (Individuals who refuse to participate in aggressive killing actions, or do not submit to the standard training in killing are declared "un-American," asocial, and they are imprisonned. Those who have killed and repent it, risk to be declared psychotic. Eatherly, (Jungk, 1961) who released the atom bomb over Hiroshima, causing therewith the greatest single killing disaster in the history of mankind was declared insane by US authorities when he made his guilt feelings public)[8].

To divert the attention of the population of the USA from the disastrous present, efforts are made by patriotic organizations and mass media to show with nostalgic – romantic means that, even though America may not *appear* to be very good now, it *is* good because it always *was* good! How good it is supposed to have been is shown among other things by glittering aspects of the "golden twenties" (without mentioning, however, that they were golden only for those who had gold, and for gangsters).

Each Christian-bourgeois society has its own nostalgization arsenal. Very effective, for instance, is the royal way to the past, especially in Great-Britain.

To keep the cold-war going, Christian-bourgeois manipulators also like to show segments of other nation's past, for example the "good old times" of feudal Russia and China, and of colonial days.

Typical, for specifically aimed nostalgification is the German "Blood and Soil" and "Heim ins Reich" literature during the Nazi era, and similar manipulations by refugee and expulsee organizations of the Federal Republic of Germany. The return spirit and a sentiment of revenge are fanned with phrases such as "your native land needs you" or "you have a right to your homeland" etc., and they are accompanied by romantic movies, lantern slides and patriotic songs. Children who have never known their parents' homeland are systematically taught to be homesick and to repossess the native land of their parents; the only authorized map of the Federal Republic of Germany is a map of Greater Germany (at 1937). This nostalgification has received the massive and active support of the Christian Democratic Government of the GFR. It was part of an insidious provocation scheme against the German Democratic Republic (cp. also the showing of steady increase of the number of refugees by administrative manipulation). Refugees were produced by giving the offspring of "refugees" the status of "refugees."[9]

During the last world war, nostalgization was used to demoralize the enemy and induce him to desert (for instance, by dropping leaflets from airplanes),

---

[8] A beautiful example for the negative attitude of the Christian-bourgeois against his fellow man is an experiment reported by W. Johnson (1946). A test group of students was given a number of portrait photographs and asked to pierce the "eyes" with an icepick. This they accordingly did. But each one of the groups refused to follow the instructions on one particular photograph – that of his own mother (which the investigator had, at an earlier date, obtained from the students for a different purpose). They mutilated unthinkingly the "faces" of strangers, but they refused to do this to their "mother."

[9] Future research should concern itself more with politico-analytical studies in the area of exploitation and manipulation of the nostalgia phenomenon. It would be valuable, for instance, to study the propaganda aspects by which certain governments motivate individuals and groups to "emigrate" or "to flee" their country. How needs, conflicts, reactive depression and uprooting problems are being exploited to increase the imperialistic and aggressive potential of the host nation. (cf. Ciananni, P. "Emigration and Imperialismus," Trikont 1967). A worthwhile objective would be the study of techniques applied by the Zionists movement to make Jewish citizens of various nations "nostalgic" for Israel – very similar to the "Heim ins Reich" movement of Adolf Hitler, – and follow-up studies of this forced (suggested) uprooting. (Certain mass media make believe that suddenly all Jewish citizens of the Soviet Union are dissatisfied with their lot and want to emigrate).

depicting moving scenes of family reunion against a beautiful rural background (Linebarger, 1948).

Manipulation aimed at inducing nostalgic involvement is also practiced in the economic sector. In the Western capitalist cultures the population is systematically conditioned to seek self-centered immediate gratification, to consume, waste and destroy goods in greatest possible quantity regardless of the consequences. In the frame of this consumption paradise the Christian-bourgeois also learns to "consume" the past to which are attributed the best qualities.

The "good old" conditions of past times are swept upward on the tide of fashion. One aspect for this is the adoption of romantic or feudal styles in interior decoration in many Western countries. Furniture in the "solid" cosy bourgeois, or the "refined" aristocratic styles are presented as something substantial, durable and cultivated! It was shown that the sale of perambulators could be increased when adorned — according to price-range with five or seven-pointed silver or gold coronets. This gave the mother a sense of being, as it were, entitled to take her "crown princess" or "prince" out for a walk. Very obvious also has been the recent clothing trend, — the grandmother and grandfather — dandy look and even the battledress appeal (with rank insignia). The market is saturated with replicas and obsoletes of former times.

VIII. Nostalgic Fixation — Pathology

Nostalgic fixation means an involvement in the past of such an intensity that the individual is no longer able to function properly.

Intense nostalgic behavior and nostalgic fixation are due to change which is abrupt, forced and irreversible (or appearing to be irreversible), which contrasts strongly with the pre-change situation, and in which isolation and pain and/or severe threat and hopelessness are the dominating features. —Among the factors that render the individual susceptible to a nostalgic fixation are young or old age, physical handicap, disease or sickness, reduced intellectual capacity, as well as factors that are fostered by the microcosmos, like emotional instability, strong dependency, lack of educational background, egocentricity, credulity, prejudicial behavior, feelings of sin and guilt, and a low frustration tolerance. A nostalgic fixation renders the individual incapable of functioning properly. The symptoms are pronounced: strong withdrawal behavior, decreased working efficiency or refusal to work, strong idealization of reference persons, objects and situations; hightened threat perception, fear of loss and support, fear that something may happen to the "loved" one(s); psychogenic and psychosomatic difficulties such as lack of appetite, headache, functional gastrointestinal disorders, sleeplessness, and dizziness, feelings of unreality. The individual lives in the past, i.e., he experiences the present from a distance and unrelated to him. Homburger (1926) and Frost (1938) relate cases of "homesickness psychosis" of German servant girls in England (e.g. also the homesickness literature at the turn of the 19th century). Young Christian-bourgeois individuals tend to react severely to separation, because of the affective overdependency on exclusive reference objects, an undeveloped cognitive faculty, with which to check and order new experiences, and because of the negative conditioning in human relations, the threat perception and fear is overwhelming.

L. Binswanger (1944) does not speak of nostalgic involvement, but his case of Ellen West is a good example of nostalgic fixation (temporal): "When the past has become all-powerful, when it rules that part of life still to come, we speak of old age. As a young woman, Ellen West was already old ... Existential aging outspaces biological aging, just as existential death, the feeling of being a 'living corpse,' precedes the biological end of life" (p. 98). (see also Binswanger, 1942 and 1955)

Of particular psychological and social significance is *aggression,* which can often be observed as a concomitant of nostalgic behavior. Attention was drawn, during the last century and at the beginning of this century, to aggression in the form of "homesickness-motivated crime" such as arson and infanticide; see Part I.

Ernst Kretschmer (1956) mentioned criminal actions caused by homesickness, committed by young girls of retarded puberty. In a patient study, Geisler (1959) relates a case of theft and the dream experience of child murder as a reaction to homesickness in a fourteen-year-old. And in a letter to me, R. Lemke (1957) speaks of misdemeanours and attempted suicide by homesick refugees. Haegi (1964) reports that the psychological stress of homesickness is responsible for the high incidence of stomach ulcers among foreign workers in Switzerland. This affliction is so common that the expression "homesickness ulcer" (Heimwehulkus) is used. According to Haegi, the same is true for tuberculosis, the incidence of which lies 80% - 100% above that of the local population.

External and personal difficulties, the inability to obtain a rational grasp on the new environment and other obstacles for understanding (e.g. foreign workers who neither know the language nor understand the culture of the host country), often cause such frustration that otherwise peaceable human beings may adopt an aggressive defense behavior. *Aggression* can be understood in the light of the function of the nostalgic illusion, in that through glorification the contrast between the frame of nostalgic reference and the new environment is intensified to such an unbearable degree, that the only abreaction seems to lie in open, hostile activities. Usually the nostalgics subject's hostility finds expression in negative comments on the customs, climate, inhabitants and other aspects of the host country, and/or indirectly in overestimation of the homeland (often vented in terms of exaggerated local patriotism).

Pathological nostalgic fixations are difficult to be recognized: the individual lives in the past and refuses to communicate; this may take a degree in which all life-sustaining activities are suspended. This form of suicide by total nostalgic involvement may occur in old people.

Probably the most striking cases of mass-apathy followed by death, in which nostalgic fixation played a part were those reported from American prison camps in China (during the US involvement in Korea). According to reports from American physicians captured at the same time, 38% of their fellow prisoners died of apathy; they lay down on the floor, drew the blankets over their heads and refused food. Within a short time they were dead (Kinkead, 1957; also Schein, 1957; a.o.). Official United States indignation over the "unsoldierly" psychogenic mass deaths and the striking high crime rate in the camps (e.g. the murder of fellow prisoners), caused President Eisenhower to appoint a top-level committee of inquiry and to issue a patriotic "Code of Conduct." Expert committees appointed by the United States Defense Department (1955) and the United States Department of the Army (1956) vied with each other in attempting to explain this national fiasco. Alongside these official investigations, there was a wave of research into the occurrences by teams of professional psychiatrists, sociologists and psychiatric workers (e.g. Gap, 1956-1957), as well as by individuals. Once it had been established that the reason for the collapse of the prisoners was not physical maltreatment by the Chinese (their diet was adequate), and reports that they were humanely treated were found to be reliable (not even the customary barbed wire fences, guard towers, watch dogs, etc. were used), the majority of experts concluded that the prisoners had been subjected to "mental torture." This "malignant" method was identified as "brainwashing." "Brainwashing," a term coined by the American journalist Hunter (1953)[10] with which he slandered the ideological reform practice "Szu Hsiang Kai Tsao" in the Peoples Republic of China (see also Lifton, 1957; Bauer, 1957). Many psychoanalysts discerned in this treatment ominous hazards, and the great danger of the Pavlov System! For one of the most grotesque interpretations of this subject see J. A. Meerloo (1951, 1952, 1953, 1954, 1955, 1956). For most of these experts it seemed unbelievable that normal American individual could prefer another system, especially the "horrible" Communistic one, to the "free" Christian-bourgeois system.

These psychological mass demises, or "give-up-itis" — as this extreme form of

---

[10]Since Hunter's book became a bestseller, and the fabrications therein stimulators for the production of many social "scientists" and psycho-analysts, a few direct quotations may show its trend:

"Another pushover for the indoctrinators [the Chinese] was the indecisive mind, especially the falsely academic kind that always sees some valid point in the other sides argument. One of the main reasons for the intensive preliminary questioning by the Reds was to locate just such individuals." (p. 280)

"A remarkable portion of the outstanding cases of mental survival was of men with a closed mind on communism ... They knew that the Reds were telling them lies, and they knew, too, that when the Reds did tell them something truthful, it was for the purpose of harming them," (p. 285)

"A mature thinkers approach to communism is that it is evil, not partly evil but all evil." (p. 287).

apathy became known among the prisoners — is a phenomenon unique in modern history.

In the context of the theory expounded here, contrast and the communication-block, i.e. the isolation experienced by the prisoners, should be mentioned as serious threat aspect. The prisoners were exposed to a completely different culture and political structure. In the American microcosmos, the Asian Communist especially is the embodiment of all that is inhuman. By endless wars of aggression, the young American male who has been conditioned to be inhuman is provided with opportunities to work off his race hatred of Communists and of everything non-American, non-Christian, non-White, etc. Military and political slogans depict the Chinese as brutal, ignorant and incapable in every way. According to the US military wisdom, "America, the greatest power on earth, will destroy this vermin — and the atomic destruction of Japanese cities had proved that the USA can do it".[11]

Small wonder then, that the representatives of this "superpower" fell into a state of shock when taken prisoner by these same "sub-humans"; the disorientation of the prisoners increased as they were neither tortured nor shot, but on the contrary given friendly treatment. Most of them did not believe this proof of humanity to be genuine, because it contrasted with the inhuman Christian practice of dealing with the enemy. — Disappointment at the collapse of their military and political power machine, mistrust, and fear of a possible bitter end, together with totally different and certainly difficult living conditions, created a climate of fear and uncertainty which proved unbearable for most of the prisoners (they could, for instance, not understand why the Chinese reacted so severly, punitively, to lying, cheating and falsehood which in their Christian-bourgeois microcosmos are standard practices). The infantile and psychopathic personality structure and the inadequate education of many American prisoners were exacerbating circumstances; many of these men were unable to read or write.[12] The disruption of spiritual local patriotic and other tonic supplies of their Christian-bourgeois microcosmos, disruption of communication with their families, absence of their accustomed modes of entertainment (strip-tease, bars, superman cartoons, comic strips, "Westerns", etc.), the upset caused by the Chinese showing the unhuman and undemocratic nature of the "American Way of Life," were additional factors for pathological reactions. For many prisoners, there remained only total flight into or the past oblivion, with death as a consequence.[13]

---

[11] Slogans which I as a visiting professor of the University of California, delegated to Korea in 1953, heard repeatedly among US troops.

[12] The Chinese conducted extensive courses in order to teach the US prisoners to read and write in their mother tongue.

[13] In this connection it should be pointed out that "homesickness" figured already as a diagnostic category in the American Military psychiatry during World War II, and according to W. C. Menninger (1948) it was the most common minor maladjustment among US troops. (see also Lavin, 1953; Regnier, 1955; Wittson, et al 1943.)

These extraordinary deaths are symptomatic of a very sick social and political order. Remarkable in this connection is the fact that there was not a single case of death among the Turkish prisoners in the Chinese camps, for whom the conditions were the same and many of whom were, moreover, wounded.

IX. Observations on Diagnosis and Therapy

The diagnosis of serious nostalgic conditions is often complicated by a socio-anthropoligical factor which mainly pertains to men. To be nostalgic as a result of separation from affective reference objects, and in terms of the personal past, is considered unmanly. This feeling is therefore concealed, thus in turn aggravating nostalgic engagement. This is especially a problem for boys who have been separated from their parents (e.g. when sent to recreation camps, or boarding schools), or for young men doing military service. For young people, to be exposed to the taunts of their fellows because they are "homesick" is one of the most humiliating experiences.

Acute nostalgic behavior may be taken for a reactive depression. Frequently a nostalgic condition is hidden behind psychogenic or psychosomatic complaints. Here a case of my praxis:

> A foreign student referred to me by a psychiatric clinic with the diagnosis "Reactive depression" only admitted to intense nostalgic involvement after six consultations. When he was asked to sketch a map of the location of his native town, he drew his own country and native town disproportionately large by comparison with the surrounding countries and towns. He then proceeded unasked to draw the district in which his mother lived, complete with streets and a sketch of the parental house, giving its exact location and a full description of its rooms. − Prior to this separation he had never been away from his hometown. Since then he had been suffering from severe migraine and pains in the heart region, disorders of which − he later revealed − his mother also complained. He had nightmares in which his mother had died, and felt he should not have left her. He was very reluctant to talk about his dead father. He did not enjoy his studies in Germany. He suffered from lack of concentration and felt that his fellow students were cold, unapproachable and unfriendly, and that they laughed at his accent and his awkward manner of expression; he said he had come to Germany out of ambition, but had now been cured of it. He only wondered what his friends would say if he went back after so short a time.

Nostalgic conditions which are disproportionately protracted and intense need careful handling, as they greatly influence the individual's general well-being, prejudice the exercise of his profession, and negatively influence others. In some cases, where this is possible the separation must be revoked, and the individual must be reunited with his wish-object. Such measures are particularly recommended in children and young people suffering from lengthy illness which necessitates stationary treatment, as nostalgic fixations may delay or jeopardize recovery

(Peiper, 1942; Schwab, 1925). The same is also often indicated in relatively undifferentiated adults. I recall here a case that was given sensational publicity in West Germany (Nürnberger Nachrichten, 1960) of the Italian worker Enrico, whose condition had, as a result of "homesickness" deteriorated so much that, in order to save his life, it was decided by German authorities to fly him back home in a military aircraft.

In therapy emphasis should be placed on explaining to the individual the function of the nostalgic phenomenon, to encourage him to speak freely about his longings, and about his fears and dislikes with respect to his present situation. He should be helped to recognize his own prejudices, and those that are likely to be directed against him, and to evaluate his situation realistically. This means among other things that he should be assisted in correcting his nostalgic illusions. Strongly recommendable are group discussion methods, and extra-occupational aids.

X. Prevention

There can, of course, be no question of preventing nostalgic behavior; this would be as absurd as to prevent thinking. As prevention is directed against nonsensical and delusional thinking, it must be directed against illusional and delusional forms of nostalgic involvement (conditions which cause severe and enduring personal discomfort and complications with the milieu, and against nostalgic dispositions which cause disturbances of social communication and prevent rational humanitarian progress). Prevention is therefore just as little a psychiatric problem as the prevention of crime is a legal one.

Prevention can be discussed under essentially two aspects which are in some respects overlapping: 1) by a limited, direct approach applicable within the microcosmos, 2) by a wide (longterm) ideological and political reform approach, i.e. a change of the microcosmos itself (toward an open system).

The first category concerns a program that can be executed by parents. To this prevention belongs a childhood-rearing which is defined by an early independence training (contraindication of overprotection), with early gradually increased separation experiences compensated by provision of ample contact with other individuals, (to counteract intense affect binding); and later, separations increasing in distance and frequency from the geographic and cultural milieu, opportunities for classless contacts, early training of a rational approach to life and the universe to strengthen the defences against delusional, especially religious conditionings, the early learning of foreign languages, and very important also, the learning of avocational interests, that is, of an activity which serves to relieve the production stress, and after retirement to compensate for the losses mentioned in a previous section. –Evidently this cannot be considered a social program because most of these prevention measures favor economically privileged groups.

In this context certain conditions of institutional care deserve attention because they tend to complicate nostalgic reactivity instead of preventing it. Old individuals of a society which is based on egocentric standards and poor human relations, should not be herded into the collective of a home for the aged in which they have not learned to function, but they should be given the opportunity to keep on living in the pulsating, even though anonymous world. For many of them it is easier to live alone in a society with poor human relations (which they have been exposed to all their life) than to live in a small group which necessitates the learning of good human relations which for old people is no longer possible.

On the other hand, the confinement to an institution may prevent pathological nostalgic involvement if this institution reproduces (continues) the essential features of the microcosm. Prototypical for such institutions are the camps, bases and colonies provided by the American government for their personnel abroad. These institutions which are run like monasteries and penitentiaries on completely autonomous lines with facilities for shopping, entertainment, religious and local patriotic indoctrinations, serve to protect the "American way of life." And since this is the Christian Puritan way, the clergy plays an important part in keeping "clean" the microcosm in these institutions which are known in occupied countries as "golden ghettos." —It is evident however that this protection of the subculture from foreign social and ideological influences, and the prevention of nostalgic reactions, is achieved at the expense of the improvement of human communication at large.

A significant prevention must aim at the elimination and counter-action of the negative (unhuman) factors which I have exposed in this paper. This means that the egocentric and credulity aspects must be continuously exposed and the hidden machinations which make and keep man dependent upon his microcosmos and nostalgically attached to inhuman traditions, must be unmasked in every phase of indoctrination. More specifically the future must be discharged of threat, it must be opened in the sense that it stands no more exclusively in the "service" of ego-gratification (with the severely threatening finality aspects), but be opened for a long-range service of collective human wellbeing. With other words, the individual must be helped to emancipate from the imperatives of the microcosmos. By helping him to reflect critically and self-critically he will become conscious of the fact that he is a conforming member of a microcosmos, and that this microcosmos is a straightjacket and inadequate frame of human reference. In the course of the rational assessment (e.g. recognition of injustice and inhuman communication) a new goal should emerge with the welfare of man as a central criterion determining the future. At the same time the attitude towards the past should become realistic, in that it loses its nostalgic (illusive and manipulated) appeal. The process of breaking with the past as a sanctuary of refuge, of becoming conscious of the meaning of existence, and of discovering the responsibility towards one's fellow-man is stressful. The processes of becoming conscious of existence and of self-liberation are the subject of some of the remarkable works of J. P. Sartre (1938, 1939, 1945).

That the realization of an open system (as contrasted to the [closed] "microcosmos") is by no means an utopia, is shown by some societies that operate on humanistic and dialectic-materialist premises. In these socialistic societies threat and anxiety conditions in their most traumatizing form of inner conflicts, (anxieties caused by sin and guilt feelings and frequently provoked by the clash between god-delusions and reality-requirements), the uselessness and finality fears, etc., are virtually non-existent. The past seems to occupy an "objective" (non-idealized) position, the present seems to be conceived as a means to an end, this end being the future to be striven for in terms of welfare for all men. The gratificational emphasis seems to be placed (projected) in the future which is shown by the postponement of material satisfactions (renounciation of a high standard of living until an adequate standard has been achieved for all men).

The concept and practice of "permanent cultural revolution" may be considered a prevention within the frame of nostalgic reference in the sense that by this method the falling back into contemplations of the past and pre-revolutionary static conditions is counteracted.

Recommendations for prevention in the supra-aspect of reform proposed, are underlined by the prevailing conditions of nostalgization. In view of the accelerated deterioration of the Christian-bourgeois empire, it can be predicted that the nostalgic trend imposed by power-groupings of the microcosmos to maintain the *status quo* will temporarily increase. The repression of the massive protest movement of students a few years ago, and the manifestations against this movement by deeply frustrated Christian-bourgeois, are examples to this point, (the price the individual has to pay for severing the umbillical cord with the microcosmos and for rejecting the nostalgic heritage, is the hostility of the guardians of the microcosmos).

In many cases the conservers and preservers of the glorious past have infiltrated the youth revolt. Where intelligent, buoyant expressions of dissatisfaction, and the mighty push toward social change ideological reform and a more humane future determined the scene, we today find frequently attempts at revision, a dull acceptance of actual conditions, and a naive admiration and mystic interpretation of things past. From the *Words of the Chairman Mao* there is a two-thousand year fall back to the *Words of "Chairman" Jesus*. "Jesus People" and many other lunatic youth sects as well as rapidly increasing groups of drug addicts substitute reality with infantile dreaming and extraordinary experiences of perception and sensation; in their dress style youngsters adopt the old look of the hightime of the bourgeois past, etc.

The nostalgic, reactionary climate of the microcosmos which keeps the Christian-bourgeois "comfortably" unaware of the induced and manipulated sources of his anxieties and which prevents him from aspiring toward an open system (humane communication) is comparable to the experimentally produced situation of a frog who is being boiled alive without being aware of it, i.e. without jumping out of the water. (this can apparently be achieved by increasing the water-temperature just below the threshhold of perception.)

XI. Recapitulation

To recapitulate the main issue of this paper which may have submerged in the course of presentation, I like to review some of the salient points of this paper. —At the base of nostalgic behavior as it constitutes a personal and social affliction lies a diseased system which I have called "microcosmos". The Christian-bourgeois microcosmos as a typical example of such a system is defined by a severly disturbed human milieu. —In the self-centered and delusional frame of reference fostered by this microcosmos, any major change, for instance separation, is experienced and learned to be perceived as threatening in terms of loss and support, "love." The "future" in this system is relatively unattractive because it exists essentially as a projection of personal and material welfare which for many is unobtainable, and if attained does not provide the expected satisfactions; the future does not act as a powerful motivator, as a projection of identification with the collective welfare and improvement of affective communication between all men. — Reasons for threat orientation are present in all phases of life within the Christian-bourgeois microcosmos through the idealistic philosophy and pathologic religious belief systems and through the practice of inequalities social, economic, religious, racial, intellectual and so on as well as by periodic war actions, and a reckless competition even among people of the same groupings. The feelings of threat, sin, guilt, isolation and loneliness which are characteristic of this microcosmos, increase in proportion to the decrease of the "market value" of the individual of the capitalist society.

In view of this finality threat and anxiety which obscur the present and discourage futuristic activity the individual tends to take refuge in a gratifying personal, and what he believes to be a personal past. The readiness to escape into the sanctuary of an illusional and/or delusional (suggested) past is the object of manipulation and exploitation by the various "guardians" of the microcosmos (clergy, politicians, chiefs of industry, etc.)

By tuning people in on the nostalgic theme with romantic, heroic, esthetic, moral, heavenly and other variations they maintain their power in the sense that people who retreat to or "live in the past are not likely to rebel against a repressive reality. Rendering people nostalgic is part of the strategy of repressive tolerance, a method of social and political control, a means to keep men unfree because it prevents more humane forms of interaction. Rational thinking and long-range futuristic engagement with altruistic goals would mean the end of the Christian-bourgeois microcosmos. The fact that the Christian-bourgeois did remain subjected to a glorified miserable past and to a delusional (religious) frame of reference over centuries up to this day shows that the age of enlightenment does not deserve its name. Egocentricity, ("individualism") and socially disturbed behavior and diseased beliefs lying at the core of the threat-orientation in the Christian-bourgeois microcosmos prevention must be applied primarily against these conditionings. Nostalgic activity is just as much an opium for the people as religious activity, the means to counteract it are similar.

Preventive attention must be directed against the metaphysical revival efforts and fabrications of Christian-bourgeois pacifists, charity thinkers, and Jesus Christ Superstar ideologists. Nostalgization appears in a "new" Christian brand of theory of social *evolution* (as antidote to revolution). This theory is based on the concept "from old make new", that is, rotten stars from the past are pieced together to form the new Christian Super-star. This is a method of (nostalgically) looking back into the future!

Post-Script

Some of the previewers of this paper* contended that its scientific quality was offset by value judgements, and the aggressive tone of language, particularly with respect to religious and political institutions, and the USA. – This critique has been applied to my writings, even though in milder form, during the last ten years. Only recently the publisher of my book "Reactions to Catastrophes" (Zwingmann, 1971) omitted for the same reasons the socially relevant part of the introduction.[14] I prefer being the object of such critique to my renouncing a way of writing which I consider inappropriate in view of the rapidly deteriorating human relations. And I continue to commit scientifically inadmissible infractions because the "ivory-tower" practice of science has disqualified itself as a social and humanization factor. More specifically I reject the criticisms on the following grounds.

My so-called "value judgements" are the synthesis of studies and observations which I gained during my life in many countries around the world. My observations were gathered not only in Europe, but in Asia, and in the USA where I lived for almost 9 years, and my association with American universities extend over some 20 years.

Every ideological and political commitment involves value judgements. The social scientist should commit himself and manifest his commitment when the situation demands it – this means that he makes value judgements. I reject the critique concerning my use of aggressive language, because I feel that the language should be clear and direct, and the tone consonant with the conditions described. Courteous description of criminal events reflects dishonest. Flowery language is the standard means of communication among hypocrites, and manipulators. If for instance I call an individual named Nixon a mass murderer than is this semantically more meaningful in terms of criteria of humanity than if I designate him with official titles.

I reject the critique also for the reason that I do not accept the prevalent definition of science and the operations of this institution. Unfortunately a large contingent of fellow scientists, cannot, do not dare, or do not want to disregard the rigid confines of the established scientific parameter. In "expert-idiot" fashion many of them continue to avoid controversial issues; they contribute to the status quo by recording and ordering data, establishing a few more or less significant relationships, and by impressing themselves and others with statistical acrobatics. For many, research is a means of self-gratification, and this reckless scientific search, which does not consider the social consequences, has for generations peacefully co-existed with Christian morality under the name of "academic freedom." The fact that the Christian-bourgeois microcosmos has been able to play such a disastrous role in human relationships is in no small degree due to "scientists" who hide behind "objectivity", and who place personal ambition above humanitarian considerations. They function as passive instruments or as active co-manipulators in power politics. If scientists were conscious of the social and political relevance of their research, men would not be destroyed as effectively and in as great a number as they are. The atomic "gift" of certain scientists was used by Christian politicians and militarists to destroy men of another microcosm. But scientists have therewith not become wiser, they continue to put powerful weapons, predominantly chemical and bacteriological, in the hands of political and military criminals, in full knowledge of their being used for aggressive purposes. At the same time, and as proof of their humanity – certain nuclear physicists have developed a

---

*Co-editor's remark: E. g. I, M. Pfister-Ammende

[14]This censure imposed by the previous owners of the publishing company was lifted by the present owners.

clean atom bomb! The irresponsibility and what I consider "reckless research" of many scientists is also documented by the fact that they have helped to enrich the consumption paradise without taking the necessary precautions against the poisoning by-products which make living in many urban areas become a health hazard. If the definition of their science had included human welfare and not just technical progress this fiasco could have been predicted and therefore avoided. As a result of this failure some scientists developed the astounding insight that if this situation continued in the future, it becomes worse! and therefore established a new branch of science called "Futurology." Parallel with the discovery of the future, wise men have discovered peace as an object of research (even though often only as an adjunct of war research).

The behavioral, social and political sciences are as guilty as the natural sciences in having, by their prescriptions, neglected the most vital issues of mankind. The majority of their representatives are directly and indirectly supporting institutions that for centuries have been operating on cycles of stress and anxiety production and quasy-reduction by nostalgization, tranquilization, and treatment of symptoms. The majority of experts confine themselves to explorations and descriptions of asocial, antisocial and sick individuals and groups, but rarely they expose the causal ideological substratum. The dominant political unconsciousness and religious delusive thinking in the so-called "Free World" are witnesses for the failure of social-scientific endeavors. Political, and above all religious institutions remain untouchables. – It cannot be the task of behavioral and social scientists, psychiatrists and psychotherapists to be neutral observers or, conservors of communicational disturbances and other disease-conditions, and to adapt or re-adapt man to a inhumane society, but to show the antisocial focus of the system and help people to liberate themselves from degrading impositions.

Scientific institutions of "futurology" and "peace" are likely to remain artefacts as long as the definition of science has not been revised in terms of humanitarian considerations. Needed are not new disciplines but interdisciplinary research, and if we intend to survive it is necessary that we give less attention to the development of technical gadgets and more to their just distribution, and less attention to spectacular conquests of the moon and other "celestial" bodies with incalculable risks to the humans involved, and more to friendly relations and the provision of humane living conditions for all men.

Origin of Contributions and References: See Page 330

PART II

Socio-psychological and Psychiatric Investigations

PSYCHOGENIC DISTURBANCES IN A LINGUISTICALLY STRANGE ENVIRONMENT

Rudolf Allers
Germany (1920)

In the course of several years of work in several military hospitals I was able to observe three examples of an apparently psychogenic condition which seems to me worthy of report. As far as I can determine, nothing similar has been described in the literature as yet. Referred to is a syndrome which on the basis of its structure as well as its probable genesis appears to be closely related to the psychosis of persons with defective hearing which Kraepelin (1909-1915) describes. Just as a person who is deaf or hard-of-hearing is unable to understand the utterances of those about him, being forced to interpret their gestures and other behavior as best he can, anyone who is in the midst of persons speaking a language he fails to comprehend is in a similar position. He too is compelled to guess, forming his impressions on the basis of information of various sorts. One might well suppose that the person lacking knowledge of the language being spoken is better off than the one with a hearing defect; for although he fails to grasp the words, he may still succeed in drawing conclusions on the basis of what he hears. He can determine if his name is being mentioned and whether others are talking about him, whereas the person with hearing insufficiency could suspect this at any time. Also, he can judge on the basis of inflection what general mood is being expressed, e.g. whether this is of a threatening or a friendly nature. Undoubtedly these considerations do play a role. They may explain too why the disturbance we shall describe occurs so infrequently. I suspect, however, that the utilization of such cues requires a degree of intelligence which seemed to have been wanting in at least two of my cases. Furthermore, speech-melodic differences in the expression of various shades of emotion appears so great as to render the reliable ascertainment of the emotional content of an utterance extremely difficult. When listening to a foreign language one may well be able to determine whether the speaker is pronouncing sentences or simply words; for only in the former case is the sequence of words embedded in a melody, in a series of intervals which can be perceived as an organic whole. To be sure, one can recite meaningless words and sounds in such a manner that they give the impression of forming sentences. (A good example of this is the "poem" by Christian Morgenstern from his "Songs of the Gallows" bearing the title "The great lalu-la") This is only the case, however, when such nonsense syllables are spoken in the linguistic melody with which we are familiar. In the polyglot armies of former Austria-Hungary I often had the occasion to hear a language being spoken from which I may have understood this word or that but never the context. I must admit that I usually was unable to detect whether a question or a statment had been intended and whether arousal - certainly perceivable as such - was of a pleasant or unpleasant nature. More than once I held a lively and friendly conversation to be a controversy. If such appraisals are so extremely difficult, even for someone whose training in foreign languages has lent him experience with diverse linguistic melodies, then it is quite comprehensible when a simple farmer, such as was involved in each of the three cases, fails completely at such a task. Therefore, I believe that, despite their hearing ability being intact, the situation of my patients can be considered analogous to that of persons with defective hearing.

Accordingly, the necessary conditions appear to have been present for the development of a psychogenic type of disturbance corresponding to the psychosis of persons with hearing deficiency. The symptoms which my cases present in fact agree to a large extent with Kraepelin's descriptions. Brief accounts of the cases will now be presented as a basis for the symptomatic relationships and other considerations we shall discuss.

Case 1. A 23 year old farmer from the Hungarian plain was admitted to a Vienna hospital in September of 1914 with a flesh wound of the forearm. He was placed in a sick room in which, other than he, only German-Austrians from Tirol and Kärnten were present. None of the doctors nor additional personnel on duty there could speak Hungarian. After the first week it struck me that the man was usually shy or depressed. His intake of food was insufficient. He lay or sat in bed most of the time, though his wound, which healed without complication, did not necessitate this. When gifts, such as cigarettes, were presented to him, he accepted them and generally said a few words; his facial expression, however, gave no indication of pleasure or gratitude. From time to time he stood up, turned to a fellow patient, a nurse or some other member of the personnel and spoke with obvious excitement, frequently pointing to someone of his fellow patients; he soon discontinued this, however, since he saw that he was not understood. Thereafter he only got out of bed at all when he was requested to do so and vigorous gestures were employed. Occasionally, he became noticeably excited, talking to himself with dark demeanor and clenching his fist in a threatening manner.

On the 15th day in the hospital he attempted to leap from the open window of his sick room in the second floor but was frustrated in this endeavor by his fellow patients; he struggled with them violently but soon gave up when confronted with superior force.

An interpreter was obtained and, with his help, rather tedious discussions with the man were carried out. These revealed that he was well oriented and completely ordered in his thoughts. He was rather unapproachable at first but could be brought to express himself more thoroughly in the course of time. He claimed that the people in his ward talked about him in a derogatory manner. Admitting that he could not understand what was said, he still maintained that they were talking about him. He was convinced that a plot was being planned to prevent his returning home and that all letters which were addressed to him were intercepted; he was likewise certain that his wife was allied with these persons, though he could not imagine how. He believed that the infidelity of his wife was being discussed and that a plan had been worked out to murder him. He was sure that the scheme was contrived further outside of the ward. What led him to this conviction could not be determined; he denied emphatically hearing voices.

During the talks the extremely depressed and apprehensive mood of the patient began to change for the better.

He was transferred to another section, where he had contact with his countrymen and with doctors who spoke Hungarian; here he rapidly returned to the norm. After 4 days he could be classed as completely rational and was freed of his delusions.

He begged to be forgiven and explained that when anyone was far from home he could come to have such "stupid thoughts."

This case can be summarized as follows: The condition it represents is characterized by an apprehensive state which seems more aggressive and depressive than depressive alone. Initially, the depressive state may have predominated; at that stage, however, it appeared as a more or less understandable reaction still falling within the norm. Indeed, as a simple peasant who was still burdened with his impressions of being torn from his normal environment by induction into the army, who was a stranger in a foreign city, unable to express his wishes and his fears, who longed to see his wife and native town and was uncertain as to his fate, he certainly had all reason to be in a depressed state of mind. To some extent it must have undoubtedly been homesickness from which he was suffering. However, during continued linguistic isolation a condition developed which was characterized by notions of persecution and by a delusional transformation of the events in his environment. As this occurred, his mood became more and more apprehensive, tensions developing on the basis of fear; for the ominous signs which he thought to recognize and to be incipient led him to expect a dreadful fate. Accordingly, he became aggressive and hypersensitive, assuming a defensive attitude toward the supposedly imminent danger and evil intentions of the persons around him.

Perhaps it is worthy of note that the patient professed not only to recognize hostile motives in the gestures and behavior evident to him in his environment but also to be aware of the plot being discussed further outside the sick room, behind the closed doors. He denied, both during the initial examination and after having gained insight into his situation, any sort of hallucinatory phenomena which could have made his assumption plausible. It seems, therefore, that a sort of projection upon his environment of his reaction to the closed doors was present; this appears similar to the attitude with which one not infrequently leaves a group of people, thinking, "As soon as I am out the door they will surely take me apart."

Further comments regarding the case need not be made at this point, since the differential diagnostic and etiological aspects will later be dealt with for all three cases together.

Case 2. A Russian war prisoner, approximately in his thirties, was hospitalized with a fracture of his lower leg. Nothing was known regarding his personal data, his exact age, etc., since he spoke a language completely unfamiliar to us and was apparently illiterate, making no use of the paper and pencil with which we provided him. During his first few days in the hospital this patient too appeared fearful and disquieted, watching with tense facial expression whoever was standing in the room; he remained quiet, however, making no attempt to gain contact with the patients or the supporting personnel. In the further course of time he became conspiciously more fearful and distraught and to some extent hypersensitive. It was noticeable in particular that he rejected nourishment and that during moments when he thought himself unobserved he hid or discarded food.

As luck had it, a second Russian war prisoner, who was able to communicate with the patient, appeared at this time. With his help and that of a second interpreter it was possible to ask the patient questions. It was learned that he was a Mohammedan Crimean who could not write and who knew his name only approximately.

The statements of the patient sounded very similar to those of the first one. He too was convinced that he was to be prevented from returning home by those around him, and the others talked of him continually, that they made signs to one another of their plans to cut his throat and kept pointing at him; he believed that his food tasted strangely and had been poisoned (incidentally, he explicitly stated that no religious scruples hindered his pleasure in eating, since the war had forced him to give up adhering to religious precepts).

He also professed to have heard people talking about him in the next room — in his language, of course — saying that he should be done away with and, at one point, that this was to occur the next day. He was unable to give a reason as to why the others held such intentions.

Asked why he had not attempted to protect himself against these threats or at least to inform the doctor or the nurse about them, he answered in a typically oriental manner: he had decided that the will of God should prevail. He seemed very happy at the opportunity of expressing his fears or, in fact, talking to another person at all. He proved to be open to persuasion and enlightenment and was ready to admit the possibility of being in error. However, he held steadfast to the reality of the words and sentences he had heard in his own language; what he had heard with his own ears could not be in error, he declared. Further enlightenment here failed as a result of the technical difficulties involved in the double translation.

The prospect of leaving the hospital soon and of being sent to a prisoner-of-war camp where countrymen of his were interned raised his spirits considerably. Eight days after the initial discussion took place he was able to be released for transportation.

By and large, what was stated regarding the first patient is true concerning this one also. In two respects, however, this patient is different from the aforementioned one. First, he appears less spirited in his emotions, or at least is less animated in his actions. This may be due to a fatalistically complacent attitude toward life which the patient shares with many persons of his religion. Whoever has had opportunity to observe Bosnic soldiers as patients is familiar with this doctrine, "the will of God, brother." Many of them see death, evacuation, return to active duty, or an operation with the same complacency or even apathy. The second difference is that hallucinations are evident here. It cannot be determined, of course, whether the patient misinterpreted, in line with his apprehensions, the actual voices emanating from the next room, or whether he produced pure hallucinations. If I allow myself a conjecture, I prefer to believe the latter, the reasons being those which were presented in the introduction. From the standpoint of linguistic melody the German and the Polish languages are markedly different from the languages of the Orient. At least, the conversation of the patient with his comrades sounded very strange to me. It seems rather incomprehensible that German (or Polish) sentences should have given rise to such illusive interpretations. Furthermore, although the patient stated that he had overheard such conversations only two or three times, conversations took place in the next room more frequently than that. Finally, the clear occurrence of acoustic hallucinations in the case which follows tends to substantiate the assumption that hallucinations occurred here too. Thus, an apprehensive and depressed condition with delusions of persecution developed here, just as in the first case.

Case 3. Not long after the second case still a third case came under observation, resembling the second in that it was again a Tartar who was involved; this was quite explainable, for Caucasian and Crimean regiments were stationed nearby.

Here too the disturbance began with apprehensively depressive behavior which was soon coupled with violent reactions. The patient, injured in the shoulder by a glancing bullet which fractured the acromion, made a sullen impression; occasionally he crept behind other patients or behind attendants and once began striking one of the latter with his healthy fist. His facial expression varied, being taciturn and darkly rejecting one moment and apprehensive the next. During a nightly round I noticed the patient sitting in bed with an intensely alert expression; he reacted antagonistically to well-meant persuasion — which, to be sure, he could not understand — as well as to gestures of similar intent, continuing to listen in a strained manner to the stillness of the night. The next day he tried to slit his throat with a knife, though he used one which was not well suited to the task.

Observation of the first two patients had already taught me how to view cases of this sort and I succeeded in obtaining an interpreter. Conversing with the patient was very difficult at first; for, however pleased he may have been to hear familiar words, he was initially rather reserved and unapproachable. Only after extended reassurance and repeated emphasis of our desire to help him did he make any exhaustive statements. What he told could just as well have been reported by the second patient. He too had the feeling that he was the object of scornful and hostile remarks on the part of his fellow-patients, who supposedly wanted to get rid of him (as chance had it, none of the others were Russians). He was sure he was to be murdered during the night. The grave was supposedly already being dug. (At the time, in fact, a spring was being dug not far from the room in which he was located.) He was convinced that during the night he had overheard persons talking about killing him before he could return home. He declared that it was malevolence alone which prompted the others to speak a language he did not understand when they were with him, for he knew he had heard them converse understandably at night. To avoid the tortures supposedly awaiting him, he had attempted to commit suicide.

Although the patient became noticeably freer in the course of the talks, he demonstrated no insight and persisted in his deluded thinking. Nevertheless, he promised not to attempt suicide. Only after repeated talks with him had taken place and he had been told that he would be sent to a group of his countrymen — his wound had healed in the meantime and he was to be released for transportation along with other prisoners-of-war — did he gain sufficient insight to begin doubting evil intentions on the part of his fellow patients. After a patient whom he had thought to be the leader of plots against him had left the hospital, his improvement increased.

At last he conceded to the possibility that he had erred. He could not be convinced that the sinister words he had referred to had not actually been spoken; however, he admitted quite spontaneously that the others may have simply tried to frighten him as a joke.

This case incorporates the characteristics of both the first and the second. The marked excitability and aggressiveness, as well as the tentamen suicidi, of the first case are combined with the hallucinations of the second. The similarity of the symptoms is so great that further remarks concerning this case would simply involve repetition of that which has already been stated.

If one compares the observations which were made regarding each of the three patients — admitting that the conditions under which the observations were obtained leave much to be desired in the way of thoroughness — striking similarity is evident. The syndrome involved can be described as follows: In conjunction with a depressed and apprehensive mood, characterized frequently, particularly at the later stages, by hypersensitivity, delusions of persecution develop relating to the fear for one's own safety or occasionally for that of one's relatives. These delusions form the basis for the individual's conception of his environment and for his illusional reinterpretation of the events within it, sometimes taking the form of acoustic delusions. The hallucinatory voices are not perceived as speaking to the individual involved but rather as dealing with him in the third person. The apprehensive mood can lead to aggression, suicide and violence. The suicide attempts of cases 1 and 2 are obviously not attributable to a taedium vitae but rather to desperation, representing a last means of escape from threatening dangers and torturing incertainties.

When the distressing situation is removed through re-establishment of linguistic contact with the environment, the symptoms disappear rapidly. Though absolute cure, as one would expect, is not immediate, a sense of relief and a degree of insight become evident at once. Only in the first case were observations continued until symptoms had actually vanished; however, as far as can be determined, return to the norm is rapid and complete. Thereafter, full insight into the illness and undisturbed recollection of it are present.

These cases offer little opportunity for etiological and differential diagnostic considerations. It does appear obvious that a psychogenic condition is involved; in fact, the first patient declared so himself. The course of the illness precludes the possibility of depression of a totally different origin, e.g. of a circular type; this is substantiated by the lack of inhibitions and the purely persecutional content of the delusions. The particular mechanism by which the disorder evolves seems clear enough. Thus, the remarks made initially need not be supplemented here.

Still, a comparison with the psychoses of persons with inadequate hearing serves to clarify our viewpoint, for these psychoses are evoked under basically similar conditions. Kraepelin, on p. 1441 of the 4th volume of his works on psychiatry under the heading "transitory psychoses (homilopathic disorders)", describes the "delusion of persecution of persons with defective hearing" as a "somewhat vague delusion of persecution, having its roots in feelings of uncertainty brought on by the severing of the major emotional and intellectual ties with the surroundings; it is characterized by strangely uncertain sensory illusions and half fearful, half hypersensitive moods." The patients reinterpret the events of their environment in terms of acts hostile toward them; they express notions of being poisoned, of others wanting to provoke them, make them sick, fetter them, poison them, etc. They are distrustful, fearful, suspicious and unhappy, utter thoughts of suicide, are frequently tense, quarrelsome and violent, withdraw from other persons and become highly dissocial. The illness is often chronic, negative experiences making it worse. "In an atmosphere that is friendly and understanding, however, the patient generally calms down quickly."

The similarities here are very striking. Some differences do exist, though I do not believe these to be of sufficient importance to destroy the analogy between the two disorders. First, most of Kraepelin's patients were well advanced in age, the hearing difficulties having existed for years. Kraepelin attributed this to the limited ability of older persons to adjust. It might be added that nearly all of his patients were living under difficult circumstances. The three cases which I observed, on the other hand, involved persons of relatively youthful age, in the third or fourth decade of life. This may have contributed to their speedy recovery. In addition, their living conditions in the trenches – all three of the patients belonged to the infantry – their prior exertions, the excitement of their induction into the armed services, etc., may have engendered a proneness to psychogenic ailments, as experience has frequently shown.

A further difference is seen in the fact that the recovery of our patients was rapid and apparently complete, this having scarcely ever been observed among psychoses of hearing difficulties. For in cases with defective hearing the causative factor cannot be removed, whereas in our cases linguistic isolation could be terminated, so that the source of disorder was overcome. If one could return the sense of hearing to the individual without it, his hallucinations and delusions would probably disappear, just as in our cases. One seems to be justified, therefore, in considering the delusion of persecution of the linguistically isolated person in the same category as the psychosis of inadequate hearing.

As far as I can survey the literature, observations such as these have not been made previously or at least have not been published. The question arises as to the reason for this. Various answers seem plausible to me. In the first place, disorders of this nature are extremely rare. Among the many thousands of sick and wounded patients I observed during the war, these are the only cases I encountered. Surely, conditions of linguistic isolation are seldom found. In Vienna it was only at the beginning of the war, when few Hungarians were present in the hospital and the transportation and care of the patients were not yet successfully organized, that a Hungarian could be linguistically isolated there. Similarly, a Russian war prisoner in a Polish hospital could only be faced with isolation of this sort if he spoke an uncommon language, such as Crimean Tartar. Also, the latter two patients were admitted during a period of only slight warring activity, when lone individuals were wounded and taken prisoner; later, whole groups of soldiers from a unit tended to be captured at once. Prison camps, of course, while providing opportunity for the observation of other aspects of the behavior of foreign-speaking persons, are lacking in the conditions which produce the "delusion of persecution of the linguistically isolated individual."

Some cases of this disorder, which after all must have occurred now and then, may have been overlooked through the fact that pyschiatric observations are seldom made in the field or in hospitals lacking in specialists. Comprehensibly enough, interest there is directed primarily at somatic diseases and injuries rather than at the psychic condition of the sick or injured person. States of homesickness and sadness, just as the understandably depressed frame of mind of the wounded or captured individual, are likely to be made responsible for such phenomena, so that the peculiarities of the latter are overlooked. Thorough observation leaves little doubt, however, that the psychosis described here is quite distinct from a psychosis with a "physiological" basis. Homesickness is a subordinate factor, probably playing a role in the total picture but obviously not constituting a major influence. Whether a particular neuropathic disposition can be made responsible for the occurrence of the illness or proneness to it, cannot be decided here. I tend to doubt this myself.

In conclusion, the three cases I have presented seem to me to indicate that under conditions of linguistic isolation a paranoid hallucinatory reaction that is partly apprehensive and partly depressive in character can evolve. It would appear that this belongs in the general class of the imprisonment psychoses and, more specifically as regards both symptoms and pathogenic mechanism, that it can be placed in a category with the psychogenic disorder of persons with impaired hearing. It is referred to here as the "delusion of persecution of the linguistically isolated individual."

Origin of Contributions and References: See Page 333

ALIENS' PARANOID REACTION

F. F. Kino
United Kingdom

Psychotic states due mainly, but not exclusively, to unusual external circumstances are commonly exemplified by such mental disorders as are occasionally met with in persons in prison, or those morbidly homesick, or suffering under the strain and stress of advanced deafness. In the great majority of these instances, however, the external conditions represent only an additional, precipitating, aetiological factor which is operating as a trigger mechanism to a mental derangement of non-specific character already present in a latent state. It may therefore be of some theoretical and practical interest to report on a group of acute and subacute psychotic states whose history, features, course and outcome characterize them as constituting a readily recognizable clinical entity of purely psychological, situational, origin.

During the years 1948-1949 a number of young men of Polish nationality were admitted to this hospital under certificate or as voluntary patients. All of them arrived in Britain after the war. Their ignorance or very defective knowledge of English was a great handicap to a deeper analysis of their mental states, though my own knowledge of the Polish language was sufficient to allow me to get in good touch with them, make them converse in their native tongue and peruse writings. In most of these cases the clinical aspect and progress were so similar and at such variance with the common features of an affective or schizophrenic disorder that the particular character of the psychotic state very soon became evident.

Short extracts from the case histories may illustrate the particularity of this mental aberration.

T.N., 28 years, single, admitted 27 February 1949 as a voluntary patient in an acute state of agitation and panic, hallucinated vividly, heard people saying that he was to be killed and thought the police were following him. He knew where he was and tried to co-operate and to answer simple questions. When reassured he asked in a frightened and subdued voice: 'Have I really got to die?' After a fairly good night (with sedatives) he was able to give a fair account of himself. He had been at secondary school when the war broke out in 1939, entered the Polish Army at the age of 18, remained with the forces for seven years, sharing first the strains of the war, the miseries of imprisonment in Russia, the Polish Army Corps, the fighting in Italy, until

1946, when he came to this country. He had never been seriously ill before, though very sensitive and homesick for his old mother in Poland. No mental disorders in his family. He was otherwise in fair health and of good physique. He became gradually quieter, and able to discuss the circumstances which led to his nervous breakdown. After discharge from the army he had done heavy manual work, digging lime, which did not satisfy him, being so inadaquate to his standard of education. He lived fairly solitarily, and the exhausting work left little time and energy to learn English. For the past few months he had had an affair with an older, married, Englishwoman and he felt that this was wrong. He had grown restless and suspicious, believed that everyone knew about it, heard his fellow workers talking about him though he could not understand their English, was sure he would be killed and there was no more hope for him. He assured me again of his innocence as to any other accusations. Gradually he became quieter, but four weeks after admission he had an acute relapse with anguish, hallucinations and delusions. E.C.T. was without effect, but good recovery followed a course of insulin comas. He was discharged on 6 July 1949 in good mental state, grateful, cheerful, sociable, and fit to go back to his work.

St. G., 25 years, single, admitted 24 September 1948 under certificate. On admission he was highly agitated, emotional, and in a state of anguish. For the next few days he remained restless, resentful and unable to give a sensible account of himself, complaining that his memory for the events of the past few weeks seemed unreal and confused. He was of good physique, and as he assured, always in good physical and mental health. No mental illness in his family. He came to this country in 1946 with the Polish Army Corps and after discharge from the forces worked as a cook in a miners' hostel among his compatriots. His knowledge of English was almost nil. About three months prior to admission he started to feel lonely and homesick, became restless and suspicious, believed that people thought him a spy, experienced strange illusions of smell and taste, the cigarettes tasted badly and he smelled an odor of corpses. He destroyed a wireless set because he thought it was prepared to spy on him. He found a lot of indirect remarks about himself in the newspapers, although he could not read English. After a fair improvement he suddenly relapsed with agitation and a suicidal attempt. Eventually he made a fair recovery, though still a little mistrustful and solitary. He was of average intelligence.

S.F., 25 years, single, admitted 24 September 1949 as a voluntary patient. On admission he was difficult to approach, tense, suspicious, frightened, surly and hostile, but after a few days more approachable though still very reserved. He came to this country in 1946 with the Polish Army Corps from Italy, where he had seen much hard fighting. He had always been physically and mentally well, and had worked latterly as a general laborer. A few days before admission he complained of severe headaches, became frightened and excited, insisted on keeping the door closed, heard clocks ticking though no clocks were near. He disappeared suddenly from his hostel, wandered aimlessly about all night, came back the next day and reported to the police; when taken by the ambulance to the hospital he suddenly jumped from the moving car, looking suspiciously at everyone. When more settled he said that he could not remember correctly what happened to him during the last few days. He thought that his friends had been avoiding him lately and talking about him in an unfriendly manner. Gradually he had become frightened. After several weeks in hospital he was more settled, though on occasions still depressed, and refusing food. He was of fair intelligence, though his knowledge of English was very poor. After a stay of several weeks he left in a fair mental state, quiet, co-operative and sociable.

St. H., 33 years, single, admitted 21 February 1949 as a voluntary patient complaining of severe headaches. He was wary and suspicious, but able to give a fair account of himself. He had served with the Polish forces, came to this country in 1947, worked in a pit and lived in a miners' hostel. The morning after admission he was in an acutely excited state, trembling, talking rapidly and relating spontaneously an extraordinary experience of the night before. He had seen the Holy Virgin standing at his bedside telling him that he was sent here to be destroyed, but she would protect him. A friend of his who visited him reported that three months before he had told him that he would be poisoned because of a Polish girl. Later he became very restless, anxious and frightened. In the hospital he remained for a while solitary, suspicious and moody but gradually became quieter, with better insight into being ill, though still inclined to exaggerate his well-being in order to get approval to leave. He said that he had noticed that during his stay here — and this seemed to have a special meaning for him — his eyes had changed their color. He stated he had always been in good health, and nobody in his family has been mentally ill. He was of fair intelligence, but his English was very poor. Five weeks after admission he desired to be discharged and went back to his hostel.

W. W., 37 years, single, admitted 16 May 1949 as a voluntary patient after making an attack on another man with a bread knife in a quarrel. He was ignorant of English, quiet, rather dull, suspicious and reserved. He denied any mental trouble before. He was of farming stock and of very good physique. He served in the Polish Army, was taken prisoner, spent five years in Germany working as an agricultural laborer, came to this country in 1948 and worked in a steel works. He believed that the other inmates of the hostel he was living in persecuted him, called him a German and tried to steal his girl friend from him. He denied any hallucinatory experiences, but remained suspicious till his discharge after a stay of six months.

All of these cases have several significant features in common which set them distinctly apart from other psychotic disorders with paranoid tendencies, namely, the pre-morbid history, the specific environmental circumstances at the onset of the illness, the characteristic clinical manifestations and the final issue of the psychotic episode.

A dependable account regarding the state of mental health in their families was not possible to obtain, though all of them denied any instances of mental ill-health among their relatives. Their personal state of health, at least for the past six to eight years, could be more readily ascertained by the known and partly documented histories of that period in their lives. Though each of them was exposed for many years to the extraordinary physical and mental stresses of war, captivity, exhaustive wanderings with the Polish Army Corps or German labor camps, none of them had had a nervous breakdown or was seriously incapacitated in his efficiency for service or labor. It will be agreed that no harder tests could be invented in order to prove a good phsyical and mental health and a high grade of constitutional make-up in a man.

With transfer to this country all the dangers and strains of war or captivity were completely removed, and these men could enjoy a freedom and material well-being they had not known for years. One would expect that such a wholesome turn in their circumstances would rather have enhanced the good state of their mental health, and made them resistant to the minor troubles commonly associated with a transfer to foreign surroundings, especially since they had already been away from their own country for many years. As a matter of fact, as long as they continued to live within their own units or groups they felt well and relatively contented. The change occurred with their transfer to workshops or pits, where they found themselves isolated in a foreign environment whose language and habits were unknown to them, making every attempt at interpersonal approach very difficult. Being accustomed at home to lively and voluble companionship, the impossibility of making conversation and friendly contact with their new companions left them emotionally upset. Misunderstandings and misapprehensions unavoidable in such a situation evoked their suspicion and mistrust. Harmless talks or remarks of their fellow workers to one another were interpreted as hostile observations, though they were unable to understand the language. Gradually this morbid state of mind grew to such intensity that a rational appreciation of the environment became quite impossible.

In one or other instance the development of the psychotic state was nutured or accelerated by some factual misconduct on their own part, which under normal conditions would hardly have led to self-reproach. Others ascribed the presumed hostility to their nationality, their conduct during the war, or the false accusations as to their political opinions. The progressive emotional tension culminated in several instances in a state of elemental panic and confusion, with impulsive running away or suicidal preoccupations. Some of them experienced vivid visual or auditory hallucinations whose content was closely connected with their delusional preoccupations, corroborating their ideas of reference or persecution. Though unreasonable, their delusions were never of a nonsensical character.

The predominant clinical features on admission were a state of agitation and fear, combined occasionally with slight confusion, deep mistrust and, rarely, emotional outbursts. Their expression and behavior were adequate to their affective state and genuine, without a shade of theatricality. It was rather the natural deep grief of an innocent person suffering under false accusations and slander. After a few days' rest (and sedatives) a fair contact could be achieved, though they did not believe in reassurances, and insisted on the reality of their fears, delusions and illusions. Hallucinatory experiences were rare. Some believed their food was being poisoned and refused it. Gradually the more intelligent of them felt the desire to talk of themselves, to assert their innocence again and again, to refer to their good conduct in the services and to testimonials from their superiors. Though they exaggerated the importance of some minor misbehavior, false self-accusations were never made. Over-estimations of their personalities, either in the form of importance or martyrdom, were not observed. In states of anguish their consciousness was slightly clouded but was never lost, and they were never stuporose. In quieter mood they were fairly well oriented, and able to give an accurate account of their remote history, and partly of experiences prior to the acute breakdown. They never had the feeling of being really ill or influenced by other people. From their conversation, letters to friends or relations, sociable conduct and fair adaptability to hospital life, it was evident that their intelligence was not impaired, though never above average.

Under non-specific psychotherapy, supported by E.C.T. and in one case by insulin coma treatment, they gradually became more settled, with more and more insight into the abnormality of their feelings and ideas, and were eventually able to go back to their former surroundings and occupations.

Discussion

The external conditions which give origin to such psychologically determined mental reaction are fortunately rare, and therefore the number of publications dealing with this type of psychotic disorder is limited.

The three cases reported by R. Allers (1920) seem to be the first to refer to psychogenic mental aberration of a similar kind. All of them foreigners, in good mental health, they were admitted to a general hospital in Austria among German-speaking patients whom they could not understand, and with nobody to translate their own tongue. They soon developed an acute psychotic state conspicious by fear, agitation, ideas of reference and persecution, with illusional distortions of harmless experiences, and with suicidal tendencies. Allers, by calling these disorders 'persecutory delusions of lingually isolated persons' emphasized the aetiological importance of language. The observations of Kurt Schneider (1930) under the heading 'Primary Delusions of Reference' are of kindred character, though he believes that the bewildering experience of being suddenly transplanted into a foreign environment is of no less importance than the linguistic difficulties. Similarly to the cases of Allers, in Schneider's cases the paranoid affect-storm developed acutely and resolved completely after several days, with full insight into the morbidity of their suspicions and fears. A case by F. Knigge (1935) belongs apparently to the same type as those described by K. Schneider. A young and healthy Hungarian girl, travelling by herself to Brazil, was suddenly overtaken in Hamburg by an acute paranoid excitement state, which cleared completely in ten days.

According to those authors their cases represented immature and emotionally unstable individuals, though of average intelligence. In a sudden and unusual situation in alien surroundings, combined with a physical and mental strain and aggravated by language embarrassment, they responded with an acute excitement state of short duration. The episodic character of the mental derangement is, in the view of the authors, of particular diagnostic significance, differentiating these 'paranoid reactive states' from the true 'paranoid processes' characterized by insidious development and chronic progression. However, Schneider, though all his cases were of this type, presumed that such reactions may also occur without such stormy development. Some of our cases may serve as an illustration to this theoretically foreseen possibility. The acuteness of the disorder, though of diagnostic value if present, is evidently not necessarily an obligatory condition. Of much more significance than the time factor is the psychopathological structure of the psychotic state and its obvious features as a genuine psychogenic reaction. In Jaspers' definition a 'genuine reaction' is one in which 'the thought content is in a comprehensible connection with the primary causal experience and which could not occur without that experience, being in its further progress dependent on that experience and its connections'. Although morbid in the exaggerations and conclusions, it remains well comprehensible in its origin as rooted in a personal experience and an almost specific situation, and in the consequences of its further development.

It is probably true that some degree of hypersensitivity or deficiency in self-reliance, or both, will often be in the make-up of persons prone to respond with a paranoid reaction under adequate pathogenic conditions. However, as evidenced in our instances, even a quite healthy and emotionally well-balanced individual, when subjected to unusual affective stress in a specifically difficult situation, may respond in the same morbid manner. In the usual interplay between constitutional susceptibility and a selective situation, the determining causal agent in these cases is rather the character or the make-up of the personality.

It is hard to say what is the primary disturbance, whether it is one of affect or of misconception regarding the attitude of the environment, since both are often closely intertwined from the start. Loneliness, external difficulties and social maladjustment will quite naturally bring on a depressive mood, which in turn will falsify perceptions and judgment. The difficulty of language was no doubt a point of great importance, but not the exclusive one. Their sudden loss of habitual companionship, the foreign surroundings with their incomprehensible atmosphere and habits, the change of occupation, the hazards of being on their own instead of being directed and cared for as before, all these various influences together were for many of them too great an emotional stress which, finding no relief by verbal expression or sympathetic consolation, broke through as a paranoid psychotic reaction.

In support of the correctness of the interpretation given, it can be stated that after 1949 mental disorders were no longer observed among Poles admitted to this hospital with psychotic disorders. After the first years had passed the difficulties of language were naturally overcome, and little by little they learned to understand their new community better and to adjust themselves satisfactorily to their new life.

Conclusions

A rare form of an acute and subacute psychotic disorder was observed during the years 1948-49 among Polish workers admitted to this country after the war.

On the strength of its aetiology, features, clinical course and issue the mental disorder is regarded as a genuine psychogenic psychotic reaction.

The suggested designation will express its particular origin and character.

Origin of Contributions and References: See Page 333

REACTIONS TO EVACUATION

Anna Freud and Dorothy Burlingham
United Kingdom

The war acquires comparitively little significance for children so long as it only threatens their lives, disturbs their material comfort or cuts their food rations. It becomes enormously significant the moment it breaks up family life and uproots the first emotional attachments of the child within the family group. London children, therefore, were on the whole much less upset by bombing than by evacuation to the country as a protection against it.

The reasons for and against evacuation were widely discussed during the first year of the war in England. Interest in the psychological reactions of the children receded into the background when, in the second year, the air raids on London demonstrated against all possible objections the practical need for children's evacuation. In order to survey completely all the psychological problems involved, the subject would have to be studied from various angles.

There is an interesting social problem involved in billeting. Children who are billeted on householders who are either above or below the social and financial status of their parents will be very conscious of the difference. If urged to adapt themselves to a higher level of cleanliness, speech, manners, social behavior or moral ideals, they will resent these demands as criticism directed against their own parents and may oppose them as such. There are children who will refuse new clothes, and hang on to torn and dirty things which they have brought from home. With young children this may be just an expression of love and a desire to cling to memories; with older children it is simultaneously an expression of their refusal to be unfaithful to the standard of their homes. Their reaction may, of course, also be of the opposite kind. The quickness with which they drop their own standards may be an expression of hostility against their own parents. When, on the other hand, children are billeted on families who are poorer than their own, they easily interpret the fact as punishment for former ungratefulness shown at home.

This situation of being billeted has a secret peace-time counterpart in the child's inner phantasy life. Most children of early school age, six to ten, possess a secret daydream — the "family romance" — which deals with their descent from royal or lordly parents who have only entrusted them to their real, more humble families. Others have secret fears of being stolen from their families and then forced to live in poor and dingy surroundings. On the part of the child these phantasies are attempts to deal with the whole range of conflicting emotions to the parents. Love, hate, admiration, criticism, and even contempt for the parents are worked out in them. When evacuation occurs at this time of life, being billeted with foster parents of a different social level may be upsetting to the child, because it gives sudden and undesired reality to a situation which was meant to be lived out in the realms of phantasy.

The psychological problem of the foster mother is evident even to those who otherwise refuse to take psychological complications too seriously. Possessiveness of the mother is, as we know, an important part in the mother-child relationship. The child starts its life as one part of the mother's body. Insofar as the feelings of the mother are concerned it remains just that for several years. Egoistic reactions of the mother normally include the child. Harm to the child is resented by the mother as if it were harm done to herself. Every human being normally over-estimates his own importance, his own personality and his own body. This overestimation on the part of the mother includes the child. This explains why an infant who is neither good-looking nor clever may still seem to posses both qualities in the eyes of its own mother. It is this primitive possessiveness and over-estimation at the bottom of motherly love which make it possible for mothers to stand the strain of work for their children without feeling abused. It is common knowledge that only love for children will prevent their continual demands, the continual noise caused by them, and the continual damage done by them from being considered a nuisance.

Foster mothers, i.e. householders, are expected to suffer children whom they neither love nor over-estimate. There will only be two courses open to them. One is to retain the attitude of an indifferent outsider, to complain about the imposition and to try and get rid of the child as soon as possible. The other course taken is to adopt a mother's attitude, which means to feel towards the strange child as if it were her own. The foster mother will in these last cases not suffer from the children billeted with her, or rather she will take the trouble involved as a matter of course, as mothers do.

But this second attitude, which is the cause of all billeting successes, contain another danger. The real mother of the child will suddenly turn up on Sundays or holidays and claim earlier rights of possession. It has been said on many occasions, and once more after the failure of billeting mothers on householders, that it is impossible for two mothers to share one kitchen. This may be exaggerated. But it is certainly impossible for two mothers to share one child.

There is a third, minor, problem which so far has been less considered. It is the problem of jealousy and competition between brothers and sisters which is presented in evacuation in the new form of jealousy of foster-brothers and sisters. Children never feel friendly towards newborn additions to their family. They sometimes pretend to do so; at other times they are mollified by the smallness and complete helplessness of the newcomer. The newly billeted foster-brother, on the other hand, is very often neither small nor helpless. He usurps rights which the other child is unwilling to give up. The billeted newcomer for his part is deeply conscious of his second-rate position and is embittered by it. There are certainly all the elements for jealousy and discomfort given in the situation.

These reactions are interesting enough to be made the subject of surveys which are carried out by child guidance clinics set up in reception areas by consulting psychologists attached to County Medical Offices. They keep an eye on trouble in the billets, smooth out difficulties and remove the worst billeting misfits. They have in their positions a unique opportunity to study the situation — especially the situation of the school children.

The Government scheme for Evacuation of unattended children was never meant to include children under school age, with the exception of some little ones who were taken along with evacuation parties as younger brothers and sisters. Evacuation of unattended children under five was rightly considered a difficult undertaking. They were supposed to stay with their mothers and only to be evacuated with them whenever necessary. When the percentage of mothers who were unwilling to leave London and stay in billets was rather large, a scheme for under-fives was added to the other. These under-fives whose mothers had to have a good reason for staying behind were sent out unattended, either to nurseries or to selected billets. The difficulty remained that vacancies under this scheme were scarce compared with the onrush of mothers who were eager to send their small children to some place of safety.

In a London nursery like ours there is little opportunity for collecting evidence about the successful billeting of under-fives. Children who are happy in their billets, i.e. who find a foster mother ready to "adopt" them, stay in the country and little more is heard about them. "Billeting failures" on the other hand, wander backwards and forwards between London and the country. Some of them may settle down in the end in residential nurseries like ours, which are created either by private initiative in England or by one of the American Relief Funds. More than twenty per cent of our cases are billeting failures of various types.

We should be more inclined to hold the billets responsible for the inability of such large numbers of children to adapt themselves to the new conditions if we did not posess first-hand evidence of the difficulties involved from our own observations of the children after their first separation from their families. The most impressive examples of this kind have been described at various times in our monthly reports. It is true that not many children present as frightening a picture as Patrick, three and a half years old, who found himself reduced to a state in which compulsive formula and symptomatic actions played the largest part; or Beryl, four years old, who sat for several days on the exact spot where her mother had left her, would not speak, eat or play, and had to be moved around like an automaton. Even apart from these unusual cases we have seen long drawn-out states of homesickness, anxiousness and despair which are certainly more than the average inexperienced foster mother can be expected to cope with. We certainly see no similar states of distress in children when we make the round of London shelters and find them sleeping on the platforms next to their mothers. Our own feelings revolt against the idea of infants living under the condition of air-raid danger and underground sleeping. For the children themselves, during the first days or weeks of home-sickness, this is the state of bliss to which they all desire to return.

There are many obvious reasons why small children should not stay in London shelters, that it is not easy to pay equal attention to the emotional reaction of the individual child against evacuation.

A child who is removed from London to the country is certainly removed from a state of greater danger to a lesser one; it exchanges unhygienic conditions of life for more hygienic ones. It avoids possibilities of infection which multiply where thousands of individuals are massed together. If the child goes to a residential nursery, it will be better fed than before; it will be given proper occupation and companionship and will be spared the dreariness of an existence where it was dragged to and fro between home and shelter with long and empty hours of queuing-up at a tube station.

It is difficult to realize that all these improvements in the child's life may dwindle down to nothing when weighed against the fact that it has to leave its family to gain them. This state of affairs is still more difficult to understand when we consider that many of the mothers concerned are not "good mothers" in the ordinary sense of the word. We deal with a large majority of mothers who are affectionate, intelligent, hard-working and ready to make any sacrifice for their children; but there are a minority of mothers who are not like this. They may be lazy and negligent, hard and embittered and unable to give affection. There are others who are overly strict in their demands and make the life and upbringing of the child extremely difficult. It is a known fact that children will cling even to mothers who are continually cross and sometimes cruel to them. The attachment of the small child to its mother seems to a large degree independent of her personal qualities, and certainly of her educational ability.

This statement is not based on any sentimental conception of the sacredness of the tie between mother and child. It is the outcome of detailed knowledge of the growth and nature of the child's emotional life in which the figure of the mother is for a certain time the sole important representative of the whole outer world.

PRACTICAL CONCLUSIONS

At first glance it seems from this material as if small children had little chance to escape unharmed from the present war conditions. They either stay in the bombed areas with their parents, and irrespective of physical danger, become upset by their mothers' fears and excitements, as well as hardened and brutalized by the destruction which goes on around them and by shelter life. Or else they avoid these dangers, are evacuated to the country and suffer other shocks through separation from the parents at an age which needs emotional stability and permanency. Choosing between two evils seems to be all that war-time care is able to accomplish for them.

On the other hand we should not be too quick in drawing such conclusions.

That evacuation under the present conditions is as upsetting as bombing itself is no proof yet that methods of evacuation could not be found which guard the children's life and bodily health, and at the same time provide the possibility for normal psychological development, and steady progress in education.

Our case material shows that it is not so much the fact of separation to which the child reacts so abnormally as the form in which the separation has taken place. The child experiences shock when it is suddenly and without preparation exposed to dangers with which it cannot cope emotionally. In the case of evacuation the danger is represented by the sudden disappearance of all the people whom it knows and loves. Unsatisfied longing produces in it a state of tension which is felt as shock. If separation happened slowly, if the people who are meant to substitute for the mother were known to the child beforehand, transition from one object to the other would proceed gradually. If the mother reappeared several times during the time when the child had to be weaned from her, the pain of separation would be repeated, but it would be felt each successive time in smaller doses. By the time the affection of the child had let go of the mother the new substitute object would be well known and ready at hand. There would be no empty period in which the feelings of the child are turned completely inward and, consequently, there would be little loss of educational achievement. Regression occurs while the child is passing through the no-man's-land of affection, i.e. during the time the old object has been given up and before the new one has been found. Two of our children have expressed this state of mind in their own words.

Bertram, three and three-quarters years old said: "I don't like you, I don't like anybody! I only like myself". Ivan, five years old, exclaimed: "I am nobody's nothing".

Mothers are commonly advised not to visit their children during the first fortnight after separation. It is the common opinion that the pain of separation will then pass more quickly and cause less disturbance. In reality it is the very quickness of the child's break with the mother which contains all the dangers of abnormal consequences. Long drawn-out separation may bring more visible pain but it is less harmful because it gives the child time to accompany the events with his reactions, to work through his own feelings over and over again, to find outward expressions for his state of mind, i.e. to abreact slowly. Reactions which do not even reach the child's consciousness can do incalculable harm to its normality.

Objection might be raised that emergency war conditions do not allow these considerations to carry weight. Still, it seems possible to base plans for "evacuation in slow stages" on psychological convictions of this kind.

If children under five have to be evacuated, unattended like their bigger brothers and sisters, they should at least not be sent out under harder conditions than the older ones. School children, even if they lose their connection with their homes, will at least retain the relationship to their school friends and to their teachers who go out with them. Under-fives who are sent to nurseries go into the complete unknown.

One could conceive a plan under which all small children would be collected in day nurseries. They would become attached to their nurses and teachers and know the units in which they spend their days while they still live at home. In times of danger these day nurseries would be converted into residential nurseries and would be evacuated collectively. Mothers who refuse to part from their small children could be offered the chance to go too as paid domestic staff. Experience has shown that only a small percentage of all those mothers would choose to do so. Under such conditions evacuation would lose its horrors for the young child and abnormal reactions to it would become extremely rare. To maintain the remnants of the parent relationship as far as possible and simultaneously to prepare the way for the return of children to their homes after the war, there should be little or no restriction of the visiting rules. In our houses parents come and go whenever their occupations leave them free to do so. Provision should be made for the possibility of such visits, as it is made for all the other bodily and educational needs of the child, as they are all considered important for the child's well being and future happiness.

It will be still harder to devise proper means of evacuation for small babies. If infants have to be separated from their mothers in the first weeks of life in the interest of war work, it is best that they go to creches near factories where mothers can deposit and collect them. This again does not solve the problem of shelter sleeping in times of danger. If babies go to residential homes these should be situated as near to the outskirts of the town as possible to encourage frequent visiting. With infants there are no "remnants of a mother relationship" to maintain, and no memories to keep alive. The baby will have to make the acquaintance of his mother during the hours or days of visiting. There should certainly be some relation between the frequency of visits and the ability reached by the infant to retain remembrance.

Origin of Contributions and References: See Page 333

DISPLACED SOVIET RUSSIANS IN SWITZERLAND

Maria Pfister-Ammende[1]
Switzerland

Contents

A. Preliminary remarks. I. Problem and situation. II. Prior history of the Soviet Russian refugees.

B. The Soviet Russian refugees in camps of the Federal Central Administration of Camps and Homes. I. Work camps in 1943. II. Isolated Russians, and Russian groups in 1944. III. Homes for Russians in 1945. 1. General behavior of the refugees. 2. Distinctive reactions as regards spontaneity, sexuality, alcohol and regulations. 3. Feelings of solidarity. 4. Ties with the homeland. 5. Mass behavior. 6. Administrative problems.

C. Summary, relations to mental hygiene.

A. Preliminary remarks.

I. Problem and situation

The Swiss authorities had to accommodate between 1943 and 1945, along with refugees of other nationalities, several thousand Soviet Russians. These were prisoners of war and alien workers who had escaped from Germany and Italy. After a preliminary stay in military reception camps or, initially, through no fault of their own, in jails, they were assigned individually to work on farms or were sent to establishments of the Federal Central Administration of Camps and Homes, thereafter called the Hostels Administration.

The care of the Soviet Russians was strongly influenced by political factors. These explain various psychological characteristics. However, since a critical

---

[1] From 1944 – 1948 the author directed the Mental Health Service of the Swiss Federal Central Administration of Camps and Homes. (Eidgenössische Zentralleitung der Lager und Heime).

evaluation of political matters is not in my field of competence, I limit myself to the facts I have found, to observations of a socio-psychological nature and to certain essential anamnestic references.

The war, the period spent in Germany and the escape had a strong effect upon these people — they were displaced persons and refugees. I concern myself, therefore, with the psychological reaction of a particular group of persons from Swiss homes and camps, those of Soviet Russian nationality. The examples I cite illustrate the reactions of deported persons and refugees, not of the Russian people in their native milieu. A portrait of the Russian people as such or of "Russians today and in former times" is neither in line with my purpose nor with my competence. I can also speak in no absolute terms of "Soviet Russians". Just as persons from the Cantons Appenzell and Tessin are both Swiss and yet are of completely different types, our Russian refugees represent all the variety and multiplicity of the peoples of the Soviet Union; the Ukrainian element was manifest particularly strongly.

No thoroughgoing differentiation is possible regarding the question, to what extent our observations can be attributed to national characteristics, to the form of government, to education or to the effects of uprooting. Since these persons were in an exceptional situation, staying with us as interned refugees, exhaustive ethnological and familial anamnestic data could not be obtained.

It would also be impossible for me to present a complete psychological account of the Soviet Russian refugees in Switzerland. I must limit myself for the most part to one aspect, namely to observations of groups, of reactions of the individual within the group and of his relationship to the group. The presence of individual differences was also evident in our explorations and observations. However, with these people who were inwardly bound to the Soviet system we had little opportunity to carry out such thorough psychological explorations as we did with numerous other groups of refugees. This was due to the situation, to the language and to a certain shyness of these people toward revealing themselves individually.

My descriptions and conclusions are based on the documentary material of the Hostels Administration, on my own observations and explorations[2] as well as on the results of detailed interviews with the Directors of our Russian establishments by psychologically trained workers. Also, valuable material and testimony of private persons who worked with the Russians was available.

II. Prior history of the Soviet Russian refugees

> "Switzerland is so hard, so many stones, so little earth, the land is so small. Russia is large, a great plain, much earth, many forests and large industries."

---

[2] I conducted part of this investigation in 1944 with the support of the Swiss Academy of Medical Sciences.

These simple words of a twenty-eight year old former war prisoner from Orsk, a photographer by profession, who escaped to our country from Italy, expresses the sharp contrast between our country and Russia which prompted the Russians to sigh, "the mountains are so heavy". The mountains, symbols of the homeland for the Swiss, were for many Russians simply "impediments" in the plain, obstructing their view as well as their feeling of well-being. They did not fascinate them but instead disturbed and oppressed them.

No less important than this geographic difference was the difference in the education and development of the youthful Soviet citizen. From childhood on he was integrated into a collectively formed society. Our refugees, most of them between seventeen and twenty-five years of age and stemming from families of farmers and workers, had been employed in their homeland in kolkhoses or factories. Many of them were deported by the Germans as school pupils or apprentices. Their parents had been born without rights as muzhiks. Thus, they belonged to the first generation in their families with regular school education and training.

The reactions of the Soviet Russian refugees in Switzerland could not be understood if one were to neglect consideration of their "European experience". These persons stemmed, as was already mentioned, from the host of war prisoners, deported persons and alien workers. A certain percentage of this last group went to Germany voluntarily. Since only very few failed to return to Russia in 1945, the number of actual collaborators must have been extremely small. A certain percentage, particularly of those alien workers who poured into Switzerland during the collapse of Germany at the beginning of 1945, may have hesitatingly decided to leave Russia. Why they went to Switzerland instead of going directly to their allies after being freed is uncertain. Were they caught in the general stream of alien workers? Did they flee to the peaceful "island" of Switzerland to gain refuge from the chaos and confusion of the last weeks of the war? Or were they disturbed by a certain insecurity since they had worked in Germany without committing sabotage? They appeared uncertain as to their later fate, this being evident in various apprehensive questions and in states of depression and fear at the time of their repatriation. We are unable to estimate the number of insecure persons among them; however, we believe that most of our Soviet Russian refugees were prisoners of war, deported persons and forced laborers. As they later came to Switzerland they knew very little about this country. They expected fascist influence here.

A Russian officer who had been an intermediate school teacher at home, escaping to Switzerland in 1943 from German war imprisonment, said: "In Germany I heard that Switzerland is living in peace, that they accept refugees but return some of them to Germany. We went nevertheless, since we simply wanted to flee to a place where there were no Germans."

Thus, most Soviet Russians came neither brimming with expectations nor anxious to make contact as did the other refugees; instead they were taciturn, distrustful, and noncommittal. — They also came, not as homeless persons, but rather as citizens of a powerful nation, still apprehensive in 1943 but then with continually growing confidence of victory. Their homeland and their country was their greatest pride.

These already collectively bound people were welded together even more strongly through their war experiences. In Switzerland, too, it was not their personal interests, but rather the bond uniting them with those of their own nation or of other nations fighting alongside them, which was of primary importance to them.

> A Russian who had fled from Germany was imprisoned in Italy and had then fought together with Italian partisans coming with them to Switzerland in sick condition, reported: "We were supposed to part. We all cried and our hearts were heavy, for we were friends and brothers. A good Swiss officer comforted us and said: 'You should not cry; where you are going is very good, a nice hotel.' I told him: 'That doesn't help. I don't want to be where it is nice but where my comrades are'."

Where such a degree of comradeship exists, resistance, where it occurs, is responded to with sharp, well-organized reactions of the group.

Some of our Russians had been in concentration camps. The results of this were particularly evident in sleeplessness, pathological restlessness, emotional outbreaks and lack of contact, and in lasting ties of the individual prisoners with one another.

Finally, as regards the prior history of the deported persons, another very important consideration should be mentioned, i.e. their deportation at a youthful age, followed by years of being uprooted during their adolescence. At the age of thirteen or fourteen they were isolated from the influence of family, school, and state. They had to perform hard labor, usually under conditions of insufficient nutrition. They lived without protection in a hostile country where a foreign tongue was spoken. Among youthful persons such influences produce either a slackening and obliteration of one's individuality or a defiant self-assertiveness, often under the cloak of a certain outward adjustment. When the iron hand of the oppressor disappears, the danger of explosive antisocial behavior is great. For then, as one can at last defend oneself, be someone and not simply remain silent, forcefully repressed aggressions flare up and restraints dissolve. Some period of time is necessary until such persons find a certain stability and inner calm, if they find it at all.

B. Soviet Russian Refugees in Camps of the Federal Central Administration of Camps and Homes

I. Work camps in 1943

127 Russians and 67 Yugoslavians were employed for half a year in clearing forests and later transported, under military guard, to a work camp. Concerning this period we possess documents but no explorations nor observations of our own. From the

documents it appears evident that this was a period of political conflict in which no stable relationship of trust between the authorities and the internees developed.

I am anxious to cite a document which I have authenticated and which stems from this period, since it indicates in what a difficult predicament the individual could find himself through lack of trust in his environment. The director of the work camp in Raron wrote to the Central Administration as follows:

> "During the night two of the internees, E., an auto mechanic, and P., an electro-welder, escaped. Yesterday noon E. came to me and complained of intensive pains in both thighs. He showed me the wound from a bullet which had pierced both thighs. Our camp samaritan, whom I consulted, was of the opinion that the wound had never been treated by a doctor. One of the bones, and the main nerve as well, appeared to have been injured by the bullet, so that E. undoubtedly suffered pain. One of his thighs in particular had swollen radically and had filled with a liquid, which was drawn off by a physician several times. I advised E. to go to the hospital and be treated there; at first he refused, since he feared that he would be operated on.
>
> With great effort I managed to convince him to go to the hospital, where he was treated personally by Dr. M., the hospital physician. Dr. M. phoned, advising that it was necessary in any case for the patient to remain in the hospital for several days, since he needed absolute rest. The treatment was to involve massage and warm air as well as other forms of therapy. Coming out of the hospital directly afterwards, E. did not report to me but supposedly sat in the barracks and cried, declaring that his legs were to be cut off. I am convinced that his fleeing can be traced to this fear along. P. appears to me to be a follower who did not want to let his sick comrade leave alone."

Thus, a twenty-four year old auto mechanic and soldier who has escaped from war imprisonment sits in the barracks weeping. Finally, he accepts all deprivations and dangers connected with an escape from internment in the year 1943. If all of this occurred because the man was to enter a hospital he was unfamiliar with, and if a comrade accompanied him during his escape, sharing his uncertain fate with him — then deep-rooted psychological relationships are evident here; possibly, if these had been analyzed and the results of such an investigation had received practical applications, various misunderstandings might have been avoided.

II. Individual Russians and Russian Groups in 1944

During 1944, more and more foreign workers of both sexes as well as escaped war prisoners found their way into Switzerland. Several hundred Russian women were assigned to the Hostels Administration. They were found both singly and in groups, together with women of other nationalities, in our refugee homes. As lone individuals among women of diverse nationalities they made a quiet and inconspicuous impression. However, psychological investigations we carried out indicated that the Russian women suffered to a considerable degree from isolation. As a result of the difference in language and in their general nature they felt themselves alien in a refugee home and often suffered under reactive-depressive states.

In 1944 I met a twenty-two year old Russian woman with her infant in a home for refugees of various nationalities. She was born in Kiev and had lived in a village near Kiev as a kolkhos worker. Her husband, with whom she had fled from Germany to Switzerland, had gone on to France to fight again as a soldier. At first Marushka spoke little. She said simply: "I am sad because I am alone so far from home, completely alone; I am so homesick." After I had spent a day with her child, she thawed out and began to cry: "I am so lonely; all the women are visited by men; I am alone! In Germany I had no time to be sad – much work, often beaten. Here I have so much time; still, I am so very sad, sad because alone, so far from home, alone with the child. Switzerland is good, but I am Russian, born in Russia; I long for Russia. Had to go to the hospital; such a good woman was there; I think of her often. She said, 'Simply work; you must not be sad.' Such a kind woman! They were all so kind in the hospital; a seventy year old man and an eighty-five year old grandmother cried as I left for the camp. I was supposed to go to Leysin to the tuberculosis sanatorium, but I don't want to be alone; I want to be here with the child. I don't want to go. Some of the other refugees here are not nice to me. In the morning they say nothing to me – not 'Good morning,' nothing. Many ask, 'How are you, Marushka?' as with a small child! 'Ca va bien?' They laugh! Why do they laugh at me? I do not speak of culture; I can not read their books, only Russian. They talk with each other. I understand what they say but can not speak. It is very, very hard;" – she cried – because I do not talk, they say 'dumb'. Here within I understand everything, but with my mouth I can say nothing. There inside it hurts! I am not dumb when I cannot speak! A woman was sick; I brought her food, knitted for her and still she said, 'dumb, Russian and dumb'. But they all visited me in the hospital, even those who said I am dumb. I work in the kitchen. I am so sad; I think, 'why dumb if I cannot speak?' Then I often hurry to my child. In Russia no one says 'dumb' if one does not understand. At night I have such terrible and sad dreams. I dream so much about home because I am alone here and my mother is dead. When I wake up, I am alone." –Other refugees, who were understanding, described Marushka as a person whose good-naturedness was exploited and who had so many troubles because others treated her badly; some women looked down upon her because she was "uneducated", whereas she was in fact intelligent and good-hearted, children being attached to her and she herself seeing and hearing everything. A Jewish woman refugee from Austria said: "A fine person, a poor devil, staying with these fur-coated women. She had nothing; therefore, to them she is nothing." –Two days later other Russian women arrived; there were touching scenes of boundless greeting. They embraced one another, laughed and sobbed confusedly. From then on, Marushka was completely changed. She laughed, talked and sang all day.

A soft, suffering and helpless human being who again had found protection and warmth in the native milieu, in a group of Russians. Here was a basic problem of many of our Soviet Russian refugees: the lone individual felt himself strange and foresaken, suffering from insecurity and feelings of persecution — reactions which have been observed in other countries as well among isolated, foreign-speaking war prisoners.[3] As soon as he was among persons of his kind, however, a group was formed, "the Russian group", in which the individual revived and flourished. No other nationality demonstrated this phenomenon so clearly. To be sure, the Yugoslavians, the Poles and in particular the Italians formed groups, but we observed this attitude of "only being able to breathe in the air of the homeland" primarily among the Soviet Russians. This dependency upon the surroundings appeared somehow ineradicable. Such intensive ties with the original life space are evident here, that this possesses for them the quality of being a "biotop" and an "archetop" in the sense of Hediger (1946): "One can scarcely escape the impression that a psychic unit, the archetop, a psychic quantum as it were, corresponds with the ecological concept of the biotop which is the primary topographic unit ... The concept of the archetop, with its similarity to the ecological element of the biotop (Hesse) and to the concept of the archetype (Jung), is thus introduced to psychologically characterize that space which an animal (or a human being) originally occupied."

In the course of time there came to be groups of 10 to 15 Russian women in some of the homes. These women were industrious and light-hearted. However, relations with them were difficult. For reasons of language they could not communicate well with other refugees. Just as this could lead to reactive depression in the case of the lone individual, as has just been illustrated, it could produce hypersensitivity toward the environment when a group was involved. In addition, as a result of difficulties in communication, they received tasks which were easy to explain but which were both dirty and very demanding. Thus, the danger existed that the women would simply be given brief directions and then left alone to work. Experience indicates that a person in charge unconsciously speaks louder and more emphatically with a person of a foreign tongue. This accentuation readily incites opposition and defiance in the person being spoken to. The Russian women then complained bitterly: "You only give orders, we only work." With patience and understanding, these difficulties could be overcome satisfactorily, and in the homes one could find various joyful groups of Russians who were liked by everyone.
—Other difficulties existed. The Russians neither understood nor accepted many of the regulations for refugees which had been established in the course of the years; this led to disputes. For whatever they failed to understand, they rejected —not quietly, if grudgingly, submitting to puzzling regulations — but rejecting them completely.

---

[3] See Allers R., PSYCHOGENIC DISTURBANCES IN A LINGUISTICALLY STRANGE ENVIRONMENT, page 49.

During a meeting in a mixed home in 1944 the Russians accused the other refugees of being cowards, since they did not raise their voices in criticism. One stateless individual replied: "For three years we have been refugees without rights. We are happy to be here at all. You have a red fist backing you up; we have nothing."

The Russians rather isolated themselves from the other refugees and formed small groups of their own.

One such group had a treasury in which their entire earnings were deposited. From this, small individual purchases, as well as clothing, were financed. The order of purchase corresponded to the need. As a result, an individual could obtain major articles of clothing much sooner, the others biding their time.

Toward strangers and those of a different language they were reserved and mistrustful. Extended contact was necessary to gain their confidence. This set them apart from the other refugees. Practically all of the other refugees were receptive toward signs of sympathy and active friendliness, opening up as soon as they detected genuine concern and helpfulness. The Soviet Russian refugee, on the other hand, withdrew from a stranger at first. After he had been acquainted with a person longer, he became trusting and approachable.

In a home of mixed nationalities in the year 1944 I spoke with refugees of Polish and German birth as well as of other nationalities. They recounted their situation and expressed their aspirations, happy to speak with someone who tried to understand them. The second day there I entered a large hall where the Russian women, who had just returned from vacation, were staying; I intended to discuss with them their wishes regarding training. They scarcely responded to my greetings, sitting together in a corner and observing me from the side as an intruder. Questioned as to their wishes, they complained violently regarding every conceivable unrighteousness. After some time they came to my table, sat down and asked questions. Finally one of them cried, "There's no point in questions; we want to go home to Russia!" The mood became one of excitement. At that moment a young woman entered the room holding a balalaika which she just received. In an instant they had gathered around her. Captivated and forgetting themselves completely, they danced and sang to the strains of the balalaika. All displeasure had disappeared; other persons had ceased to exist! —About half a year later I encountered the same group in another home. Beaming happily they called to me: "You were with us in La Rosiaz! Oh, since then we have seen and experienced a great deal!" And with that they began talking to me, not the least bit shy or distrustful.

In the course of time it was decided that the Russians should be brought together in particular establishments where they would be trained. E.g. a group of eighteen Russian women, together with approximately sixty refugees of other nationalities, were trained in home economics. Near Luzern an actual Russian training home, where Russian and Swiss instructors taught, was founded. At first, since the regulations there were quite stringently enforced, the atmosphere was cold and formal; distrust was mutual. A positive attitude gradually developed, however, so that a highly satisfactory training program could be implemented. Courses in tailoring and sewing were conducted, forty Russian women taking part. They showed strong interest, in fact to some extent an actual thirst for knowledge.

> A camp directress reports: "Such a quest for knowledge I've seen nowhere else except among former concentration camp prisoners from Buchenwald. No one skipped classes. They often stood in front of the door before the school was opened."

A vocational uncertainty such as we frequently observed among youthful refugees of other nationalities was completely lacking among the Russians. Their occupational desires were well considered, serious and concrete: engineer, commercial employee, pilot, physician, chauffeur, etc.

III. Homes for Russians in 1945

During the first half of 1945 thousands of alien workers, displaced persons and war prisoners poured into Switzerland. The Hostels Administration was commissioned to take on approximately 2000 Soviet Russians. They were housed in eighteen rather antiquated hotels distributed over the whole of Switzerland. Five were for women alone; the thirteen others were for families as well as for single men and women. In August 1945, they returned to their homeland in special trains.

Since 1943 the entire situation had changed appreciably. Accordingly, the full weight of the experience gained in the course of the years in working with the refugees could be applied in caring for these people. Possible psychological difficulties were considered and preventive measures taken: A cooperator with long experience in connection with camps, and a positive attitude toward the Russians, was appointed as responsible coordinator and inspector. Experienced directors (4 couples, 3 men, 11 women) were chosen as heads of the camps. The camp staffs cooperated closely with the Soviet liaison officers and with the Russian spokesmen in the individual establishments. In addition, suitable refugees of other nationalities were employed in a supporting capacity. Before the arrival of the Russians the newly-appointed directors met at a convention to which the Russian liaison officers were also invited. In lectures and discussions on psychological and administrative themes the directors were made aware of the distinctive nature of their task and of the basic characteristics and the "European experience" of these refugees. They were instructed in some guiding principles for the management of the homes: Because of the language difficulties, clear and simple instructions were to be given. Nothing should be promised which could not be carried out. Distrust should not be met with harshness; rather, solutions should be sought with an air of calmness and trust. The giving of directions should not be viewed as a test of authority; instead, the ideal director would be the person who endeavored to bring about a mutual shaping of the home in an attitude of comradeship. This was to be achieved by mutual discussions of current problems and close cooperation with spokesmen. Whenever difficulties arose, it was important that the director be ready to keep starting and building anew. —Following instructions of this sort the Russian delegates spoke of the Russian manner of thinking and their collective ways of life. "The collective attitude permeates our life. We want every person above all to be of service to the society", they explained. At later meetings thorough discussions between Russians from the various homes and members of the Hostels Administration were held.

Thus, through combining a basically favorable situation with careful administrative and psychological planning, we attempted to provide for the physical and mental needs of these persons. Clumsiness and mistakes did still occur. In general, however, an atmosphere of good will prevailed and the Russians were free to live their own mode of life.

In the following pages I shall attempt to convey our observations and impressions of how these Russians reacted during their stay in Switzerland in the year 1945. *What I intend to describe are reactions we observed among displaced Soviet citizens in Switzerland, and not those of "Russian persons as such".* Some of these reactions may reflect Russian nature. Others represent symptoms of the uprooting of young persons between seventeen and twenty-five years of age.

General Behavior

In Russian homes orderliness and cleanliness were the general rule. Only certain large establishments with antisocial elements had difficulties in this respect. In many homes the newly-arrived Russians refused to lie down in clean beds before bathing or washing themselves thoroughly. They were emphatic in their cleanliness, washing and bathing themselves as much as possible. —Their rooms were liveable and clean. However, their efforts at grooming broader areas of their surroundings were varied. In some establishments their orderliness encompassed the entire home. In others it ended at the windows of their rooms; what was not wanted was simply thrown out of the window. We observed this form of negligence as a symptom of uprooting and demoralization rather frequently among refugees who had been shipped here and there for years. —Insofar as possible they tried to lend a special character to their surroundings, decorating their walls with many pictures. Whereas most other refugees carried their family pictures with them, the Russians hung a photograph of their relatives in Russia above their beds. Alongside this hung a picture of Stalin or of a Russian military leader, as well as an array of simple, usually colored postcards depicting flowers or views of various sorts. —They were untiring in the designing and producing of clothing and of simple, colorful decorations for their own theatrical performances and for visits, holidays and parties. One of their strongest desires was to celebrate parties.

Their food requirements were substantial. Each person consumed, along with other types of food, approximately two liters of soup and two kilograms of potatoes a day. Dishes which were strange to them they rejected outright. They

referred to spinach, e.g., as pigs' food or grass and could only seldom be enticed to eat it. What they particularly loved was "borschtsch", a Russian stew containing cabbage, meat, etc.

Their material wants were concentrated upon useful objects: watches, luggage, clothing, shoes and kerchiefs. They were thrilled with photographs of themselves and the women particularly with permanent waves. Their tastes in clothing were from our viewpoint old-fashioned; they delighted in laces and frills.

A particular attitude toward work and wages was evident. The essential jobs in an establishment were generally easy to distribute. They did not always work rapidly but were diligent and active. Supervision was usually not necessary; if the explanation was sufficient, a task was usually carried out in the proper manner. They did not strive for flexible shifts from one task to another but preferred an unchanging work plan within the group. However, they had strong interest in additional work which brought them extra pay. Then they really worked untiringly and could go on without stopping hour after hour.

> In one establishment they arranged to get up at four in the morning, complete the necessary chores and then report to their additional job, working there the whole day without a break, cutting turf, paving roads, harvesting hay, collecting cones from fir trees, etc.

A personal and inward relationship to the work they performed was almost completely lacking. For practical purposes, they viewed it simply as an opportunity for earning money. This can be attributed to two factors. These persons had spent years doing forced labor for the enemy. In addition, they had no intimate relationship to our country, a factor which I shall later discuss. They looked upon their private employer as a "stranger" or often as "the capitalist" who paid for their services; they worked for him because they needed money to buy various things. This money was immediately translated into goods and finally into alcohol and permanent waves. Efforts to save money were not evident.

The emotional ties between parents and children were strong. They cared for and attended to their children, in ways different from ours. We experienced examples of the Russian love for children again and again.

> In one reception camp the room of six Russians was the playground for the children. A twenty-one year old former Russian war prisoner, who was as strong as an ox, was the best and jolliest nursemaid for the numerous Italian children. Although each understood scarcely a word that the other said, they loved each other dearly. One never saw the man without a small child in his arms. During my six-hour exploration the Russians rocked one Italian child after the other.

They were intimately bound to their family in Russia, particularly to the mother. Frequently one heard the question, "Is my mother dead?" They tried to imagine what it would be like when they entered the living room of their home again. Here the marked fear of returning to a destroyed and abandoned home town became evident.

Concerning their religious ties they varied considerably, depending upon their upbringing. Older persons and refugees from rural areas made a pious impression. They wore small medallions of the Virgin Mary and prayed. Refugees from the city, on the other hand, generally appeared indifferent.

Peculiarities

The bearing of these people can be summarized as follows: It was elementary, natural and direct. The amplitude of their emotional fluctuations was considerably greater than ours, a latent period between stimulus and reaction seeming to be lacking. Emotionally guided in their thinking, they were quick, sharp, direct, uncompromising and unbridled in their manner of reacting. Weighing of one's thoughts and only then deciding upon a particular course of action was foreign to them. There was only an immediate and certain "yes" or "no". Criticism was sharp and prompt. When not defensive in their approach but giving free rein to their natural bents, they were like spontaneous children of nature, bursting with vitality. They sang during monotonous work just as untiringly as they danced in their free time to the sounds of an instrument. During celebrations they reacted with childlike delight.

A piano, a radio or a grammaphone was played almost continuously from five in the morning until ten at night. If a particular record pleased them, it was played constantly, so that listening to it frequently became a burden to the Swiss administrative personnel. Occasionally, the stress was simply too great for the bookkeeper and the record then sailed out the window in a high arc, much to the dismay of the Russians, who simply could not comprehend the thoughts of this man.

On the 1st of August, the Swiss National Day, rockets went off in the home in broad daylight. "I couldn't wait any longer," admitted the guilty person repentantly, though he beamed at the detonation. In another home everyone literally bent on his knees for a rocket.

Thus, they knew no emotional barriers, living, loving and protesting loudly and directly.

During the departure of the Russians, a Russian officer gave orders very strictly and decisively. The Russians obeyed silently. Various Swiss employees had clothing to distribute among the homebound refugees. A woman colleague had the clothes tried on and sought out what was appropriate for each individual. This took longer than the officer wanted. He spoke violently to her in Russian, although she understood no Russian. She was astounded at his tone and said indignantly: "Such an unreasonable man! What does he think he's doing?" Half an hour later we sat peaceably with the officer in the repatriation train. Asked why he had been so enraged, he replied with astonishment: "Enraged? Not at all! That's the way we Russians are; we say everything directly."

If one was not familiar with this sharp and emphatic manner of many of our Russians, one regarded as "defiance and indignation" many actions which were simply different, more direct forms of behavior.

During a tumult a Swiss officer from outside came into the reception camp to restore order. He spoke with the woman who was the leader of the agitation. She gestured furiously and kept screaming in his face: "We don't want . . . ., we reject . . ., we demand . . . . etc." He listened to her for some time. As she finally stopped for breath, he asked quietly and in a friendly manner, "Why do you keep screaming at me so?" She stopped her screaming, stared at him with astonishment, then laughed, gave him a friendly clap on the shoulder and said: "I'm not excited, I'm Russian." Everyone laughed, and got along well with one another after that.

However, we should not designate every form of animation and loudness as "Russian". Uprooting alone often brings on restlessness. We observed that many of the refugees were inwardly and outwardly restless and unable to concentrate well.

An example of their direct manner of acting follows:

In St. Moritz suitcases were much more expensive than in Zurich. The director of the home in Celerina advised the Russians to wait and buy the cheaper suitcases in Zurich, but they simply could not wait. As soon as they received their pay, they immediatley went and bought suitcases.

Among themselves, too, they showed the same tempestuous reactions and could be extremely harsh, in fact brutal, with one another.

Thus, in one home they threatened a young woman who had stayed away overnight with a Swiss: "We'll take her by the hair and throw her in the chasm." The director of the home had to prevent them from doing this. In the same harmonious and well-directed establishment they had decided that no one should work individually outside of the home. Nevertheless, two women left and returned during the night. The director of the home reports: "The women were enraged at the two. Suddenly they brought them in, bleeding from the head, arms and hands. They had beaten them and thrown bottles at their heads. Later I heard screaming. In the room a water bottle lay on the floor and next to it one of the young women, who writhed and groaned. Four others had thrashed her. I was shocked that they had gone so far. The woman was covered with red marks and lay in bed for two days; I had to isolate her. —When they did something, they did a complete job of it".

Their ingenuous manner expressed itself in their very natural attitude toward the body. Little sensitive as such, they were very concerned when an accident or serious illness occurred, showing an extreme and spontaneous fear of a terrible end.

Among men and women we observed strong sexual drives. Although marriage relationships generally remained stable, a looseness of free sexual relationships was evident. This often stemmed from purely genital needs. The partners changed frequently, whereby they simply remarked: "She is no longer my girl" or "He is no longer my fellow".

The directress of an establishment sent Russian men from a military camp nearby away as they attempted to visit women in the rooms. She reported: "They came back. I ordered them away again. They looked at me dumbfounded and left; later I no longer had illusions. They have a completely different, more direct attitude toward sex."

In a mixed home several young women confided openly to the directress: "If sick, then all over, so better now. When we're twenty-five years old, then we shall sleep at night."

A fifty-year old woman refugee who worked as a night watchman in a home for Russians described her experiences in a letter:

"They go to the village happily, earn money, drink and sleep — three girls with three men in a room. In the morning they leave the house smiling, or walk around inside of it smiling even more. After having accepted me, a twenty-two-year-old fellow honored me with the proposal that we sleep together. Since he could speak no German, he discreetly availed himself of a translator. I had great difficulties in convincing him that I refused, not because he was a Russian, but rather because he would surely not have the comical notion of wanting to sleep with his mother. Everyone laughed at this point and the situation was saved. As a result, I am now called 'Stariababa = grandmother'. and I call my admirer, who has consoled himself with another, 'Stariadiadia = old uncle'. Besides that, they all give me a kiss from time to time. I take that in stride since I am rather well acquainted with them now. But when others from X come and want to embrace me too because I am their 'comrade', then that goes a bit too far. Still, I have to smile and not take things too seriously. When I enter the room of a group of men who are singing at 12:30 at night, they all courteously invite me to sit down, each of them standing up to offer me his seat and his glass, from which I am obliged to sample "schnaps", a terribly sour red or white wine. But they are immediately quiet and that is what I want. No one says an impolite word. Once a tall fellow came into my room at 11 P.M. without knocking —and I must admit that my heart stood still for a moment as the fellow stared at me without saying a word. Then came a torrent of Russian words and, as I shook my head, he explained that he could not find his girlfriend but that he would prefer staying with me, since I was lonely. 'Much nicer, just you and I.' I preferred looking for his girlfriend, however. That was the first night in Switzerland that I slept with locked doors. They now understand that I have no desire to go along with them and leave me unmolested. From time to time one of them says: 'If you want to come, don't be afraid; you will sleep very well!'"

Such reactions were not the rule but were conspicuously frequent. In addition we observed genuine and stable erotic relationships, just as among other nationals. —What goes on here? I consider these loose customs to be the result of various factors: As already mentioned, these were young persons who had been removed from the usual influence of family and upbringing. During their puberty they were suppressed by the brutal outward force of prolonged forced labor or war imprisonment. Now they had fled these oppressive conditions and met fellow countrymen of the opposite sex here in Switzerland. As this occurred, they were still far from their homeland with its customs and laws. Their future was uncertain.

As was already mentioned, some of the alien workers were fearful of retaliatory measures; all of them suffered from uncertainty as to the condition in which they would find their home town, their house and their family.

In March 1945 the director of a home received a book from fourteen men and women participating in a training course; in it they had written as follows (in Russian, translated by us):

> Наша жизнь впереди неизвестна
> Она закрыта вся черной тьмой
> Быть может после первой разлуки
> Неувидимся больше с тобой

> Our future life is uncertain,
> it is shrouded in darkness.
> Perhaps after this first parting,
> we will never see one another again.

Such an uncertain situation is not conducive to the development of permanent emotional relationships. More likely is the suppression of the inward feeling accompanied by strong sexual desire. Thus, I believe that the following factors coincide in producing this superficial sexual exchange: forced uprooting of young persons, undermining of custom and law through deportation, the experience of having been free in Switzerland, obstruction of feeling as a result of uncertainty regarding the future, together with strong youthful sexuality. An evaluation of these factors in the individual case would have to be carried out by Russian psychologists.

I know of no instances of rape by Russian refugees in Switzerland.

The same factors appear to me to be responsible in large measure for the problem of alcohol among the refugees. In the homes and camps of the Hostels Administration no alcoholic beverages were served. The care of the Russians was also oriented to this principle of temperance, which in a few establishments could be implemented without difficulty; however, in other establishments many of the refugees could not be diverted from their craving for alcohol. They drank everything, particularly great quantities of schnaps. This they obtained from stores and taverns in the neighborhood by paying for it, by use of threats or promises, or in some cases by theft; they drank among themselves in small groups, either in their rooms or at parties. At the same time, they showed little interest in the public forms of entertainment in their Swiss environment. They were seldom in dance halls and bars but preferred drinking in small gatherings of their own. They scarcely ever sat in taverns. When they were drunk, they were loud and threatening. Commands or restrictions issued to a drunken Russian had the effect of being dangerously provocative; the drunken person did not know what he was doing. He became violent, smashed windows and doors and hurled objects of various sorts until he could be subdued by his countrymen. Then he slept off his intoxication and afterwards went for a brisk walk.

Also, alcohol sometimes played the role of "the great consoler" when certain experiences they had in Germany were recalled.

A former prisoner of war habitually became drunk when he thought of the massacre of the fellow soldiers in his company. He was troubled again and again by the question as to why he alone had not met his death (a question which troubled some survivors of such massacres for years (W.G. Niederland 1961). A thorough discussion of this matter with the director of the camp brought an end to these thoughts, and after that he no longer resorted to alcohol.

A characteristic attitude toward rules and regulations was evident. A Russian woman brought a large bouquet of flowers to the directress, who asked her where she had obtained them. She answered with a broad smile: "Stolen — don't be afraid; no one saw it." Again, an intelligent Russian told the railway guard in a friendly way, as the man caught him without a ticket, that he would send him the money. Here we observed quite different legal notions than we possess, probably also the result of years of uprooting.

The directress of a home owned a bicycle. Nothing pleased the Russian men and women more than to race through town on it. Every attempt of the very well-liked directress to reserve it for herself failed. Neither impudently nor provokingly, but with a joyful attitude of absolute innocence, the Russians romped around on the bicycle.

Difficulties arose regarding public food resources such as fruits from the field and orchard as well as fish. Despite continual admonitions from our directors, there were repeatedly persons who violated the laws and thus came in conflict with the local population. Whoever has lied and stolen for years to supply his needs or conduct sabotage, as many of these Russians had in Germany, does not get over that quickly.

The attempt to make certain regulations understandable to them proved difficult. Their notions and assumptions were simply different from ours. The regulations for wages of refugees, with their exact stipulations, were too much for them, as e.g. the rule that a guest in the home had to report beforehand and turn in meal tickets.

An intermediate school teacher could not be made to understand why a guest of his had to turn in meal tickets. He argued that one of the refugee women was away that day, so that everything would cancel out. Finally he became angry and called it all a provocation.

Deductions from pay for individual work outside of the home, i.e. payment of the refugee working and earning money outside of the home toward the board and room provided him in the home, could often not be obtained. Not that the people were malevolent — they simply did not let themselves be convinced. If one nevertheless insisted upon it, then they showed strong defensive reactions. If the measures were carried out against the will of the Russian, he became obstinate and showed a strong distrust of the other person.

An otherwise friendly Russian became completely rabid because a deduction was to be made from the pay he had earned for individual work. Every attempt to explain the regulations to him failed. He came to the directress again and again: "I am a good person. Why are you so mean to me?" Sunday at 9 o'clock in the evening he came into the office and declared that he would not leave until he had received his money. He sat in a chair and waited for hours ... at last the directress complied. Afterwards, the man showed her a suit he had bought with the money, and said guilessly that he had not bought schnaps and therefore had not wanted the money for drinking. —He could not understand the deduction and considered it to be thievery of the part of the directress. "He could not understand it because his way of thinking was different", remarked the directress.

What was the reason for these difficulties? Were things demanded of the Russians which they were really unable to understand? Did their different manner of thinking, then, make our regulations incomprehensible to them? Did they have no wish to understand them? Is it to be suspected that some persons who had shown a collaborationist attitude in Germany attempted, through a correspondingly more emphatic and rigid approach, to find an alibi for themselves here in Switzerland before returning home? Along with such easily conceivable reactions of insecurity, the difference in language and in their essential nature seems to me to play an important role. These persons were strangers from a distant land with other customs and practices. Harmonious relations between people of very different backgrounds depend upon their mutual ability and desire to understand the sociological determinants and the intimate characteristics of one another. Each national and regional group has its typical customs. These one must know and take into account, in fact I would almost say "learn by heart", just as one learns the conjugations in a foreign language by heart. Various difficulties of understanding solve themselves in this way. The liaison officers, the refugees of other countries who helped us, and to some extent the Russian leaders too, made strong attempts to find a path to mutual understanding. But in everyday affairs skillful mediators for such problems, who mastered *both* languages and really knew and understood both sides, were lacking.

The same thing applies to the evaluation of our country and our customs by these refugees. In general, our governmental organization and our way of living were strange to them. However, they reacted sympathetically and spontaneously when they saw poverty with their own eyes. Thus, after an enlightening talk by the camp director, refugees in the highland valleys of the Canton Wallis no longer trampled on the "tiny bit of grass" of the mountain farmers and even declined to accept gifts which generous persons offered them. When working as farm hands, however, some Soviet Russians referred to the farmers as capitalists because they called their horse and their plow their own. —Often they failed to understand our system of rationing food and our problem of lack of food. They were here as strangers in a different and unknown world.

We now concern ourselves with another characteristic of these people, i.e. with their feelings of solidarity and their ties to the native soil. I have already cited an example from the year 1944 illustrating the depressed condition of isolated Russians when their native milieu was lacking. We saw how this was transformed into a feeling of security as soon as several of them came together. In 1945 in completely Russian establishments a wealth of collective reactions of every possible degree could be observed.

They stayed within the framework of a social group. Lone individuals were nonexistant. In contrast to most of the other refugees, who viewed a room of their own as a place of privacy or a kind of home, single rooms could not be found among the Russians. These were transformed into double or triple rooms or into rooms for five or six. No one went for a walk alone; they always went in groups of five or six. Taking a bath alone was completely unknown to them; at least two and often as many as four women were in the bathtub at once.

Along with these outward signs of unity, many other reactions lending insight into the genuineness of their solidarity appeared.

> A woman who was otherwise not well-liked cried and screamed, believing that a needle she had sat on had become lodged inside of her. A throng of people gathered around, everyone crying. They assiled the director, demanding that she be sent to the hospital. They were ready to pay everything themselves. They placed a belt around her body to prevent the needle from reaching her heart. The next day the woman was brought to the hospital. No needle could be found. As the director inquired at the hospital regarding the results of the examination, the others swarmed around the telephone like bees, almost crawling inside the receiver and shouting into it five at a time, elated at the happy result, laughing, crying and shouting all at once.

This solidarity was evident in the unflagging care of sick Russians. They took shifts, a helpful woman always staying next to the bed.

> On account of illness at the time of their repatriation, one woman had to wait for a later opportunity to go. After the others had consulted with one another, one woman who was not particularly close to the sick woman remained to stay with her, "so that she would not be so alone."

In these examples we observe the collective reaction against adversity, a profound and mortal fear when a member of the group suffers, and an intimate solidarity with the fate of the other person. In contrast to certain primitive peoples who abandon the afflicted tribesman and ban him from the group as "res sacra misera," i.e. as object of the wrath of invisible forces which they fear (Levy-Brühl, 1927), we observed an unwavering emotional bond between these Russian refugees at the very height of their suffering and misfortune.

Also in the case of occasional, secretly-conducted abortions, and at their drinking parties, they remained true to one another. The woman in question was quietly nursed by the group, just as those who were drunk were supported by the shoulders, laid in bed and cared for until they were sober. The following example reported by a directress illustrates that this was often anything but simple.

> "One of them was just like a fish when he had been drinking – quick and agile. Four to six others tried to put him to bed. They became quite brutal in their attempt to bring him to his room, stomping on him and dousing him with water until the whole dance floor was flooded. They never were the least bit angry or excited at those who were drunk, performing such tasks as a kind of sport. Bringing these persons to their rooms, they usually laughed, much as children laugh at an intoxicated person. Windows and doors became shattered in the process. Only when something had been broken were they ashamed at their drinking."

At their parties they sang, danced and drank together in one great fellowship. One really sensed how much they belonged together and needed one another, and what being together meant to them. How much stronger their feeling of solidarity was than their consciousness of individuality could clearly be observed in numerous telephone calls from one camp to the other.

> Many telephone calls of the following sort were received: "Call a Russian woman to the phone, please." "Who is calling?" "I am." "Who?" "A Russian!" "Which woman do you want to speak with?" "That doesn't matter." Then some man or woman came to the phone and talked for half an hour, smiling happily and elatedly chatting with the unknown countryman on the other end of the line.

Solidarity was also clearly demonstrated during the fortunately seldom police actions for arresting a Russian who had infringed upon the law. Genuine mass reactions ensued, the entire group protecting the individual and creating a tremendous tumult. Men and women quivered and shook with excitement; women here and there sobbed despairingly. We will mention other forms of mass behavior later.

Along with these expressions of a deep-seated feeling of solidarity, I found in several homes organized communities formed on a voluntary basis. Strict equality was emphasized; accordingly, they wanted all to receive the same pay, rejecting the gradations which were forseen in the official pay regulations. They preferred wages of .90 Fr./hour for everyone to wages of 1.00 Fr. for only one of their number, just as they preferred that none of them receive clothing rather than have only some of them receive it. What they also did not understand was that as a rule women received lower wages than men. "Same work, same pay" seemed self-obvious to them. —Mistakes of individuals were largely concealed from the outsider; within the group, however, they often were strongly censured. They subordinated themselves to their own countrymen, whereas they reacted quite sensitively to a gruff tone from an outside person. When disciplinary measures were put into effect or disputes fought out, the acting parties or the entire group were often very harsh, even brutal. One calls to mind the threat we mentioned, "We'll take her by the hair and throw her in the chasm."

> After an uprising in a military reception camp one of the women who had led the revolt agreed with the Swiss officer to a sort of truce. She returned to her compatriots, stood on a bench and addressed them in a spirited way. Various others, still aroused by the insurrection, began shouting against her. She leaped down and slapped one of the shouters in the face. Then she climbed up on the bench again and continued talking until she had expounded everything.

An enormous difference is evident here in comparison to intellectually-inclined middle and western European refugees, who in general would have reacted toward a harsh speech of a fellow refugee even more harshly than toward one delivered by a Swiss.

> Thus, an Austrian refugee in a training camp of mixed nationalities shouted at a man who distributed food at the dining hall with an air of arrogance and superiority: "Behave decently! You're made of the same dirt that we are; you're a refugee too." Such a statement would never have been uttered in a Russian refugee camp.

In most establishments the Russians made intensive efforts to achieve an ordered manner of living together. The spokesmen and liaison officers played an important role here. The spokesmen were persons of every conceivable sort, their influence depending upon their personal attitude and sense of responsibility, as well as on their psychological and organizational cleverness. Some sought to mediate and explain, others to advance the sense of fellowship among their countrymen, demanding harsh measures against asocial individuals. Many of the spokesmen, and certain liaison officers too, were familiar with the demoralizing influence of deportation, imprisonment and war upon their young countrymen. They tried to counteract these harmful influences by education in social adjustment. Also, there were sergeant-types who tried to gain authority with loudness.

The capable spokesmen had strong influence and helped the camp staffs appreciably. The directress of a middle-sized establishment said:

> "At the first sobranje (business meeting) the spokesmen who formed a committee of one woman and four men, were elected. The division of responsibilities was achieved quite simply and corresponded to the individual propensities of these persons. One of them held moral sermons; another made announcements of a more practical nature. All in all, they worked well together. Their goal was to help the Russians to live satisfactorily with one another. Honored by their election, they took their task very seriously."

The directress of a large establishment remarked:

> "It would not have worked out, or many things would have been much more difficult, if the spokesmen had not helped us. They accomplished many tasks to which we would never have come. Running a large establishment

without them was impossible, not only in a technical sense but also in regard to the prevailing attitude and climate of opinion. They announced everything which was to be made public, attended to discipline and saw to it that the necessary jobs were carried out. They made our task much easier."

At the sobranje, sessions for the purpose of discussion, they often showed great discipline. This can be attributed partly to the cooperation of each individual, and partly to the commands given by the leaders and the will expressed by the majority. We were always astounded at the effect which the sobranje had upon these people: free discourse and discussion took place and they learned to subordinate their desires to those of the group. We saw what a valuable help such common discourses represented for group organization, and what a powerful, binding influence they had upon the individual.

After all that I have said, I scarcely need to dwell upon their *attitude toward their homeland*. The strength of these people lies in their unity with their soil.

> While delivering a talk in a home, a Russian liaison officer announced, "Russian soil awaits its children." Thereupon everyone laid his head on the table and cried, men and women alike.
>
> The waves of homesickness were rather strange. A director who spoke Russian told me that sometimes in the evening, for no apparent reason, they all at once stood up and quietly went to their rooms, to sit there pensively and yearn for their homeland. A few hours later, or the next day, this mute and collective feeling had vanished. The director declared, "I never did understand how it came about that they were all overcome by just the same feelings at the very same time."
>
> A leading Russian artist, who had lived in Switzerland for several decades, told them in the course of a lecture that he loved Russia and Switzerland alike. In this way he hoped to bring Switzerland closer to them. They rejected him bluntly: "Why does he stay here voluntarily if he is Russian? A Russian can't decide to live away from Russia."

Robbing them of their homeland would have meant robbing them of everything, for their allegiance to it was profound and genuine. Surely, the common element in their thinking played a significant role here. Russian air and soil were for them "biotop" and "archetop" (p. 83). Among individual psychopaths and uprooted persons we would undoubtedly have experienced a considerably greater degree of asocial behavior — of loose sexuality, alcoholic excesses and degenerate principles of legality — if these people had not been sustained by their strong ties with the Russian soil and their yearning for the homeland. When we consider what many of them had gone through in Germany and how brutally they had been torn from their homeland at an age when they were not yet mature, then we can imagine something of the inward strength which protected them from being totally uprooted and destroyed by their war experiences.

Of particular interest is the *attitude of these refugees toward refugees of other nationalities*. When they were confronted with another refugee who was friendly in his bearing, they were warm and brotherly to him. However, they had little interest in the problem of refugees in general; this was due among other things to the fact that they did not share with the others the basic situation of being without a homeland. The prisoners of war in particular considered themselves not as "refugees" but as "Soviet Russians", as citizens of a powerful and victorious nation, who had been forced by the war to come to this country. They were spared the bitter experience of being without a country; for this reason they felt no "solidarity of the refugee" with the other persons near them who were faced with this lot. They considered each person who adjusted to their way of living as a friend and brother: "When we get shoes, Daniel should get them too; when we get a coat, Daniel should get one too." They isolated themselves from this person, however, if they encountered unfamiliar viewpoints on his part which he was unwilling to drop.

Finally, I will consider *mass behavior* briefly. Properly seen, these refugees were not conformists, but spontaneous, colorful human beings with different collective ties from those to which we are accustomed. Genuine solidarity with the group does not involve loosing one's identity. —I observed mass reactions in all the refugee camps. Among certain groups of refugees, the Italians and the Soviet Russians in particular, such reactions were more conspicuous than among other groups. The Soviet Russian refugees, being quick, intense and emotional in their reactions, responded violently and consistently to certain external influences. Many forms of mass reaction were evident, as e.g. that of subservience to a psychologically clever liaison officer; we personally observed an outbreak of mass-psychosis triggered off by the strict measures of the Swiss camp commander at a military reception camp. —In large establishments mass reactions came about through lack of personal contact between the refugees and the staff. The individual felt himself persecuted or lost in the crowd and in certain situations he defended himself with disproportionate force to achieve definite ends. The agitation which accompanied feelings of persecution was readily transmitted to the others, so that mass reactions ensued. Among the Russians these feelings of persecution were understandable enough, since in a material sense they were for several years the worst treated of all forced laborers in Germany.

> In a large establishment which was beset with problems, 200 pairs of shoes were to be distributed. The directress of the camp reports: "Our original plan was that those who were working should be taken care of first. That appeared to us to be technically simpler than letting them all into the room at once. The room had two doors. In the truest sense, the people lay in waiting for the shoes; at the moment, this constituted their entire life's purpose. An hour before distribution crowds stood at the doors. We just barely managed to enter the room ourselves. Outside they clamored. We wanted to let in ten persons but twenty came. We had them try on the shoes and that was the mistake; at this point the crisis occurred: They stormed the doors, whereupon one hundred fifty persons rushed into the room, pushing,

pulling each other by the hair, puffing and shouting but not touching the shoes. After an hour they were still standing there. At last the spokesmen drove them out. After a quarter of an hour the hundred fifty persons suddenly entered from the veranda. "Do what you want", I said and left the room. Five minutes later not a single shoe was left. It was like an insane asylum! —They roamed around afterwards for as much as two hours until they managed to exchange their shoes for appropriate ones. It easily happened that a person had three shoes or a yellow and a black one or four for the left foot. —When the second shipment came, our procedure was much simpler. We simply distributed as many pairs of shoes as there were people. Afterwards they were to exchange among themselves. There were eleven pairs that were extra. We gave these out but received them back immediately. They didn't want to have as many shoes as possible nor did they want to steal or to be dishonest; rather, their only desire at the moment was 'shoes'."

Who would not think of Silones' Peppino Goriani at this point? "... Sometimes everything was topsyturvy in the city and, without his wanting to be, he was there ... For example the day when Peppino Goriani saw a large crowd of people storm the stores in the Cola di Brienzo ... He was in the middle of things and so it was that he entered a shoe store; but when he was outside the shoes in his hand did not match: two women's dancing shoes, both for the left foot, and a large riding boot for the right foot ... What should he do with them? He set off on the search for the person who had taken the shoes that went with these ones ..." (T. Silone, 1930)

My description of behavior apply to the Soviet Russian refugees in the homes of the Hostels Administration. Living among these persons were their spokesmen but not the liaison officers, the latter not living in the homes but coming and going. As militarily interned persons they were not subordinate to the Hostels Administration. Along with their work in cooperation with the Hostels Administration they had additional tasks, in particular that of making preparations for the repatriation of their countrymen. Their goals were therefore different from those of our directors, whose entire task involved making the stay of these refugees in Switzerland a satisfactory one. The reactions of the Soviet Russian refugees toward the liaison officers were many-sided. They ranged from genuine devotion to mute obedience.

In August and September 1945 the Russians returned to their homeland. At the same time there were some persons who traveled back with the others without having come from Soviet Russia, being children of Russian immigrants of the First World War.

> A young woman whose parents had emigrated in 1925 had come from southern Germany to Switzerland as a refugee together with other Russians. She wanted desperately to go back with the rest of them to Russia. The Russian leader, a student, rejected this. He explained that no one who had been gone from Russia for 25 years was allowed to go. Nevertheless, the

woman rode with the others to the Swiss border; here she appealed to a Russian major, crying and sobbing that she wanted to come along. He gave her no answer. She rode on with them; the next day the Russians gave her nothing to eat; she was not supposed to come. She went from one officer to another and finally she was allowed to come along.

Administrative Problems

The directors of the homes were faced with the task of providing a truly homelike atmosphere for these people, of attending to the necessary administrative and bureaucratic matters and of mediating between the refugees and the local population.

At the preliminary meeting of the camp staffs, which has been mentioned already, I warned against reacting personally to signs of distrust and against becoming excited when one was not properly understood or failed to understand something; similarly, I advised against deeming an individual responsible for those actions which might be attributed to the peculiarities of his group. I stressed particularly that negative conclusions regarding the group as a whole should not be drawn on the basis of the delinquent behavior, stealing or whatever, of particular individuals. Finally, I emphasized the importance of a friendly welcome.

Our directors attempted to solve the problems, each in his own way. Here I let them speak for themselves:

> "My wife and I welcomed the women at the railroad station with flowers. Weeping and reluctant they stepped off the train. It was a miserable day with miserable weather (at an altitude of 1400 meters in a poor mountain valley). Thirty or forty of them wanted to leave with the next train. I suggested that they come along, took the two heaviest suitcases, set off in the direction of the home, and they followed me. A meal was served immediately, then I showed them their rooms with the freshly-made beds. Only then did they dare to breathe freely. From then onward they were in good spirits. The first night they refused to go to bed until I had unlocked the bathroom door, for they said that after a bath they would be cleaner when they lay down in their fresh beds. The next morning they arose at 5 a.m. cleaned and dusted everything and bustled around furiously. By 9 o'clock everything was spotless. When they went to breakfast each morning my wife and I stood in the hall. Those who went past greeted us and we greeted each of them personally. This took considerable effort but much depended upon it. Indifference had no place here."

(A director-couple)

A director reports:

> "We did not introduce ourselves as the staff; we simply were there and helped out in the office. At meals there were also no differences made and I left everything unlocked; they had to gain the impression of everything being completely open ... As soon as we had gained the trust of these people, they left everything up to us. They entrusted us with their children after a week."

It soon became evident in many ways that the task entailed enormous difficulties. Think of the *language difficulties* alone!

In one home two Russian women were to clean the office. The work supervisor gave brief directions in Swiss-German dialect. The two women stood there mutely. The supervisor became impatient, and repeated the directions in a sharp tone of voice. Hereupon the Russian women became stiff and obstinate. Just then another staff member appeared, said "Come" and began cleaning in one corner of the room. "So . . ." she said with appropriate gestures. A smile of understanding passed across the faces of the Russian women, who then mopped and dusted until everything glistened.

Some of the Russians could speak German reasonably well, but in a curt, loud and halting manner, employing only the infinitive form of the verbs. Their utterances were therefore somewhat hard and blunt; in order to avoid being irritated at their apparent gruffness some of the staff had to remind themselves repeatedly that this was the tone and language of complete foreigners.

Another difficulty lay in the already mentioned difference in their attitude and manner of thinking. This created problems for many of the camp directors. Some of them were able to adjust to it completely but this required great effort.

A directress stated: "Of course we find them difficult, but this is only because of the effort involved in adjusting to them. What we find complicated is adjusting to them. I am perfectly convinced that they are less complicated than we are. With our overdeveloped individualism it is difficult for us to gain contact with them. They simply think differently. And that often leads to difficulties. In a given situation they draw different conclusions than we do. We could not orient ourselves to them in advance because we did not know how they would react. In dealing with other refugees we could predict what they would do and consider possible difficulties beforehand."

Here we see the roots of various misunderstandings. Our directors were anxious to establish contact and understanding; only few of them, however, were familiar with the Russian language and mode of thought. When they were confronted with large numbers of these people (380 in the case of the directress mentioned above) and endeavored to explain to them regulations such as those regarding deductions from pay for individual work, they were often unable to cope with the difference in attitude and way of thinking. If agreement was not acheived, the danger of further dissention and misunderstanding remained.

Particular difficulties arose in *large establishments* when *psychopathic grumblers* were present. In a home with a hundred persons mutual contact could be achieved through group discussions. If there were 350 persons in the home, this was much more difficult. Here such elements could gain footing and occasionally assume leadership, with the result that conflicts occurred repeatedly.

Difficulties also presented themselves when *devious individuals* attempted to seize control.

> In two of the camps conflicts arose because other women were not agreed to the weekend orgies planned by certain individuals. They dealt with the matter by organizing their own house police and dispelling the boyfriends of others before they could enter. After that, there was peace and quiet.
>
> In various homes conflicts were brought on by some individuals who behaved asocially, stealing watches in stores, "getting a hold of" schnaps, etc. This resulted in very difficult situations, mastered best with the help of their spokesmen and the liason officers, who punished the guilty parties severely.

One stumbling block which basically exists in all human leadership, among teachers, officers, directors of homes, etc., should be mentioned. I refer to *difficulties within the person of leadership himself*. Persons with directive functions are always subject to the danger of projecting their own conflicts and faults upon their environment. It is then the others who are at fault; one's own harshness is viewed and justified as "the result of improper actions of others." This danger was reduced by the fact that the directors of our Russian establishments were carefully chosen. When they were overtired and tense, however, they had difficulty in controlling their irritations, their sensitivities and their proneness to responding aggressively. – Despite their good will, some proven directors were simply unable to adjust to the difference in these people.

> The director who understood this better than any of the others and whose establishment was considered by the Russians themselves to be ideal explained afterwards: "They do not adjust, it was we who had to adjust. Afterwards I was completely exhausted."

Thus in the course of time, resentments could develop; these represented the hypersensitive reactions, so to speak symptoms of uprooting, of strongly individualistic persons against the collective atmosphere surrounding them. Resentments were also caused by the abrupt, harsh way of talking of the Russians. If such resentments were combined with fearfulness toward aggressive elements, then the differences in viewpoint could lead to an aloofness which could scarcely be overcome. In one case this induced the entire staff to leave the home. Such actions motivated by fear, understandable as they may have been, neglected the nature and the mode of living of our Soviet Russian refugees. This is shown in a letter written by a refugee woman of another nationality to an outside person the day after this occured:

> "The serious side of the matter is the fact that these are bitter and fearful young people – uprooted, negligent and demoralized – millions of whom we will see in so-called normal everyday life after the war. Some of them were deported by the Germans at the age of sixteen, some still earlier, some later. A portion of these young people were in the infamous camp of Auschwitz and were forced to look on as best friends of theirs who had suffered crippling work accidents were burned alive, the rest of them having to gather and watch this 'theatrical presentation'. The doors of the oven were

left open... Do you suppose that these young people will ever forget it? Do you consider them to still be normal? They are no longer afraid of death; neither are they afraid of crime. Whoever fails to understand this will never gain influence over them... The great mistake of the staff was to abandon the camp. Those who they left behind were honestly hurt and asked me without exception, men, women and girls alike: 'Why do you stay? Aren't you afraid of us? Are we so much worse than the others?' It is known that the Russians are particularly sensitive."

On the other hand, I saw striking examples of directors who did not lose their sense of perspective and even at critical moments endeavored to establish contact, mastering even the most perilous situation. Also, I sometimes saw how quick-wittedness and a strong measure of humor could save a muddled situation. — Another important practical measure was the appeal to the pride in Soviet Russia.

"Our later impression of Russia and its way of life will be determined by what we observe of you here", said one director. And a directress won over her refugees with the following words: "Russia demands of you Soviet citizens discipline. Only with discipline have you won the war." The Russians were proud of their discipline and declared of other camps: "Uh, no discipline!"

Concerning the management of these people, it is to note that a brief command given by a non-Russian, e.g. by a director, had no appreciable effect. Everything had to be explained carefully and made plausible. If they understood, everything was fine; if they didn't, they became distrustfully rejecting, as I have illustrated with examples.

In the establishments as a whole serious conflicts seldom occured. Frequently we observed just the opposite and a genuine "Russian" community developed within the home. Grumblers had no influence here.

I saw this impressively demonstrated in one establishment housing approximately one hundred Russians who were rather notoriously known from their period in the reception camp as being "asocial". Within the home, an esprit de corps prevailed; the two or three grumblers found no footing. The directress, together with the Russian leaders and the non-Russian refugees, had really won their trust.

If such trust had been achieved, it was achieved completely; thus we experienced in no small number of establishments a kind of local pride in the home.

In one home the director asked the women before they departed: "Listen, how would it be if we left the laundry and linen just as it was when we arrived?" Thereupon they slept in their beds for three days without linen, washing, ironing and mending everything.

In such communities the refugees had an intimate relationship to the staff. A director reports:

"I once went to the mountains for three days. When I returned, they stood in front of the house with flowers in their hands. They presented me with a bottle of fruit-juice as well."

Here we see an intimacy and a direct warmth within the group such as was evident in the refugee homes of no other nationality. Neither before nor afterwards were the other refugees in just such an advantageous position as the Russians in 1945. In 1943 groups of Russians opposed their surroundings; in 1945, however, they could cease viewing the camps as a place of detention and, therefore, develop a positive attitude toward it. It really became "their" home, a refuge after years of suffering and fear.

However, even in these congenial and contented camps the task was not simple. Only two of our eighteen directors were able to bridge over the differences without great effort. The others had a certain feeling of isolation, this being difficult for them to pin down exactly. Some of them felt: "We didn't really get personally close to them; this remained a puzzle to us. Tremendous adjustment was necessary on our part. Thinking individually was simply inappropriate here; we had to think and act collectively. We were completely absorbed in work with them, and yet we had a much more personal contact with the other refugees." Particularly the women were deeply devoted to their directresses, often kissing and embracing them. But intimate contact with individual refugees or friendships such as we were accustomed to with other refugees were seldom established. This could be attributed to the difference in language as well as to an ignorance of those reactions which were typical of them; knowledge of such reactions is only attainable by extended mutual contact.

One way of gaining their trust was to intercede for them when their environment reacted negatively. The local population varied considerably in its attitude toward the Russians. In some localities very fruitful contact was established; in other localities difficulties developed. For one thing, the rural Swiss population often took offense at the difference in attitude and manner of these people. Also, misconduct under the influence of alcohol, sexual excesses or thefts on the part of individual delinquents tended to be generalized to all Russians. Finally – particularly in remote areas – the strictly churchgoing population rejected the Soviet Russians on the basis of inner convictions. Here was a thankful task for mediation on the part of the directors. The director of a home for women reports:

"One day their spokeswoman Nina came to me and said that the people here in X behaved strangely. She said they made a sign whenever they saw a Russian (the sign of the cross). Here was a chance for the women to see whether I stood up for them. How I would react interested them noticeably. I donned my hat immediately and went to the pastor to confer with him. The Sunday after we attended church. I told them to dress well; I came in formal black myself. Everyone was there in the church. Afterwards the stationmaster from the railroad station told me we had been a great success."

C. Summary

I followed the fate of the Soviet Russian refugees during their stay in Switzerland over a period of two years. They left behind a deep and lasting impression. On the basis of observations made during this period, the perspective which the years hence have given me, and the comparison with the experiences gained in caring for other refugee groups, I would draw the following conclusion: We were confronted with a strong and spontaneous people whose qualities were those to which Tolstoi referred in describing the Russian people: "We do nothing half-way. When we love, we love completely. When we hate, we hate completely. When we smile, we smile completely." They needed to be together with their countrymen as much as they needed air to breathe. They were harsh in their hatred and defensiveness, just as they were direct and spontaneous in their affection. Their trying experiences in Germany had left their effects. A certain percentage of them returned in a fearful and uncertain frame of mind, expecting to be faced with strict measures on account of their having been "foreign workers" in Germany. Many of the others, the actual deported persons and war prisoners, were psychically harmed, full of inward restlessness and tension, some of them showing asocial behavior. Yet after they returned to their homeland to breathe its air and live in its routine again most of them probably had overcome, through the strength of their character and their solidarity with one another as well as with Russian soil, much of the harm done to them.

Caring for these persons proved to be a psychologically difficult but thankful task. The events in the year 1945 indicate that with a satisfactory general situation this task could be solved. During that year we saw that people of such different nations and styles of living as the Swiss and the Russians were able to live and work together. Through the cooperation of responsible persons from both groups, these people, harmed by war and in search of asylum in a strange land, could be offered a home which was more than simply a roof over their heads and bread on the table.

I have drawn up this report without deep psychological analyses and conclusions regarding mental health. Within the limits of this report only facts can speak — and I feel that they speak impressively for the importance of mental hygiene as a means of bridging the mutual gap between persons of our own and of other groups. At the conclusion of my remarks I draw no abstract inferences but cite the simple and yet centrally relevant words of a man who in his years of quiet work with refugees sought and found a bond linking one individual or nationality to another. As director of a Russian camp he was able on the basis of his understanding to span in a short time the differences I have alluded to, and to transform through his work and attitude a problematical establishment into a home. His words are:

"What the Russians cannot bear is distrust. Part of the Western world has viewed them as inferior persons altogether. As soon as they sensed equality, human love, openness and truthfulness, however, and that this was genuine, everything was in order. They were among the finest persons I have ever met and I am convinced of their value and strength. Right from the beginning I liked them. It was one of the most thankful tasks that I have known. I had a particular sense of satisfaction in feeling that I understood on the same basis as I did the others these people who were so strange to me. The most gratifying experience was the transformation which took place in a short time as distrustfulness was replaced by trust."

Origin of Contributions and References: See Page 333

HUMAN UPROOTING

D. Müller-Hegemann
German Democratic Republic

A Viewpoint on its Psychopathology

The term "Entwurzelungs-Depression" (depression resulting from uprooting) has come to stay as a term in German psychiatry, and together with similar psychopathological phenomena has on many occasions aroused interest in problems of uprooting, and thus also in the finding and rediscovery of human roots. Some years ago H. Ruffin drew attention to the drastic changes in environmental and living conditions affecting vast numbers of people as a result of deportations, expulsions, loss of homeland, family, possessions, work, honor and respect, and the threat to both body and soul in prisons, concentration camps, or during attempts to escape. Special note should be taken of his remark that the older generation forms a considerable proportion of survivors who suffer from feelings of failure, and who have been described in accounts of depression caused by uprooting, of diminished responsibility and other psychotic reactions, with loss of contact colored by apathy.

The "house-moving depressions" suffered by older women, described more than thirty years ago by J. Lange, may be recalled in this connection, for additional reason that changes of residence have recently been given aetiological consideration in psychologically disturbed cases. Of the more recent publications, those of Hall, Bovi and Müller-Fahlbusch should be mentioned as showing that change of residence is by no means generally recognized as an important reason for mental disorders. Our own investigations of 604 cases of psychosis (see "Sozialpsychiatrisch-epidermiologische Analyse . . .", 1969), revealed an aetiopathogenic link with change of residence in only a few isolated cases, and always in elderly patients.

Not included were such factors as serious quarrels with neighbors and social isolation, since these were associated with change of residence only to a very minor degree.

It seemed necessary to touch upon the subject of change of residence, as this usually involves only everyday difficulties, and it is therefore hardly possible to speak of "uprooting" in this connection. The exceptions here again are older people, for the most part such as have become attached to their homes over long periods. Every housing authority has instructions to give most careful consideration to such people, even when there is a serious housing shortage, to prevent suicides and other serious complications.

A problem of far greater significance for our subject is migration, where change of residence weighs far less than the need to adapt to an almost entirely new way of life. There is so much literature on this subject that it can only be briefly touched upon here. "Migration, Mental Health and Community Services," edited by H. P. David — 1966, contains valuable information indicating that since the epidemiological investigations of Odegaard, Malzberg and others, the findings available give no uniform picture of migration as presenting an aetiopathogenic group of factors. Like other authors, M. Pfister-Ammende leaves us in no doubt in her article on "Migration and Mental Health Services" that this is a major problem affecting the mental health of the people concerned, also for foreign workers, and from the point of view of international welfare organizations. She recalls that as a result of the Second World War more than 30 million people suffered persecution and uprooting and that in recent years, too, immense population movements have taken place. She mentions the 570 thousand refugees from ten African countries who found asylum south of the Sahara, and the millions of foreign workers in the various industrialized countries. Her statement, that in Canada, Singapore and Israel there was not always an increase in the rate of admission of immigrants to mental hospitals, is of particular interest.

There can be no doubt that the proportion of psychic morbidity among immigrants and their children depends on numerous factors, the most important of which are the social structure and national characteristics of the receiving country, the constitution and disposition (including the strength of their roots in the homeland) of the immigrants, and, to a considerable degree, the attention paid to their mental welfare. The social isolation of single persons and of groups, a concommittant especially of life in an environment where a different language is spoken, always presents a danger. Evidence of this can also be found in the well-known work "Social Classes and Mental Illness" by Hollingshead and Redlich who write that 70 per cent of "Class V" with the highest rate of psychotic illness consist of new immigrants and their children. These people are cold-shouldered by the long-resident Americans because of their specific origins and are to a great extent isolated from the rest of the community.

M. Pfister-Ammende has carried out investigations on 450 cases of mentally sick persons (see "Psychologie and Psychiatrie der Internierung -1961") drawn from two groups: one consisting of 7,500 refugees of various nationalities and one of 8,900 Swiss repatriates. A comparison showed that the rate of mental illness was much lower among the repatriates. The tendency to suicide was far less marked and there were far fewer cases of psychopathy and depression. Nevertheless, the psychic morbidity of these repatriates was higher than that of the average Swiss citizen. These differences show that the rediscovery of roots can also lead to mental disturbances but that these voluntary repatriates, who had obviously remained attached to their homeland, were in far less danger than refugees and deportees forced to accustom themselves to a quite alien environment.

From my own experience, on the basis of the above-mentioned analysis of 604 psychotic cases, the following can be said: The statistically significant predominance of female over male patients (428 : 176) taking population proportions into account, can mainly be ascribed to the fact that the consequences of two world wars have not been overcome and that the lonliness over the years has in fact had a crushing and depressive effect on millions of women. 11.7 per cent. of the female and 8 per cent. of the male patients could be classified as "re-settlers", that is to say persons who found a new home in the German Democratic Republic after the second World War. This percentage is not essentially different from the population proportions, nor are there any clearly defined differences in the case of diseases such as schizophrenic, manic-depressive and reactive psychoses (women 11.8 per cent., 19.5 per cent., 15.3 per cent.; men 11.7 per cent., 14.3 per cent., 11 per cent.). There is no doubt that resettlement deserves attention as an aetiopathogenic factor, for in a number of cases difficulties of adjustment were reported. But this factor pales into insignificance in comparison with other far-reaching changes such as appear in migration, which are dealt with separately.

In those cases, failure to adapt to life in big cities, such as Berlin, runs like a continuous thread through long periods (sometimes from before the second World War) following the move from definitely rural areas, from other parts of the former Germany or, to some extent, from other countries. Here the percentages are 6.6 for women and 1.7 for men. The percentages are significantly higher in the case of reactive psychoses: women 11.9 and men 11.1 per cent. Partial social isolation regularly plays a role here. The following case of reactive psychosis (accompanied by the beginnings of involution) may serve as an illustration:

> The patient, E.H., a woman, born in 1921, grew up in stable surroundings in Czechoslovakia. There are no known cases of serious illness in her own or her family's history. She was trained as a dressmaker and worked with success in a medium-sized firm. In 1946 she was resettled, because of her German nationality, in what was then the Soviet Occupation Zone, spending some months with her family in a resettlement camp. The family had remained together and survived despite hunger and many difficulties. They then received a permit to move to a medium-sized town, where she qualified further for a post as instructor in a vocational training school. She moved to Berlin in 1958 but, though she received a residence permit after a long delay, could only find accommodation in a border district where she lived for about eight years. Since she was unable to receive visitors there, she also rented a room in Berlin, changing her address a number of times. She had, however, few personal contacts, and especially few in Berlin; nor did she manage to achieve a permanent and valuable relationship with a man. "After the war, one waited and hoped, and then nothing came of it after all . . ." she said. She had wanted more than anything to be a housewife and mother. She had a few distant relatives in Berlin and she also met one or two female colleagues there

from time to time. With one of these she had had a close association, until she discovered that the woman wished to enter into a Lesbian relationship with her. She then abruptly broke off the friendship. She had obviously suffered from sexual frustration for years, as well as from partial social isolation. To compensate for this and also to meet her not inconsiderable expenses, she overworked at her job in a fashion house, doing excessively long stints on special work for customers, and often getting only five hours sleep or less. She tried to find a suitable apartment to help make up for the lack of family atmosphere, but unsuccessfully. She had many difficulties at work. She believed that people intrigued against her and broke up the group she was in charge of. After the whole situation had been discussed in public, she lost all her self-confidence.

She told us that during the months preceding hospitalization, she had found brightly colored black and yellow worms in her hygienically unsatisfactory room. Later she became convinced that she was surrounded by a whole group of Lesbian women who were attempting to force her to join them. She also said that she had heard on the radio that she was to be murdered. —In December 1966 she became seriously mentally disturbed and wandered aimlessly through the streets. Hospital treatment followed from 19 December 1966 to 16 February 1967 in the Wuhlgarten (now Wilhelm Griesinger) Hospital in Berlin. In particular she expressed paranoid ideas of being spied on and pursued; she also suffered from accoustic and optical hallucinations. She was treated with generous doses of propaphenin and prothazin and she had six sessions of electric shock treatment, after which the acute symptoms abated. She insisted on leaving the hospital without having gained an insight into her illness.

Shortly after, she became capable of establishing much-needed contact with other people, but she still did not arrive at an understanding of her illness. The diagnosis was paranoid-hallucinatory psychosis in pre-climacterium.

At a later examination in May 1969 it was ascertained that shortly after her discharge from the hospital she had resumed her qualified work and was doing it successfully. She had in the meantime obtained a small modern apartment and thus gained a firmer hold on life. She still had difficulties with her colleagues, because they let her feel that they knew she had been in a mental hospital, and she continued to suffer from partial social isolation. Nor had she gained a proper insight into her illness. On the contrary, she considered that she had been forced into a situation leading to hospitalization in December 1966 as a result of suggestions made by others — here the colleague with Lesbian tendencies played a major role. Emotionally she appeared easily approachable. She gave the impression of being a motherly type, with traces of inhibition. Her periods were said to be still regular. Taking developments as a whole into consideration, the diagnosis was then altered to "reactive psychosis".

After thorough investigation of the patient, coupled with psycho-therapeutic advice, the following comment can be made: resettlement in very difficult times did not result in mental disturbances of any kind, although the patient must be considered mentally unstable on the basis of her general biography. The general distress prevailing at the time, the combined efforts made to overcome it as soon as possible, and good family relationships were, as in very many similar cases, protective forces. Psychotic symptoms began to appear with incipient involution only when, after she had survived the hard times and her personal needs had begun to increase year by year, family bonds were loosened and the patient, a single woman, fell into a state of frustration regarding marriage and other intimate relationships; it was then that a disorganized mode of existence, accompanied by partial social isolation, began to take increasing toll.

Further observation of the patient, however, led to expectations that, given regular care, she would be able to find new roots in her present social environment.

There are without doubt cases of drastic uprooting in which the prospect of finding new roots is very slight because the limits of human endurance have been reached. The following case may illustrate this:

> The patient S.L., born in China in 1910, a Chinese woman with American citizenship, was admitted to this hospital for treatment in 1967 and 1968, on each occasion for a few weeks at a time. The reason for this was a condition characterized by serious excitement and marked anxiety. In the further course of the illness what appeared to be catatonic restlessness was observed. She had paranoid ideas, suffered from delusions that she was being pursued and would be murdered. Hysterical symptoms appeared from time to time. It was especially noticeable at the beginning of the psychosis that she was intransigent and emotionally inaccessible. After abatement of the psychotic symptoms she was somewhat more prepared to make contact with others, but this was rendered difficult by the fact that during the first period of hospitalization she had spoken practically no German, while during the second her German was still poor. A markedly distrustful basic attitude persisted.
>
> The patient's entire family lives in the People's Republic of China. In 1933 she went to Moscow for political reasons, lived there until 1936 and then went to the United States in connection with her work in the arts, where she married an American citizen. The marriage has remained good throughout many years in difficult circumstances. At the end of the war both had such serious political difficulties in the United States, that as soon as they were granted exit visas they left America and went to China. Here they at first found opportunities for work, but from 1959 to 1960 they encountered political difficulties of a kind hard to describe. The patient was also under intensive pressure to dissolve her marriage and resume Chinese citizenship. Her husband went to London in 1960 to renew his passport. At that time, in a state of very serious depression and with the prospect of never seeing her husband again she became mentally ill for the first time and had to be treated in a mental hospital for some weeks. After about one year, she was permitted to leave the country and was able to join her husband in London. She lived there for a time and then came to the German Democratic Republic with her husband in 1963. They have no children. Both work here, but the patient has

had little success in settling down, a fact which also emerges from her lack of interest in making friends or in learning German. She has a very close relationship with her husband, who appears to be mentally very stable. All the psychotic phases occurred when her husband had to leave the country in connection with his work and she was left to her own devices. She then appears to have experienced extreme anxiety, followed by psychotic symptoms.

It should be mentioned that no signs of organic disease could be found and that up to 1960, when the mental stress became especially severe, there was apparently no sign of mental illness.

A report of the course of this illness seemed appropriate because it was ascertained that experienced colleagues who treated the patient in the hospital, following my treatment in 1968, did not even consider the possibility of a reactive psychosis, but diagnosed a special form of "endogenous" psychosis.

It appears to be clear that the patient's link with her husband remains as the last "root," that is to say hope, for a life without deep mental disturbance, and after all the shattering past experience of uprooting the danger of a relapse remains acute, especially since involution plays an increasing role.

In the early stages of senium, difficulties of adaptation, also known as "psychic rigidity", can assume such proportions that relatively minor changes may lead to a kind of uprooting with serious mental disturbances. The following example from my own experience may illustrate this:

R.B., born 1902, a qualified bookkeeper, was given treatment in the former Wuhlgarten Hospital on three separate occasions from 1964 to 1966, each time for several months. He had held a responsible position in a West Berlin firm, where he had worked for forty years, and was known as an extremely hardworking and dependable person. He had always drunk two or three bottles of beer in the evening, but had never been an alcoholic. As he had always resided in East Berlin, he had been obliged to look for a new job after the frontier was closed in 1961. According to his own detailed account, it was not only the change of work after so many years in the same firm, but above all the basically different economic, technical and administrative as well as social conditions in the German Democratic Republic which were to blame for his failure at work. Within a very short time, the once respected and responsible bookkeeper had become a minor employee, able to work only under supervision. Consequent depression and abuse of alcohol resulted in the loss of his new post. Pronounced alcoholism then developed, and attempts to work in other jobs also ended in failure.

The man admitted to hospital for examination was somewhat prematurely aged, but still able-bodied. Apart from myocardial damage, the patient showed no organic changes nor any signs of dementia. Depressive symptoms connected with enforced inactivity were clearly present.

The usual treatment for alcoholism was not successful. During repeated hospitalization intensive rehabilitation in the administrative department of the hospital was undertaken. The patient showed goodwill, but considerably reduced ability to adapt was noted, so that he could not be considered a fully capable worker. After the third period of hospital treatment, he suffered a rapid relapse and was unable to do regular work. In 1966 he moved to West Berlin to be with his children and he is therefore no longer under our control.

Alcoholism as described here, with marked depression based on partial uprooting, can only be fully understood in conjunction with advancing involution. Involution and senium can, in accordance with the above, be described as a phase in life in which uprooting constitutes a special danger.

In conclusion, mention should be made of unusual phenomena observed in persons persecuted by the Nazis who were subjected in youth to the indescribable horrors of deportation and concentration camps. Reports in a number of publications (see Muller-Hegemann, 1966) speak of permanent changes in character, with acute distrust of other people and difficulty in making contact, frequently accompanied by paranoid reactions, lack of emotional expression and excessive excitability. In later years such persons remained very often rootless. As no similar phenomena were observed in very small children who had been persecuted but had been unable to grasp the full extent of the horror, or in persecuted adults, we may conclude that it is during the formative years, i.e. after infancy and before reaching adulthood, that social and national roots are best formed. The picture of people who in childhood and adolescense daily experienced extreme oppression and humiliation, who went in fear of their lives and watched others die in agony, is a warning to the world never again to permit such inhumanity. However, such cases remain the exception to the general rule, which is that during involution and senium the danger of uprooting is greatly increased, while the chance of finding new roots is much reduced.

Origin of Contributions and References: See Page 334

MENTAL HEALTH ASPECTS OF VOLUNTARY MIGRATION

Abraham A. Weinberg
Israel

Notwithstanding the vital role population movements have played in the history of human civilization, our knowledge of the social psychology of these phenomena is still limited. This is also true of the inter- and intranational migrations of our times. Their impact on mental health is even less known. A short survey on some facts and experiences in the field of voluntary migration with emphasis laid on international migration may throw some light on this hitherto hardly explored field of mental health.

Migration today is usually divided into two categories: voluntary migration or planned transplantation and involuntary or forced migration, comprising displacement, forced labor and flight (refugees). One has often called voluntary migration "free" migration when thinking of the mass movements during the last two centuries, mainly of Europeans migrating to the Americas, Australia, New Zealand, and Africa. Lately, however, and especially since the first World War this free migration has been transformed to more or less controlled migration. Nations want to regulate the number and types of persons leaving, and perhaps even more, to control the number and types of persons entering the country. The United States, during the nineteenth century the most important country of mass immigration, restricted greatly through its migration laws of 1921 and 1924 the entrance of migrants. Other countries in need of new citizens give preference to certain groups of immigrants, whilst preventing the entry of others. Thus international migration has decreased considerably though many countries have still room for millions of people.

Voluntary migration is not always as voluntary as the term may imply. It is often difficult to discern whether a person emigrates of his free will to the country of his choice or because of anxiety about imminent persecution which never or only in the distant future might materialize. In the latter case, he would psychologically be a refugee though his migration could be called a voluntary one as there was no real cause for flight.

In this paper we will restrict ourselves to some mental-health aspects of voluntary immigration in comparison with those of involuntary immigration.

There are many reasons why voluntary immigrants may have better chances for successful adjustment, acculturation, and integration than involuntary ones. We shall discuss the mental aspects under three headings: selectivity, preparedness for change, and inner security.

Selectivity. – Voluntary migration means in many respects selective migration. It has often been thought that voluntary migrants are generally more intelligent, more energetic, and better equipped for migration. According to Hofstee (1952) this need not necessarily be so. It seems especially not to be true in the case of intranational (internal) migration from one rural area to another. Migrants from rural areas to towns are positively selected in respect to intelligence and intellectual achievements when there is a relatively great demand for highly qualified work in the town.

Where unskilled laborers are sought in town, migration might not be selective. We can assume, in agreement with Hofstee, that international migration is also not directly selective with respect to intelligence, and that whatever indirect selection there may be depends on the comparative opportunities in the country of origin and the country of immigration.

Selectivity may exist in that voluntary migrants often differ in their personality from the average individual of their native community; they rebel against the strict norms of behavior, or have political or religious convictions of their own. Amongst them are, apart from the adventurers, the ideologists and the pioneers seeking new ways of life in another country. That among the latter very many energetic and persevering people are to be found, has perhaps nowhere more clearly been demonstrated than in the case of the pioneer settlers in Palestine (Israel).

Preparedness for Change. – The adjustment of the immigrant to his new environment is related to his level of expectation. Immigrants who are disappointed because of too high expectations are more prone to fail in their adjustment than those who found conditions in the new country above or according to their expectation. This generally acknowledged fact has in Israel (Palestine) been confirmed by Guttman (unpublished) and by my investigation among voluntary immigrants from Holland (Weinberg, 1949, 1953, 1953, 1954). Immigrants who before their immigration were adequately informed of the socio-cultural environment are, ceteris paribus, more prepared for change than those who did not get such information. Preparedness for social, cultural and economic change promotes adjustment; unpreparedness influences it unfavorably. An example of lacking preparedness for change is the fourth immigration wave to Israel which occurred in the years 1924-26, following the legislation of discriminatory laws against the Jewish middleclass in Poland. These people transplanted their way of living to the cities of Israel, contributing greatly to change their institutional role and when an economic crisis came in 1926, they left the country by the thousands, in contrast to pioneer immigrants of former wavers who resettled even under unfavorable conditions, prepared to change from former roles of students and middleclass town-dwellers to those of farmers in cooperative or private agricultural settlements.

In the inquiry among immigrants from Holland, on the other hand, it appeared of no significance for their successful adjustment whether they carried on the same occupations as in Holland or another one, provided they possessed the necessary vocational abilities or training.

Multiple immigrations, which occurred with 79 of 396 investigated immigrants from Holland, did not influence adjustment. I have observed, however, cases of migrants who suffered from a psychoneurosis upon arrival in a country after repeated migrations. These were cases of Jewish refugees or so-called voluntary migrants who left their country of origin because of fear lest the existing discriminations might change into forthright persecutions, as later really was the case. Much depends on the inner security of these migrants, the reasons for their multiple migrations, and their socio-cultural distance from the new society.

In this context, another factor influential on adjustment or maladjustment is the possibility or impossibility of return to the country of origin or of migrating to another country. An immigrant who knows he can return to his old environment and is still in close contact with his family or friends may be impaired in his preparedness to change and save or reconquer his inner security by leaving the country of immigration. Many who did so were well accepted by their former environment enjoying perhaps even a special status of "experienced" people of the world; others, however, discovered that they did not fit in any more into the old environment and became "marginal." On the other hand, the absence of close ties with the old environment but still the awareness of having the old country as "last refuge" may enhance the immigrants' inner security and with it their chances of acculturation and eventual integration, i.e., the state of being adjusted to, accepted by, and belonging to the community.

Many people immigrating against their will sabotage themselves unconsciously. They suffer often from so-called "bad luck" because of their unconscious refusal to succeed in the country they did not choose as their new homeland. E.g. they do not learn the language or when attempting to, fail. Many who immigrated to Israel before the second World War because of the dangers of the Nazi regime are learning Hebrew only recently. They have become aware that they do not want to leave or are not able to do so because of economic, family, or age reasons. Now they study Hebrew successfully as one of the means towards acculturation and integration.

Inner security. — It is a widespread opinion that migrants are suffering from a sense of insecurity both in the homeland, where it induces them to leave, and in the country of resettlement where it diminishes or impedes their integration and so endangers their mental and physical health. This may hold true for involuntary migrants and also for many who lived under strain, due to economic difficulties on their farms or in their business, to unemployment, to discrimination, or to fear of persecutions, and left "voluntarily." But if migration is truly voluntary, feelings of insecurity need not exist.

A man who condemns ethnic, political or religious prejudices without being involved himself, who wants to build up a new life somewhere under more favorable conditions, be they economic, social, or cultural or who is led by idealistic or pioneering motives, may feel quite secure before migration and retain this feeling of inner security in the new country, too. This does not mean that an immigrant is not more prone to suffer from insecurity than the native, for through his transplantation he has been cut off from his homeland, part or all of his relatives and friends and derives no more security from his old environment. He has to build up a new status among alien people, learn an alien language, and understand alien habits and customs, perhaps adapt himself to a different climate and landscape.

When the difficulties are too great for his adjustment to social, cultural, and economic change, he may become marginal; he no more belongs to his old environment, though still strongly attached to it, and is not integrating into the new one although in reality living within it or, more correctly, on its margin.

In case he can not adjust himself to the new community and is not able or willing to return to the old one, he finds himself not belonging to any community; he is uprooted. The significance of uprootedness for mental health has been described by Maria Pfister-Ammende (1952), L. Tyhurst (1951), and others (Handlin 1953). The chances of becoming mentally uprooted are presumably less for voluntary immigrants than for involuntary ones. In our material, the incidence of mental illness in relation to voluntary immigration could not be assessed, our investigation is still continuing. Migrants seem to have a greater incidence of mental disease than the resident population (Taft and Dobbins (1955), Murphy (1952), Pfister-Ammende (1953).)

Regarding criminality, new immigrants have proved to be no less law abiding than residents and sometimes they even show less criminality. The well-known increased criminality of the second, and, to a lesser degree, of the third generation of immigrants seems to occur especially in those families who entered too soon into the new society, as well as among immigrants living in secluded quarters in big cities, especially in slum areas.

A voluntary immigrant who felt secure in his home country may be faced with specific and difficult problems and, especially in the beginning, not always know how to tackle them. Even if he understands the language, he may not always comprehend the ways of expression of his new countrymen. He may feel uncertain sometimes without, however, becoming innerly insecure.

For a proper understanding of the process of adjustment and acculturation one has to distinguish between an inner insecurity — anxiety which is derived from lack of belongingness, i.e. lack of love, understanding, and support in childhood or later — and the feeling of uncertainty consequent to strangeness of existing economic, social, cultural, and political conditions. Too frequent and embarrassing uncertainties may lead to inner insecurity or cause a latent insecurity to become overt.

The investigation among voluntary immigrants from Holland, as well as a pilot study among students of the Hebrew Intensive Course, proved that many voluntary immigrants do not suffer from inner insecurity. This fact has also been borne out in an attitude research by Louis Guttman, who did not find any difference in the percentage of immigrants and residents who feel secure.

This concept of inner security of healthy voluntary immigrants has a bearing on the understanding of some phenomena of immigrants' behavior and research and practice of mental health of migration. Migrants tend to travel in groups, to contact after arrival old immigrants from the same country, to cluster together temporarily in tenements or town areas, to settle permanently in groups or in the neighborhood of former countrymen, to enter (or to found) immigration associations, to read (or to publish) papers in their mother tongue containing news from their country of origin etc. Thus the immigrant remains, at least for the time being, part of a group representing for him the land, the fold, the habits and customs of old, symbolizing his parental home. He preserves his inner security by only gradually coming into contact with his new social and cultural environment, helped and guided by his former compatriots. In this way he can explore the new surroundings at ease and prepare himself for his new role in society. At the same time, the receiving society does not have to accept the newcomers en masse, which might lead to the former's own disintegration.

Too great a distance between immigrant groups and the receiving population may result in a permanent separation and subsequent formation of minorities within the resident society. In this way inner security of the members of the minorities often may be retained because the discrimination or oppression is not suffered individually but collectively.

When great distance in religious, ideological, and other cultural traits exist, or when there are obvious physical anthropological differences, so-called "social visibility," strong prejudice may result, which inhibits or severely hampers assimilation. Prejudice and the resulting discrimination or even segregation, i.e. exclusion of the discriminated members of a group from public facilities and education, badly influence the mental health of immigrants.

Where the distance between immigrants and the receiving society is rather great, but the two groups are interdependent, e.g. economically, assimilation may not develop beyond a superficial contract called "accommodation" which results in a more or less stable form of symbiosis. An example of successful symbiosis exists, for example, in Canada between the settlers of Anglo-Saxon and of French origin. The history of the Jews gives us examples of temporary symbiosis.

It is, therefore, not advisable to attempt to hasten the assimilation of the immigrant because of the danger of his becoming "marginal," if not fully uprooted. On the contrary, as Saenger has pointed out, "the demand for speedy Americanization together with the punishment for behaving in foreign ways may retard assimilation" (Saenger, 1953). Such an attitude fosters the retiring of the immigrant into a ghetto of his own group and the formation of racial pride in order to compensate for his insecurity.

voluntary immigrants do not suffer from inner insecurity. This fact has also been borne out in an attitude research by Louis Guttman, who did not find any difference in the percentage of immigrants and residents who feel secure.

This concept of inner security of healthy voluntary immigrants has a bearing on the understanding of some phenomena of immigrants' behavior and research and practice of mental health of migration. Migrants tend to travel in groups, to contact after arrival old immigrants from the same country, to cluster together temporarily in tenements or town areas, to settle permanently in groups or in the neighborhood of former countrymen, to enter (or to found) immigration associations, to read (or to publish) papers in their mother tongue containing news from their country of origin etc. Thus the immigrant remains, at least for the time being, part of a group representing for him the land, the fold, the habits and customs of old, symbolizing his parental home. He preserves his inner security by only gradually coming into contact with his new social and cultural environment, helped and guided by his former compatriots. In this way he can explore the new surroundings at ease and prepare himself for his new role in society. At the same time, the receiving society does not have to accept the newcomers en masse, which might lead to the former's own disintegration.

Too great a distance between immigrant groups and the receiving population may result in a permanent separation and subsequent formation of minorities within the resident society. In this way inner security of the members of the minorities often may be retained because the discrimination or oppression is not suffered individually but collectively.

When great distance in religious, ideological, and other cultural traits exist, or when there are obvious physical anthropological differences, so-called "social visibility," strong prejudice may result, which inhibits or severely hampers assimilation. Prejudice and the resulting discrimination or even segregation, i.e. exclusion of the discriminated members of a group from public facilities and education, badly influence the mental health of immigrants.

Where the distance between immigrants and the receiving society is rather great, but the two groups are interdependent, e.g. economically, assimilation may not develop beyond a superficial contract called "accommodation" which results in a more or less stable form of symbiosis. An example of successful symbiosis exists, for example, in Canada between the settlers of Anglo-Saxon and of French origin. The history of the Jews gives us examples of temporary symbiosis.

It is, therefore, not advisable to attempt to hasten the assimilation of the immigrant because of the danger of his becoming "marginal," if not fully uprooted. On the contrary, as Saenger has pointed out, "the demand for speedy Americanization together with the punishment for behaving in foreign ways may retard assimilation" (Saenger, 1953). Such an attitude fosters the retiring of the immigrant into a ghetto of his own group and the formation of racial pride in order to compensate for his insecurity.

involved himself, who wants to build up a new life somewhere under more favorable conditions, be they economic, social, or cultural or who is led by idealistic or pioneering motives, may feel quite secure before migration and retain this feeling of inner security in the new country, too. This does not mean that an immigrant is not more prone to suffer from insecurity than the native, for through his transplantation he has been cut off from his homeland, part or all of his relatives and friends and derives no more security from his old environment. He has to build up a new status among alien people, learn an alien language, and understand alien habits and customs, perhaps adapt himself to a different climate and landscape.

When the difficulties are too great for his adjustment to social, cultural, and economic change, he may become marginal; he no more belongs to his old environment, though still strongly attached to it, and is not integrating into the new one although in reality living within it or, more correctly, on its margin.

In case he can not adjust himself to the new community and is not able or willing to return to the old one, he finds himself not belonging to any community; he is uprooted. The significance of uprootedness for mental health has been described by Maria Pfister-Ammende (1952), L. Tyhurst (1951), and others (Handlin 1953). The chances of becoming mentally uprooted are presumably less for voluntary immigrants than for involuntary ones. In our material, the incidence of mental illness in relation to voluntary immigration could not be assessed, our investigation is still continuing. Migrants seem to have a greater incidence of mental disease than the resident population (Taft and Dobbins (1955), Murphy (1952), Pfister-Ammende (1953).)

Regarding criminality, new immigrants have proved to be no less law abiding than residents and sometimes they even show less criminality. The well-known increased criminality of the second, and, to a lesser degree, of the third generation of immigrants seems to occur especially in those families who entered too soon into the new society, as well as among immigrants living in secluded quarters in big cities, especially in slum areas.

A voluntary immigrant who felt secure in his home country may be faced with specific and difficult problems and, especially in the beginning, not always know how to tackle them. Even if he understands the language, he may not always comprehend the ways of expression of his new countrymen. He may feel uncertain sometimes without, however, becoming innerly insecure.

For a proper understanding of the process of adjustment and acculturation one has to distinguish between an inner insecurity — anxiety which is derived from lack of belongingness, i.e. lack of love, understanding, and support in childhood or later — and the feeling of uncertainty consequent to strangeness of existing economic, social, cultural, and political conditions. Too frequent and embarrassing uncertainties may lead to inner insecurity or cause a latent insecurity to become overt.

The investigation among voluntary immigrants from Holland, as well as a pilot study among students of the Hebrew Intensive Course, proved that many

One should, however, keep in mind that sometimes migration, instead of leading to insecurity and uprootedness, may influence mental health favorably.

In the freer atmosphere of the new country many immigrants fully develop their potentialities to their own benefit as well as to that of their fellowmen.

Socio-Psychopathological Research.[*] — Research on the reactions of man to social and cultural change and on intergroup relations is still in its very first stage of development. One of the reasons lies in the lack of understanding of the urgency of such research on the part of many who would be in a position to facilitate its being carried out. The most important reason, however, is to be found in the difficulty of getting comparable results. Quantitative compilation of results obtained in inquiries on qualitative data is only in its beginning and has not yet sufficiently penetrated into social psychiatry. An attempt to obtain comparable results was made in an investigation on problems of adjustment of immigrants from Holland to Palestine in 1941 and 1942. Although this method provided insight into many problems of adjustment, it had to be further developed. Moreover, the need was felt for an additional device for the study of the attitude of the individual and his relations to his group. We found the device in one of the newest methods in attitude research in sociology, Guttman's scale analysis (1950) and facet design (Stouffer 1950; Guttman 1954). The combination of this scaling device, in the form of a written closed questionnaire, with my comparative depth-interview was very revealing. In many cases, however, additional investigation with the aid of projective and other tests was desirable: (a) for the examination of adjustability, (b) for psychiatric diagnosis, (c) for vocational guidance in addition to other tests. In 20 cases, the Szondi test was applied; in 3, the Rorschach test; and in 15, other tests.

The investigation was carried out among students of an "Ulpan," an intensive five-month Hebrew course; part of them were living in, part coming for the daily lessons from 8 A.M. to 12:30 P.M. The students are new immigrants, tourists, and immigrants who, though living here for some years, only now have started to learn the language. It is intended to carry out the research during more courses, depending on the budget available. This is desirable not only because of the need of a sufficiently large number of interviewees, but more so for the following reason: An intensive depth-interview is practicable only with a selective sample — apart from the fact that it is too costly and cumbersome with a random sample. The students of this Ulpan do not form a representative sample of immigrants to Israel. Guttman's method is usable with a large random sample. The coordination of these methods of extensive and intensive research serve important purposes:

(1) The application of the written closed questionnaire on the lines of Guttman's method administered to groups has proved to be a timesaving device;

---

[*] This investigation has been made possible through the generosity of the late Mr. Eduard Vis, and I am indebted to Professor Louis Guttman, Director of The Israel Institute for Applied Soical Research in Jerusalem, for his most valuable help and advice.

(2) The replies to the questions in the closed questionnaire can be verified by the data of the depth-interview;

(3) A comparative evaluation of the two methods might lead to an improvement of both, the extensive and the intensive ways of research;

(4) Consequently, methods of extensive research may be developed as to enable us to study intricate mental health problems of a large population.

Results. — The closed questionnaire was furnished in four languages, Hebrew, English, French and German. The first time the students answered the questionnaire was two months after the course started March 3, 1952, the second time toward the end of the course, May 20, 1954. We gave the questionnaire twice, in order to find out whether the opinions and attitudes of the students had altered during their stay in the Ulpan and to what extent they were able to form a community within the Ulpan. There was a total of 91 in the Ulpan, 38 men and 53 women. Of the total, 44.4 per cent lives in the hostel attached to the Ulpan; 21.8 per cent were below 25 years of age; 43.6 per cent were between 26 and 40 years old; 28.2 per cent were between 41 and 55 years old; 6.4 per cent were above 56.

The majority of the students came from Europe (two-thirds), 20 per cent from America; 8 per cent of the students were not Jewish. 60 percent came to Israel in 1953; 28 per cent came to Israel in 1952; 12 per cent came to Israel before 1952. Of the 91 students, 77 per cent were immigrants; the rest tourists. During the five-months' course, some students left and some entered late. Fifty-nine students took part from the beginning to the end.

The immigrants and the tourists answered all questions of the questionnaire alike except the questions pertaining to immigration. Concerning the adjustment of the students to conditions in the Ulpan, we did not differentiate between immigrants and tourists. We found that we had to distinguish between different categories of migration:

1. Voluntary emigration

2. Involuntary emigration

3. Voluntary immigration

4. Involuntary immigration

Involuntary emigrants can be divided into refugees, displaced persons, and forced labor.

Among our involuntary emigrants we found only refugees.
49 people were voluntary emigrants and voluntary immigrants (1/3);
2 people were voluntary emigrants and involuntary immigrants (1/4);
6 people were involuntary emigrants and voluntary immigrants (2/3);
9 people were involuntary emigrants and involuntary immigrants (2/4).

Of 4 we know that they were voluntary emigrants but they did not reply to the question of immigration.

The problems of voluntary or involuntary emigration were examined by a number of questions arranged according to the ranking principle of the Guttman scale. Because of the great concentration of the students within one type (72 per cent of the respondents belong to the type who wanted most to leave their country of origin), we had as yet no opportunity to examine the "perfectness" of the scale. Inasmuch as it was possible to speak of a scale and its shape, we defined as most negative in the ranking those respondents who replied that in their country of origin their economic existence was endangered and that they left their country only to a certain extent of their own will. In contrast to this type, which we will designate later as Type A, there was a negative type who did not fit into the shape of the scale. This not-fitting-in resulted from the contradiction that on the one hand, it was expressed that in their country of origin their lives were threatened and on the other hand, the reply that they left their country only of their own free will. This type will be described below as Type B. In group A, as well as in group B, were 5 students.

After a further study of the scale and the universe of the content, we tried to explain the above phenomenon with the help of the following hypothesis: it is obvious that both types were forced to leave their country of origin through external circumstances, but it is also quite obvious that none of them was actually driven out; that the last decision to leave was left to them.

However, while Type A's acknowledged their unwillingness to leave their country, Type B's stated that they decided to leave of their own free will. We assumed that the factor, influential of the different types of persons, which induced them to differing attitudes in a more or less similar situation lies within the personality, i.e. that those belonging to Type A suffer from inner insecurity, in contrast to those of Type B who possess definite inner security.

In order to test our hypothesis, we examined it in two independent ways in two separate directions: by examining the case histories obtained by depth interviews of the respondents concerned and by comparison of the dispersion of the replies by Type A with those of Type B. In all the subjects dealt with by the questionnaire, we got a confirmation of our hypothesis.

1. It appeared in the depth interview that all five respondents of Type A suffered from inner insecurity, in contrast to the two respondents of Type B we were able to interview, who both were innerly secure.

2. In comparing the replies we obtained from the two types regarding the remaining subjects of the questionnaire, we found that there are differences between the two types in respect to subjects connected with inner security or insecurity, while differences in other subjects were not observed. There are differences in the following subjects:

a. Psychosomatic disturbances (nervousness, disturbed sleep, frightening dreams, stomach trouble, headaches, palpitations). Type A disturbed; Type B undisturbed.

b. Decision to enter the Ulpan: Type A did not enter on their own decision; Type B entered on own decision.

c. Social life in country of origin: Type A was not sociable; Type B was.

d. Social life in the Ulpan: Type A was not so well integrated in the class; Type B was.

e. At-home-feeling in the Ulpan: Type A does not feel at home; Type B does.

After having obtained these two confirmations of our assumptions, we decided to check on the correctness by applying its conclusion. If it is true that inner security or insecurity is obviously evident within the two types of involuntary migrants, then this factor must also be influential within the rest of the migrants, viz. the majority of the voluntary emigrants and immigrants. We examined the results of 39 depth-psychological interviews which had been held amongst the Ulpan students and divided the students accordingly in two groups: 30 migrants with inner security and 9 migrants with inner security. We compared again the dispersion of the replies of the two groups with regard to the various subjects of the questionnaire. The results were exactly the same. We found again differences with respect to all the subjects for which differences had been found between Types A and B in precisely the same direction. From this experiment not only additional confirmation was obtained of the correctness of our assumption, but also this important conclusion: The adjustment of the investigated group of immigrants seems to depend on the inner security of the migrant (in other words, his mental health), rather than on his migration being voluntary or involuntary. There remains the influence of the form of migration as such, but to our regret, the number of persons investigated so far is too small for venturing an opinion on the influence of this variable.

The conditions of the Ulpan were very favorable for the investigation. Teaching and attitude of the teachers were positively commented on by the students. The teachers were even considered as mixing freely within the students' community. Discrimination was almost non-existent. At the beginning integration of the classes was better than towards the end; the cooperation in matters of study became less, but the cooperation in other matters became greater. Social life in the Ulpan as a whole did not, however, appreciably alter. This might be due to the fact that, in the course of time, students became less secluded within their classes and mixed freely amongst all the students of the Ulpan. Our observation taught us that interests of the students were shifting from the studies to the economic difficulties ahead. In the congenial atmosphere of the Ulpan, under the influence of the stimulating, vivid, even cheerful teaching, and with a prospect of learning the language, the opening to a perhaps prosperous future, they feel at first more optimistic, in a better mood. Maybe many of them and especially the insecure, feel freed from the daily worries and relax as in a holiday resort. Towards the end they feel, on the whole, less optimistic though still more than before the entrance into the Ulpan. They have learned surprisingly much Hebrew in so short a time. They are better equipped for the struggle of existence, but have to face reality in Israel. For many occupations, opportunities are not too good; in the cities there is a housing shortage and unemployment. The small decrease in percentage of optimistic immigrants is quite in accordance with what one may expect. Closer scrutinizing of the individual cases for which we have as yet not had any opportunity may reveal particulars of these phenomena.

Treatment and Prevention. – In cases of seriously impaired mental health in new immigrants, psychiatric treatment should be given before or immediately after the entry into the country of resettlement, at any rate always as soon as possible. A single mentally-ill person may endanger the resettlement of his family; a disturbed family, the mental health and chances of successful resettlement of a whole group. Socio-therapy and group psychotherapy in psychiatrically supervised immigrant villages or community health centers in areas of immigrant settlements should be considered, as soon as symptoms of inner insecurity and maladjustment are developing.

Still more important is socio-prophylaxis. All means should be applied which may promote undisturbed, speedy acculturation provided that nothing should be done to unduly hasten the assimilation of new immigrants.

Suitable means of communication are essential for promoting smooth acculturation. Though stress should be laid on learning the country's language, publications in the immigrant's mother tongue should be allowed. Personal contacts, radio, films, television (where possible) should be used towards this end. Personal contact between governmental officials and social workers and immigrants is of the greatest significance.

A listening ear, a humane approach, a friendly attitude, an empathetic participation, without over-protectiveness or possessiveness, in the migrants' problems may make the immigrant feel that he is welcome in his new homeland. For the insecure migrant such an empathetic behavior may mean the beginning of regaining his confidence in his fellowmen in general and in government in particular. Courses in mental health work for immigration officials and voluntary workers should be held in every immigration country.

Settlements of more than one group should be encouraged but without permitting too much diversity (heterogeneous settlements).

As children adjust themselves more easily and completely than adults, stress should be laid on their education towards citizenship of the new country. The education of the children should be within the parental surroundings and due care should be paid to parent-child and parent-school relationship.

In conclusion, it should be stressed once more that the dangers threatening the mental health of voluntary immigrants are great, even for those who are selected, healthy, i.e. innerly secure, and prepared for the social, cultural, and economic changes awaiting them in the new country.

Preventive mental health work with immigrants should therefore also include the apparently mentally healthy; curative mental health work should be applied as early as possible. Such mental health work and the necessary research should be fostered and coordinated within the framework of the United Nations.

Origin of Contributions and References: See Page 334

AFRICAN WORKERS IN FRANCE AND PROBLEMS OF ADAPTATION

S. Diarra
Senegal

Since the end of the second World War, there has been a steady influx into France of manpower from the African countries south of the Sahara. Sporadic at first, the number of immigrants began to increase rapidly from 1958 on, and in the summer of 1963 amounted to one thousand. It was estimated at the time that between 20 to 60 thousand such immigrants had settled in France, two-thirds of them in the Paris region.

These manpower movements affect chiefly the zones forming the common frontiers of Senegal, Mali and Mauritania. However, agreements concluded between France and these three African countries mainly concerned seem to have resulted in a stabilization of immigration, with the result that in 1966 the net balance of newly-arrived African workers was not noticeably high.

The transplanting of Tukulors and Sarakolles straight from rural Africa raises many problems in France. Illiterate and unskilled, these migrants are brought into brutal contact with the rapid rhythm of industrial life which exacts a satisfactory output. They have to face serious health problems – they are not used to the climate, their food is inadequate and their living conditions are wretched. Constituting as they do a marginal group, a kind of sub-proletariat, they have brought with them to France the social structures of their home villages.

A. Adaptation to Industrial Work and Human Relations
1. Adaption

Most of the employers interviewed agreed that given equal skills, the African worker's output would equal that of the French workers. However, the lack of skill and illiteracy of the majority make it difficult for such workers to adapt to industrial work. A staff manager in a big car factory, who has been employing African workers from countries south of the Sahara for over ten years, said the immigrants who had come over in the fifties adapted easily to the work. They all speak French which makes it easy for them to integrate into industrial activity. After preliminary "preparation" in a training course or a stay in an urban center, some of them achieve a decent output. He said, however, that the new arrivals were less dexterous, and had no knowledge of French. They do not, therefore, adapt easily to work in a factory. Their inexperience of danger makes it impossible to put them to work on machines. Accidents are frequent during the first six months.

"The period of adaption needed to ensure a reasonable output is longer than that needed for a European or a North African, and training must be very carefully supervised", said the staff manager of a big boiler shop which employs approximately three hundred Africans from countries south of the Sahara. Many employers add that when such workers are given psychologically correct attention, the results are likely to be satisfactory. They are moreover docile and easy to deal with if they are treated with firmness and flexibility, but also with kindness. They may even become skilled workers, provided they are surrounded by competent, patient and indulgent supervisors."

In undertakings where it is possible to work in teams, it is considered preferable to place African workers with a satisfactory output in a team with one or two more advanced individuals, who can act as interpreters for their illiterate compatriots. Some workers become very adept. At the start of their period of adaptation the new arrivals are given the job of feeding the conveyor belt for the manufacture of parts. At the end of a year, they specialize and are given jobs as oilers, crane-operators, truck drivers and trimmers. Some who have been working in the car industry for up to fifteen years and have taken vocational training courses, have managed to achieve skilled status.

2. Human Relationships

Employers agree that African workers from countries south of the Sahara have certain good qualities. They are gentle and willing, correct in their behavior, punctual, docile and persevering, and they make good workmates. Were it not for the language problem they would – it appears – be easy to guide. And according to the staff manager of a factory producing steel furniture, the language difficulty can be overcome by the presence of one or two Africans with a rather better education who can act as interpreters and settle labor and social questions satisfactorily.

Higher grade staff is usually willing to give such African workers a try-out, if only because of the intense shortage of labor for the meaner type of job. But the lower grades almost always view experiments of this kind with reserve. If the experiment proves positive and the African workers prove satisfactory, both as to output and behavior, prejudices gradually disappear and a good relationship is established between the workers and those in charge. Such is the case in a tannery where these Africans constitute half the permanent labor force (250 out of 500). Some concerns no longer employ North Africans, but prefer to employ an increasing number of Africans from countries south of the Sahara. "French workers no longer object to the hiring of Africans from those countries, since they have been forced to make the comparison between such workers and those from North Africa who, unfortunately, behave rather badly", said the staff manager of a big printing works which employs approximately eighty Black African workers. When a trial proves unsatisfactory, because of the difficulties these workers experience in adapting to industrial work, the staff becomes impatient and often concludes that such African labor is unemployable. "We engaged several Africans from countries south of the Sahara in 1962", said one employer. "We gave them a try-out but it was not satisfactory, so we decided not to take on any more. They are not reliable, their health is indifferent and if one leaves, many others follow in his wake." Another said: "We gave them a trial which ended in failure. The relationship between wages, output and quality of work was so disproportionate when compared with that of the metropolitan workers, that it was impossible to continue on such a basis." Frequently ignorance of the French language makes relations between the staff and those African workers difficult. Difficulties of communication can result in misunderstandings which may cause incidents between some of the African workers and their team-leader or foreman. The staff manager of a concern at Epinay-sur-Seine defined the problems raised by employing labor from African countries south of the Sahara as follows: – "These African workers have to be very carefully supervised and allotted tasks of a specific nature adapted to their possibilities and to their understanding. The French workers know little about them: there is widespread ignorance of their religion, of their highly developed sense of justice, of their community life. They are easy to handle, provided you know something of the mentality of people from that part of Africa."

Relations with French labor are generally good. In the beginning, some European workers "who find it difficult to get used to this contiguity" are reserved. For the unskilled workers, however, these Africans are not dangerous competitors, as the European worker is usually better qualified.

But relations are very different with the North African workers. At best, they may appear to be good between the two communities; in fact, there is more or less open hostility between them. Competition, often very strong, exists between these two communities, both on the labor market and in respect to accommodation. The North Africans who were the first on the scene, feel themselves increasingly threatened in respect to jobs habitually reserved for them in various undertakings. Clashes are frequent during the hiring of workmen, particularly in undertakings where co-option is the customary method of recruiting workers of the lower grades. This method which is frequent among North Africans, helped to ensure priority for certain families or douars, the members of which were given the vacant jobs. The return of the Kabyles to Algeria after independence made it possible for Africans from countries south of the Sahara to step into jobs thus released. The return in 1962 of certain Algerians to their former jobs in France gave rise to incidents which were often of a violent kind. The new-comers who have themselves adopted the practice of co-option have no wish to relinquish the jobs abandoned by the North Africans. The upshot is altercations which degenerate into pitched battles, sometimes at the place of work, but mostly in the districts where the immigrants live in proximity. There is permanent tension between them, and fights may break out at any moment. As the relationship between the North Africans and the Africans from countries south of the Sahara is, with respect to accommodation, that of lodging-house owners towards dissatisfied lodgers, hostility is everywhere rife between the two communities. It is extremely difficult to place them in the same team at work, because of the possibilities of a clash.

The foregoing was confirmed by an official of the society of Algerian workers in France: " The main reason for the hostility (between the two communities) is economic. The Algerians are afraid that the Black Africans will step into their hard-earned jobs. On their return to France, some weeks after independence, many of them were horrified to see that the number of newcomers had increased almost fivefold." This hostility between North Africans and Africans from countries south of the Sahara, forces certain enterprises who are used to North African labor to turn down other African workers. In some branches of activity, however, there is no competition between the two communities. Building sites and public works are cases in point, because the Africans from the countries south of the Sahara abandon jobs where they are exposed to the rigors of the climate, particularly during the winter.

3. Manpower Fluctuations

Many deplore the unreliability of this category of manpower; others, on the contrary, declare themselves satisfied with its reliability. It has emerged from many discussions that manpower fluctuations are a characteristic feature of certain branches of activity and of certain jobs where the pay is poor in relation to the great effort demanded. Moreover, there are other causes of discontent, such as dismissals because of illness, bullying and layings off at the conclusion of temporary work. Sometimes the African workers leave without giving a reason. Here, however, the distance of work from their domicile plays a part. Long daily journeys become exhausting after several months, particularly when the job is in itself exhausting. Many workers have to travel daily right across Paris to get to their work in a suburban concern. Overwork is thus one of the reasons for their unreliability. Frequently, also, the cause is rivalry within a community. This competitive mentality can be observed particularly among the young, who like to compare their earnings with those of other members of the group, each one wishing to earn a higher monthly wage than the other. What counts above all is the monthly income of the immigrants who care little for working conditions. "The gregarious instinct is very developed, and uniformity of earnings, whatever the job, would be willingly accepted, with complete disregard for justice", comments the staff manager of one project. Those that earn less than their colleagues thus tend to leave their job before making sure of another. It is worth noting that in projects where large numbers of Africans from countries south of the Sahara are employed – all earning the same – there are few manpower fluctuations.

B. The Problem of Accommodation

After concluding their daily work — often a job demanding mere physical effort — the African workers return each evening to the family abode, where they live under wretched conditions, but where a quite remarkable system of organization prevails.

Living conditions show most clearly how wretched is the life of these workers. It is, of course, true that the accommodation of the North African workers reflect the same misery, and the scandal of the shanty towns still persists, despite campaigns in the press and specialized studies in which the deplorable living conditions of their occupants have been denounced. But the tenements inhabited by those who come from the countries south of the Sahara are in general less obvious than the North African butments of the Paris region, for example. They are not shelters erected on wasteland, but sordid premises which defy the most elementary rules of sanitation and which hide behind the stolid frontage of houses in working class districts.

It is in Paris and the region of the Seine that the housing problem of the African workers is particularly serious. Over ninety per cent of them live in communities in order to enjoy a solidarity based on mutual help. They occupy dilapidated hotels or make-shift premises arranged as dormitories, most of which evade the regulations governing furnished apartments because of their clandestine character. Cellars, garrets, coffee rooms and dance halls, sheds, former stables, unused workshops and factories are transformed into places tightly packed with African immigrants from the steppes of the Sahara. These places are to be found in districts with a very large North African population. Nine-tenths of them are owned by Algerians, and the remainder by Moroccans, Frenchmen, and even Black Africans who thus hope to free their compatriots from the ascendancy of the North Africans. The latter, and also some French owners, occasionally entrust the management of their dilapidated properties to Africans from countries south of the Sahara, in the hope that they will bring them a large number of lodgers belonging to the same ethnic group.

There is a similarity between the aims and methods of the immigrants from North Africa and those from Black Africa. The latter have the same aspirations as their North African predecessors. Having, like them, arrived completely destitute, they try to set up house as cheaply as possible. Usually the two strata of immigrants live in close proximity, and lodgers change as the premises inhabited by the North Africans are vacated, either because they return to their country, or because they are moved to hostels created for them by the authorities or by private institutions. The tenements thus vacated by the older strata of North African immigrants are naturally the most insanitary and the most dilapidated. Merely to see them is to be struck by a general impression of overcrowding and squalor. The African workers crowd into rooms of only a few square meters, where there is no ventilation and where the beds are stacked on top of each other, right up to the ceiling.

In order to face up to the manifold difficulties which beset them during their stay in France, these immigrants have their own community organization in each building, where the solidarity which unites them allows them to fight against isolation and to benefit from material as well as spiritual mutual aid.

Occupying as they do the position of a "fringe" group, these African workers have brought to France the social structures of their countries of origin. Predominately illiterate, knowing nothing of the institutions and the way of life of the European population, they consider the world which surrounds them as foreign to them. The only place where they can find human warmth and where they feel safe, is the circle in which they live. Once outside the group, they become distrustful of everything. Theirs is a world apart, with its own traditions, its structures, its laws and its chiefs. This situation also results from the specific character of a migration solely of men, who have come to France without work contracts or any resources whatever. They come nevertheless, in the hope of amassing sufficient savings to meet their own needs and those of their families who have remained behind in Africa. Their main worry is thus to live as cheaply as possible in France, in order to save as much as possible. They therefore form groups according to their village of origin and ethnic affinity. Usually a community living in the same dormitory consists of people from one and the same village. The ties formed in Africa are thus maintained and consolidated in France, where the trials of a new and difficult existence are faced in common. Often the difficulty of finding accommodation in the same building forces the immigrant to form small groups which are dispersed throughout the Paris region or in the outlying communes.

C. Organization of Community Life

A furthur concept implied in community organization, is that of the ethnic group. Usually, migrants from a given village belong to the same ethnic. This is the case with the Tukulors from the middle valley of the river Senegal. With common customs and a common language, they understand each other better and their feeling of solidarity is greater within the same group. The Sarakolles too, prefer to be together so as to escape the painful feeling of lonliness which they experience as soon as they are isolated from their compatriots, particularly in a country where they do not understand the language.

1. Village Structures

(a) Authority

The conditions under which these immigrants come to France encourage the setting up of village and ethnic communities, especially as each immigrant has, on arrival, the address of a brother, a cousin or a friend to whom he is tied by links formed in Africa. New arrivals are thus welcomed according to the rules of hospitality and enter a milieu already familiar to them. Such organization, based on the village, and traditional in character, necessitates a chief. As a result, at the head of each collectivity, there is a headman whose authority is unanimously recognized and respected as is that of the village chieftain in the regions from which the immigrants come. He is, moreover, known to his compatriots by the name "village chieftain". He is not, as is often assumed, the oldest inhabitant, or a skilled marksman, nor is he the one with the greatest prestige because of his experience of life abroad or because of his knowledge of French. Rather is he the representative of traditional authority, whatever his age. He is a member of the founder-family of the village. The head of the immigrant community is thus above all a spiritual authority who guarantees the institutions of village society abroad. He is the intermediary between the parent community and that formed by its members in France. Sometimes several members of the patriarchal family which traditionally supply the headmen are present in one and the same community. In such cases, the representative of the village is designated according to the genealogical principle which governs the accession to any chieftainship, authority being excercised vertically, from the oldest to the youngest within the same generation. In the patrilinear classification of the offspring of the same ancestor, it is the oldest of the first cousins who will head the community. When he returns to his village, a brother or a cousin will succeed him. Where villages are represented by several community groupings, there are as many headmen as communities, each community being ruled by a member of the family of the village chieftain. For example, the Camara rule the communities which consist of Africans from the village of Aourou in Mali, the Diallo those coming from the village of Manael in Senegal, the Sakho those from the village of Diawara in Senegal, and the Gandega those from the village of Serenati in Mali.

The head of each community is surrounded by members of other influential families from their village of origin. They play a role similar to that of the notables in the village council. The presence of marabouts, who have an undeniable influence, both religious and moral, on the African communities in France has also been noted. In the absence of the representatives of the village chief, they assume the role of the head of the community. In the early days of the phenomenon of mass immigration, some of the marabouts lived on their compatriots for whom they fashioned talismans, mainly intended to ensure success in money matters. But, increasingly, they seek paid work like the rest of the community, instead of leading a parasitic existence, exploiting their religious knowledge among the group of which they form part.

(b) Solidarity

The power of decision rests with the head of the community, but this right entails duties. He is responsible for internal discipline, for seeing that instructions and decisions taken by common agreement are carried out. He it is who settles disputes which may arise between two members of the collectivity whose moral authority is vested in him. Mostly he has a secretary-treasurer, sometimes one who can read and write French, to assist him. Usually this will be a Griot attached — in accordance with ancient tradition — to the family of the village chieftain. The Griot does the bookkeeping in respect of the community's income and expenditure. Life in the community requires, in fact, that each wage-earning member participate in the general expenditure. All wage-earning lodgers must contribute monthly:

— rent (an average of 40 francs);

— a sum towards food for the community, laundering of sheets, the purchase of coal for heating in winter (the amount varies according to the size of the community);

— a share towards the mutual aid fund, amounting to about 5 francs per person per month.

Within each community material and moral solidarity is a rigid code. This is evident above all in the assumption of total responsibility for those who are out of work. New arrivals, the sick, the unemployed have a right to bed and board. They pay no monthly rent, for to their compatriots it is inconceivable that they should share expenses, when they are receiving no money and have no resources. The same applies to food which, according to the African tradition of hospitality, is shared with any individual who has been admitted to a collectivity, without the principle of a financial contribution towards an expenditure being raised. In addition, new arrivals receive pocket money from the members of the community, in particular from their relatives and friends, to allow them to meet the cost of travel necessitated by the search for work. The occupant of a bed will not hesitate to share it with a compatriot until one is vacated. All members of the community have the same rights and duties. The evening meals are always taken together and the financial participation of all those who are working is a strict obligation, even if some of the members eat at the works' canteen or go to North African restaurants. They are not required to attend the common meal, but they must pay their share.

In all the communities, only members of inferior caste, such as Griots, blacksmiths and cobblers with no claim to nobility are not required to pay their share of the food. In return they do the shopping, prepare the communal meals, look after the dormitories, do the washing up, and run errands for the community. Sometimes they also do the laundry. The unemployed and new arrivals, for whom the community assumes total responsibility, help the members of the lower castes in their daily tasks in each dormitory.

The services rendered are a kind of return for the advantages they enjoy. But after they have been gainfully employed for two months they are required to contribute to the common expenditure. The idea is that they should keep their entire wages for the first month, to allow them to buy essentials, such as warm clothing for winter, working clothes or bedding. As from the second month, they will start paying back debts contracted with friends or relatives to cover the cost of the fare to France.

The solidarity of the community with the unemployed or the very sick has limits, however. If an individual is a long time finding work, he is allotted a fixed period within which to try his luck. This period never exceeds one year. Thereafter he is sent back home by his compatriots, who pay the cost of his return journey to Africa. This also applies to a person with a serious disease, regarded by the community as incurable. In 1963, a sick African who had spent a long time in a sanatorium was put on a plane to Africa by his compatriots in Paris, since according to custom he must not finish his days in a foreign country, but must return to his village to die. He was placed in the care of a cousin who was to accompany him to his home and then return, after a week in Africa.

To meet the expenditure incurred by such decisions, the community has an emergency fund into which each wage-earning member pays a monthly sum. This fund has various uses. It makes it possible to help those who have to cope with unforeseen monetary difficulties. In such cases individuals are given a loan at a rate of interest of approximately 5%. The fund also pays the return fare to Africa of patients whose condition is considered hopeless, as mentioned earlier. The same applies to the unlucky ones who cannot find employment and who are a heavy burden on a community which has to support them for several months. Above all the fund is reserved for disasters, particularly fires which, unfortunately, take a heavy toll of tenements inhabited by immigrants during the winter months. The emergency fund also pays the funeral expenses of a member who has died in France or in Africa.

Sometimes this fund will make it possible for members of a community which has established itself in France to set up a joint undertaking in their village of origin. For instance they may purchase canoes for use on the river Senegal or fishing tackle for the community. It is evident from all this that the solidarity between individuals born in Africa and coming from the same village, is consolidated during their stay in France and continues on their return to traditional African society.

Hand in hand with economic solidarity goes moral solidarity. A rigid discipline rules the life within each collectivity. Order, the cohesion of the members and respect for tradition are maintained by a system of fines which is more or less drastic, according to the community. The expulsion of an individual is the supreme punishment. Those who infringe upon unanimously accepted principles must pay a fine, the amount of which varies according to the seriousness of the offence. In one of the communities visited, serious insults incurred a fine of 55 francs. If the injured party retaliates with an insult, instead of referring the matter to the head of the community, he will have to pay 50 francs. When wounds have been inflicted or a steel weapon or firearms used with murderous intent, the opposing sides have to pay the sum of 250 francs. Thefts are punished by beating and exclusion from the community. Any behavior considered as injurious to the community as a whole, entails payment of a fine of 100 francs.

Solidarity is evident in yet another form in the daily life of each group. Those who know how to read and write will translate the many letters which their illiterate companions receive from home. They also write the messages to be sent to

Africa or applications for work to the employment bureaus of undertakings likely to have work for newcomers. They deal with administrative questions, particularly any transactions in connection with health insurance. Some communities however, have nobody who can really speak and write French well enough to ensure the liason between the immigrants and the authorities. In such cases, private organizations, such as the "Reception and Promotion" organization, deal with administrative problems or write the letters intended for the African villages.

A form of solidarity which is particularly appreciated, is the organization of savings — the major worry of all immigrants. In every dormitory the institution of the "tontine" is widespread. Individuals who work in the same enterprise and earn the same wages save together in groups of three and four to provide for each one in turn. At the end of each month, as soon as the workers have been paid, a member of the group collects a kind of subscription from the others, the amount of which has been agreed in advance and is usually between 200 and 250 francs. This sum, acquired by each member in turn, allows the beneficiary to send a large money order to his family in Africa. The relatives who receive this money thus have the impression that the sender is earning a very high wage. The "tontine" system which makes it possible to send large sums of money home creates a great sense of rivalry among the young who have not yet been in France and increases their haste to be gone.

A survey carried out in Paris shows the hardships that immigrants will submit to in order to save a third or fifty per cent of their monthly wage. It must be emphasized that such savings are possible only thanks to the unwearying solidarity created by the organization of life on a community basis. The monthly expenditure for a wage earner will be as follows:

Item	Amount
Lodging	40 F
Food	80 F
Various subscriptions	30 F
Transport	30 F
Pocket money	
Clothes, purchase of	100 F
Laundry	
Miscellaneous	
Total	280 F

Monthly wages vary between 400 and 600 francs, and savings thus fluctuate between 120 and 320 francs a month. These are then turned into money orders for the families left behind in Africa. But such items are not sent monthly, because the immigrants dislike sending money orders for less than 200 francs. Those that send small sums of money believe, rightly or wrongly, that their prestige suffers in the eyes of the villagers. That is why the "tontine" system is so widespread, allowing as it does large amounts to be sent. A wage-earner may thus send between 600 and 800 francs every four or five months to Africa, according to whether his savings group consists of three or four of his compatriots. Part of the money goes to the sender's family to cover the contribution to the expenses of the patriarchial community, and part is entrusted to a friend who has remained in the village. It is the latter's duty to see that the money bears fruit. He may, therefore, buy oxen with it, and they will constitute capital available to the investor on his return to Africa. This form of accumulation of riches is very widespread in the African emigration zones, particularly in the valley of the river Senegal.

(c) Evolution of Traditional Forms

It should be pointed out that not all the migrants are subject to the community structure described above. Some have broken with the traditional social organization, the more easily since they come from towns or have been living for longer or shorter periods in African towns. Most of them have been to school and have been converted to Christianity. They do not live in a community, but in cheap hotels or in rooms. Having come to France to acquire training, they feel no need to associate with other immigrants for the sake of economy. That is the case of those coming from the coastal countries, namely the Ivory Coast, Dahomey, Cameroon and Togo. The Mandingos from Casamance must also be mentioned, though most of them are illiterate. Community life is a peculiarity of the Sarakolles and the Tukulors who remain firmly attached to their traditional social structures. But there are some communities which are more loosely-knit than others, and where the headman's authority appears to be weaker. Certain individuals tend to elude the control of the community; while still participating in the common expenditure, they gradually cease to follow the custom of entrusting their savings to the headman or to their elders. Usually, at the end of each month, the youngest members of the community hand over their wages to a cousin or an older brother to escape the temptation to spend them. They receive the money necessary for essential expenses and when they have accumulated a considerable sum, a money order is made out and sent to Africa. Increasingly, however, the young people — who are exposed to the temptations of modern life — wish to dispose freely of their income. They buy transistors, motor-assisted bicycles, record players, and they go to the cinema. Not wishing to cut a sorry figure in the streets, they pay great attention to dress in preparation for their Sunday walks. In order to do this they will not hesitate to spend money on clothes.

D. Organization of leisure

No thought has, however, been given by the African workers — as a secondary demonstration of community solidarity — to the satisfactory organization of leisure. Their ignorance of the French language is the greatest obstacle to participation in the various activities offered to the European population, particularly cultural entertainment, as provided by the theatre and the cinema. Most of the workers come straight from the African bush with no prior contact with modern life in the urban centers of their country of origin. In general, the immigrants do not use their leisure in the same way as does the world around them. Their customs and their mentality differ from those of the Europeans and this leads them to fall back on themselves; They tend to talk until very late into the night, after days of exhausting work. Saturday afternoons and Sundays are reserved above all for the exchange of news on the week's work and discussion of the letters which have come from Africa. A note of gaity is introduced into these talks by musicians who make music on instruments brought from their native villages. Moreover, quite often a radio — used exclusively for the transmission of music programs, preferably Arabian — is to be found in each dormitory. Not being able to understand the news, the Africans prefer to listen to music from Arab countries since, as most of them are of the Moslem faith, they are more receptive and more used to Arab tunes. Another distraction is sometimes provided by a record player which, hour after hour, will reel off the familiar tunes from their country of origin, recorded by certain recording companies. But these distractions are usually those of the younger generation; the older people prefer to talk. They consider the cinema a luxury, which uses up hard-earned money. But "Westerns", science fiction films and above all Arab films are becoming increasingly popular with the young, in spite of the disapproval of their elders.

Apart from the long talks held in the dormitories, the Sunday walk is the most popular way of passing the time. They walk in small groups and look at the shop windows. This provides them with both relaxation and an opportunity to see the things they would like to possess. These walks take place mainly on Sunday afternoon, Sunday being often their day of rest, though some also have the Saturday afternoon. However, after a week of exhausting work, they usually prefer to remain in their dormitories until Sunday. Visits between communities from the same village are frequent during the weekend. After a week during which they have not seen each other, friends will go right across Paris or even to the suburban communes to pay or return a visit. Often after talks which go on late into the night, some of the visitors sleep at their host's place, having no means of returning to their dormitory after the public transport — particularly the underground — has stopped. The leisure of the African workers is thus devoted to activities within the community, and this tends to isolate them still more.

Conclusions

The housing difficulties of African workers coming from countries south of the Sahara are beginning to find a solution thanks to the "Social Action Fund for Foreign Workers" set up under Decree No. 64 701 of 10 July 1964. This is an adaptation of the "Social Action Fund for Algerian Moslem Workers in the Metropolis and their Families". Specialized institutions try to put dilapidated lodgings in order, at a cost which is within the means of the African workers. The latter undertake to pay a fixed monthly rent of 40 to 60 francs, according to the state of the lodging placed at their disposal. So far 1,500 to 2,000 communal rooms have been occupied under this kind of arrangement. Clearly this solution is inadequate, when one considers the number of workers who are still badly housed. It should be emphasized, however, that the French authorities hesitate to provide permanent lodging for African workers, because of what they consider to be the provisional character of the present immigration phenomenon. When we made our survey, we ascertained that in the regions from which these migrants come, there had been a noticeable decline in manpower and a falling off in the development of the country. Vast territories have lain fallow, because the farming of crops has been abandoned, the people having developed the habit of waiting for money sent to them by the migrants in order to pay for their livelihood.

The migratory movement has provoked a change in the structure of the population which is reduced to the two extremes of the pyramid: the old and the very young. Moreover, the prolonged absence of the married men causes matrimonial problems and increases the divorce rate. A change is also noticeable in the dowry system, because the migrants compete among themselves for prestige in the eyes of the families of their future wives. Formerly it was the custom for questions of dowry to be settled by the old people; now they see their power gradually slipping from them, because of the increasing importance of the financial means sent home by the migrants, on which, to a considerable extent, their community life depends. Profound changes are thus taking place in the traditional way of life — the authority of the older people is now being questioned, and they attempt in vain to stop these changes.

In recent years, however, a more positive development has been noticeable. We have already mentioned the purchase of cattle, the setting up of small local undertakings to replace the big European commercial enterprises. This development is evident above all in the progressive replacement of flat roofs or thatches by the more solid corrugated-iron roof which provides greater protection during the rainy season.

Several years will no doubt be needed, before a satisfactory relation is obtained between the outside resources furnished by the migrants and the amounts invested in the development of the country — a development which could lead to a stabilization of the autochtonic populations.

Origin of Contributions and References: See Page 335

DIFFICULTIES OF ADJUSTMENT IN IMMIGRANT CHILDREN IN GENEVA

R. Rodriguez
Switzerland

The immigration of workers from the south into the interior of Europe is now a common occurrence. Such immigration places a considerable strain on the family, and ability to deal with it depends not only on its intensity (the extent of socio-economic, linguistic and cultural difficulties, and emotional uprooting . . . . .), but on the family's readiness to face up to the problems created by the new situation.

In this article we shall discuss, in the light of the behavior of children of Spanish and Italian immigrants, the varying ways in which such families react to immigration and adapt to life in Geneva. We shall attempt to analyze the way in which certain attitudes have proved adequate and others deficient — to the extent of hampering the family's adjustment to the new environment.

Children of Spanish or Italian immigrants constitute about 10 per cent of the child population of Geneva. These children represent 20 per cent of those attending the Child Care Department (SPM), and they appropriate approximately 50 per cent of the social assistance provided by the SPM.

We propose to discuss the characteristics of this immigrant child population, which is handicapped in relation to the aggregate of children living in Geneva.

Immigrant children are rarely brought to the attention of the SPM before they begin attending school, and therefore our study will deal mainly with school-age children; our findings will show, however, that disorders observed in these children have their roots in the pre-school age, and that the ability of some parents to face up to the situation during the first years of the child's life has limited the occurrence of mental and functional disorders.

We have divided the Spanish and Italian children into sample groups representative of these two populations, in order to compare them with control groups of local children, with groups representative of the entire child population, and with each other.

We have emphasized the psychopathological characteristics of maladjusted children, while taking account of environmental conditions, and conditions prior and subsequent to their immigration to Geneva.

Features of the Family Environment

These features are common to both Spanish and Italians.

Socio-economically speaking, these children live in working class families and immigration to Geneva has occurred during the past 10 years, which means that they were subject to the legislation which prohibited foreign manual workers from bringing their families to Switzerland during the first years of their stay and which obliged the wife to go out to work.

Low wages and the need to save cause these families to spend only the bare minimum.

Housing conditions are often poor, and families are only entitled to low rent housing after several years' residence.

Culturally speaking, the parents' schooling has been confined to primary education, often incomplete.

Many of the families speak a regional dialect, in addition to their national language.

Only one-fourth of the parents speak adequate French.

The major part of the immigrant population is unaware of the numerous social, cultural and leisure facilities offered by the Canton of Geneva.

Television is very often the sole source of information and the main leisure occupation for the families.

Moreover, while most of the families have no intention of returning to their country of origin in the foreseeable future, they maintain close contact with their former environment.

Although these comments apply to both the Italian and Spanish populations, there are differences in the reaction of each to the stress placed upon them by immigration.

Among Italian parents there is a marked tendency to place their children in boarding establishments having a staff which is insufficient, unspecialized, but Italian-speaking. The child enters the establishment in the first years of its life and remains in this situation for long years, without legal or economic justification. There is also a tendency to send the children back to Italy, to their grandparents, in order to solve the difficulties resulting from migration.

Spanish mothers find it difficult to part with their children, preferring to remain in Spain until the father is permitted to set up house with his entire family in Switzerland. The grandmother — usually the maternal grandmother — is then generally sent for, to look after the smaller children while the mother is out at work.

Italian mothers adapt more easily, and learn the new language more readily than Italian fathers.

With the Spanish, the contrary is the case.

Psychopathological Findings

We shall first consider the group of Spanish children.[*]

1. When comparing a group of Spanish children (74 children) attending the SMP with the group representative of the entire child population attending an SMP sector at the same time, we noted the following:

— No mental syndromes affecting only Spanish children were observed. As in the group representative of the entire child population attending the SMP, a low proportion of psychotic and maladjusted cases was noted, as against a high proportion of neurotic subjects.

Psychosomatic disorders, such as vomiting, anorexia and recurrent bronchitis are more frequent among children of immigrants.

— Enuresis was noted among twenty per cent of the Spanish children, as against 5 per cent in the control group.

— Language difficulties are far commoner among Spanish children but, as shown in the table below, this is due to the percentage of Spanish children who suffer from the consequences of a poorly integrated bilingualism.

Language Difficulties

Difficulties	Control Group %	Spanish Group %
Specific	30	33
Bilingualism	6	42
Others	7	10
Total	43	85

— In children of the sample group the mental structure is generally less mature than in those of the control group. Spanish children attending the SMP have a less varied and more primitive range of defence-mechanisms; the type of object-relationship is more archaic.

— While 70 per cent of the control group make normal progress at school, in the immigrant group 70 percent have difficulties, often considerable. This is the case even though the various intelligence quotients of these children (quotients obtained on the basis of tests which measure the intellectual potential rather than acquired knowledge), follow a gaussian curve identical in both population groups.

2. If we compare the immigrant group with an equivalent group of Swiss children, i.e.: a group composed entirely of children of Swiss manual workers who attended the SMP at the same time, we note:

---

[*] L'adaptation scolaire chez les enfants d'immigrants espagnols à Genève (Acta Paedopsychiatrica), 34, 1967.

— An equivalent lack of emotional maturity in both groups.
— Sixty per cent of children of Swiss manual workers are backward at school, a proportion that approaches that of children of Spanish immigrants (70 per cent). Many of these children have or will become "school defectives".

Backwardness at School

Backwardness	Control Group %	Manual Worker Control Group %	Spanish Group %
1 Year	20	30	33
2 Years	8	20	25
3 Years	2	8	12
Total	30	58	72

3. When comparing the sample group of Spanish children with a different group of the same nationality, whose progress at school was normal and who had never attended the SMP, we noted the following:
— Those of the latter group had mostly come to Geneva before reaching school age. Their specific feature is that they had contact with French-speaking children of their own age. In most cases this was made possible by attendance at kindergartens or nurseries where French was spoken, and also by better schooling from the start.
— A large majority of the well-adjusted children received help with their homework from French-speaking persons (neighbors, students, teachers); this was not so in the case of the children of the sample group.
— Children who had come to Switzerland with their mothers adapted more easily than those who had remained in Spain while the mother worked in Switzerland. The greater proportion of the control group had never been parted from their mothers throughout the period of immigration and of adjustment to the new environment. On the other hand, the group attending the SMP had most often been parted from their mothers for a period of between one and three years.
— For the well-adjusted group, the use of two languages was no obstacle to adaptation to school. It should be pointed out that they were bilingual only as regards the spoken language, and were learning to write only in French. Moreover, for them the French language was not merely of cognitive but also of affective value. These children spoke habitually in French, not only with their French playmates but with children from their own country of origin. The Spanish language was often reserved for communication with the less adapted of the two parents (usually the mother).
— A considerable proportion of the maladjusted children had been cared for by a grandmother during pre-school age (35 per cent). This was seldom the case among those of the well-adapted group (5 per cent).
  A recent study of various sample groups of Italian children (to be published

in collaboration with *Mme Cattin*, psychologist), produced the following results:
— Among children not living in institutions, the findings are similar to those recorded in the case of Spanish children. We shall therefore not dwell on this group.
— On the other hand, as was to be expected, children placed in institutions present far more frequent and extensive disorders. We shall now compare sample groups of Italian children living with their families with groups of Italian children in institutions.

4. Comparison between a group of Italian children attending the SMP (children from institutions excepted), and a group living in institutions with Italian-speaking staff, shows the following results:
— Somewhat more than half the number of children who spent long periods in an institution during pre-school age show signs either of psychosis or serious maladjustment (desertion or hospital syndrome), whereas the percentage is very low among those attending the center who were not in institutions. On the other hand, emotional disorders among the latter are usually of the neurotic type (80 per cent of those attending).
— Among those living in institutions, the proportion of mentally defective children is 32 per cent, as against 17 per cent of those living with their families.
— Children not living in institutions usually attend the SMP for language defects (speech and writing), while those in institutions attend because of general difficulties in schooling. Among the latter, functional disorders are observed, in addition to language difficulties.

Children over 7 years old living in institutions are all backward at school to a greater or lesser degree, according to the case.

5. Finally, we made a comparison between a group of pre-school age Italian children attending a nursery-kindergarten where French was spoken, with a group of the same age living in an institution with an unspecialized, Italian-speaking staff. None of the children in either group has ever attended the SMP.
— Fifteen per cent of the children attending the nursery were subject to behavioral disturbances, whereas 80 per cent of those in institutions presented behavioral disturbances of a disquieting nature, seeming to tend towards a psychotic structure (inversion), or maladjustment (instability, continuous fidgeting).
— If we compare the results obtained with the children of the two groups, in tests in which verbal factors played little part — such as Rey's mental automatism, Dame de Fay, and the Bender and Figure tests — we find the curves on the following page.

The curve shows that children attending kindergarten give results commensurate with their age; among the children in institutions we were struck by the degree of backwardness revealed by the mental automatism test, which shows the state of acquirement, integration and mobility of images of the external world; we were also struck by the backwardness revealed by the Dame de Fay, a test which reflects acquirements translated into mental images of the child's own body.

The results from the same children in the Bender and Figure tests, although inferior to those of the other group, approached the average. Unlike the previous

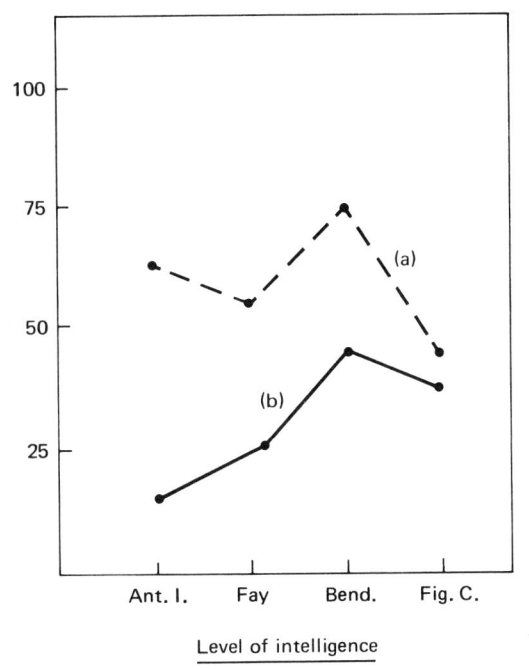

Level of intelligence
a) Children attending kindergarten
b) Children in institutions

ones, these two are performance tests, requiring graphic imitation of geometrical figures in different positions and topological relations.

The backwardness of children living in institutions, who have a basically sound intellectual potential, would appear to affect mainly integration and mobility of mental image.

The children of this group who obtained the best results in the mental automatism and Dame de Fay tests are also those whose behavior is most adequate.

Summary and Conclusions

From these findings we shall retain certain points which we consider essential.
– The immigrant child can overcome the difficulties connected with immigration and adapt rapidly to its new surroundings. The success of adjustment is closely linked with the attitude of the parents towards the child during the period of strain which immigration represents for the family group.

Comparison between the group of Spanish children attending the SMP and the well-adjusted group has demonstrated:
– disastrous effects of separating the child from its mother at the time of immigration and during the period of adaptation to new surroundings;
– that it is preferable not to call on the grandmother to act as mother-substitute for young children, since, because of her usually very primative reactions and low

intellectual level, she tends to hinder rather than further the child's adaptation;
— the positive part played by attendance at nursery or kindergarten with a competent and sufficiently numerous French-speaking staff. In our opinion, this educational environment allows the child to adapt early and progressively to its new environment, without the parents being deprived of the affective role they should play in the daily lives of their children.

In order to facilitate adjustment at school, it is also important that the immigrant child be given individual attention by a French-speaking person, who, while helping with school work, will above all form an object of intellectual identification for the child, enabling it to master feelings of omnipotence and culpability which it may experience towards its parents; such feelings may be prematurely intensified in children by their mastery at an early age of intellectual tools such as French, arithmetic and drawing, with greater ease than their parents.

The fact that among the Spanish or Italian immigrant populations there are children who have successfully adapted, would appear to prove that bilingualism need present no problem, provided the child is not mentally backward and does not suffer from specific language difficulties or emotional disturbances. When, however, children are maladjusted, this duality aggravates the abovementioned disorders and tends to prevent the child from gaining, cognitively and affectively, from its surroundings.

A comparison between maladjusted Spanish children and the general child-public attending the SMP has shown that Spanish children have a greater tendency to convert their fears into bodily symptoms and to retain embarrassing somatic habits (enuresis). This latter tendency would appear to permit a better emotional balance between the child and a mother who is too engrossed in her own problems of adjustment.

The fact that, as a general rule, Spanish children attending the SMP are low achievers at school to a degree equivalent to that of children of unskilled Genevese manual workers, points to the presence of analogous factors in both groups. That both belong to families that are not well-off and are generally rather unlettered might in itself justify difficulties at school. We are, however, tempted to think that in the great majority of cases in these two groups, emotional factors inhibiting the child's receptivity are closely connected with the lack of any contribution from its background. These factors would also seem to explain the numerous cases of emotional immaturity to be found in both groups. The object-relationship which these children have established with their parents appears to deviate from the standards of normal evolution. These perturbed relationships necessarily have repercussions on the child's intellectual acquirements as well as on its emotional structure.

A study of children placed in institutions, as is the case of the last two sample groups of Italian children, has revealed two important elements: a lack of intellectual contribution from the environment, and poorly developed object-relationships. Hence the massive personality disorders noted in these children.

Our findings on the backwardness of pre-school age children living in institutions, as regards integration and mobility of the mental image, might well open the way to a study of the structure of mental and "school" defectiveness; this, however, goes beyond the context of a study on the adjustment problems of the children of immigrants.

Origin of Contributions and References: See Page 335

NOSTALGIC BEHAVIOR

A Study of Foreign Workers in West Germany[1]

Charles Zwingmann
Switzerland

Again and again there are complaints by the general public and management about the untrustworthiness, uncleanliness, asociality and immorality of foreign workers. These complaints point to a psychological phenomenon which has not yet been understood in its entirety — or at least been underestimated: the nostalgic reaction, commonly known as "homesickness".

The expression "nostalgic reaction" was chosen by the author, who also explored the phenomenon systematically, because the expression "homesickness" is psychologically misleading (Zwingmann, 1959). Here we limit ourselves to the problems of this affect syndrome, and its importance as it pertains to foreign workers and their behavior. In this special frame of reference, the nostalgic phenomenon is discussed as a reaction to a geographic separation from the familiar milieu. Characteristic for the nostalgic reaction (which is commonly operative during the emotional acclimatization crisis), is the psychological representation of the milieu left behind, and the wish to return to it. The nostalgic reaction is often noticeable only some time after the separation, since the worker is usually cognitively too busy — immediately after the separation — with the assimilation of new impressions.

Generally, the nostalgic reaction is a far more complex and important socio-psychological event than has been hitherto recognized. What is especially important in the situation of foreign workers, is the observation that less differentiated people are affectively more stress-prone than more differentiated people. Of prime significance to us here is the fact that the nostalgic disposition is a product of the Christian-bourgeois microcosmos and that the institutions within that microcosmos encourage and use nostalgic involvement as ideological, social and political control. Among South-European workers (the Italians and the Spanish, especially) the nostalgic disposition is heavily influenced by credulity aspects.

Among many young people within Christian-bourgeois societies there exists a

---

[1]This work was originally prepared for a speech to a group of laymen. It is oversimplified and should be considered complementary to this author's work THE NOSTALGIC PHENOMENON AND ITS EXPLOITATION (Pp. 19-47).

conflict between the security and the protection which the parental home and the establishment offer, and the wish to become independent, to get to know the world in which prestige and most of all, money, are to be gained. When this desire for independence was "realized" (only externally) through separation, but no emotional bonds have yet been formed with the new milieu, there arises the psychological necessity to keep in touch with the "love objects" left behind, at least at a symbolic level (which is frequently achieved through pseudo-optic representations). These nostalgic attachments usually disappear to the degree to which the adaptation to the real (present) environment increases.

The foreign worker is particularily predisposed towards nostalgic involvement since his new environment makes it difficult or impossible for him to establish gratifying relations in his new surroundings. This is especially true in West Germany, where the foreign worker finds himself hampered by his conditioned contact-inability, lack of rational-ideological background (etc.) and by the prejudices directed against him.

Immediate Determinants of the Nostalgic Reaction

The assessment of a nostalgic condition requires among other things the following data:

1. Was the separation voluntary or forced?

This means, f.e., did the laborer come to Germany by his own initiative or was there some kind of pressure exerted upon him, f.e., by his family (because of economic want) or by some other circumstances?

2. Is the personal goal structure of the laborer influenced by the separation?

A worker who goes into a foreign country to get better training in his own specialty, i.e., whose stay in a foreign country fits in with his professional goals, is usually less affected by the nostalgic reaction than a worker whose stay serves only the fulfillment of his material ambitions. For the latter the stay in the foreign country simply means an unpleasant interruption of his usual habits, so-to-speak, a "necessary evil."

3. Are there sufficient possibilities for communication?

Isolation caused by the absence of news from home (e. g. because neither the worker himself nor his relatives are able to write or to properly express themselves in writing) may have considerable nostalgic consequences. The same is true (even though) to a lesser degree for isolation as a result of the language barrier. For most foreign workers it is very difficult to establish social contacts with people of the new milieu.

4. What differences exist between the home milieu and the new milieu?

In many ways we find strongly contrasting differences between Germany and the South-European countries. Among others we observe:

(a) *Climatic-topographical Contrasts.* The importance of climate and specific conditions of weather and their influence upon the emotions of man are well known. If even people in the Northern hemisphere tend to react to the difficult climatic conditions of their areas (especially the fog) depressively, one can imagine with what intensity the Southern Europeans suffer under the frequently gloomy and wet climate of Germany. It is not surprising that they long for the warm and sunny climate of their home country. There is also a considerable discrepancy between the oftentimes barren and colorless landscape of German industrial cities and the colorful home countries of the foreign workers.

(b) *Differences in Work Tempo and Rhythm.* In the philosophy of life and in the attitude toward work there are frequently considerable differences between the German worker and his South-European colleague (which, however, are diminishing in the younger generation). Grossly generalized one could say that the German "lives in order to work" and the South European "works in order to live". The South European starts the day later, has a longer lunch break, and works later in the evening. This difference in rhythm requires of the foreign worker a readaptation as far as his usual meal times are concerned and, what is more important, brings with it the problems of those long evenings, which are void of activity. Special difficulties arise since the accustomed leisure time activities are lacking, most of all, because of weather conditions in Germany which frequently do not allow outdoor pleasures.

(c) *Differences Within the Belief System.* For instance the God-image in West-Germany tends to be more impersonal and abstract than the Southern Italian and Spanish image. Whereas the God of Christians in other areas tends to be conceived as the allmighty "boss," the South Italian and Spanish God is more the father type and also the saints are part of the family. The "communication" between God and his earthly children is more intimate and as prescribed, sheep like.

(d) *Contrasting Attitudes Towards Orderliness and Cleanliness.* Here the Southern Europeans are most heavily criticized by many West-Germans. This probably is due to the fact that the German is in this respect somewhat compulsive. The differences can be seen most clearly in the interior of the home. The German regards the decorative aspects of his home as most important. The emphasis is upon "Gemütlichkeit". This phenomenon is not known to the South European; he seems to neglect these aspects, the reason for it being that he can and does live more outside of his home than the German. For the South European, the whole village, the market place and the street are his home where he feels well, where he sings and talks, plays and barters. His home is not much more than a place where he eats and sleeps. In contrast to that, the German lives mostly within his four walls and prefers to keep distance from his neighbors.

(e) *There are also differences in the family relationships* which are of decisive importance for the understanding of the nostalgic phenomenon. Among South Europeans we find a strong family bond of mutual dependence: financially, socially and emotionally. Against this, the German way of life frequently appears schematic and sober.

(f) *The differences in emotional expression,* have to be viewed in the same light. In contrast to the West-German, the South European is demonstrative. He likes to smile and to laugh, and he is not even afraid to cry once in a while. In this respect, the South European considers the German stiff, methodical, unfriendly, sometimes even inhuman and cruel.

To this we must add apparent drastic differences in customs, moral attitudes and in the philosophy and world-outlook. The German likes to brag about his self-assuredness, his punctuality, his honesty and his endurance. To him the South European appears insecure, volatile, superstitious, unreliable, a person whose love for truth is questionable and so forth.

All these differences real and apparent are subject to prejudice formation. What we mean with this can be seen from interviews with some Arabian apprentices who are in addition object of strong political discrimination. We cite (Carl Duisberg-Gesellschaft 1956-57):

I.B.: " ... and house wife always quarrels with me, uses bad words. Once I broke cup. She says, 'you don't know china from your own home, you all eat with fingers from pot'."

S.R.: " ... and then I sat in the street-car. Old lady came in, no more room. I got up so she could sit. She looks at me and looks away quickly and she not sit down. There German blond man gets up and gives her his seat and she sits down".

E.A.: " ... and also laborer in factory to me: 'you have it good, you have black color, you need not wash, because one sees not dirt on you'."

M.S.: " ... in our city was fire, on Israeli cemetery. Everything burned down. Police came to us, look through room, we were at police station whole week, many hours, questioning. We nothing had to do with it. In newspaper it reads: Probably two Arabian students. All people in factory, in stores, look at us and speak quietly."

S.A.: " ... in restaurant, where we always eat, says owner to me very loud and all hear: 'do not take it so hard that you are black, it is not your fault.' In my own home country I would have beaten him in the face. Had I done it here, then tomorrow in paper it would read: German beaten up by Arab. So I went without word, although he hurt me and my people. Me in my heart never forget this. I am proud of my color and proud that Egyptian."

Object- and milieu-bound people, as well as undifferentiated individuals, show a greater readiness to react nostalgically than intellectuals. They tend to remain at home psychologically even if they are not there physically. A lack of cognitive and affective mobility permit neither their psychological separation from home nor the establishment of emotional roots in the new environment. The majority of South-European workers belong, because victimized by religious conditionings, in this group.

In serious nostalgic cases it is important to look at the family background of the foreign worker. Frequently it is not, as is generally supposed, the happy childhood with good emotional relations between the parents and the children which cause severe nostalgic reactions, but the unhappy home where the child never had the possibility to form affective bonds and never had the experience of security. The nostalgic reaction in this sense then is a pseudo-phenomenon, for it is not the home for which the person longs, but it is the threat of the new situation which pushes him back toward the home as the only refuge.

Symptomatology of the Nostalgic Reaction

One of the reasons for which the nostalgic phenomenon has not received adequate attention is a diagnostic problem, i.e., the diagnosis of the nostalgic reaction is complicated by the reluctance of the person concerned to admit his nostalgic involvement. If a man admitted that he was homesick and wanted to go back home, he would probably acquire the reputation of being "unmanly". Only children and women may have this feeling! The suppression of the nostalgic wish gives rise to the hypothesis that some of the asocial acts committed are indirect expressions of the nostalgic longing.

Variations in the working capacity of man are to be expected. They are individually different and therefore cannot be controlled externally. If they are repeated with a certain regularity we can report them statistically. Such variations in foreign workers, however, resist calculation. If, however, the importance of the nostalgic reaction is recognized then it should be possible to bring sometimes considerable decreases in working efficiency to a tolerable level. In order to achieve this, a knowledge of the personal and collective reference events (birthday, name-day, local and national days of celebration, etc.) are essential. No matter how the employer himself judges such relational events, disregarding them can lead to serious nostalgic consequences. It may happen that the laborer simply does not come to work on such a reference day (he is "sick") and in the pain of his nostalgic loneliness he may reach for the bottle more than is good for him. The result is thus a missed day of work and a lowering of the working efficiency during the following day. Such difficulties could have been avoided if the employer had paid a little attention to the one concerned. A word of encouragement or a small friendly gesture might have sufficed. Holidays — which are not considered such in the new environment — may occasion an epidemic rise of the nostalgic reaction. Such "mass-epidemics" have been described among others by Flicker and Weiss (1943).

An interesting symptom of the nostalgic condition is the retrospective change of fantasy. This "nostalgic illusion", as the author has called it (1959), consists of a subjective overestimation (idealization) of personal or suggested past and a simultaneous downgrading of the new environment. To the nostalgic person the sky does not appear as blue as at home, the flowers are not as fragrant as in one's own garden, the cake does not taste as well as mother's and the bells do not sound as beautifully as in the village at home! The understanding of this nostalgic illusion is of importance to the employer, for he often thinks that the improvements of the purely material conditions alone would chain the worker closer to his working place. —In the "homesickness" literature we frequently find descriptions of cases in which the colonial masters were surprized when their slaves showed homesickness (in the "beautiful" new environment) for the primitive conditions, the unhealthy climate and the gloomy circumstances of their country. They could not understand, f.e., that Eskimos died of "homesickness" after they had been brought to civilized Europe and were fed good meat instead of raw fish! Similarly, the modern employer often thinks of his worker as ingrates when their living quarters are abused. He is angry when the new facilities for foreign workers are used for a purpose for which they were not intended, e.g., when the bathtub is used for potato storage, when the living room is degraded to a laundry room and when the bedsheets are used as cleaning rags for shoes. His anger is understandable when one considers the social climate within which many an employer moves: as a tourist he has stayed in first-class hotels of South-European countries and thus missed completely the sociological and cultural-anthropologgical conditions. Most often he does not even take the pains to show interest for these conditions on a theoretical level. If he did this, he would probably find out that external cleanliness, as it was drilled into him, is not the measure of all things. Often, also it is an unpleasant discovery for him that the emotionally conditioned nostalgic reaction cannot be influenced by material factors and that the South-European laborer resists a "Germanization" with all of his nostalgic energy, just as much as many a German immigrant in the USA resists "Americanization" and resolves his nostalgic longings by returning to his less-mechanized and automatized home country, despite the fact that the new world offered him a higher standard of living and a better chance to "make" money.

In summary the nostalgic reaction is frequently accompanied by the following symptoms:
1. Decreased working efficiency
2. Fear that something could happen to the members of the family.
3. Lowered capacity for empathy.
4. Guilt feelings (mostly concerned with the fact that the family was left behind).
5. Fatigue and loss of vitality.
6. Increased suggestibility, sensitivity and irritability, often mixed with paranoid tendencies.

7. Inability to concentrate.
8. Increased sickness – and accident proneness (an especially important factor in industry). According to an investigation concerned with accident statistics in an American steel mill, the frequency of accidents among foreign workers was twice as high as among American workers (Chaney and Hanna, 1918).
9. Decreased frustration tolerance.
10. Feelings of hostility.

Since the last mentioned symptom and asocial and antisocial behavior stand foremost on the "black list" of the so-called "host" population a few observations to this subject are in order.

The concept "home" in the German sense of "Gemütlichkeit" of a home or an apartment, as noted previously, is unknown to the South European. For him, the market place, the whole village or any part of his city are his home. He is not limited by his four walls, but he lives mostly outside of his home; there he also finds his parents, his brothers, and sisters, his relatives and his friends. If he does the same thing in Germany, i.e., if he leans against the wall of a house and if he strolls through the streets he is said to be a vagrant; if he goes to the bars where he looks for the social and emotional contacts known to him from his market place, he is thought of as a "typical South-European bum." If he sleeps in the waiting room of a railroad station, then he is said to show "typical gypsy manners, which are characteristic for his race."

Slanderous remarks of this kind tend to reveal the essential inhumanity of the Christian-bourgeois microcosmos. The "hosts" can see in this behavior neither the anxiety engendered by the provocation characteristics of the West-German society nor the great desires of the displaced person to recreate the social climate of his native milieu. A special role in this connection plays the railroad station as a symbolic link to the home land. Here at the tracks it begins, and here at the tracks it ends.[2]

The frequently unsuccessful search for friendly human relations in the new environment forces the laborer to resort to compensatory means of ego-preservation (e.g. by power-demonstrations)! Unfortunately, the consequences are contrary to his intentions (prejudice against him is reinforced), and subsequently the nostalgic involvement is intensified. Hostility, antisocial behavior and sometimes even suicide (Frost, 1938) derive from the nostalgic inability to adapt to new conditions and to assess these rationally, as well as from the uncritical upgrading of the home milieu. Serious crimes reported to have been caused by homesickness young girls appeared in the literature as early as the last century (Jaspers, 1909). Flicker and Weiss (1943) in the USA speak about disciplinary problems and serious

---

[2] As answer to my taking up the defense of the rights of foreign workers in a newspaper (Zwingmann, 1971), that is to congregate at the railway station of Frankfurt/Main, I received a flood of angry and hostile letters from German citizens.

law infractions of nostalgic soldiers and Lemke (1957) mentions frequent cases of delinquencies in homesick refugees, among others theft and abnormal sexual behavior.

Prevention and Treatment

These observations should not lead to the conclusion that nostalgic behavior is abnormal. The nostalgic phenomenon is a normal part of the Christian-bourgeois microcosmos. In this system retrospection is even an emotional imperative since it assures emotional continuity during the adaption phase. A conflict between the social and emotional gratification which is offered by the home environment, the necessity to emancipate and to find acceptance in the new group is unavoidable. In this microcosmos the hunger for success (property greed) usually wins out over the affect and social needs of the individual.

One may consider the nostalgic reaction an illness only when the quantitative and qualitative aspects of it are disproportioned to its cause. This is, f.e., the case in the foreign worker who manifests even after several months of intensive retrospective episodes somatic symptoms (such as headaches, sleep- or other vegetative disturbances), who isolates himself from his environment or who seeks a relief of tension by engaging in asocial activities. In this case, the nostalgic reaction is no more a mechanism to bridge the crisis of acclimatization, but serves as a crutch; it is no more a means to an end but it has become an end in itself.

A convincing argument for the significance of the nostalgic phenomenon is that it can complicate illness and delay or prevent the process of therapy. This is not only the case in children, as Schwab (1925) and others have observed, but also in relatively undifferentiated adults, to whom the foreign laborer usually belongs. In very serious cases the nostalgic fixation may even lead to a complete suspension of motivation and death. A fixation of this seriousness may be provoked by life-threatening events (disease, deprivation, accident etc.) because these events increase the isolation and helplessness, and therefore the dependence of the individual. – One such case of nostalgic fixation received international attention several years ago. As the result of injuries from an accident the Italian worker Errico became so nostalgic that it was feared he would die. The West-German government therefore decided to fly him back to his home town (Nürnberger Nachrichten, 1960).[3]

The psychiatrically untrained industrial physician who is ignorant of the dynamics of the nostalgic reaction and relies upon standard diagnostic schemes, is likely to apply symptomatic treatment, i.e., he is concerned with the "somatic facade" and even if he takes "homesickness" in consideration, he is not likely to take attach etiologic importance to it. – The nostalgic individual tends to camouflage his

---

[3]The surprise of the administrative and medical officials however was great when Errico at his arrival and reunion with his compatriotes did not react joyfully but in hostile manner. – According to this interpretation the over-valuation of his nostalgic image (n. illusion) had apparently been so great, that the confrontation with reality resulted in a shock, because his weakened physical and psychological condition made a correction of the illusion impossible.

true pains and present physical illness. These somatic complaints are often interpreted as simulation and pretense for not wanting to work. But even when the complaints are misinterpreted by the physician he should not reject him but look for causal factors. – The treatment of incapacitating nostalgic involvement should make positive and humane use of the hightened suggestibility of the individual.

Following these observations we can now say that the problem is not the prevention of the nostalgic reaction as an emotional bridge during the adjustment crisis but to recognize and understand it in order to preclude a development into a nostalgic fixation.

According to the experiences of the author, it can be assumed that an important number of working accidents for which the causes remain undetected and efficiency reductions may be traced directly to the widely unknown and misunderstood nostalgic phenomenon.

As a preventive measure against more serious nostalgic conditions, newly arriving foreign workers should be prepared to experience nostalgic involvement with the following informations:

Most people when separated from their reference persons and objects will think about them. To be nostalgic is a normal reaction to separation. (The word "homesick" should be avoided, because of its suggestive sickness effect.)

When one looks back into the past during a state of emotional want it appears more beautiful than it really was and would be if one was there and that by contrast to the new environment is frequently judged more critically and even rejected.

When one gets nostalgic to speak freely about his experiences, his fears and hopes and especially encouragement to be openly critical of the host milieu (mores).

Furthermore the social and cultural differences and similarities between his own country and the "host" nation should be explained to him, and he should be informed about the prejudices which are likely to be directed against him.

Attention should be directed to potential "release situations" and intensifiers of nostalgic reactions and milieu – specific measures should be developed to decrease nostalgic dependence.

Also it appears useful to familiarize the foreign worker with the geographic beauties and peculiarities of the German landscape, and to help him find appropriate leisure-time activities.

Among unmarried foreign workers the sexual problem is somewhat critical. The establishment of contact with the other sex is frequently not only difficult for him because of the language barrier, but also because of national and occupational prejudices; they are directed against him as a South European, (member of an "inferior race") and as an unskilled laborer. In this dilemma he finds himself frequently in the arms of certain "ladies" who take the money from him for the sake of which he came to Germany in the first place. The sobering effects of such experiences are usually enhanced nostalgic episodes.

The question of diet for foreign laborers requires attention, because it also plays an important role in nostalgic preoccupations. The preference for food is learned in early childhood and has a deep emotional significance because of the close association between feeding and food preparation with the primary reference persons (especially the mother), the home and by generalization the home country.

Taste preferences of the adult are therefore quite resistant to change. Even older people who have been living in foreign countries for many years long for the "specialties" of the parental home and their home land. This should not mean, however, that for financial reasons Italian workers in West Germany should be only fed spaghetti, for spaghetti are not the only national food in Italy.

For individuals who have been recognized as being nostalgic, group-discussions are highly recommendable because the climate of the group has itself a home re-creative effect.

Unfortunately many of the preventive measures are bound to remain relatively inefficient in view of the essential inhumanity and ideologic rigidity of the Christian-bourgeois system which needs to breed hostility against any element that might upset its autoritarian hierarchic order, and to these belong traditionally workers, particularily foreign workers from Southern hemispheres (perhaps, and also, they approach most the despised proletariat).

Origin of Contributions and References: See Page 335

PART III

Epidemiological Research

EMIGRATION AND MENTAL HEALTH

Ørnulv Ødegaard
Norway

Dr. Benjamin Malzberg's (1935) interesting study of mental disease in New York State according to nativity and parentage gives me the opportunity of calling attention to a similar study of my own (1932). My findings were practically the same as those of Malzberg, but the conclusions differed somewhat, which may make a comparison useful.

The material of this study differed from Malzberg's in some important respects:

1. Among the heterogeneous masses of the foreign born, one group, racially, socially, and culturally fairly well defined, was selected — the Norwegian born of Minnesota.

2. The rate of first admissions among the Norwegian born of Minnesota was compared not only with the native born of the same state, but also with that of the population of Norway. This made it possible to attack the problem from more angles, and also to exclude many sources of error.

3. Diagnosis in psychiatry is still so much a matter of personal opinion that it seemed inadvisable to make statistical comparisons where the diagnoses were made by different psychiatrists, in different hospitals, or even in different countries. Therefore, representative samples were selected (about 1,100 cases from the state hospital at Rochester, Minnesota, and about 2,000 from the Gaustad state hospital in Norway) and the diagnoses were made by the author himself, in each case after careful reading of the case history. This selected material proved very useful even for the study of factors like occupation, residence, and material condition, which are not shown in the tables of the official statistics.

The main findings are presented in the tables that follow.

Table 1. — Rates of First Admissions to Insane Hospitals, All Diagnoses, Classified by Nativity

Material of present study	1909-19	1919-29	Malzberg's New York material	1929-31
Norwegian born of Minnesota	100	100	Foreign born	100
Native born of Minnesota	78	75	All native born	84
Norwegians of Norway	59	58	Native born of native parentage	69

Table 2. — Rates of First Admissions to Insane Hospitals, Classified By Diagnosis and Nativity

	Material of present study		Malzberg's New York material		
	Norwegian born of Minnesota	Norwegians of Norway	Foreign born	Native born	Native born of native parentage
Schizophrenia	100	50	100	68	51
Manic-depressive psychosis	100	110	100	79	70
General paresis	100	73	100	98	78
Alcoholic psychosis	100	34	100	94	69
Senile psychosis	} 100	13	100	75	55
Arteriosclerosis			100	81	65

All rates of admission are given in per cents of the rates for the foreign born, to permit of an easy comparison with Malzberg's New York material. All rates are standardized, to exclude the error caused by the differences in age and sex distribution.

Table 1 shows that the Minnesota Norwegians tend in the same direction as Malzberg's New York foreign born: the rate of admissions per 100,000 per year is considerably higher among the immigrants. Attention is drawn to the interesting fact that the rates are still lower for the Norwegians of Norway: these rates are roughly comparable to Malzberg's rates for the native born of native parentage. The explanation is very simple: the native born of a state like Minnesota are all of them descendants of immigrants in the second, third, or sometimes fourth generation, and they still live in an environment which has many of the traits typical of newly settled communities.

The high rate of admissions may, it might be argued, be an artifact — it may be that mentally diseased immigrants are more readily committed to state hospitals, for instance, because they belong on the average to the lower social and occupational classes, or because they are more predominantly urban in residence.

Such an explanation might be true in some states, like New York, but it is unlikely that it would play any important role in Minnesota. The Norwegians born in this state are predominantly rural, and their social status does not differ much from that of the native born or that of the population of Norway. Of course comparatively few immigrants are able to enter the well-to-do business and professional classes, but the percentage of the population that belongs to these classes is so small even among the natives that their hypothetically low rate of admissions cannot possibly influence the statistics to any great extent. Moreover, private sanitoriums for upper-class patients are scarce in Minnesota, and in Norway such institutions are included in the official statistics. According to the author's experience as a physician in mental institutions in both countries, the chances that an insane person will be committed is practically the same in both.

The conclusion must be that the difference in rates of admission is much too marked to be explained in this way. The fact then remains that there is really a higher incidence of mental diseases among the immigrants. There are two possible explanations for this fact:

1. The mental and physical hardships of emigration and of immigrant life may cause mental derangement in persons who would otherwise have remained sound.

2. The emigrants may comprise a higher percentage of psychopathic or early psychotic types than the rest of the population of Norway. This might, for instance, have some connection with the tendency toward restlessness and social maladjustment which is characteristic of such personalities.

It is evident that these two possible factors are both at work. The problem is merely to determine their relative importance — the well known psychiatric problem of constitution versus environment.

Among the diagnostic groups, only two contain a sufficiently large number of cases to be of statistical importance: the schizophrenics and the senile and arteriosclerotic cases. These two clinical groups differ so fundamentally with regard to pathogenesis that the problem of constitution versus environment must be discussed separately for each of them.

The senile and arteriosclerotic disorders are more than seven times as frequent among the Norwegian born in Minnesota as in Norway. From what is known of the etiology of these conditions, it seems improbable that constitutional factors should be responsible for this tremendous difference. A detailed study of the present material confirms this: the incidence of psychopathic heredity as well as of psychopathic traits in the pre-psychotic personality is substantially less among the Minnesotans.

Factors of a social nature are probably more important. In Norway there may be a greater tendency to keep such patients at home instead of having them committed. The unsettled social conditions of the immigrant community, as well as the comparatively poorly developed system of old people's homes, makes this more difficult in Minnesota. A study of the duration of the disease previous to admission, however, seems to indicate that this social factor may not be as important as might have been expected. These patients are actually admitted at an earlier date in Norway than in Minnesota, which would hardly have been the case if the tendency to avoid commitment had been much stronger in Norway.

The most likely explanation is that the high incidence of the psychoses of advanced age among the Norwegian born of Minnesota is due to the mental and physical strain of immigrant life. The labor is more strenuous than in Norway, with longer hours and more rush. The change toward a diet more rich in meat, eggs, and pork, at the expense of cereals, milk, and fish, may even play some role. And last, but not least, the mental strain upon people in the forties and fifties is much worse in America, owing to the highly developed industrialization and the inefficiency of the systems of pension and social protection. It is quite natural that all these difficulties should be felt particularly heavily by the immigrants, who have had a comparatively late start in life.

An important statistical point in facor of the environmental hypothesis lies in the fact that the age at onset of the psychosis is definitely lower among the Minnesotans than in Norway, as will be seen from the following table:

Table 3. – Age of Onset of Senile and Arteriosclerotic Psychoses Among Norwegians in Minnesota and in Norway

Age of onset	In Minnesota	In Norway
40-44	1.86	0.93
45-49	4.29	0.93
50-54	19.37	12.04
55-59	21.11	10.18
60-69	38.52	53.70
70 and over	14.85	22.22
Total	100.00	100.00

Schizophrenia is about twice as frequent among the Norwegian born of Minnesota as in Norway. (See Table 2) Malzberg's New York material shows practically the same result when the foreign born are compared with the native born of native parentage. The environmental explanation may be used even for this reaction type: the mental and physical hardships of immigrant life may lead to a schizophrenic deterioration in personalities who may be predisposed, but who in their own home country would have managed to maintain a mental and social balance. A detailed study of the material gives no positive support to this hypothesis, however, and a number of facts seem to point in an opposite direction:

1. The age at onset of the disease is the same in both population groups. If difficulties of adaption, and so forth, had played any significant part, the psychosis would have tended to start at an earlier age in the immigrant groups than in Norway. (The difference in age distribution has to be corrected in advance, of course.)

2. The schizophrenic reaction does not show any particular tendency to begin during the first five years of the patients' stay in America, as would probably have been the case if the said difficulties had been important pathogenic factors.

3. Among the "causes" for the mental deragement given by the patient themselves or their relatives, very few are in any way connected with the immigrant situation. Even if such "causes" given by lay people are generally irrelevant, this fact nevertheless seems to indicate that the strain of immigrant life has not been a particularly important problem in the minds of these patients, at least not consciously.

4. The symptomatology of the disease is remarkably seldom colored by the fact that the patient is an immigrant; the clinical picture of schizophrenia seems to be exactly the same as in Norway.

These facts may not be absolutely conclusive, but nevertheless they mean that the constitutional hypothesis has to be given serious consideration. In this connection it is important to point out that the incidence of manic-depressive insanity is remarkably low among the Minnesotans — even lower than in Norway. In Norway, there are about 1.5 schizophrenic admissions to each manic-depressive, but for the Norwegian born of Minnesota the proportion is 3.5 to one.

The etiology of these "endogenic" psychoses is far from clear, but it seems to be an established fact that their clinical picture depends mainly upon the constitutional make-up. Environmental factors very likely play a part in provoking the outbreak of the psychosis, but from then on the course and symptomatology of the disease are determined: if the patient belongs to the leptosomic-schizoid type, he will tend to develop a schizophrenia, and if his make-up is pycnic-syntonic, his psychopathological reaction will be of the manic-depressive type.

Consequently, if we explain the increased incidence of schizophrenia among the immigrants as a result of environmental factors, how shall we be able to account for the fact that the incidence of manic-depressive insanity does not show a similar increase?

The constitutional hypothesis offers a natural solution. The schizoid type of thinking, feeling, and social relationship must furnish a far more likely background for emigration than the syntonic make-up. The social contact of such personalities is poor, and it is consequently comparatively easy for them to break away from home, friends, and familiar surroundings. They have little ability to make a good social adaption in early youth; this results in conflicts with parents, sweethearts, teachers, and employers, and may lead to unemployment, or at least may render it difficult for them to make a career satisfactory to their own ambition. Their sensitive minds react strongly to every real or imaginary misfortune, generally with a stubborn and brooding bitterness, mixed with wounded pride. In this way it seems psychologically most likely that many maladjusted schizothymic personalities should choose emigration as the best solution to social defeats and adversities in the old country.

But the tendency in such personalities to emigrate is not exclusively, or even mainly, a result of their difficulties of social adjustment; even their positive and valuable traits carry them in the same direction. Their ambition and courage, their romantic dreams of greatness and adventure, their ability to sacrifice the present for a remote and insecure future, their intolerant idealism and unwillingness to compromise when it comes to personal, political, or religious ideas — these are all of them character traits that have brought America thousands of its best citizens.

Any one who is familiar with the teachings of Kretschmer and his followers will be able to amplify this sketchy picture, and must agree that the schizothymic constitution is the best possible soil for the idea of emigration. The syntonic type, on the other hand, is in this, as in every other respect, the direct opposite.

A closer study of individual cases gives ample support to this hypothesis. Again and again, the case history shows how a schizoid personality or an incipient schizophrenic psychosis was the direct or indirect cause for emigration; whereas no such facts have been available for the syntonic personality or the manic-depressive psychoses.[1]

In view of these facts it seems to the present author that a complete understanding of the problems of emigrants and their mental health is impossible without introducing the constitutional hypothesis — not instead of, but as a supplement to the environmental one. For instance, the importance of economic conditions, of the labor market, and so on, for emigration is so well established that a discussion of this side of the problem may be omitted here, but it should be stressed that among a group of Norwegians of the same economic and social status those who have a schizothymic or schizoid make-up are more likely to emigrate.

As for the mental diseases of immigrants, a similar interaction of constitutional and environmental factors seems to offer the best explanation of their relatively high incidence. The tremendous excess of senile and arteriosclerotic psychoses probably is a result of predominantly environmental factors — the physical and mental strain of immigrant life, which is particularly hard upon the age groups above forty. For schizophrenia and manic-depressive insanity, on the other hand, the specific difficulties of immigration seem to be of less importance than the constitutional make-up of the immigrants themselves. This does not necessarily mean that these diseases are absolutely independent of all environmental factors. More likely the explanation is that the importance of such specific difficulties has been somewhat exaggerated. After all, the social change which a European experiences in America is, comparatively speaking, of a superficial nature; this at least is true of the Norwegians who emigrate to the agricultural Northwest. The social factors that influence human beings so deeply as to affect their mental health are of an international character.

---

[1] For case histories, see the monograph by the author previously referred to.

Origin of Contributions and References: See Page 336

NORWEGIAN EMIGRATION, RE-EMIGRATION AND INTERNAL MIGRATION

Ø. Ødegaard
Norway

Introduction

Epidemiology is the field of medical science which deals with the occurrence and distribution of diseases. Its methods are principally those of demography, its aims are those of ecology, and its field is located where these two disciplines overlap.

The emphasis upon the total environment of the patient and the pathogenetic agents has made the epidemiological approach increasingly useful in modern medicine, particularly in fields such as psychiatry, in which the interrelation between patient, disease and environment is the key to most problems.

Now psychiatry deals with *personal* problems even more than other branches of medicine, and therefore the intensive study of individual cases (be it by biochemical methods or by depth psychology) is the method of choice, and will so remain. But this should not blind us to the fact that every individual is part of a population, and that all psychiatric patients are dependent upon the collective forces which are active within the group. The very uniqueness of each psychiatric observation makes deductive reasoning from individual cases rather hazardous, and the need of statistical controls are frequently felt. It must be admitted that the subtle reactions of the human mind do not lend themselves easily to the rigidity of mass statistics. But the obvious conclusion is that there should be in psychiatry, as everywhere in human biology and sociology, a cooperative balance between the individual and the collective – a combination of intensive and extensive methods, whereby one always controls and guides the other.

The statistical investigation of mental disorders is complicated by a great number of variables, and it is natural that efforts should be made to avoid this difficulty by choosing comparatively homogenous populations. On the other hand this may lead to a simplification which narrows the scope of the project. The American studies of the highly special sect of Hutterites and the French investigation of the North African immigrants to Paris show clearly that such highly important special studies need to be supplemented by the investigation of more complete or normal populations.

One is then faced with the problem of the size of the population to be studied, and here two distinctly different methods have been developed within psychiatric epidemiology. In the *census method* a certain population is studied intensively by tracing and examining each individual case of mental disorder, or preferably even each person in the group whether diseased or not. Many sources of error can be overcome or at least minimized by this approach, such as the problem of diagnosis, and the difficulty that only a certain proportion of mental disorders lead to hospitalization or to any kind of medical attention at all. This time-consuming method has been applied to fairly large-size populations, up to 100,000, but even then the number of actual patients is too small for the detailed statistical analysis which is mostly desirable. As an example may be mentioned that a comparison between the single and the married with regard to mental morbidity must take into consideration at least the factors of sex, age and psychiatric diagnosis, which means a subdivision of the original material into something between 96 and 320 sub-groups.

The other method is based upon the use of *admission statistics* to psychiatric hospitals, which has the obvious advantage that a sufficiently large number of cases can be secured without much difficulty. On the other hand one has to depend upon the varying clinical diagnoses of a great number of highly individualistic colleagues, and the non-hospitalized cases remain an unknown factor of possibly great importance.

The present paper gives a summary of epidemiological research which has been carried on in Norway for the past 30 years. It is based upon admission statistics, but whenever possible intensive study of smaller groups with special problems is included, as an attempt to overcome some of the errors and limitations inherent in the extensive method. Since 1936 the statistics of the psychiatric hospitals in Norway have been based upon personal index cards. Similar cards for previous years have been prepared from the records of the hospitals, so that the register is actually complete back to 1916. The cards are prepared by each hospital according to detailed instructions, and sent yearly to the Central Bureau of Statistics – one card for each admission, discharge or re-admission. All mental hospitals, private and public, are included. Other psychiatric hospitals are included only as far as psychotic patients are concerned. Neurotics are hospitalized only to a very small extent, and so admission statistics are considered rather useless in this particular field.

The cards from each calendar year are first used by the bureau for the preparation of the yearly statistical report on the mental hospitals of the country.[1] Next the cards are forwarded to the social psychiatry research institute, which is located at the Gaustad mental hospital. Here all available information about the

---

[1] Norges offisielle statistikk. Mental Hospitals.

successive admissions and discharges of each patient is entered upon individual index cards, whereby it is possible to follow each patient from his very first admission to his final discharge or death. This system has the advantage of giving some information about the outcome, but naturally with reservations. The fact that a patient was discharged to his home ten years ago and has not been re-admitted since then, does not exclude that he is actually a chronic mental invalid who is taken care of by his relatives without any public medical assistance.

Another definite advantage is that the initial diagnosis will often be corrected on discharge or on a subsequent re-admission. Particularly there is a tendency to avoid the ominous diagnosis of schizophrenia in psychoses of comparatively recent origin, and a successful therapy will encourage the hospital to make a favorable prognosis and a correspondingly optimistic diagnosis. In Norway this frequently results in the diagnosis of "reactive psychosis", which means a paranoid or affective or confusional reaction which occurs in a person of more or less deviating personality after more or less heavy personal stress. Long-time observation, however, will in many of the borderline cases reveal schizophrenic trends which were hidden during the initial stages, and the therapeutical success may prove to have been merely transitory.

A special study was made of the 9125 first admissions 1950-54. By means of the registration system these cases were followed until the end of 1963, and all changes in diagnosis were recorded and analyzed. In the 2900 cases with more than one admission the diagnosis was changed in 32 per cent. Changes from some other diagnosis to schizophrenia were found to be four times as frequent as changes in the opposite direction. This shows a clear tendency to avoid the diagnosis of schizophrenia in the beginning of a hospital stay, while the future course of the disease will still seem uncertain. A large scale personal follow-up examination of patients discharged from the Gaustad Hospital has confirmed this. The most notable finding was that the diagnosis of paranoid psychosis had to be changed in more than 40 per cent of the cases because the course of illness was found to have taken a schizophrenic turn.

It must be admitted that the uncertainty of psychiatric diagnosis is a problem in the use of admission statistics. In psychiatry pathognomonic symptoms or specific diagnostic tests hardly exist, and frequently the choice of diagnosis depends upon clinical hunches or intuition rather than upon exact observation. This applies particularly to the concept of schizophrenia. Kraepelin himself worked with this problem for 40 years without being able to give us a final solution, and at present different psychiatric schools use different definitions. The average American psychiatrists tend to use a much wider concept of schizophrenia than their continental European colleagues, and the inclusion of all or most paranoid psychoses into the group of "dementia praecox" is less accepted in France and other latin countries than for instance in Scandinavia. In practice these discrepancies have not led to much confusion, however, because the more extreme standpoints are held by a comparatively small number of non-conformists. It is characteristic that the more widely used psychiatric text books do not differ much in their differential diagnostic system. Within the small psychiatric group in Norway diagnostic practice tends to be comparatively uniform, because we all have a closely similar background of training and education, but even here this source of error should not be overlooked, and all data concerning the relative incidence of various diagnostic groups should be regarded with reservations. This is particularly true of the delimitation between schizophrenia and the somewhat indefinite and heterogeneous group of "reactive psychoses".

We should realize, however, that diagnosis is a problem in all branches of psychiatric research. It leads to serious errors whenever patient material from several sources has to be pooled, for instance in the study of therapeutic results. Neither can this problem be overcome by the method of using only material which has been diagnosed after personal examination by one single psychiatrist, because the difficulties return when the result of this particular investigation are compared with others, and such a comparison is in practice inevitable.

It may not be commonly realized that in epidemiological research using mass statistics this source of error is actually less important and more easily controlled than in other fields of psychiatric research. In the Norwegian material the diagnosis represents a cross-section of the concepts of 30 or more different hospital chiefs, and consequently the influence of extremist standpoints is more or less neutralized. Besides, our statistical analysis is to a large extent independent of the diagnostic variations. The observation that schizophrenia is more common in the single than in the married is for instance likely to be independent of the differing opinions about the exact delimitation of this diagnostic group.

More serious is the problem of hospitalization. For several reasons only a fraction of the psychotic patients are ever admitted to a psychiatric hospital, the more important reasons being shortage of beds in institutions, and ignorance or prejudice on the part of the patients and their relatives. Recently extramural treatment has become an important factor. The probable result is that a somewhat varying part of the benignant cases (particularly depressions) avoid admission, because they improve sufficiently without any hospital care. The more malignant and chronically progressive types are far less likely to avoid hospitalization *in the long run,* but admission may be delayed for many years, and owing to the excess mortality of the insane this means that a certain number will die before they become included in our hospital statistics.

The variations in hospitalization are most marked, however, for senile and arteriosclerotic psychoses and for related cases of an organic nature. These patients are likely to be regarded as mere nursing problems, who should preferably be kept away from the over-crowded mental hospitals and cared for in a simpler and less costly way, because we have no effective therapy to offer for these cases, and because they are as a rule not dangerous to themselves or to public safety.

Epileptics and mental defectives who are not actually psychotic are nevertheless frequently unable to take care of themselves, and sometimes they represent serious social problems. When, as in Norway, proper institutions for these patients are lacking, considerable pressure is put upon the mental hospitals to receive them — a pressure which is resisted more or less successfully by the hospital psychiatrists, who prefer to reserve their scarce beds for the more hopeful acute functional psychoses. There result great variations in the hospitalization of such cases, mostly according to the degree of over-crowding and hospital shortage.

To offset these shortcomings, admission statistics have the advantage of being based upon a precise definition: admission to a certain group of hospitals. It is actually difficult to see how any other criterion can be found which is equally concrete and indisputable. In the more intensive census investigations there is a tendency to include even the slighter degrees of mental maladaption, and while this is undoubtedly of the greatest interest, the delimitation of the material will then have to be based upon more or less personal judgement on the part of the examiner. Most likely, variations will result which are easily comparable to those caused by differentials in hospitalization.

It is our conclusion that the problem of hospitalization should not discourage us from using admission statistics. The problem may as a matter of fact be less serious in epidemiology because there we have possibilities of bringing the errors under control. The influence of added hospitals or hospital extensions can be studied directly. Variations in the duration of the disease previous to admisson may offer a clue: If the average duration is short, it indicates a tendency to have the patients hospitalized and vice versa. Even the influence of the distance to the nearest hospital has been proposed as a possible factor,which is easily studied by epidemiological methods.

Norway is in many ways suited for epidemiological investigations.The population of 3.5 million (1960) is not too big for a study of the entire nation, and at the same time the number of first admissions (around 2500 per year) is sufficient for a rather detailed statistical analysis. Racially the people is uniform, apart from the small group of 20,000 Lapps in the arctic provinces. In language and culture the continuity goes back for many centuries, and politically the country has been stable for 150 years. Immigration from other countries has not played any role in historic times. In 1960 there were a total of 62,000 foreign-born in the country, most of whom were born in neighboring Denmark and Sweden. Overseas emigration (mostly to America) was an important demographic factor from 1870 on and until 1930,but has been virtually non-existant since then. Vital statistics have been well organized since the middle of the last century, and the high educational standard of the people guarantees the quality of the primary statistical material. Normally a census is held every tenth year, but because of the war the census of 1940 had to be postponed until 1946.

In the psychiatric sector, mental hospital statistics and census surveys go back more than a hundred years, and psychiatrists have generally taken an interest in this particular field. The mental hospitals have never been able to take care of more than half of the mentally-ill, the remainder being cared for in colonies and nursing homes or in family care under the supervision of public health officers. This shortage of beds has limited the admission of typical nursing cases like seniles and arteriosclerotics, but otherwise the tendency has been for all psychotics to be hospitalized at least for some time, using the extramural care as a secondary one. Psychiatric hospitals specially dedicated to the less serious psychoses and the neuroses did not exist until 1918, but during the past twenty years they have had an increasing influence upon the admission rates for depressive and allied psychoses. While the hospital facilities and the general standard of medical care and social development varies from one part of Norway to another, definitely backward regions cannot be said to exist.

In spite of the convenient uniformity which is outlined above, Norway offers possibilities for the study of a wide range of environmental variations, from the modestly metropolitan Oslo area with 600,000 inhabitants- the rich agricultural East - the densely populated and industrialized South-East- the rugged fjord landscape along the western and north-western coast- the isolated mountain valleys- and finally the northern countries north of the arctic circle.

Emigration

The immense emigration from various European countries to America has contributed much to bring epidemiological methods into psychiatry. Among the many unfavorable traits in these foreigners which were registered by the frequently hostile native born, the high incidence of mental disease and other mental defects was one of the most discussed. Statistics which showed incidence rates two or three times the normal were widely used in the political fight to restrict or stop immigration. It was one of the first achievements of psychiatric epidemiology to be able to show that these alarming figures were grossly misleading, because the difference in age distribution was disregarded: Among the native born a much larger proportion were children below the age of 15, and consequently protected against the common psychoses. But even after correction of such statistical errors, the overseas migrants have significantly higher admission rates according to nearly all investigations.

In 1933 the present author published a special study of the Norwegian-born in the state of Minnesota. A summary of the main results was given in 1936 in an article which is reprinted in this volume [2]. In a chapter on Emigration published in 1961, the author did not have much to add, nor many changes to make. After having rejected the hypothesis of differential hospitalization as a main cause for the variations in incidence of mental disorders, two alternative explanations were presented: *social stress* connected with immigrant life in Minnesota and *social selection* in connection with the motivation behind emigration from Norway. The

---

[2]EMIGRATION AND MENTAL HEALTH, page 155.

argumentation is closely similar to that given in 1936, but a repetition of some of the material is justified.

For a further approach to this problem a study of the various types of psychosis is of basic importance, but a direct comparison was impossible because the diagnostic systems were too different in the two countries. All Norwegian-born first admissions to one of the three Minnesota state hospitals (Rochester), about 1100 cases, were therefore personally diagnosed by the author from the information given in the case histories. This supposedly representative sample was compared with a similar sample of 2000 first admissions to a mental hospital in Norway (Gaustad) from the same period, and to the best of the author's ability diagnosed according to the same system. Relative admission rates are given in Table 1.

Table 1.

	Minnesota	Norway
Schizophrenia	100	50
Manic-depressive psychosis	100	117
Other non-organic	100	114
Senile and arteriosclerotic	100	13
Alcoholic	100	34
General paresis	100	73
Other organic	100	24

The most striking difference is found for senile and arteriosclerotic and other organic psychoses. It is unlikely that constitutional differences should be responsible for this tremendous difference. Most likely there was in Norway a greater tendency to keep such patients at home, partly because tradition demanded it, and partly because the more settled social conditions made it easier. A study of the duration of the illness previous to admission shows, however, that admission is delayed for a longer time in Minnesota, which does not seem to indicate that the tendency towards hospitalization is stronger here. Most likely the mental and physical strain of immigrant life, which is particularly heavy upon people of late middle age, is a contributory factor. The age at onset is actually much lower in Minnesota than in Norway, which is a further point in favor of such environmental influence.

Among the functional psychoses schizophrenia is found to have an admission rate twice as high in Minnesota as in Norway while the non-schizophrenic functional psychoses (most of them manic depressive) have slightly higher admission rates in Norway. This relative predominance of schizophrenia among the immigrants is not likely to have an environmental explanation. Why should stress lead to schizophrenia rather than to non-schizophrenic psychoses? After all, the latter are not supposed to be *less* dependent upon environmental factors than the former. A further study of the material did not give any direct support to the environmental hypothesis. The age at onset of schizophrenia was found to be the same in both groups, and the psychosis did not show any particular tendency to break out during the first five years of the patients' stay in America. Among the "causes" given by the patient or his relatives, very few were in any way connected with immigrant life, which at least signifies that such problems have not consciously been particularly important in the minds of the patients. Furthermore the symptomatology of the psychosis was remarkably seldom colored by the fact that the patient was an immigrant, but seemed to be practically the same as in schizophrenics in Norway.

The hypothesis of selective emigration, on the other hand, offers a natural solution. The so-called schizothyme or schizoid type of thinking, feeling and social relationship furnishes a natural background for emigration. These personalities are not very closely tied to home, friends or familiar surroundings. They will often have difficulties of adaption in youth, and consequently do not make an early career which satisfies their ambition. It should be stressed that the tendency of such persons to emigrate is not exclusively or even mainly a result of personality *handicaps*. Even positive and valuable traits will carry them in the same direction: ambition and courage, romantic dreams of greatness and adventure, stubborn idealism and unwillingness to tolerate social, personal or religious oppression — these are character traits which have brought America thousands of its best and most typical citizens. It can hardly be doubted that such personality traits are associated with schizophrenia — either as pre-psychotic personality traits, or as initial symptoms in schizophrenic psychoses of insidious onset. A closer study of individual cases gives ample support to this hypothesis. Again and again it can be shown that a schizoid personality or an incipient schizophrenic psychosis was a direct or indirect cause for emigration, whereas no such facts could be established for the syntonic personality or the corresponding manic-depressive psychosis.

This naturally does not exclude the importance of unemployment and economic difficulties as a background for mass emigration, nor does it exclude mental stress connected with immigrant life as an eliciting cause for mental disorders. It does mean, however, that a complete understanding of the emigration problem is impossible if the mechanism of a social selection based upon personality traits is disregarded.

The possible influence of emigration upon the epidemiology of mental diseases in Norway has two aspects. In the first place the excess morbidity among the emigrants will lower the morbidity in the home population, under the assumption that these excess psychoses would have occurred even if the emigrants had stayed home. This assumption may hold true for about two thirds of the cases, but most likely not for senile, arteriosclerotic and alcoholic psychoses and for general paresis. During the 45 years from 1886 to 1930 (when overseas emigration dropped to quite insignificant figures) the total overseas emigration numbered 514829 persons above the age of 14. (For children no excess morbidity need be assumed). On the basis of their age on emigration and the calculated expectancy of mental disorder for Norway it is possible to arrive at the rough estimate that this emigrated population represents an extra 6000 first admissions to mental hospitals (most of them from schizophrenia) which would have taken place in Norway if these persons had not emigrated. Over a period of 45 years this means that the total number of first admissions might have increased as much as ten per cent. This influence of emigration has made itself felt in a diminishing degree up to 1945 or possibly 1950, that is, fifteen to twenty years after emigration from Norway virtually came to an end.

Another aspect is *selective re-emigration.* Only a small number of immigrants are deported to Norway as insane, but many return of their own accord, and in certain parts of Norway the proportion of such "returned Americans" has at times been as high as 8.5 per cent of the adult population. Many return according to plan because they have had success and made what money they need for the purchase of a farm etc., but others may be forced by failing physical and mental health. On the basis of material collected by *Melsom* from two counties in Southern Norway with a particularly large population of returned emigrants, the author has calculated a rate of first admissions of 1938 as against merely 603 for the local population. This would seem to mean that the excess morbidity is even higher in returned emigrants than in those who remain in America, which is of course not surprising. Most likely this may have influenced the admission rates in certain parts of South-Western Norway, particularly previous to 1930.

Migration Within the Country

The study of internal migration and mental disease has been hampered by insufficient information about the migrations of the general population. In most countries the census will register place of birth and place of residence, but nothing is known about the intermediate movements. Nevertheless our Norwegian material has shown certain interesting and apparently meaningful trends. In the following the first admissions to Norwegian psychiatric hospitals 1958-63 are related to the population data from the census of 1960.

In general the rates of first admission are significantly lower for the migrant part of the population, i.e. for those who at the time of the census were not resident in their community of birth. Table 1 shows that this is true even of those who have migrated merely from one rural community to another within the same county – a "short distance migration," which is unlikely to have led to any important change in the personal and social situation.

Migration from cities to rural districts forms an interesting exception in that these migrants have higher rates than either the rural or the urban non-migrant population. This type of migration is relatively infrequent, and it is common experience in psychiatric epidemiology that groups which are somehow atypical tend to have higher incidence of mental abnormalities.

Table 2. First admissions per 1,000,000 per year.
"Short distance" means a migration within the same county.
In Norway there are 20 counties, with an average
population of 200,000.

	Men	Women
Non-migrant rural population	873	1005
Short-distance rural-rural migration	685	642
Short-distance urban-rural migration	1175	1200
Long-distance rural-rural migration	735	898
Long-distance urban-rural migration	1219	1055
Non-migrant city population	1085	1049
Migrants to cities from rural districts	895	1002
Migrants to cities from other cities	945	997

Oslo, the capital and only larger city in the country, presents a reversal of the usual pattern in that migrants to the city have higher admission rates than the Oslo-born. This is particularly true of immigrants from other cities, a finding which is hard to explain from the point of view of the social stress hypothesis.

Table 3. Migration to Oslo

	Men	Women
Non-migrant population of Oslo	1180	1108
Migrants to Oslo from rural communities	1246	1278
Migrants to Oslo from other cities and towns	1535	1580

As "sub-urban communities" have been singled out communities which are still classified as rural, because they have so far not been incorporated in the city from which they have received the greater part of their population. In these sub-urbs the admission rates are extremely low. The explanation is probably that they are generally of a fairly high social standard. The typical sub-urbanites are youngish married couples with considerable drive and with a reasonably good income. Evidently this population is likely to represent a positive selection with regard to mental health, while at the same time their favorable living conditions will protect them against stress. In any case this finding is solid proof of the close association between internal migration and mental health.

Table 4. Migration to Suburbs

	Men	Women
Non-migrant population of suburbs other than Oslo	833	792
Short-distance rural-suburban migration	485	730
Short-distance urban-suburban migration	377	567
Long-distance rural-suburban migration	368	633
Long-distance urban-suburban migration	557	740
Non-migrant population of the suburbs of Oslo	575	662
Migrants from rural districts	503	865
Migrants from cities (including Oslo)	633	612

The pattern is not consistent, however. In the first place the difference in favor of the migrants is much less marked in the female sex. Possibly the explanation is that the selection involved depends more upon the personal qualities of the men than upon those of their wives. Furthermore, the pattern is less clear for the suburbs of Oslo: Here the admission rates are equally low for migrants and for non-migrants, but these rates are only about half as high as in the neighboring city of Oslo. Possibly the non-migrants in the suburbs owe their low morbidity to the fact that they are second-generation offspring of out-migrants from Oslo who had the characteristic low rate of mental disorder.

The Norwegian census of 1960 is available on tape, which made it possible to study in detail variables such as age, marital state and occupation which are not included in the tables on migration printed in the census reports. It was found that the excess morbidity of non-migrants has its maximum between the ages of 25 and 50 years, i.e. in the age groups with the most stable socio-economic conditions.

The pattern of lower migrant morbidity is found in the single as well as in the married, and so it could not be a mere statistical artefact caused by the higher marriage rate of the migrants. We did find, however, that the excess morbidity of the non-migrants was most marked in *married men* but in *single women*. It seems probable that many married women move from one community to another because of the qualifications of their husbands rather than from any personal choice. This would tend to make a favorable selection less likely in agreement with our findings.

The migrational pattern does not seem to be much influenced by *social class*, but a few interesting occupational groups are found to deviate from the average. In *owners and managers* the admission rates are considerably higher in migrants than in non-migrants. Now this somewhat heterogeneous middle class group contains many individuals who exist more or less passively on inherited means. For them migration will quite often have the character of an early retirement, and will naturally tend to be associated with an unfavorable selection and higher mental morbidity.

As far as *psychiatric diagnosis* goes we find the same pattern for schizophrenia as for manic-depressive and other functional psychoses, but the city of Oslo forms an interesting exception from this general rule. Here schizophrenia is particularly frequent among the immigrants, while manic-depression predominates in the Oslo-born, and the intermediate groups of paranoid states and reactive psychoses take an intermediate position. This reminds one of the diagnostic pattern which was found for Norwegians who had emigrated to Minnesota, and it suggests that a similar mechanism of selection by personality type is at work even in the immigration to Oslo. The capital might easily have some special attraction for pre-schizophrenic individuals.

The senile and arteriosclerotic psychoses are of interest because we have reason to believe that variations in their admission rates are related to differences in the tendency to have such old patients hospitalized rather than to true incidence. Now we find that in Oslo, with a relatively complete hospitalization of these patients, there is no difference between migrants and non-migrants. Outside of Oslo, on the other hand, migrants have the higher admission rates. Apparently migrants are particularly sensitive towards the social factors which determine differences in the hospitalization of the psychoses. Here again the parallel with the Norwegian-born of Minnesota is striking.

There may be a tendency in those migrants who develop a mental disease to return to their home community or to be sent back by others because of the illness, but before they are hospitalized. Such cases will figure in our statistics as non-migrants, when they should rightly be regarded as migrants – at least in the cases in which the patients were predominantly passive and sent home at the instigation of their employers or the authorities, or fetched home by their relatives. In order to throw some light upon this problem 756 case histories of patients suffering from functional psychoses were studied with regard to the pattern of internal migration, particularly around the onset of the psychosis. 436 of these patients were resident in their community of birth at the time of first admission, and consequently classified as non-migrants. But 7.6 percent of the men and 16.4 per cent of the women were found to have returned to their home quite recently in connection with the outbreak of psychotic symptoms, and in all these cases it seemed probable that there was a causal connection rather than a coincidence in time. Generally these patients returned to parents or other relatives in the country because they had failed in their work in some city in another county.

On the other hand, 11 per cent of the patients classified as migrants could be shown to have left their community of birth and taken up new residence for some reason connected with the onset of the psychosis: general restlessness and maladaption, specific conflicts with their environment or definite psychotic symptoms. Most of these patients were long-distance migrants to cities, frequently to Oslo.

The two trends probably eliminate each other: the number of patients who are brought back to their community of birth by the onset of a psychosis is about equal to that of patients who migrate during the initial stages of such an illness. This would seem to mean that the lowered admission rates in migrants and the higher in non-migrants are not likely to be caused by factors immediately connected with the initial stages of the psychosis. The social selection, if any, is more likely to be based upon pre-psychotic traits or undiagnosed psychotic symptoms of fairly long standing.

It should be mentioned in this connection that 29 of the 756 cases were over-seas emigrants who returned to Norway in connection with the onset of mental illness; mostly they were deported from the U.S.A. 12 of them were probably already psychotic at the time of their emigration. Such cases are probably over-represented at the Gaustad hospital, because of its location in the main port of Oslo. They represent a source of error of uncertain direction, and should rightly not have been included in the material at all because they have no counterpart in the census population.

A special group of 207 single women patients who had been employed in domestic work was selected for special study, because it could be assumed to be particularly mobile with regard to residence and employment. 64 of them or 31 per cent were found to have migrated around the time of onset of illness: 28 moved back home, mostly from Oslo, 28 left their home communities for some city and the remaining eight were overseas migrants. Only five of them were short-distance migrants, and even in this exceptionally unstable group mental disorder is evidently seldom related to this type of migration.

It may seem surprising that *overseas* migration should be connected with an increase in mental morbidity, while for migration *within the country* the opposite is the case. Actually there are many reasons why these two forms of migration should be connected with different types of social selection. Overseas emigrants have to make a far more complete break with their previous existance, and have to face their future without the aid of definite plans or preparations. A migration within Norway does not have the same character of being a final and irrevocable step, and at the same time the change of residence has generally been planned beforehand in some detail, work is assured and a house is rented, etc.

In this connection it should be noted that the admission rate is considerably raised in the foreign-born of Norway, despite the fact that most of them have immigrated from the neighboring countries of Sweden and Denmark. This migration across the border to a country with language and customs which are not too unfamiliar, is connected with a selection which is similar to that of overseas emigration.

Discussion

This sketchy analysis represents merely preliminary results of an investigation which is not finished, but it does suffice to show that internal migration is related to mental health (as measured by the incidence of hospitalized psychoses). On the whole the morbidity is higher in non-migrants, which contrasts with the excess morbidity which was found for overseas emigrants from Norway. It is hardly surprising that such hypothetical mechanisms as social selection or social stress should work out differently in different types of migration. Even for migration within Norway we have found the pattern to be very complex. Clearly internal migration does not consist of one single stream with one specific source and one definite direction. Some of the many currents emerge from the analysis of our findings:

1. Among the non-migrants there are some who have remained in their community of birth because of some personal mental handicap. This is undoubtedly so for mental defectives and epileptics, and probably for schizophrenics and pre-schizophrenics, but the same mechanism may be at work even in most other diagnostic groups.

2. Migrants from one rural community to another have a low morbidity, in particular if the migration is of the short-distance type. The same trend, but less

pronounced, is seen in migrants from one urban community to another.

3. Migrants from cities to rural districts are comparatively few, and they have a relatively high morbidity. Possibly certain mental patients are moved to more rural surroundings by their relatives because of their mental symptoms.

4. In the steady stream of migrants to Oslo the morbidity is definitely increased. This is particularly true of migrants who come from other towns and cities.

5. The lowest admission rates are found in the numerous migrants from a city to the surrounding suburbs.

6. Internal migration is less common before the age of 20, and in these young migrants a high morbidity is found.

7. Mental disorders of old age seem to be more common in migrants, which could indicate that the tendency to have mental patients hospitalized is stronger in migrants than in non-migrants.

8. In population groups with a high proportion of migrants, the admission rates for these migrants tend to be low. This seems to be an expression of the more general law that people who behave atypically by moving against the most common currents of migration, have a higher morbidity from psychoses. Another instance of the same type is that in typically rural population groups with relatively few migrant elements the non-migrants do not present any excess morbidity.

Some Main Points in Recent Research

During the past ten to twenty years the relation of migration to mental disorders has been studied in many countries, and the results have varied. *Malzberg et. al.* (1956) found for New York State higher admission rates among the foreign born, but the difference was significant for women only and mainly in the age groups above 60 years.

In the *Midtown-Manhattan study* (Srole et al. 1962) the immigrant population was divided into three groups:

1. Those who came to USA as children and who can therefore not be regarded as self-selected migrants.

2. A transitional group who emigrated as young people in the company of their parents or kin.

3. The self-selected migrants who came over unaccompanied or in adult age.

If selective factors were decisive, group 3 should have the highest morbidity and group 1 the lowest, whereas in fact no difference was found.

The post-war immigration to Israel (*Halevi* 1963) has for many Jewish groups taken place without any possibility of selection, because the group was moved in its entirety (for instance from Yemen). The statistical findings are not conclusive, but they seem to indicate that the morbidity in these "100 per cent immigrant groups" is lower than in the more selective groups and also lower than in the native-born.

Eitinger (1959) *and Eitinger* and *Grünfeld* (1966) have studied the incidence of mental disorders in displaced persons in Norway and found it to be five times as high as in a comparable control population. These migrants have no doubt suffered much, but at the same time the element of selection is far from excluded. In many cases it could be shown that the patient had been maladjusted already in his home country. During the first years after migration there was a preponderance of short-termed reactive psychoses, but after some years the diagnostic distribution approached that which is typical of Norwegian patients.

As to *internal migration, Malzberg et al* (1956) found higher admission rates for migrants to New York State than for native New Yorkers. The excess morbidity was particularly high for those who had lived in New York for less than five years. Similarly *Lazarus et al* (1963) found higher admission rates for migrants in New York as well as in Ohio and California.

Jaco (1960) studied inter-state migration in Texas in some detail, including even patients treated by private psychiatrists. He was able to exclude from his material "transient" residents of Texas, and for the remaining "true migrants" he found the same incidence of psychosis as in the non-migrants. The fact that migrational data were unknown in one third of this material is a serious source of error, which is likely to have made the admission rates too low for migrants (*Malzberg* 1962).

In the *Midtown-Manhattan study* population groups born in New York City, in other cities in the state and in smaller towns were compared. Admission rates standardized for age and socio-economic status were used. The morbidity was found to be highest in the group born in New York City and lowest in the small town group. The authors tend to regard the small town-metropolitan migrants as a favorable selection with an upward socio-economic trend. They also feel that children who grow up in relatively small urban societies have the best mental health chances.

Helgason (1964) found a higher incidence of psychoses in non-migrants, especially for men. The incidence of schizophrenia and epilepsy was particularly low among migrants to Reykjavik (the only major city on Iceland), while for manic-depressive psychosis no difference was found. Helgason feels that selection is the most likely explanation.

Stenbäck and Achte (1965) found that in Helsinki schizophrenia was less frequent among migrants from other parts of Finland, while for most other psychoses the opposite was the case. *Karlsson* (1966) found admission rates to be lowest among recent migrants, but this difference was not found for schizophrenia. The discrepancies between his findings and those of Stenbäck and Achte could be due to his use of admission rates standardized for age.

Dalgard (1967) has conducted an intensive study of mental disease and pattern of migration in Oslo. A representative sample of 1105 hospitalized patients with functional psychosis was compared with a control study matched for age, sex, occupation and marital state as well as for residence within Oslo. In the male sex he has found a slight excess morbidity in people born in Oslo, but only in the higher social class, whereas in the lower class the pattern was reversed.

In women marital state was found to be more decisive than socio-economic status: the highest morbidity was found in single non-migrants and in married migrants. (Our findings were the same).

Generally Dalgard found a high migrant morbidity in population groups with relatively few migrant elements, which may support the hypothesis of selection. There was also evidence of stress, however, in particular associated with status inconsistencies: Groups moving upward or downward in social characteristics are more liable to develop funtional psychoses.

Astrup et al. (1966) have studied the migration pattern in 706 carefully examined patients with functional psychosis who have been re-examined at least five years after discharge from the hospital. Before first admission 45 per cent were found to be resident in their community of birth. On follow-up this percentage had increased to 57, which means that many migrant patients tend to return to their original home after having gone through a mental illness. This tendency was found to be independent of diagnosis. A considerable proportion of the patients were found to have moved previous to first admission, but after the onset of the psychosis; some had moved back to their community of birth. However, an approximately equal number moved away – presumably driven by mental symptoms or their social consequences.

Postscript

The author feels that certain conclusions can be drawn from his own experience and from the studies made by others.

As in all epidemiological research, a combination of extensive and intensive investigations is the method of choice. In the extensive studies large population groups can be examined and a variety of types of migration can be compared. The information about each member of the population will, however, necessarily be scanty, and the case-finding will be limited to patients who have come under some kind of psychiatric care. The intensive studies will reveal the detailed pattern of successive migration in the individual case, and to some extent they can even give us information about personal motivations and problems and so throw light upon the problems of selection and stress. From a statistical point of view the intensive studies have the advantage of more solid morbidity figures, and adequately matched control materials are a possibility.

In extensive statistical investigations on migration more demographic information is needed than is usually available in official statistics. As a minimum one needs data on the distribution of the migrants and the non-migrant population with regard to age, sex, marital state and occupation. Crude rates where these variables are disregarded may be misleading. Information on time of residence is also highly desirable, at least in the form of "under or over 5 years".

Choice of Field

The relations of migration to mental morbidity varies from time to time, from country to country and from one population group to another. Our aim is therefore not to establish a pattern which has general validity. It is of importance that epidemiological fields as widely different as possible should be investigated. Among the most important are countries or regions where the migration associated with beginning industrialization and urbanization is still going on. Highly stable as well as rapidly changing populations are both important objects. Particularly interesting are population groups which are moved from one place to another in their entirety without any possible selection (hundred percent migrants). At times nearly experimental situations arise, as when small groups are moved because of some planned industrial development such as dam building (Sudan). Some migrations lead to social problems of such dimensions that a solution is a pressing need, which opens up possibilities for a utilization of epidemiological methods in practical social medicine (The immigration of Puerto-Ricans to New York, of North Africans to Paris, of political fugitives to several countries).

Conclusions

Sometimes it may be a primary aim to do away with prejudice and superstitions about migrants being particularly valuable or worthless people, and to replace such beliefs with a scientific curiosity as to how they differ from non-migrants. Next comes the study of the health risks inherent in most migrations and of the ways of preventing them.

The problem of selection versus social stress is a central one here as well as in social psychiatry in general. It is of course nothing but a special form of the universal problem of nature and nurture. A study of migration may help to unravel this knot, but we should keep in mind that a final solution is probably in principle impossible. So far we may be justified in claiming that clear instances of selective migration as well as of disease-provoking stress have been shown to exist. In planning for the future both aspects should be considered, with the emphasis upon preventive social psychiatry rather than upon restrictive legislation.

Origin of Contributions and References: See Page 336

CONCENTRATION CAMP SURVIVORS IN NORWAY AND ISRAEL

L. Eitinger
Norway

Introduction

The severe psychic and physical stress situations to which human beings were exposed in the concentration camps of World War II may very well have had lasting psychological results. The purpose of this investigation was to discover the nature of this sequelae, their symptomatology, and to identify the specific factors in the stressful situations responsible for these morbid conditions.

Methods

To this end 600 Israeli and Norwegian concentration camp survivors were studied (Table 1). The Norwegians constituted a fairly uniform group, born and bred in Norway, who after the war returned to their native country. The Israelis were drawn from almost every country in Europe which had been under German occupation during World War II, but chiefly from Poland, Hungary, Czechoslovakia and Germany. They had all immigrated to Israel, most of them after 1948. The Israeli group was exposed to the severest form of psychophysical ill-treatment, while the Norwegians belonged to the more "priviliged" groups of prisoners. However, neither of the two groups is truly representative, since those persons who

Table 1. The distribution of the groups and the percentages of psychiatric conditions caused by war experiences

Groups		Number of cases	Percentage of psychiatric conditions caused by war experiences
Norwegian	clinical	96	45
	team	152	80
	work	80	—
Israeli	psychotic	104	60
	neurotic	92	72
	work	66	84
Total		590	

Table 7. "Premorbid personality" of subjects, including previous illness (in percentages)

	Norwegian			Israeli		
	Clin. gr.	Team gr.	Work gr.	Psych. gr.	Neur. gr.	Work gr.
Even, unremarkable personality	50.4	82.8	95.0	74.9	77.2	81.9
Personality sensitive, "nervous"	26.7	9.2	3.8	12.5	17.4	16.6
Personality unstable, disharmonious	21.9	7.7	1.2	5.8	5.4	1.5
Others and unknown	1.0	1.3	–	6.8	–	–
Total number of cases	96	152	80	104	92	66
Illnesses of significance						
Somatic illnesses	35.3	19.6	23.7	14.3	4.4	3.0
Psychiatric illnesses	9.4	2.4	2.4	5.7	1.1	1.5
Earlier alcohol addiction	15.6	3.2	–	–	–	–

Hereditary taints, deviate character traits in childhood, premorbid personality traits, alcoholic addiction and previous mental disorders were remarkably similar in the three Israeli groups and in two of the Norwegian groups, but the Norw. clin. gr. included the most patients with tainted family histories and with premorbid deviating personalities.

Tables 8, 9, and 10 show some data concerning the internment in concentration camps and the conditions there.

Table 8. Conditions of concentration camp internment (in percentages)

	Norwegian			Israeli		
	Clin. gr.	Team gr.	Work gr.	Psych. gr.	Neur. gr.	Work gr.
0 to 1 year	40.6	13.8	36.2	47.3	46.7	39.4
1 to 2 years	25.1	21.1	43.8	24.9	20.6	15.2
2 to 3 years	25.1	35.5	17.5	10.5	17.3	30.3
3 years and more	9.2	29.6	2.5	17.3	15.4	15.1
Duration of internment (cumulative)						
0 to 2 years	65.7	34.9	80.0	72.2	67.3	54.6
2 years and more	34.3	65.1	20.0	27.8	32.7	45.4
Experience in concentration camp						
Subject to special torture	19.1	45.3	6.2	4.8	11.9	9.0
Head injuries	23.9	48.2	3.8	20.1	30.4	10.6
Total number of cases	96	152	80	104	92	66

Table 9. Loss of weight of the subjects (in percentages)

	Norwegian			Israeli	
	Clin. gr.	Team gr.	Work gr.	Psych. gr.	Neur. gr.	Work gr.
"Living corpse"	8.3	32.8	–	23.1	40.2	33.3
Comparatively reasonable loss of weight	52.2	63.1	100.0	40.3	59.8	66.7
Uncertain information	39.5	4.0	–	35.5	–	–
Total number of cases	96	152	80	104	92	66

Table 10. Incidence of somatic illnesses in the concentration camps among subjects (in percentages)

	Norwegian			Israeli	
	Clin. gr.	Team gr.	Work gr.	Psych. gr.	Neur. gr.	Work gr.
Skin infections	8.3	34.2	15.0	9.6	39.1	39.3
Illnesses of the respiratory system	26.0	46.7	26.2	16.3	24.9	27.2
Illnesses of the digestive system	18.7	63.8	33.7	22.1	46.7	51.5
Rheumatism	18.8	34.2	28.7	12.4	36.9	29.6
Encephalitis (?)	8.3	19.7	–	4.8	5.4	10.6
Spotted fever	3.1	12.5	1.2	13.4	29.3	24.2
Other infectious diseases	6.4	29.8	8.7	3.6	7.2	11.4
Edema	11.2	40.1	7.5	8.6	34.7	33.3
Total number of cases	96	152	80	104	92	66

The most prisoners with more than two years of captivity were found in the Norw. team gr. while the fewest were found in the Norw. work gr. The most patients with head injuries and those who had been exposed to special torture were found in the Norw. team gr. Loss of weight down to the "living corpse" stage was greatest in the Israeli groups and the Norw. work gr. The Norw. team gr. had the greatest number of illnesses during their internment, probably due to the fact that its members were subjected to the severest stress but had the greatest power of resistance, while the Jewish prisoners with so many and such serious illnesses had no chance of survival.

With regard to extraordinary mental stress situations, it is also the Norw. team gr. which rates highest; the Norw. work gr. lowest, while Israeli groups cannot be compared because of the very real danger of death in which they live.

At the end of the war, only 10 to 20% of Israelis had more than two living members of their families, and 75 to 80% were the sole surviving members of their families. There was not a single Israeli who had not lost at least one of his close relatives.

survived until the present investigation, by their very survival for so long, have undergone a certain process of selection.

Not only are the investigated groups not representative for all concentration camp survivors in Norway or Israel, but the two main groups are not comparable as to method of selection, clinical diagnoses, or contact with the investigator and the intensity of the examination. These reservations should be kept in mind when considering the conclusions.

Unlike the Israelis, the Norwegians had, before their arrest, lived in relative security and with fairly adequate nutrition, they were arrested (with few exceptions) for what they had done and not for what they were. Most suffered their greatest stress during the period between arrest and entering the concentration camp, in the form of head injuries and other results of torture. On the other hand, this period was of secondary importance to the Israeli group. In the camps, the Norwegian groups were indeed exposed to similar treatment as the Israeli groups, but for them internment did not entail exploitation of their strength before final annihilation, as was the case for the Israeli groups. They were not exposed to the same acute mental stress as the Israeli groups, such as total isolation from their families with the knowledge that most of them had been killed. Somatically, the Norwegian groups were exposed to illness, injuries and malnutrition to almost the same degree as the Israeli groups. The greatest difference occurred after liberation from the camps, when the Norwegians returned home to almost normal conditions of life, while the Israelis, having lost their homes and contacts, were isolated in the truest sense of the word.

Each group was divided into three subgroups. There are three Norwegian and three Israeli groups:

Norwegian clinical group (Nor. Clin. gr.) consisted of patients who were admitted to the University Psychiatric Clinic, Oslo, for various psychological complaints. The facts of internment in concentration camps was revealed when the case history was taken and the results of the stress connected with it were only a few cases considered the "real" reason for their hospitalization. The case histories were very detailed, and the information given by the patients was supplemented in almost every case by data from relatives or others who had known the patients' vita ante acta. Routine physical examination and laboratory tests were performed. Other examinations, including psychological tests, electro- and pneumoencephalography, and consultation with specialists were carried out when indicated.

The so-called Norwegian team group (Nor. team gr.) consisted of patients examined by the "Medical Board of 1957," who at the time of the investigation had given up the struggle with their daily social problems. The majority had been through very difficult conditions of internment, but their complaints often appeared diffuse. Their were no clear somatic changes, and the evaluations by the examining physicians were both varied and heterogeneous (1). In this group, the somatic and social aspects were especially emphasized and the psychiatrist was only one of the many specialists who assessed the patients. The Norwegian work group

(Nor. work gr.) consisted of a control group of apparently healthy, able-bodied individuals, who had been in German concentration camps but, despite this, had been fully employed since their release except for inter-current illnesses. They were subjected to a detailed psychiatric interview following a questionaire based on experience with ex-internees. The same questionaire was used when interviewing the Israelis. No previous case histories were available for these subjects, nor was there any information from relatives. Physical examination and examinations by specialists were not usually necessary in this group.

The Israeli psychotic group (Is. Psych. gr.) consisted of psychotic patients who were hospitalized in Israeli psychiatric hospitals, and who had been in concentration camps.

The Israeli neurotic group (Isr. neur. gr.) consisted of patients with mild nervous complaints, who had attended outpatient departments, usually for several years, and some of whom had been admitted to psychiatric departments. The case histories were always very detailed and informative. All had had thorough physical examinations. Many had had psychological testing, and when indicated, special examinations, including electroencephalography, but not pneumoencephalography. During my interviews with these patients, besides taking a detailed history and performing the usual psychiatric examination, I concentrated on their war experiences, of which I tried to get as detailed a picture as possible.

The Israeli work group (Isr. work gr.) consisted of apparently healthy persons. I examined occupants at two kibbutzim (collective farms), many of who had been in concentration camps. Technically, this was comparitively easier than to

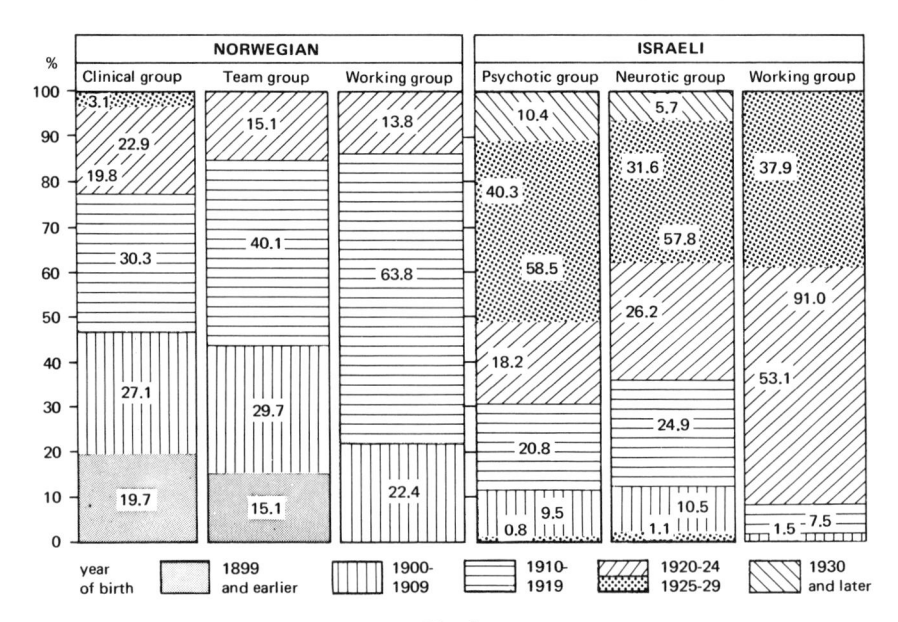

Fig. 1.

find representative groups among the rest of the population. However, a more important consideration was the fact that the special living conditions of the kibbutz helped to exclude a number of misapprehensions which might otherwise have biased the material.

It is obvious then that selections were made in the groups examined, according to very different points of view, so that no conlusions can be reached regarding the quantitative incidence of late sequelae — or the lack of them — in former prisoners. The only common factor in these six groups is that all the subjects had been concentration camp inmates. The duration of internment, its severity, the torture and illness suffered during captivity, and the resulting disorders varied from group to group. The starting point, however, was not how much or how little each individual member of the group had endured, but their physical and mental status at the time of the investigation.

The Israeli groups had lived in poorer social circumstances, and the level of their education and training was considerably lower than that of the Norwegian groups, as might be expected from the lower standard of living prevailing in Eastern Europe (Tables 2-7 and Fig 1).

Table 2. Childhood background of subjects (in percentages)

	Norwegian			Israeli		
	Clin. gr.	Team gr.	Work gr.	Psych. gr.	Neur. gr.	Work gr.
Hereditary tainting	26.0	11.8	10.0	12.4	7.6	13.6
Disharmonious childhood home	23.9	19.7	16.2	28.8	32.6	30.0
Poor social conditions during childhood	20.8	21.7	22.4	44.0	40.2	42.4
Deviating traits of character during childhood	30.2	9.2	7.5	12.2	11.3	10.1
Total number of cases	96	152	80	104	92	66

Table 3. School education of subjects (in percentages)

	Norwegian			Israeli		
Type of education	Clin. gr.	Team gr.	Work gr.	Psych. gr.	Neur. gr.	Work gr.
Elementary school (up to 7 years)	45.3	48.9	27.5	70.2	66.5	64.4
Elementary school (7 to 12 years)	37.1	39.8	43.8	22.1	25.9	27.9
General Certificate of Education (13 years)	12.4	7.9	26.3	4.9	6.5	4.6
Higher (university etc.)	5.2	3.4	2.4	2.8	1.1	3.1
Total number of cases	96	152	80	104	92	66

Table 4. Civil status of subjects at the time of their arrest/beginning of persecution (in percentages)

	Norwegian			Israeli		
Civil status	Clin. gr.	Team gr.	Work gr.	Psych. gr.	Neur. gr.	Work gr.
Single	52.1	44.8	72.4	84.7	84.0	94.0
Married	47.9	55.2	27.6	15.3	16.0	6.0
% successful marriages	78.0	78.0	86.3	100	100	100
Total number of cases	96	152	80	104	92	66

Table 5. Classification of subjects' occupation at the time of arrest/beginning of persecution (in percentages)

	Norwegian			Israeli		
Occupation	Clin. gr.	Team gr.	Work gr.	Psych. gr.	Neur. gr.	Work gr.
Unskilled laborers	26.1	19.7	13.8	20.2	10.2	7.5
Skilled laborers	26.1	32.8	26.2	21.8	20.0	15.2
Seafarers and fishermen	7.2	11.4	–	–	–	–
Businessmen and office workers	31.3	32.2	51.2	16.3	12.4	12.2
Others including school children	9.3	3.9	8.8	41.7	57.4	65.1
Total number of cases	96	152	80	104	92	66

Table 6. Father's occupation in Israeli groups (in percentages)

Father's occupation	Psych. gr.	Neur. gr.	Work gr.
Unskilled laborers	6.7	5.5	1.5
Skilled laborers	18.4	27.2	39.2
Businessmen and office workers	66.3	62.0	56.3
Others and unknown	8.6	5.3	3.0
Total number of cases	104	92	66

The psychotraumatic importance contained in these figures is indeed difficult to evaluate. Numerous reports stress the significance of the family's protective function in disaster situations. Hill and Hansen (2) reviewed these investigations and their work shows clearly that a family has more resistance and is better equipped to face disaster when it remains intact than when members of the family are scattered.

The anthropological study of Zborowsky and Herzog (3) showed that family cohesion is more important for Israelis than most European populations. The total disintegration of community and family cohesion will thus radically affect the individual and increase apprehension.

Findings

The results of this investigation appear to show that a certain amount of mental stress, such as that to which the Norw. clin. gr. and work gr. and a few patients of the Norw. team gr. were subjected, does not break down the personality, does not blunt the ability to feel with others and can, to a certain extent, develop the personality in a positive direction, such as to increase the wish to help others. On the other hand, when mental stress surpasses the individual's endurance, and destroys the individual's social norms and values as occurred in the Israeli groups and many of the Norw. team gr., deep changes in the structure of the personality may result which may be irreversible. There were no uniform opinions within the Israeli groups as to why individuals thought they had been able to survive. However, most of the psychiatric cases tended to ascribe their survival more to chance rather than other survivors, who inclined to attribute their survival to interpersonal help.

Guilt feelings among the Norwegian groups were usually related to their rather privileged position but in rare cases, resulted from breakdown under interrogation and the like. In the Israeli groups guilt feelings varied in cause from the most irrational of reasons to very concrete ones. The question of lack of active resistance to oppression was considered in great detail, and in many cases believed to be the basis for neurotic feelings of guilt, especially because this question has been discussed publicly so often.

Among the signs of illness present, emphasis has been laid on the so-called concentration camp syndrome, whose symptomology has been described elsewhere (4,5). This syndrome is correlated with what has been termed "cumulative stress situations." It appears, therefore, most frequently in the Norw. team gr., which includes the greatest number who had suffered head injuries, encephalitis, spotted fever, internment of longer than three years, loss of weight down to the "living corpse" stage, or a combination of these. There were only a few mild cases of this syndrome in the Norw. work gr., which was affected relatively mildly by captivity. Gronvik and Lonnum (6) demonstrated a remarkable parrellelism between symptomatology of the concentration camp syndrome and organic cerebral changes, and the present investigation supports this finding. The cases of concentration camp syndrome in which the patient had not been exposed to traumatic physical factors, can be explained on the basis of Wolff's investigations of the effect of chronic psychic trauma on the highest integrative functions (7).

Table 11 shows how many of the psychiatric disturbances in the different groups are related to experiences in the camps. We did not find any manifest illness in the Norw. work gr. Fewer than half of the Norw. clin. gr. had disturbances caused by war experiences while the rates were much higher for all the other groups.

In the Norw. clin gr. the eight endogenous psychoses (with one exception) did not appear to have any causal relationship with internment (Table 11). Among the 11 reactive psychoses were four for which internment apparently exacerbated the disorder and its disabling course. Among the 33 patients with neuroses, 12 were apparently aggravated by internment, while in the other 21 cases the war experiences probably were the most important causal factors of the neuroses. The 24 patients with organic brain disease were divided into two distinct groups, one consisting of seven, with known causes for the disorders, the other of 17 patients whose organic brain disease resulted from their war experiences. Among the 19 psychopaths there were none on whom the war experience appeared to have had any effect as manifested by the clear character deviations.

Table 11. Clinical picture of illnesses and their possible connection with concentration camp internment

	Norwegian Clin. gr. Total	Norwegian Clin. gr. Caused by war experiences	Norwegian Team gr. Total	Norwegian Team gr. Caused by war experiences	Norwegian Work gr. Total	Norwegian Work gr. Caused by war experiences	Israeli Psych. gr. Total	Israeli Psych. gr. Caused by war experiences	Israeli Neur. gr. Total	Israeli Neur. gr. Caused by war experiences	Israeli Work gr. Total	Israeli Work gr. Caused by war experiences
Psychoses:												
Endogenous	8	1	6	3	–	–	62	34	–	–	1	–
Reactive	11	4					26	15				
"Neuroses"	33	21	17	14	–	–	–	–	74	54	62	55
"Organic reaction type"	24	17	104	101	–	–	9	9	18	13	–	–
Serious character disturbances "psychopaths"	19	–	8	–	–	–	4	2	–	–	–	–

Of the 104 cases of encephalopathy in the Norw. team gr. 101 cases resulted from war injuries. Only three of the 17 cases of neuroses revealed premorbid personality traits which could partly explain their present condition: while in the other 14 cases war experience must be blamed. On the other hand, this was not the case in the eight psychopaths. In three of the six psychotic cases stress of internment was the precipitating factor which led to chronic illness.

There were no actual psychiatric disorders in the Norw. work gr. and although there were a number of oversensitive reactions etc., most subjects had well integrated personalities.

Since in the Isr. psych. Gr. 60% of the cases were schizophrenia, the possible causal relationship to the stress of internment was given special attention. Of the 62 patients with schizophrenia, 21 patients with hereditary tainting, deviating traits during childhood or later, as well as tuberculosis in childhood were excluded. Of the remaining 41, 30 cases were considered to result directly from their internment, and four had undergone noticeable change of personality at that time. Only seven could lead a fairly adequate life for a few years after the war. This finding that 34 out of 62 cases of psychopathy resulted from internment is in keeping with those of Schneider (8) and Kolle (9) with regard to exogeneous etiology in such cases.

In the 26 reactive psychoses we were able to show a direct causal connection with war experiences in 12 of the 16 depressive reactions, in three of five confusional states, but in none of the five paranoid reactions. In all nine cases with definitely proved organic psycho-syndrome, connection with internment was doubtlessly the cause. Of four patients with personality disorders, two felt that their condition was not related to their internment as their deviating behavior had started in childhood. To repeat the life-history of the third one dispassionately is almost impossible.

Isr. psych. gr. Case 34, born in Poland in 1928. His father died early and his mother moved back to her parents where the boy lived until the outbreak of the war. Neither the home conditions, nor the financial circumstances were particularly good, but the grandfather was a mild and religious man to whom the patient felt attached. During the war, the family was moved first into the ghetto, later during an "action" the grandfather was captured, and the boy saw the Germans scorch his beard off and then kill him. He rapidly developed an uncanny gift for hiding during all the raids and managed to remain alive for four months after the ghetto had been liquidated. He "lived like a rat," came out of his hiding place in the ruins during the night, and stole what he could find. He was finally caught, and taken to Auschwitz. He admits openly that he had become reckless and without scruples: "Wanted to stay alive at any price." In order to get some soup, he agreed to drag the corpses out of the block, and he gradually obtained a "very good" job in the camp, sorting out the belongings of those who were killed. For a time he was a "living corpse," but he gradually improved and, when he was evacuated to Mauthausen he was "as strong as anybody." Immediately after the war, trying to get to Palestine illegally, he was caught and interned on Cyprus. He came to Israel in one of the first transports in 1948, and volunteered immediately for the military forces. Here he was also "daring," reckless, was regarded as a badly disciplined but "good soldier." At one time, his unit was ambushed. Most of his comrades were mowed down, but he managed to escape. In 1949 he suffered a concussion during the fighting, and twice later in 1955. After demobilization, he proved to be completely unable to adjust. He was untruthful, unstable and dishonest; he began to steal and was only interested in satisfying his immediate needs. He had no training and not enough stability to get any. He was finally hospitalized in a psychiatric ward and during the interview in 1962, he appeared cynical and reserved. He looked upon the whole world as a concentration camp. "They all behave exactly as they did in the camp, everyone thinks only about himself, they just grab all they can lay hands on. The only difference is the way they speak and their clothes. Apart from this there is no difference." He only laughed when asked if there was anyone he trusted, and to the question of whom he hated here, the answer came like a ship-lash: "Everyone."

How many of these personality disorders can be attributed to the concentration camp is a moot question. The different incidents are so entangled and so deeply tragic that I am inclined to look upon this young human wreck more as a concrete symbol of the total lack of meaning of war and persecution than as a "psychiatric compensation problem."

Among the Isr. neur. gr. were 20 patients with neuroses easily explained by current conditions. The possibility that internment in concentration camps changed the tendency of the patient's reactions was considered, but the conclusion was that the neuroses of these patients must be regarded, on the whole, as independent of war experiences. In 13 of the 18 patients with organic psychosyndrome, there was an indubitable connection between war injuries and the present conditions, while another origin was found in five only.

As many as 54, or more than half of the Isr. neur. gr. suffer from conditions which cannot be classified according to the usual clinical diagnostic criteria. Disturbed sleep, anxiety phenomena, and depressive moodiness are among the most significant and most frequent symptoms in this group, but none of these symptoms have the same value as in ordinary psychiatric disorders. I have concluded as have others (9-12), that we face very deep-rooted changes which have affected the whole personality without being able to designate any specific area of predominant injury. Even very lengthy and intense psychotherapy has not been able to bring about any real improvement in these tragic changes of personality.

Discussion

Strauss (13) has called these conditions Entwurzlungsdepressionen (depression of uprooting) thereby suggesting that the central pathogenesis is the absolute break, the patient being deprived of contact with the family, environment, and homeland. If this opinion is correct, the same disorders should be presented by other refugees from Europe. In Israel (and probably also the USA) there are many who came before the war from the same environment as the concentration camp survivors. Their families were also murdered and their homes ruined. None of the Israeli psychiatrists I consulted reported any immigrant to Israel who had not been in a concentration camp who showed symptoms similar to those described above.

Indeed they reacted with depression, moodiness, and sorrow, when they realized in 1945, the full extent of the disaster, and that their families were exterminated. These natural reactions disappeared as was expected after a relatively short time.

The chronic state of hopelessness — Strauss's Entwurzlungsdepression — appear then only in those patients exposed to the stress situations of the concentration camp, injurious both mentally and physically.

Both Kolle's "break in the life line" and, especailly Venzlaff's erlebnisbedingter Persönlichkeitswandel are more appropriate expressions for the material presented, although they describe very little of the actual origin. Elucidation of this question is difficult, when we consider how complex are the causal conditions both from a mental and physical point of view. All of the 54 patients had suffered from severe illnesses during their internment, more than a third had had spotted fever and more than half had reached the "living corpse" stage. With two exceptions, all had lost relatives and friends and were practically alone in the world. In more than half, psychiatric symptoms suggested organic cerebral disorders. Because confirmation by neurological electro- and pneumoencephalographic and psychological examination is lacking, it is unnecessary to consider the purely organic origin of these conditions. The physical and mental persecutions and injuries suffered should produce total changes of personality, without our being able to point to the specific predisposing, or causal pathogenetic factor element.

This view is strongly supported by another cooperative investigation in which the material consisted of case studies of several hundred survivors of the Nazi holocaust in Europe in Talbieh Hospital, Jerusalem (14).

In the Isr. work gr. there were only three symptom-free individuals, a remarkably few for an active working group in this age distribution. There was one case of manic-depressive psychosis, and in seven others there were conditions, other than captivity, which could explain the psychiatric findings. Two had typical compulsion neuroses clearly precipitated by war experiences, and more than two-thirds of the whole group presented psychiatric changes which strongly suggest the conditions in the Isr. neur. gr. About half of these were relatively mild symptoms and the others more serious. An exact comparison between these sub-groups showed differences in two respects only, serious weight loss down to the "living corpse" stage and complete isolation after the war. The question how these troubled people can function in such a demanding community as a kibbutz is very relevant. The secure social and interpersonal conditions may allow them to function on a satisfactory social level.

Another explanation is that owing to the relative youth of the group impairment of mental faculties is overcome more ably. Thus, members of the Norw. team gr. compensated for their initial impairment symptoms during the first years after the war, but serious changes were revealed later.

If it is true that with good premorbid equipment one is more likely to come through serious stress situations unharmed, it may be presumed that the Norw. team gr. and the Norw. work gr. were well armed to meet the stress of war. All three Israeli groups — apart from, or because of, their youth (still an unsolved problem) — should have been equally well armed and prepared, while the Norw. clin. gr. should have had the least chance of resisting a serious traumatic situations, and since there was no basic difference between this group and e.g., the Norw. team gr. (which suffered the most), it is probable that the premorbid personality is of less significance in estimating the severity of the trauma we are dealing with here, and that, in the first place, it is the degree and duration of the traumata which are decisive for the tragic final results.

Conclusions

In drawing conclusions we must remember that concentration camp survivors cannot be compared with any other patients hitherto described in psychiatric literature. Throughout the whole history of the human race there have been wars and the victorious annihilated the conquered. Slavery has also existed in various forms throughout the ages. Hitler's Germany was not the first to use slave camps to break down the enemy's will to fight. But Hitler's regime was the first to apply the finesses of modern technique to carefully planned destruction of both the individual and the group, while well-planned propaganda techniques were used to hide the murderers.

There are, however, two aspects in connection with concentration camp survivors which are unique. One, that this is the first opportunity to examine on a large scale, people sentenced to death, in whom the slow but efficacious execution of these sentences was in progress, but was interrupted by cessation of war. The other, which applies exclusively to the Israeli groups studied — is that while the individual was subjected to "slow execution," both his family and background environment were destroyed. The few who survived were not only subjected to severe immediate psychophysical traumata, but they were later — absolutely without any form of anchorage in the world.

The first factor distinguishes concentration camp survivors from all hitherto described groups of persons who may possibly have been exposed to extreme situations, while the seond makes it impossible to compare Jewish concentration camp survivors with any other group, unless this existential and essential factor of isolation is taken into account. The further conclusions must also be considered from this point of view.

The so-called concentration camp syndrome with the symptomatology described earlier, seems to be correlated mainly with mechanical or toxic trauma to the brain, or both. This investigation thus supports the theory that this syndrome is of organic origin. At every examination of concentration camp survivors, a detailed history and a thorough neurological psychiatric and psychological evaluation should be made to detect the organic psychosyndrome. The absence of this syndrome does not exclude the possibility that prolonged and deep mental traumata may have caused irreversible personality changes. The symptomatology of these personality changes varies considerably, and may resemble the organic psychosyndrome.

People of average mentality are capable of carrying on despite mental stress situations which may not affect their mental health to any great extent, provided that their personal and environmental anchorage is kept intact, and that the stress situations do not persist for too long.

Premorbid deviations appear to play a certain part in the development and maintenance of both endogenous and especially of reactive psychoses, but serious somatic and special forms of mental stress seem to have an equally great significance in the manifestation of reactive psychoses.

Organic brain disease can often be traced back to the effect of interrogations and hard labor, and also to frequent infectious diseases together with malnutrition and famine edema. Parallels drawn between these injuries and "ordinary" head injuries in civil life are of little value. Both the pretraumatic state of the brain (usually altered by famine edema) and the hopeless post-traumatic situation, makes comparison almost meaningless. The premorbid personality plays a smaller role in the development of chronic neurotic conditions than we at first supposed, in any case smaller than the sum of the psychosomatic traumata to which the prisoner was exposed.

In the Norwegian groups, which have formed the background for the conclusions presented hitherto, it was possible to distinguish between the various traumata up to a point, and to correlate them with the permanent injurious effects revealed. In contrast with this, in the Israeli groups the traumatic effects were not only much more intense, but more complex and involved, for which reason the psychological and somatic aspects of the traumatic effects are completely inseparable. This is also shown clearly in the illnesses demonstrated.

This complex psychological traumatization by internment of young people seems to be a far more important contributory cause of schizophrenic psychoses than is generally supposed. The same applies even more so to the chronic reactive psychoses. The opinion that these psychoses "will pass" when the precipitating agent has disappeared, finds little support in the present investigation.

The most predominant sequel to the concentration camp captivity seems to be the deep wrought personality change, a mental disability which affects every side of the psychic life, the intellectual functions and, especially, emotional life and the life of the will, involving difficulties of adjustment and consequent complications. The most characteristic symptoms of this condition include chronic anxiety states, with nightmares, sleeplessness, disturbing day time thought associations and memories, by chronic depression, inability to enjoy anything, to laugh with others, to establish adequate interpersonal contacts, to work with pleasure, to fill a position – in short, inability to live in a normal way. Its different components may not be apparent, but a reliable history and a thorough examination will usually reveal the condition. The present investigation could not reveal with certainty the actual etiology of the condition, but Chapman's (11) and Wolff's (7) investigations of the disturbances of the highest integrative functions seems to confirm our results. Whether there are also definite organic brain changes must be decided by further detailed investigation.

As far as the complexity and difficulty of the problems involved allow, I have tried to support and to prove the different theories stated in this paper in a nearly axiomatic way, in my monograph (15).

One can perhaps also object and say that the problems which are considered here can only have an historical significance. C. G. Jung's opinion that rational culture necessarily runs into irrational destruction of culture has, during the 50 years which have passed since it was formulated, proved to be too true (16). We, therefore, unfortunately have no guarantee that the concentration camp syndrome is a disease of the past.

Collis has published a brief and extremely dispassionate account of his observations a few days after the liberation of the Bergen-Belsen camp (17). This shrewd physician became aware at once of their problems which concern us so much today. "The problem of what to do with these forsaken, almost lost souls is immense, but one which if not tackled and solved will make all our efforts a mere waste of time, for then it were kinder to have let them die than to have brought them back to mere existence and more sufferings in a hostile world, where they no longer have even a hope of being able to compete in the struggle of the survival of the fittest, and must inevitably go down . . ."

These words of Collis contain deep prophetic truth which demands that the responsible authorities and physicians shall succor these forsaken lost souls.

Origin of Contributions and References: See Page 337

MENTAL DISEASES AMONG REFUGEES IN NORWAY AFTER WORLD WAR II

L. Eitinger
Norway

The aim of this investigation, which was concluded in 1956/57, was to examine the psychiatric diseases among the refugees who remained in or came to Norway after World War II. (Refugees who came to Norway before World War II are not included.) It has generally been observed that there is a higher incidence of mental disturbances among refugees, and an attempt is made to shed light on this question. The author has also tried to find out the possible pathogenic factors which might have an influence on the incidence of the different diagnostic groups and on some especially outstanding specific symptoms he found among refugee patients.

In order to place the present material in its correct perspective, the general post-war refugee problems are discussed, the quantitative importance of the tasks included is shown, and the various international conventions which were established after the war for solving these problems and tasks are briefly described, (Kornrumpf, 1954, Murphy, 1955).

Norway with a population of about 3.5 million had at the end of World War II a refugee population of about 140,000, most of them forced laborers from Poland, Russia and Yugoslavia. Most of them returned to their homelands, but some of them refused to go back, preferring to stay as refugees in Norway, partly for political, but mostly for personal reasons. In addition to this group which remained, Norway accepted refugees from the DP-camps in Germany. Only a few were accepted according to their working ability and skill; the Norwegian government had concentrated mostly on so called "minus" or "hard core" refugees, i.e. refugees who were disabled in one way or another and therefore had been rejected by screening-commissions from many other countries and thus, to all appearances, being doomed to spend the rest of their lives in a DP-camp.

Eitinger stresses very strongly *the difference between an emigrant and a refugee.* The first one has a free choice, which means many possibilities of motivation, the premorbid personality, the reaction pattern, etc. are thus of great importance. A refugee has no choice, he has to leave his country because his freedom or life is in danger and he has to go to any country willing to accept him.

All the other factors are practically of no importance. It is, however, striking that the psychiatric literature on this topic is so scarce, with the exception of the important studies of *Murphy* (1955) and *Maria Pfister-Ammende* (1955).

The material on which the study is based comprises all post-war refugees who have been treated in Norwegian psychiatric institutions. The patients were found by tracing the Norwegian Central Register (containing the names and principal information of all patients admitted to Norwegian psychiatric hospitals and departments) and by individual inquiry from all the hospitals about any patients who were born outside Norway. From this rather comprehensive material the refugees were traced. Furthermore the files of the Norwegian refugee organizations were checked and only in one case was found the name of a psychotic patient which was missing in the material. (It was a paranoid woman who had returned to her homeland, convinced that everybody in Norway wanted to kill her.) Apart from this one patient, the material regarding psychotic and neurotic refugee patients hospitalized in Norway from January 1st 1946 to December 31st 1955 must be considered as complete.

The neurotic outpatients dealt with in this study are, however, not a representative sample. They consist only of the patients examined at the psychiatric outpatient clinic of the Oslo University Hospital and finally outpatients treated by the author personally. Neurotic patients treated by other doctors could not be included in the material. (The refugees who had been under forensic psychiatric observation are also dealt with in the material presented.)

After studying the case histories of all the patients included in the material, those who at the time of the investigation were still in Norway, had been personally examined by the author, either in the mental hospitals where they were patients or in their homes. In all patients one met an initial suspicion, which in most cases did not disappear until the author had disclosed his own background as a former refugee and concentration camp survivor.

In addition to the medical investigation, the patients' files at the different refugee organizations, at the police departments and at the Aliens Registration Office were examined in order to get as much as possible of "objective" information.

There were two different control groups. The first one is a Norwegian matched group selected among the patients of the Oslo University Hospital's psychiatric department and consists of the same amount of Norwegian patients, of the same sex and the same age groups, admitted at the same time as the refugees with the same diagnoses.

The second control group, which rather should be called a "background group" is an "average refugee transport" selected by the same lines as most of the other "transports" of refugees brought to Norway and examined in toto personally (by the author). Here again all the objective sources, files and police reports were checked. (In addition a prognosis for adaptability was made and controlled after about one year's stay in Norway).

The pathological material consists of 95 patients, i.e., 60 psychotics (50 men and 10 women) and 35 non-psychotic patients (26 men and 9 women). The distribution of sex and age in this material differs greatly from the distribution found in other groups of psychiatric patients. The ratio neurosis/psychosis is the same for all nations and religions except for Jews and Czechoslovaks, where one finds relatively more neuroses.

Fifty per cent of the refugee patients had only attended primary schools, and more than 40 per cent had not even this minimal education. The Poles and Russians had the lowest level of education. Compared with the Norwegian controls, the refugee patients' level of education was far below average. The same applied also for the socio-economic state. This was furthermore stressed by the fact that 56 out of the 90 patients were unskilled laborers and only 45 were in regular work at the time they were uprooted. Twenty-three were uprooted at the very beginning of the war in 1939 and 24 emigrated only after the end of World War II. Not less than 90 had been in different camps before their arrival in Norway (16 in concentration camps, 48 in forced labor camps, 7 in prisoner-of-war camps) and all the 90 later on in DP camps.

More than two thirds of the refugee patients were without any contact with their families or anyone else in their homeland.

It was suggested that "positive" motivation, expectations of the new country, readiness to make sacrifices and efforts to cooperate in the integration differed according to the reasons for emigration and uprooting. These were divided into 3 groups: "individual-political" (only 3 men belonged to this group), "race and collective political" (69 of the patients belonged to this group) and finally "accidental, non-political" (21 patients belonged to this group). Even if the figures seem to indicate that the "positive motivation" present in the "individual-political" group was leading to fewer psychiatric complications, no conclusion can be drawn since there are no adequate figures available concerning the whole refugee population and the reasons for their uprooting. The same reasoning can be applied to the knowledge of the Norwegian language as being indicative of adaptability and desire to cooperate and integrate. Thirty-two of the refugee patients had practically no knowledge of Norwegian, 51 had very little and the remaining 12 were either good or fluent.

The civil status at the outbreak of the disease showed that 44 patients were unmarried, 10 divorced and 12 married several times. Only 34 were married to a partner of the same nation, 10 to Norwegians and 7 to partners from other nations. Of the 51 married, 14 men had wives in their homelands, 4 did not know anything about the residence of their partners. While the overall ratio married/unmarried is about the same for the refugee patients and the Norwegian controls, the number of divorced, widowed and those married several times, is nearly three times as high as among the latter (28 to 11).

Anamnestically "pure somatic" diseases were found in 53 cases and psychosomatic diseases in 34 cases. Premorbid character traits which could point in a paranoid direction were detected in 24 patients.

At the outbreak of the actual illness the patients were remarkably often brought to the psychiatrist by their working comrades or by the social workers of the different relief organizations. More than two-thirds of the psychotic refugees were admitted during the first three months of their illness, while the same number of Norwegian controls had to wait more than half a year from the first symptoms until they were admitted to the hospital. While 20 out of 60 refugee patients were admitted during the first 6 weeks of actual illness, only one Norwegian patient reached the hospital as quickly. One quarter of the Norwegian patients were treated and kept at home for more than a year before the family finally decided to make an application for admittance. The environments' threshold of tolerance towards refugees seemed to be much lower than towards Norwegian patients. On the other hand this means that the psychotic refugee patients were better off with regard to earlier treatment. (There was, however, no difference concerning the neurotic patients.) A relatively high number of refugee patients had to be transferred to the "maximum security wards" of a mental hospital for "extremely difficult" patients. This is explained by the linguistic isolation, the perplexity and the lack of adaptability even in the ordinary mental hospital. These difficulties are also reflected by the fact that the refugee patients remained mush longer in the mental hospitals than the controls, but the results of the treatment, assessed at the time of release from the hospital are about the same for both Norwegian controls and refugees. (Ødegard, 1956)

> To clarify the number of refugees in Norway during the observation period was no easy undertaking. Several reasons for this were the chaotic circumstances immediately after the war, the lack of detailed records of the forced laborers refusing to return to the country of their origin, the absence of special registers for refugees (until 1951), etc. The author perused therefore the archives of all governmental institutions which had worked with refugee organizations, and finally all the "transport-lists" available.

By adding up all the actual numerical information available, one finally arrived at an "average population" of 1879 persons, of whom 60 became psychotic during the observation period, i.e. 3.19 per cent (males 3.53 percent, females 2.16 per cent). This frequency is about five times higher than could be expected compared with a matched Norwegian population. (For schizophrenias less than 5 times higher, for reactive psychoses nearly 10 times higher.) Of the possible "general reasons" for the higher incidence of psychoses among the refugee patients are mentioned their lower educational and socio-economic status, and the fact that they belonged to occupations with lower standards of practical and theoretical training than the Norwegian controls.

The author has also tried to find out more "specific reasons" and has concerned himself to a large degree with *the question of isolation*. The term "isolation" is used in very different meanings in the psychiatric literature. The "Verkehrspsychosen" and the psychoses of the deaf expounded by Kraepelin (1899) are among the first manifestations described. The difference between isolation in a patient's own, old, familiar milieu and in a new strange milieu is, however, stressed. Isolation in a familiar milieu results in a lack of stimuli and may by misinterpretation of sensory impressions lead to paranoid thinking (in persons who have a disposition to this reaction type). Isolation in a quite strange environment (be it either linguistic, national, social, etc.) will lead to an abundance of, an "over-flowing" of stimuli. The personality is literally flooded with outside impressions which will have a threatening effect on an individual who is threat-oriented. The motley multiplicity of these impressions which appeal to every sense and degree of experience will demand such great adaptability that individuals less well equipped intellectually or affectively will not be able to resist this flood of outside stimuli and impressions: they will react pathologically to it. The quantity of stimuli is so great that a "corrective and modifying effect" (Cameron 1943) on an individual's behavior cannot come into action. An "interchange" of experiences is out of question in such a quantitatively oblique relationship as confronts a person isolated in a strange milieu. This again will result in a feeling of insecurity as well as a projection of this insecurity to the surroundings. The overwhelming impressions cannot be absorbed and "digested," and a breakdown of the total personality will be the result. This theory is supported by the sociological studies on role-taking and on the importance of group-formation for the development of personality. Furthermore it is shown that an individual normally does not constantly receive new stimuli from his surroundings to which in one way or other he must adjust.

> The majority of our everyday reactions occur without our reflecting upon them. The mechanism in our psyche can easily be compared with the "automation" which characterizes a part of our physiological existence. We walk, stop, move in the traffic and go on without thinking about the mechanism of our actions. A good car-driver reacts "automatically" to all traffic obstacles without thinking of putting the brakes on, changing gears and so on. If — instead of reacting mechanically — we were to "let all stimuli into the brain", examine them carefully, consider the reactions and then finally perform them, our lives would become considerably more difficult. Thus this sort of mechanizing and automation seems to be a relieving and protective mechanism both with regard to mental and physical reactions.

In isolated refugees the manifold of external impressions do not create any feeling of solidarity, of an understanding of the situation or of the inner meaning of the impressions, and first and foremost, no understanding of the individual's position in the whole of this unknown and overwhelming system. It is precisely this lack of ability to receive, to understand, to develop and to react to the surroundings which causes this apparent but nontheless very familiar paradox of feeling isolated, as being totally alone as Lilly's (1955) experimental persons in the water tank, while one is actually surrounded by masses of talking, laughing, active fellow-beings, be it on Karl Johan street in Oslo, on Picadilly Circus in London or on Fifth Avenue in New York. This "overflowing" of "undigested" stimuli in complete isolation combined with feelings of insecurity results clinically in confusional and persecutoric-paranoid psychotic pictures.

There might also be other reasons specific for refugees, explaining the high incidence of psychoses. Most of the refugees came from part of Europe where the question of national ethnic majority or minority always has been of the greatest importance in the consciousness of each person who has grown up there. This will reflect upon the feeling of insecurity in a strange national milieu such as the Norwegian one (Bernstein 1959). The difference in religion (almost all the refugees were either Catholics or Jews, all the Norwegians Protestants) seemed to be of pathoplastical influence in Jewish refugees only. The very serious persecution these refugees had been subjected to because of their "race" seemed to be sufficient explanation (Cohen 1954; Bakis 1955).

Furthermore all the patients had spent some years in different camps. It is well known that these have had a devastating influence on their inmates, lowering of physical and psychic power of resistance in the concentration camps, demoralization and resignation in the DP-camps.

Finally, the period of establishment is not without its difficult problems. (Hoffmeyer & Wulff, 1952) The experiences of the individual refugee are determined not so much by the "official" attitude as displayed by the government and in friendly articles in the newspapers, but much more by personal events, small competitions in the workshops and the like. Economic dependency and restrictive laws concerning all foreigners are also important factors augmenting the inner insecurity and thus the tendency to psychotic paranoid reactions.

The *diagnostication* followed the usual Scandinavian criteria. (Langfeldt, 1954). According to these 14 patients with *schizophrenia* were found. The symptomatology was at first tainted by the prevailing situation, but in the course of the disease the typical schizophrenic symptoms broke through and dominated the picture. The therapeutic results in the schizophrenic patients were very bad (NB – Before ataraxica-period), but this must be expected considering the overwhelming difficulties of interpersonal relationships, lack of acceptance in the foreign milieu and unsatisfactory care of the patients after discharge from the mental hospitals.

There were no manic-melancholic psychoses and no psychoses in idiots and imbeciles represented in the material. It is supposed that patients with manic or melancholic exacerbations scarcely had a chance to come through a camp alive during the war. Their behavior – manic or melancholic – would never be understood and would lead to punishment with fatal results. The same explanation is valid – mutatis mutandis – also for idiots and imbeciles. There were 4 psychoses in patients with an organic brain syndrome. (One of these was probably a chronic brain atrophic state caused by ill treatment in the concentration camp – added later.)

The diagnosis "psychosis reactiva" was used in patients where the psychotic states were neither typical schizophrenic nor manic-melancholic, and no organic traits could be found. This group consisted of 42 patients (32 men and 10 women) and thus showed an incidence nearly 10 times as high as could be expected in the average Norwegian population. Also relatively, i.e. in proportion to other psychoses, the reactive psychoses among refugees show a higher incidence than in average materials published in Scandinavian publications where this diagnosis is used.

More than 40 per cent of the patients with reactive psychoses fell ill during the first year and about two-thirds of the total during the first three years after the end of the war (or the refugees' arrival in Norway). Three patients had had psychotic reactions before the actual exacerbation in Norway and 5 had shown an extremely labile personality structure. In these patients the stress of the milieu had a releasing influence, but considering the background of the personalities mentioned, they hardly can be considered as causal. In the other 34 patients the actual difficulties of their life situation, the experiences of the war and the postwar period could be traced as rather obvious causal factors. (Several case histories have been used to demonstrate these facts.) In patients who became psychotic after a longer period than 3 years, it was possible to trace the difficulties of the immigrant-situation as decisive for the outbreak of the psychosis in only half of the cases. It thus seemed that the difficulties during the first three years of the "root-taking"-period are experienced as especially severe and traumatizing and the social and mental-hygienic arrangements for refugees in this space of time thus seem to be of the greatest importance. – The therapeutic results at the follow-up investigation were about the same for the refugee patients as for the Norwegian controls.

In addition to the "more classical diagnoses" also some special syndromes were investigated. Among the 60 refugee-psychoses 52 cases of paranoid psychoses were found, among the Norwegian controls 28 cases only. The distribution of the *persecutory* paranoid symptoms was even more remarkable. While 9 "refugee schizophrenias" had persecutory paranoid ideas, only 3 Norwegian schizophrenia patients showed corresponding persecutory delusions. Among the 42 refugee patients with reactive psychoses 22 showed persecutory delusions with only 3 Norwegian controls. In addition there were 2 persecutory paranoid patients among the 4 patients with organo-genic psychoses (none among the Norwegian controls). The case-histories showed that the *feeling of insecurity* was a common trait in the genesis of the paranoid delusions of different grades, the trait that instils the individual with doubt regarding his relationship with his surroundings and which, with the help of projection, leads to the delusion that the surroundings are hostile.

In schizophrenic patients the paranoid delusions often started the illness, but in the course of the disease they turned out to be of secondary importance only. Feelings of inferiority towards Norwegian girls (wives) also formed the base on which paranoid delusions grew in persons with that disposition. Organic inferiority (in the material presented, especially blindness because of a transport of 55 blind refugees) was also a starting point for persecutory delusions, just like other situations which strongly stressed the insecurity and isolation of the refugees.

In addition to these rather "indirect" pathogenetic mechanisms for persecutory delusions, also more "direct" ones were taken into consideration, having their origin in the political situation with its possible actual persecutions, "shadowing" by political opponents and so on. Relatively peripheral happenings might be releasing factors for a paranoid reaction.

The symptoms which quantitatively followed paranoid reactions were complaints about somatic disorders. (Other authors as *Tyhurst* (1951), *Pfister-Ammende* (1955) and *Bibering* (1951) had made the same findings.) Conversion symptoms occurred in 45 cases, i.e. in nearly half of all cases, among the Norwegian controls in 19 cases only. Three possible pathogenetic factors were considered: somatic preoccupation, primitive reactions and finally feelings of insecurity, the latter one appearing to be the most important and predominant pathogenetic factor. Somatic sensations and complaints were "understandable, acceptable" and "safe" to talk about and could thus be communicated without the patients "risking" too much, while their psychic symptoms were considered rather difficult to understand and therefore "unsafe" to communicate.

Disturbances of consciousness occurred in 14 cases out of the 42 patients with reactive psychoses in the refugee-patients and in only one of the Norwegian controls. The pathogenesis is explained by the fact that the amount of stimuli exceeded the abilities of the individual to "digest" them and caused a failure in the basic adaptation, a "break-down of the personality," i.e. a confusional state.

Finally, jealousy reactions occurred in the refugee-patients in 10 cases as against none in the Norwegian controls. Eight of them were married or engaged to a partner of another nation. It was shown that jealousy reactions were expressions of general insecurity feelings which the refugees had towards their Norwegian partners.

The non-psychotic patients of the actual material cannot be considered as representative for the incidence of non-psychotic psychiatric diseases among refugees. Conversion neuroses occurred in more than half, and depressive neuroses in a third of all cases, while compulsion – and anxiety neuroses were not represented. Nearly all the former mentioned neuroses manifested themselves in the first two years after the refugees' arrival in Norway (or after the end of the war) and this finding demonstrated again the importance of an adequate handling of the refugees in the beginning of the settlement-period in a new country. The very good therapeutic results indicated that these cases were mainly caused by the actual situation and an improvement could be obtained by a change of this.

It was suggested that patients with more serious character-deviations reacted with deeper, i.e., psychotic disturbances to the severe stresses of refugee life. This suggestion would also explain both the large amount of reactive psychotic states and the relatively few neurotic reactions rooted in deeper personal deviations.

The earlier mentioned *transport of "hard-core" refugees* – who should serve as a "background" material and who were subjected to a detailed personal clinical and social psychiatric investigation – consisted of 44 persons (29 men and 15 women) over 15 years old and was composed mainly of Polish and Czechoslovak refugees. They have been screened according to the same lines as Norwegian screening commissions had used in earlier refugee transports. All of them were so called "minum" or "hard-core" DP-camp inmates; Norway was for most of them the last chance after they had been refused by several commissions from many countries. A few had already tried emigration to other countries, but without being able to adapt themselves there. The persons examined had thus very varied and extremely dramatic and often tragic life histories, even when merely compared with other war- and camp survivors. They had a number of somatic and psychic disturbances (31 and 26 cases respectively out of the 44 examined), their expectations and the degree of understanding of the difficulties to come and of their possible solution were in more than half of the cases rather unsatisfactory or even completely unrealistic.

Based on the anamnestical information, on all the available files and reports, on the clinical and social psychiatric investigations, a prognosis regarding the further adaptation for each person examined was attempted. Nineteen (14 men and 5 women) were assumed to be able to adapt themselves relatively quickly in Norwegian industrial life, leading a socially satisfactory existence without burdening the refugee organizations with their problems to any great extent. Eighteen (11 + 7) were assumed to need the help of an organization for some time and in many different ways, without being capable of solving their own problems to any great extent, and 7 (4 + 3) were assumed to have such difficulties of adaptation as would lead to psychiatric or serious social complications. The prognoses were reviewed one year later and showed that they have been "too good," only 75 per cent of the prediction having been correct. The social adaptation of married women appeared to a very large extent to be dependent on that of their husbands, much more than on their own capabilities.

A direct comparison between the transport described above and the patient in the actual material can hardly be considered as quite correct. However, some important findings seem to be common and some general factors can be pointed to:

A remarkable fact is the large number of psychic symptoms, complaints and disturbances. The number of somatic complaints is, of course, also large, and the Norwegian authorities responsible have done a great deal to clarify and treat these disorders; but little attention has been paid to possible psychic disturbances. This is, unfortunately, almost typical of our community. This fact is of special interest in connection with the refugees. The refugee organizations have never employed psychiatric experts in the screening of applicants for emigration. Nor have psychiatrists been consulted with regard to the general treatment of newcomers. It is true that extremely disturbed and disturbing patients, and later also patients with neurotic difficulties, have been referred for psychiatric examination and treatment, but the many cases which are not revealed in manifest disturbances remained undiscovered and untreated. During interviews with organization officers, social workers, and consultants, one always met the greatest readiness to co-operate and a genuine regret that so little psychiatric assistance was provided in refugee work. The reasons for this are partly the general lack of psychiatrists, but also — and this should be emphasized — because of a somewhat inadequate estimation of the importance of psychic factors in the problems which arise in connection with the adaptation of refugees, in spite of the apparent understanding shown by the organizations. The few sparse attempts at obtaining psychiatric assistance have been made because of actual difficulties, and not because of a general assessment of the situation. It may perhaps be considered a "consolation" that in this respect the refugees are no worse off than Norwegian citizens; but the greater need, the variety and frequency of the problems, reduce this form of "consolation" to less than a pious self-delusion.

In this connection it is perhaps correct to look closer at the "forming of the prognosis" in the "transport" -population. The question of prognosis is of importance only when seen in relation to what one expects from the immigrants in Norway. There is usually no actual formulation of these expectations; but, on the basis of informal conversations with social workers and consultants, we can say that the least we expect of a newly arrived refugee is that he will be able to manage by himself, financially and socially, as soon as the first starting difficulties have been overcome. By these "first starting difficulties" we mean work and housing. These minimal expectations also include the supposition that the newcomer will submit to the laws of the country and feel so much social responsibility that she or he will undertake the same duties as every Norwegian citizen in the common life (at the place of work, in apartment houses and so on). On the basis of these – perhaps vaguely formulated – suppositions, alcoholics, quarrelsome psychopaths and chronic psychotics will in all probability be rejected by Norwegian screening commissions.

By the investigation of the transport, one psychotic and one alcoholic psychopath were revealed, as well as 2 men with such a mistaken estimation of their own capacity and possibilities that one could immediately foresee serious difficulties in the process of their adaptation. According to the conditions in force, the first 2 should have been rejected, the other 2 accepted with reservations – that is, one should be aware of the special problems they would later present. Anamnestically, further information was obtained about the use of alcohol in 3 other cases. In spite of this, a relatively good prognosis was expected, but the follow-up showed that this was a mistake.

These examples are not mentioned in order to show the superiority of one judgment over another, but only to suggest that with relatively few means one could probably have gained experience which could form a foundation for later selections. The fact mentioned above, that the social adaptation of married women is to a great extent dependent on their husbands' social adaptation, seems also to be of importance in this connection.

Conclusion

To conclude the psychiatric investigation which was undertaken, it may be stated that the refugees who came to Norway showed a great number of psychic symptoms and problems. These made their influence felt in all situations, especially with regard to the placing in occupations, adjustment to environment and so on. The psychic difficulties were far greater than one was inclined to suppose beforehand, and they therefore demanded a greater effort on the part of the refugee organizations than they were able to provide.

Post-war refugees on the whole with the frustrating backgrounds we have described above, and refugees to Norway in "good-will" transports especially, must be said to have a very labile psyche. They can to a certain extent be described in the same manner as those military persons depicted by Hunt et al. (1952) as "marginal psychiatric cases." These individuals can no doubt manage to adapt themselves to the demands of their military service; but they are constantly a heavy burden on the medical, and especially on the psychiatric services, the welfare officers, and on their superior officers. Refugees who came to Norway from German DP camps must be expected to be an "extra burden" of this kind. The numerous difficulties which face welfare services confirm this. Some of these services are perhaps not sufficiently aware of the extraordinary psychological problems presented by the refugees. In any case, the personnel at their disposal is often not adequate to meet the demands which these psychiatric "marginal cases" present, and the high incidence of mental disease among the refugee population finds here one of its explanations.

Origin of Contributions and References: See Page 338

MIGRATION AND THE MAJOR MENTAL DISORDERS: A REAPPRAISAL

H. B. M. Murphy
Canada

The first studies by Ødegaard (21) and by Malzberg (16) of the high mental hospitalization rates of immigrants stimulated three principal theories concerning the interrelationships between migration and mental illness. These are:
1. That certain mental disorders incite their victims to migrate.
2. That the process of migration creates mental stresses which, in turn, precipitate mental disorder in susceptible individuals.
3. That there is a nonessential association between migration and certain other predisposing or precipitating factors, such as age, social class, and culture conflict.

Later, when the spotlight shifted from external to internal migration, and similar high mental hospitalization rates were found for the internal migrants (17, 12), there was a tendency to regard the stresses of migrational experience as the most likely explanation, with selection playing a secondary role. The matter cannot be regarded as settled, however, and it is appropriate to seek some reassurance that we are not pursuing a phantom; reassurance, that is to say, that the gap between migrant and non-migrant rates of mental hospitalization is not due to some quite extraneous factor. This mistake was made once, when immigrants were ascribed a gross excess of mental disorder through neglect to allow for the fact that their population had a quite abnormal age distribution. It seems thus desirable that we examine various other ways in which migrant samples or situations can be aberrant, before assuming that migration and mental disorder are in any way related.

In this paper we will be concerned only with hospitalization data, despite their serious limitations. There are two reasons for this. One is lack of time to do more; the other is that, although there are many better sources from which to study the nature of some sociopsychiatric association, there are no better sources as yet available for examining whether or not such an association exists. The significance of other measures of mental disorder can be debated, but mental hospitalization accompanied by the diagnosis of psychosis is undeniable evidence that such disorder is present. Since the pictures presented are sufficiently similar to suggest a shared pattern, evidence will be reviewed for both foreign-born immigrants and for internal migrants, despite the recognized possibility that different factors may be involved. Data from the United States will be reviewed first, and then some material from other lands.

What are the variables which might both affect mental hospitalization rates and be abnormally distributed in migrant situations? Age is the most obvious, and little more need be said about it here than that its influence is so great that it needs to be controlled in relation to every other combination of variables considered. But there are many other variables with similar if less familiar action. Among these are sex and marital status; social class and the associated factors of occupation, education and income; geographic location and residence; cultural, religious and racial variables; the different types of household and family; and, less easily defined, the various other membership groups to which an individual orients himself. All of these variables have been shown to influence the risk of mental hospitalization; not all, but many, have also been studied in relation to the mental hospitalization rates of migrants. We shall now review the available evidence for these variables.

Residence

Under the term residence are subsumed a number of variables of possible relevance. First, there is the country or state whose data have been analyzed. Is it typical with respect to psychiatric services, legal conditions attending hospitalization, attractiveness for the migrant, etc., or are there special features about it which might affect the rates? Next, there is the question of area within a state. Do migrants congregate especially in urban areas or in rural ones, in localities with good psychiatric services or in localities with poor ones? Then, within cities, there is the question of ecological zone, as Faris, Dunham (7) and their followers have shown. Some parts of some cities appear to yield significantly higher rates of mental hospitalization than others, regardless of the nativity and socio-economic status of their inhabitants, but migrants often collect in such areas. And finally, there is the matter of actual household residence, since single-person households yield higher hospitalization rates than family households and migrants, again, tend to be found in excess in the single-person category.

With respect to state or district of the United States, there was for a time the question of whether New York data, on which the initial studies of internal migration mainly depended, were representative of the country in general. With its relative abundance of psychiatric services and with its metropolitan glamor, it seemed possible that New York would attract from other states both people in search of psychiatric treatment and others whose motives for migration were particularly unrealistic. Two mental health surveys, one in Baltimore in the late 1930's (25) and one in Texas in the early 1950's (9), provided some grounds for doubting the representativeness of the New York material, but comparative data from other states have since become available. Figure 1, derived from the paper by

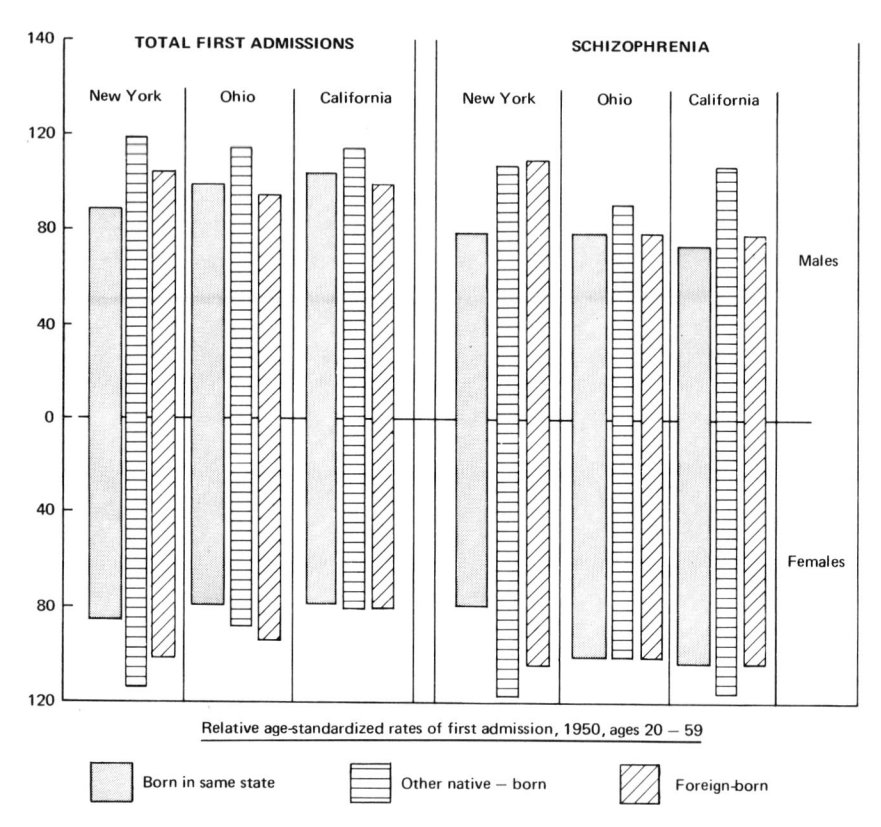

Fig. 1. Comparative incidence of mental hospitalization in the States of New York, Ohio, and California; for schizophrenia and for all first admissions; by sex and nativity status; whites aged 20-59 only (11). NOTE: Rates are relative to the overall first admission rates for each state separately, not to the overall rate for the three states combined. It cannot be deduced from this Figure, therefore, whether age-standardized rate in one state, for any category, exceeds that in another state cited.

(Fig. 1) Lazarus, Locke and Thomas (11), presents relative age-standardized rates for migrants and for non-migrants in New York, Ohio and California. One sees that although an interesting difference appears with respect to schizophrenia, the picture for total white first admissions in Ohio and California is essentially the same as that for total first admissions in New York. That is to say, native-born male migrants have higher age-standardized rates than either the foreign-born or the non-migrants, and the female migrants, whether native or foreign-born, have higher rates than female non-migrants. Since age-specific rates and rates for the non-white population confirm these findings, we can say that the excess of mental disorder in migrants is not a characteristic found in New York alone.

Further, we can say on reasonable grounds that the association is not a characteristic only of large urban centers. In 1948, Lemert published data from

Newberry Hospital in rural upper Michigan showing that the foreign-born had much higher hospitalization rates than the native-born (14). In that study, the question of isolation and culture conflict for immigrants loomed large and age differences were only roughly controlled, but later studies confirmed the finding. Both in Ohio (15) and in New York (17), migrants living in what are called the "non-metropolitan" zones, like migrants living in the "metropolitan" areas, were found to have higher age-standardized rates than non-migrants.

With respect to zones within the metropolitan areas, the picture is also reassuring, though it awaits further study. Faris and Dunham (7) showed that the foreign-born portion of Chicago's population had higher hospitalization rates, both for schizophrenia and probably for hospitalizations generally, than the native-born in most of the eleven ecological areas into which the city was divided. Variations between areas are large enough to be interesting, but the whole subject calls for re-study, preferably with household data included. Nevertheless, the overall picture seems clear.

Sex and Marital Status

Figure 1 indicated clearly that an abnormal sex distribution, alone, was not distorting the picture. Marital status, however, requires brief discussion, since married persons are usually considered to be less mobile than unmarried, and they also have lower mental hospitalization rates.

For a long time there was no analysis of marital status in relation to mental hospitalization and migration. However, Everett Lee has demonstrated that, for New York and for the twenty to fifty-four age range only, marital status has probably little effect on the picture, either for schizophrenia of for total admissions (13). Above the age of fifty-four, it remains possible that marital status might have an effect. Widowhood is more likely to be followed by institutionalization in an old person who has previously migrated than in an old person living in his native community. However, that is of minor relevance to the general problem.

Education, Occupation and Social Class

The next variables are those which one might consider most likely to produce spurious differences between the rates for natives and for migrants within the United States. Immigrants are traditionally lower class, welcomed for the fact that they accept work which the local-born despise or shun. However, with the exception of the moves of Puerto Ricans to the mainland and of southern Negroes to northern cities, internal migrants and more recent immigrants may not follow quite the same tradition. Nevertheless, there is no doubt that mental hospitalization rates are much greater for the lower than for the upper and middle classes.

However, the two attempts which have been made to examine the socio-economic influence on migrants' hospitalization rates indicate that the effect

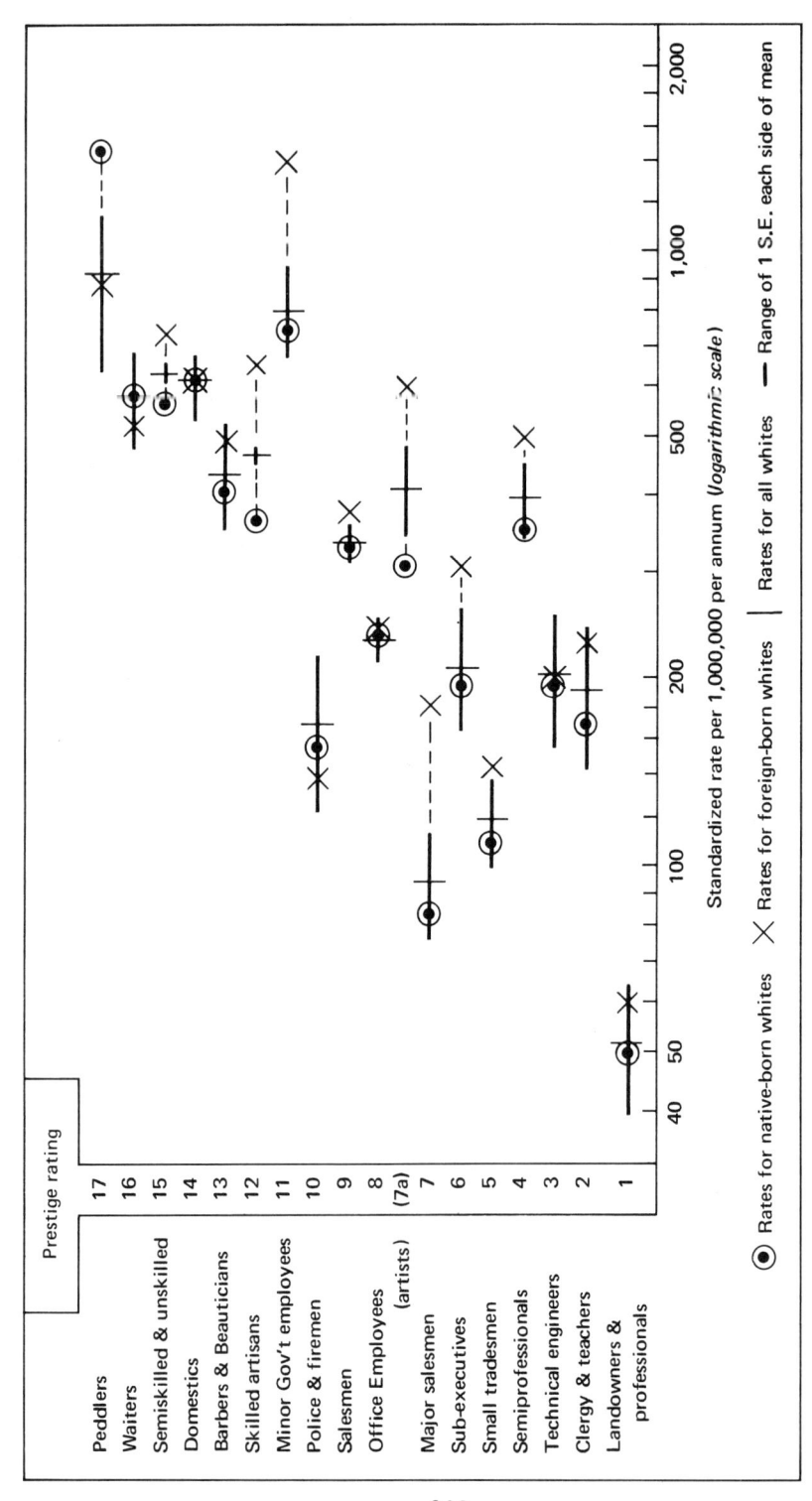

Fig. 2. Foreign-born and native born rates of first admission for schizophrenia; by occupational stratum; males only; Chicago 1922-1934. (Recalculated from Clark (3).)

is much less than might have been expected. The first of these studies, by Clark in Chicago (3), showed that in most occupational categories, age-adjusted rates of schizophrenia for the foreign-born were higher than those for the native-born. (See Figure 2) There were one or two intriguing exceptions to the rule, and the picture is unsatisfactory in that only nativity differentials were studied, and that the data are limited to schizophrenia. But, while the study needs replication, its broad findings do not contradict the general picture.

The second of the studies is the one previously cited by Lee (13). There one finds that standardizing for educational level does reduce the gap between migrant and non-migrant rates, but only slightly. One would expect that use of a more detailed educational scale or more elaborate measure of social status would further reduce the differences but these data make it appear seriously doubtful that they would be entirely eliminated.

Diagnostic Category

The question of diagnosis does not come within the compass of this paper, since the indicator of mental disorder being used here is the fact of hospitalization and not specific constellations of symptoms. Nevertheless, one would like assurance that migrant rates are not inflated by admissions for minor disorders which, in the case of non-migrants, get treated mainly in clinics and private offices.

The categories most susceptible to such adventitious inflation are the neuroses, character disorders, and disorders associated with alcoholism and drug-taking. A simple check on their possible influence can be made, thanks to the work of Lee (12) and Malzberg (18) for New York, by examining the resultant rates after admissions for such disorders have been excluded. For both sexes, it turns out that the age-standardized rates for the within-state born population are significantly lower than for the out-of-state. It can therefore be said that migrant rates are *not* being inflated in the suspected manner.

This answer still does not exclude the possibility that migrants diagnosed as schizophrenic are less seriously ill than non-migrants and it does not deal with the interesting point that in certain diagnostic categories no migration differential appears. These matters, however, lie outside the scope of this paper.

Race and Ethnic or Cultural Group

The foregoing sections practically exhaust the intervening sociological variables for which we have relevant demographic data. There remain those variables which can be regarded either as genetic or as cultural. First, there is the question of race. In the United States, mental hospitalization rates for Negroes are usually much higher than rates for whites and a larger proportion of Negroes in a migrant sample could raise the hospitalization rates for this group. However, nearly all recent studies of migrant hospitalizations tabulate whites and non-whites separately, and demonstrate that migrants have higher rates in each category.

With respect to the proportion of different ethnic or cultural groups within white migrant populations, the more recent studies are silent. Earlier, however, Malzberg (16) had shown that the foreign-born had higher mental hospitalization rates than the native-born, regardless of ethnic or cultural origin, thus indicating that this was not a relevant factor in the external migration picture at least. For internal migration, it remains possible, and still untested, that migrants come especially from ethnic or cultural backgrounds with known high rates of hospitalization — the Irish, for instance. This seems unlikely, however, and we may say, once again, that these extraneous factors do not appear to be able to account for the higher hospitalization rates found in migrant groups.

Consideration of ethnic groups, of course, leads on to the question of group memberships. However, since there are no recent data from the United States on this subject, it is better to drop the point for the moment and to say, in summary, that there is no evidence that the association between migration and mental hospitalization within the United States results from the action of a clearly extraneous factor.

Foreign Data

If the conclusion reached immediately above is valid, the utility of examining foreign hospitalization data may be questioned. Surely it would be more apropos to drop hospital studies, with their limited meaning, and turn to other approaches.

The answer is that there exists a whole important category of variables which the preceding summary did not touch and which at the present time can be reviewed only through hospitalization studies, namely variables relating to the receiving population. The reasons for the omission are simple. It is exceedingly difficult to find within one state or country whole populations of contrasting character with the numbers which the studies require. Moreover, when contrasts are attempted, there is the temptation at the present stage of our work to emphasize the similarities found, not the differences. In the studies reviewed there have been a few indications that different receiving societies might have different effects on the migrant/non-migrant rate differential. Thus, the New York picture differs somewhat from those of Ohio and of California with respect to comparative schizophrenia rates (11). Clark's paper (3) on schizophrenia in Chicago showed that there were a few occupational strata where the expected native/foreign-born difference in rates did not appear. Faris and Dunham (7) showed that there was one type of locality in Chicago where immigrant rates were actually lower than those of the native-born of native parentage. Yet such variations might have arisen by chance and, individually, they provide little basis for argument. However, if a general association between migration and mental health is to be postulated, then it is desirable to demonstrate that the relationship holds regardless of situation. Hence, it is desirable to inquire whether the limited data available, from countries where the receiving population has a different structure or different value systems, are in accord with the picture found in the United States.

As many may know, all overseas findings are *not* in accord with the picture in the United States, Norway offering the most familiar exception. There, continuing the interest in migration that for years made his name so well known, Ødegaard published in 1945 (22) and in 1960 (with Astrup) probably the most detailed analyses of migrant hospitalization rates available to date (1). His data are fully presented elsewhere in this volume but their essential points for this paper can be summarized in Figure 3. One sees there that only for Oslo do migrants have higher rates than natives. For all other parts of the country, people born locally have higher rates than those born elsewhere. Our conclusion at this point, therefore, must be that in Norway migration is associated with raised rates of mental hospitalization only when the migration is to the capital city. Migration to any other area, regardless of origin of the migrant, is associated with lower rates of mental hospitalization than is non-migration for the same area. As in the United States, of course, the measure of migration is not completely accurate since people moving and then returning to their community of birth by the time of the census

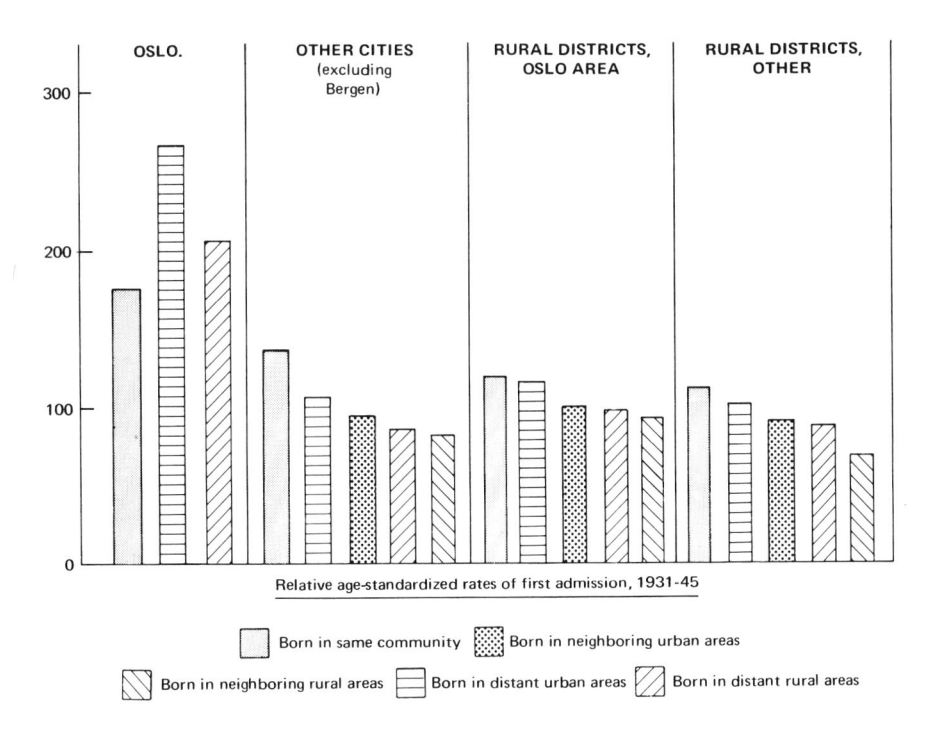

Fig. 3. Incidence of mental hospitalization in Norway; by residential and nativity status; 1931-1945. (From Astrup and Ødegaard (1). See original paper for category definitions.)

are treated as non-migrants. However, this point also is examined by Ødegaard and the impression obtained from the clinical data presented is that remigration is not frequent among mental patients, and therefore, is not likely to have distorted the picture.

The difference between the pictures for Norway and for the United States can lie principally in the characteristics of the migrants, the migrational situation, or in the receiving society. One's first inclination is probably to think of a different selective process at work in Norway from that in the United States, a process which does not negate the general relationship between migration and mental health but which obscures it. However, if this were the case, we should expect to find that Norwegians moving to other lands reflect the same selective influence, and that other peoples moving into Norway do not exhibit it. This is not the case. As was shown thirty-five years ago (21), Norwegian immigrants to the United States had a

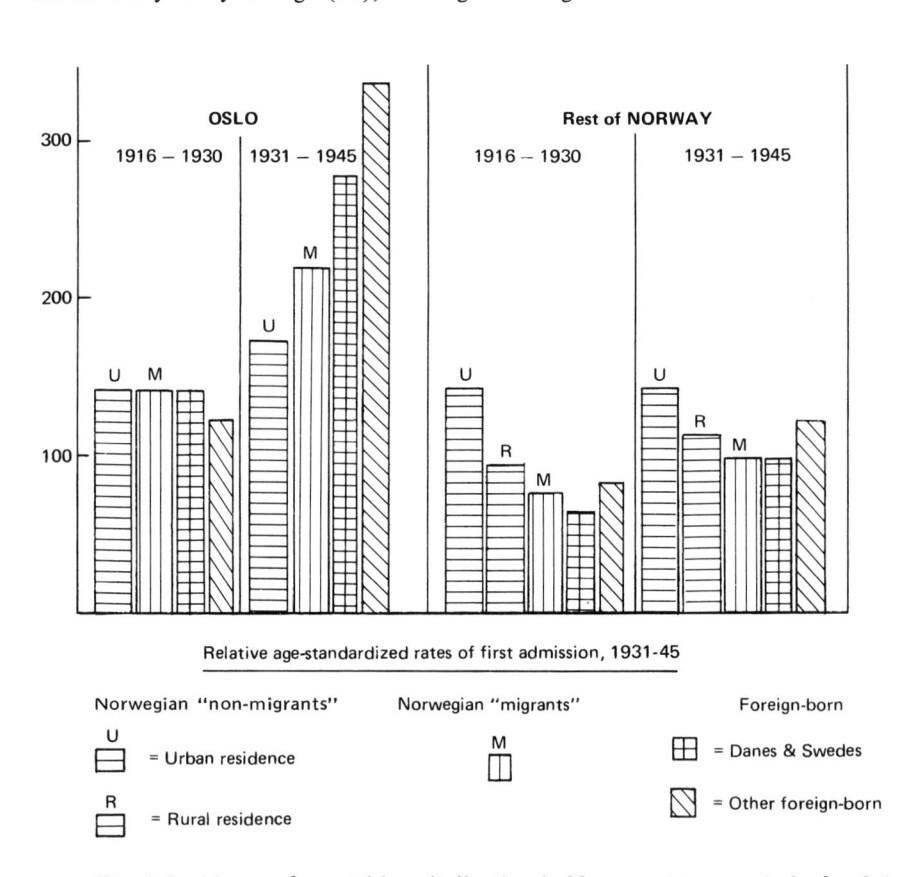

Fig. 4. Incidence of mental hospitalization in Norway at two periods; for Oslo and for rest of Norway; by country and locality of birth. (From Astrup and Ødegaard (1).)

higher rate of mental hospitalization than people in their homeland, and as Astrup and Ødegaard have demonstrated more recently (1), Swedes and Danes moving into the general countryside of Norway have lower age-standardized rates of mental hospitalization than Norwegian non-migrants in the same areas (See Figure 4). Only Oslo exhibits a pattern like that of the United States in place of the more general Norwegian pattern of hospitalization rates. Here the foreign-born rates exceeded those of the local inhabitants in the 1931 to 1945 period; but in the 1916-1930 period even this was not so. Thus, the probable inference to draw from these most interesting figures is that the *receiving* situation in Norway is an important factor, with Oslo diverging from the national norm through its greater urbanization or through its greater cosmopolitanism.

However, that is but one country. What is the picture elsewhere? There is no other country where statistics as satisfactory for our purpose can be obtained, but there are suggestive data from a number of locations. In the Paris region, there seems little doubt that in the 1950's North African immigrants had much higher rates of hospitalization (controlled for age differences) than the general population (4). However, these migrants had a caste position similar to that of the American Negro; they had little education and were in the lower social classes; and they were disturbed by the struggle for independence going on in their homeland. These facts tell us relatively little, therefore, about the influence of migration *per se* on French mental hospitalization rates.

Elsewhere in Europe, studies deal either with abnormal populations or are insignificant in scope or depth. Thus, Eitinger's study of refugee immigrants to Norway (6) and my own of refugees to Britain (19) both show that newcomers have very high rates of mental hospitalization but, in both instances, the migrants were quite emotionally disturbed by loss of country, and in the Norwegian case they were also frequently disabled through blindness or amputation. In Finland, a partial study of internal migration was carried out (10) which, as far as it goes, seems to agree with Ødegaard's Norwegian findings rather than with findings in the United States. Kaila found that the part of the country with the greatest inward migration had the lowest hospitalization rates. However, his approach is too indirect and leaves too many factors unexplored.[1]

When one leaves Europe for Israel, however, one finds better data which yields interesting interpretations. Israel has accepted, since its foundation, Jewish immigrants from all parts of the world, largely irrespective of health. In the earlier years, these were mainly Europeans who suffered heavily during the war; in later years, they were mainly from Asia, Africa and the Near East. The next figure (Figure 5) shows some rates which I was able to calculate concerning them.

---

[1] Later Finnish studies appear to indicate that there is no association between migration to the capital city, Helsinki, and either an excess or deficit of mental hospitalizations. But there are weaknesses in the manner in which the samples were chosen. (See K.W. Karlsson: Migration and mental illness in Helsinki. *Proceedings of the IV World Congress of Psychiatry, Madrid, 1966.* Excerpta Medica Foundation, Amsterdam, 1968. Vol. 3, p. 1479-1481.)

ISRAEL

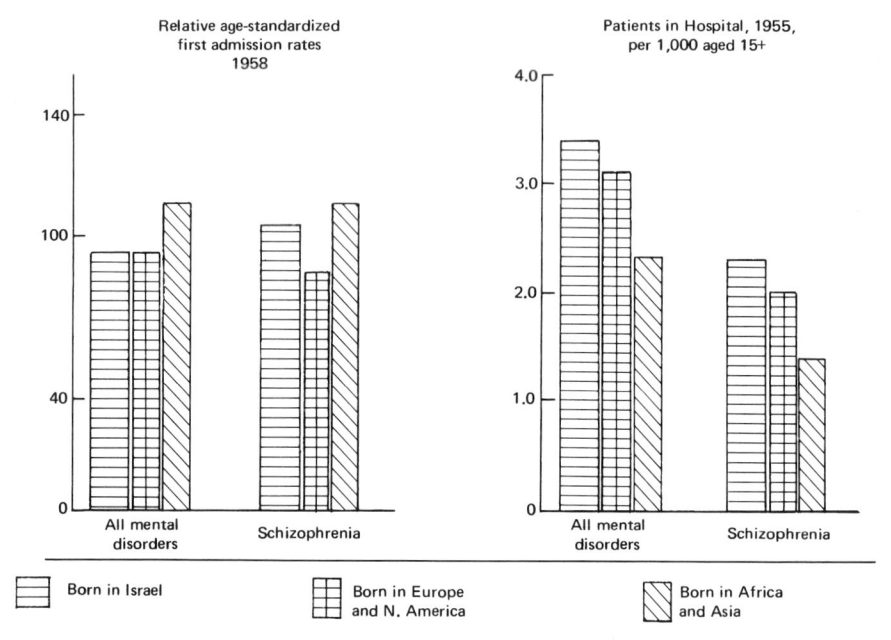

Fig. 5. Incidence and prevalence of hospitalized mental disorders in Israel; by birthplace; for schizophrenic and for all mental disorders. (Calculated from Halevi (8), Sunier (24) and Statistical Abstract of Israel (23).)

Immigrants from Asia and Africa show higher hospitalization rates than the local-born Jew, but one should allow for their having much lower educational and occupational status than the rest of the population, and if this were done the difference might disappear. Immigrants from Europe, who are much closer to the local-born in education and social status, on the other hand, have despite their traumatic war-time experiences no more mental hospitalizations than the local-born (in proportion to their numbers in each age group) and have significantly less schizophrenia. Thus the picture in Israel, as far as it can be gauged, is certainly not in accordance with the findings in the United States.

Searching for an explanation, it seemed possible that the immigrants' mental breakdowns had occurred earlier, in the years immediately after migration. (When I was in Israel in 1950, the authorities expressed some alarm at the amount of mental disorder appearing in the immigrants from the European Displaced Persons camps.) However, for this to be an adequate explanation, one would expect to find that although the hospitalized *incidence* was now low or average, the hospitalized *prevalence*, or number of patients *in* the hospital on a particular day, would be proportionately much higher for the immigrant than for the local-born, which does not appear to be the case. In the second part of Figure 5 are depicted some data collected by Sunier in 1955 (24). The data are not age-standardized apart from the exclusion of children, but they show that the European immigrants had lower prevalence rates than the Israeli-born, even though the former had definitely the higher mean age level.[2] Israel has many peculiarities in its current social situation, however, and might be regarded as too atypical an area from which to generalize.

Conditions in Canada, on the contrary, are very similar to those in the United States, and the Canadian Department of Citizenship and Immigration carried out an analysis of 1958 admissions as a pilot test for a later study.[3] Figure 6 gives some

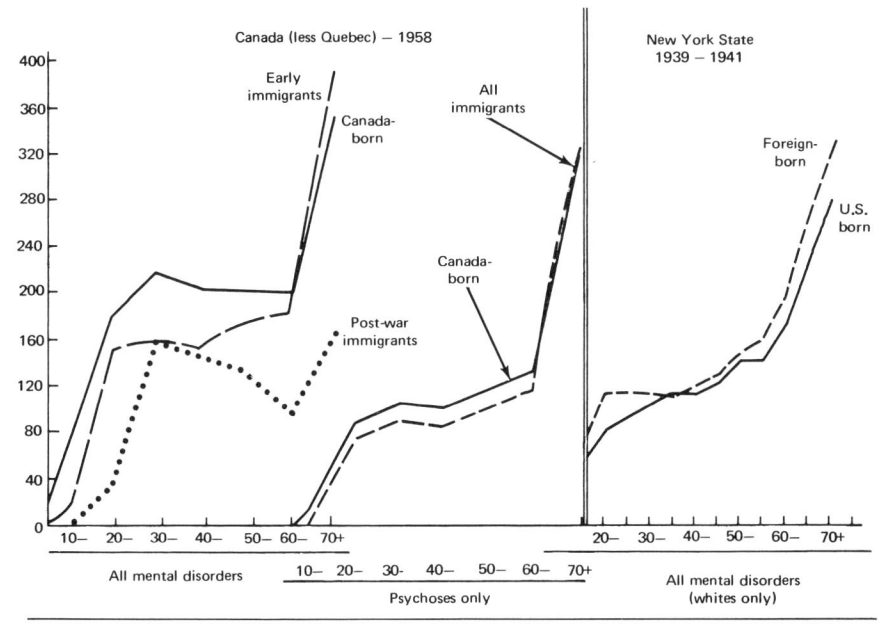

Fig. 6. Incidence of mental hospitalization in Canada, 1958; for Canadian-born and for two groups of immigrants; by age; with comparative curves for psychoses only and for New York State, 1939-1941. (Canadian rates for all Canada except Province of Quebec; morbidity card data only (Footnote** on page 13.) New York data; for whites only, from Malzberg and Lee (17).)

---

[2] A census of mental hospital in-patients carried out in 1964 and since elaborately analyzed has now shown that the local-born have higher age-standardized prevalence rates not only than the European-born but than the African-born and Asian-born as well, even though the local-born have much the higher educational level. This is an unexpected finding until one remembers that Israeli-born adults are a minority within their own country. See H.S. Halevi et al.: *Census of Mental In-Patients,* Ministry of Health, Jerusalem, 1969.

[3] This 1958 analysis has never been officially published but comprises Report GSI-*Mental Health of Immigrants, 1958*. Ottawa, Department of Citizenship and Immigration, Economic and Social Research Division, 1964.

results from that analysis, after allowance had been made for provincial distribution of both population and cases.

As one sees, the immigrant population of Canada is producing proportionately not more mental hospitalization, but less, than the native-born population, age for age. The difference in rates is less for the psychoses than for other categories of mental hospital admission, and it is possible that if we had rates only for schizophrenia the difference might disappear. Yet this possibility must not be allowed to distract from the most striking feature of these graphs, namely the curve for the post-war immigrant group above the age of thirty. This group is an urban rather than a rural one, with an occupational distribution quite similar to that of the Canadian urban population as a whole. It is medically screened, of course, but presumably not more strictly than its counterpart in the United States. Its older members, being often dependent relatives of earlier immigrants, are the least strictly screened of all. The picture presented by this group today, therefore, appears to be genuinely different from that found in the United States in previous decades. Possibly, the post-war immigration to the States would show the same picture, since the gap between immigrant and native rates has been decreasing steadily over the past forty years or more (5, 17). However, if we only take the earlier Canadian immigration, a difference is still shown from the United States picture of 1939-1941. It seems justifiable, therefore, to conclude that in Canada in recent years the overall pattern of mental disorder in immigrants and the native-born differs significantly from that generally found in the United States.[4]

What other studies are there? Only two, up to the time this paper was originally written, and neither of them is satisfactory. The first is from Australia and suggested that non-British immigrants had mental hospitalization rates for psychosis which were several hundred per cent higher than those of the Australian-born population (2). However, it had several methodological errors which made its conclusions questionable, and that difference is probably greater than is really the case.

Even if we were to cut the rates for the immigrant group by half, however, they would remain above that for the native-born. So it must be taken as highly probable that certain immigrant rates in Australia do significantly exceed those of the natives. The highest reported rates in the study are for the same East European refugee type of population that had exhibited such high rates in Britain (19) but Italian, German and Dutch immigrants also have rates considerably higher than the Australians, whereas Italians and Dutch in Canada seem to have especially low rates.[5]

The second unsatisfactory investigation is one I attempted in Singapore. It is

---

[4] See the following chapter for more recent Canadian data.

[5] A fresh study avoiding the previous errors has been carried out and supports some of these inferences. (J. Krupinski & A. Stoller: Incidence of Mental Disorders in Victoria, Australia, according to Country of Birth. *The Medical Journal* of Australia, 1965, *2*, 265-269.)

unsatisfactory since nativity had not been routinely recorded at the hospital prior to my research, and therefore, for this variable I had to work with only an eight-month intake during which time the point was specially recorded for me. However, since at that time Singapore's population was about 50% immigrant, it was still possible to calculate rates for both immigrants and natives, for Chinese only. These calculations suggest, despite the small number of patients involved, that the immigrants had probably *less* mental hospitalization, allowing for age, than the local-born, even though there did appear to be an undue concentration of hospitalizations in the first years after arrival. Another point which appeared was that the immigrant cases, age for age, showed no predilection for schizophrenia. Rather, their disorders were of the acute confusional and manic type described in immigrants to North America in the last century but rarely seen there today. No great weight can be put on these findings, but they suggest that the Singapore picture is similar to that of Israel and of Canada, and dissimilar to that of the United States and of Australia.

Conclusions

The studies in the United States suggest that there is, in that country, an association between migration and mental hospitalization that cannot be explained in terms of peculiarities in the structure of the immigrant or migrant populations. At the same time, reports from other countries suggest that this association is not a universal phenomenon. The latter are not numerous or full enough to permit wider generalization on the subject, but they do indicate that migrants and immigrants can sometimes have hospitalization rates as low or lower than those of the native-born population. Obviously, more studies outside of the United States are called for.

In the meantime, I wish to draw attention to one feature of the material I have been citing, since it might suggest a new line of research within the United States. It is that, where immigrants constitute a large proportion of the population, as in Israel and in Singapore, their relative hospitalization rates are less high than where they constitute a small percentage. This inference is supported locally within the United States by the studies of Faris and Dunham (7) and of Lemert (14). The former showed that in districts of Chicago where the foreign-born were in a majority, their hospitalization rates were quite low, lower, for some disorders, than the city-wide rates for the native-born of native parentage. Lemert showed that, for rural Michigan, there was a negative correlation between the percentage strength of an ethnic minority and the level of its hospitalization rate. Elsewhere, a similar picture was found in Britain, where Polish refugees showed an inverse association between local group size and relative incidence of mental hospitalization (19).

These observations all refer to immigrants, and they might appear to have more relevance to culture conflict than to the question of mobility, which is the topic of this paper. From Singapore, however, I possess a related finding which suggests that the association may depend more on group membership than on culture conflict *per se*, and that it could, therefore, be relevant to internal migration also. In Singapore, the great majority of the population is Chinese, and culture conflict between groups speaking different dialects of the Chinese language did not arise. Yet when the hospitalization rates for these dialectal groups are plotted against their size within the community, by sex, highly and fully significant inverse correlations appear for certain diagnoses, as shown in Figure 7. This finding agrees with a number of other features from my Singapore material in emphasising the importance of group membership for the mental health of the Chinese, but I had hitherto regarded the association as largely peculiar to their culture. Now I suggest that the phenomenon may have wider application and be worth looking into, elsewhere.

Yet, group membership is, of course, not the answer to all the vagaries of the data I have been reviewing. Whether it is relevant to the Norwegian scene I do not know, but it does not seem adequate, alone, to explain the apparent differences between the Canadian findings on the one hand and the United States and Australian findings on the other. Immigrants are not in a majority in Canada, and both in the United States and in Australia there have always been large immigrant communities in the cities and countryside, available to the newcomer should he want them. Yet, when one considers these three countries, there are two factors pertinent to group membership which the United States and Australia had in common and which Canada has not.

One is a "melting pot" policy. In Australia, at least in 1950 (19), there was a strong official insistence that the newcomers should spread themselves throughout the land, should learn the local language and customs as rapidly as possible, and should not be treated as different in any way from other "New Australians". That official policy appeared to reflect public attitudes, which had earlier been considerably hostile to immigrants even of British stock and which, at this date, were prepared to accept the immigration only if the newcomers made themselves as much like Australians as possible in the shortest time. These are attitudes which were familiar, in earlier decades, in the United States, and still probably strike many people there as not unusual. Due mainly to French-Canadian influence, however, such public attitudes have never been widely prevalent in Canada nor have they been able to influence official policy. Thus, at least with regard to immigrants, it is possible that although a migrant could attempt to maintain ethnic group membership in all three countries, the climate of opinion in the first two discouraged this by making it seem disloyal, whereas in Canada such behavior was regarded neutrally or even with approval.

The origin of Canada's different attitude towards ethnic minorities is largely historical but, in part, it may be linked to a deeper question of cultural values. Australian and United States cultures strongly emphasize individuality or independence and regard dependency feelings as close to sinful and certainly as a sign of immaturity. In French Canada this is not the case and the rest of Canada may have

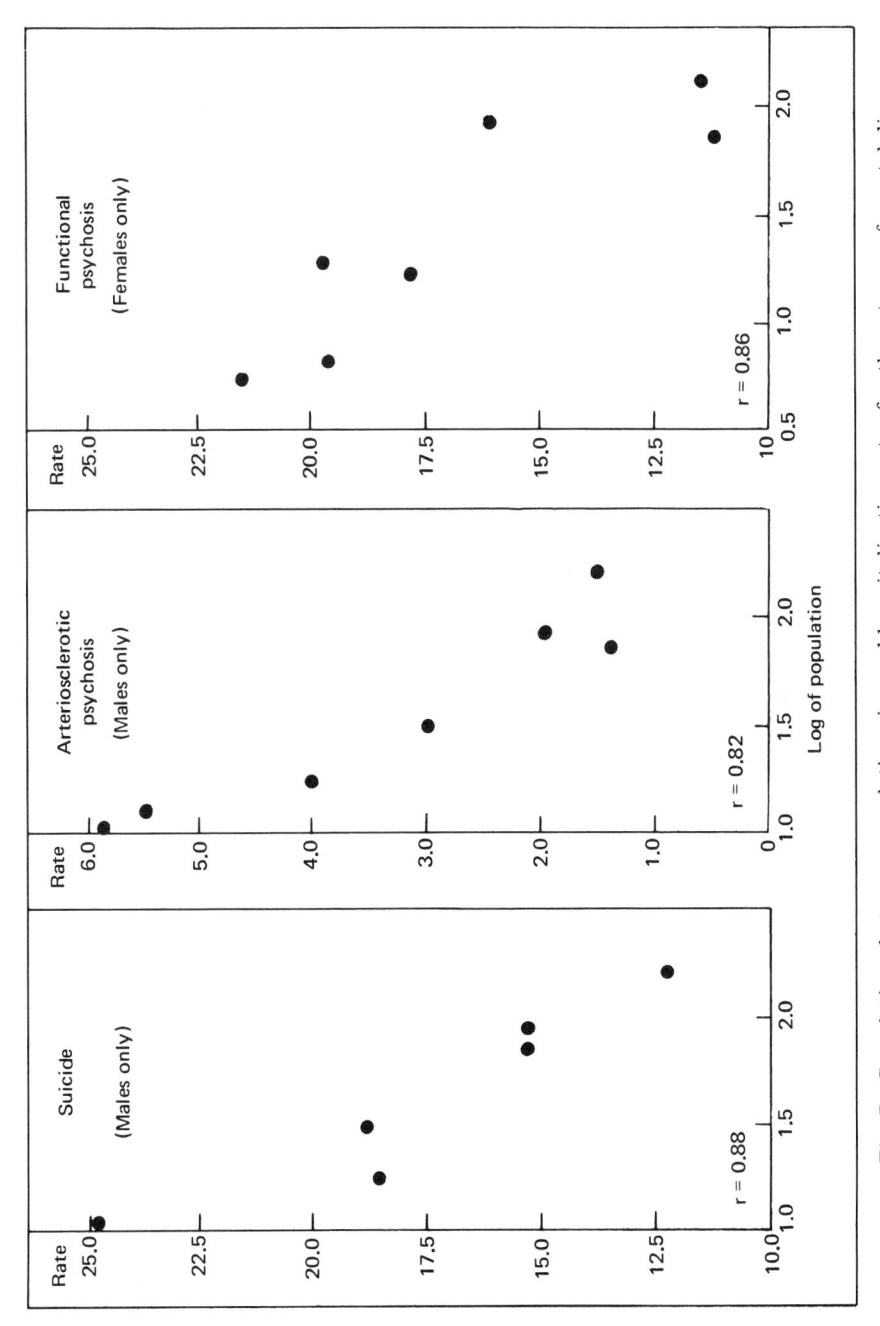

Fig. 7. Correlations between population size and hospitalization rates for three types of mental disorder in Chinese dialectal groups in Singapore; by sex and type of disorder. (From Murphy (20).)

been influenced by this. For East European Jewry one may doubt whether this was the case and among the Singapore Chinese one might say that the reverse was the rule, since the family and related social units took precedence over the individual both in terms of needs and in terms of modes of action. Now, this may have some relevance both to the selection of migrants and to the experiences encountered during migration, even migration to the next town. Where the family, community or other group is consulted before any major change is embarked on, then two things are likely to occur. First, approval may be withheld if the individual seems unstable and the venture thus likely to fail or to reflect adversely on the group. Secondly, the resources of the group and its contacts will be utilized in the migration and, where possible, the individual may be encouraged to attach himself immediately to a new group, to accept dependency or tutelage within it for an initial period, and only gradually to make acquaintance with what is really unfamiliar in the new situation. If one compares this with the situation where the individual makes his own decisions and his own contacts, as with much internal migration in the United States, it can be seen that there are advantages and disadvantages in each system. Possibly the individualistic system affords the migrant both greater rewards and greater penalties.

The data reviewed do not permit me to draw stronger conclusions. They do, however, raise the question of whether or not some of the apparent associations between migration and mental disorder which researchers in the United States have found is a product of the cultural setting within which the migration is taking place.

Origin of Contributions and References: See Page 339

THE LOW RATE OF MENTAL HOSPITALIZATION SHOWN BY IMMIGRANTS TO CANADA

H. B. M. Murphy
Canada

In the previous chapter it was stated that, whereas immigrants to the United States have repeatedly been found to possess higher rates of admission to mental hospitals than the local-born population, immigrants to Canada apparently have lower rates than the local-born. If this difference, which was based on preliminary and as then unconfirmed Canadian data, was correct, or if the ratio of immigrant to native-born rates of mental hospitalization was dropping below par in other countries besides Canada, then much of the theorizing which had previously taken place respecting the apparently excess vulnerability of the immigrants to mental disorder must be put in doubt. For this reason it is proposed to examine the latest Canadian findings in some detail in this chapter, in the hope of deciding whether increased vulnerability, either to mental disorder as a whole or to schizophrenia in particular, is a true accompaniment of migration.

The first question which must be asked concerns validity. As stated above, the Canadian findings reported in the previous chapter were only tentative, being based on a pilot study relating to an inter-censal year, 1958, when population data were necessarily imprecise. After their publication, Benjamin Malzberg kindly sent me his own unpublished analyses of Canadian data for the period around the census year 1951, and these apparently contradicted the 1958 findings. Although perhaps supporting my suggestion regarding the importance of minority group size — since the lowest immigrant/native-born hospitalization ratio was found in that part of Canada with the highest concentration of immigrants — they showed that for Canada as a whole the immigrants' rates were, after age-standardization, considerably higher than the native-born ones (8). However a re-reading of his paper revealed that in some provinces over a quarter of the patients had had no data cards made out for them, and this seemed likely to have induced some bias. In allowing for these patients it had been necessary to assume that their age-distribution and ratio of immigrants to native-born was the same as for other patients, but a knowledge of the situation suggests that the non-cooperating hospitals would be seeing a considerably lower proportion of immigrants than the cooperating ones would, by virtue of their geographic location. For instance, (they were mainly in the east of Canada, whereas immigrants go mainly to the center and west.) For these reasons I felt that the rates calculated by Malzberg could not be accepted as they stood, but that they still constituted a sufficient challenge to the 1958 calculations for the latter not to be relied on. Also, even if the 1958 picture were to be validated in 1961, Malzberg's earlier results, particularly for Ontario, suggests that it might represent a relatively recent change.

The major lesson of Malzberg's paper, namely that sources of data must be closely scrutinized and estimates undertaken with great care, was taken to heart by the researcher, Charlotte de Hesse, who had done the 1958 analysis and was embarking on a more detailed study of mental hospital admissions in the census year 1961. The Dominion Bureau of Statistics had much better cooperation in this latter year, except from the Province of Quebec, and non-reporting was no longer a problem, but all data cards were reviewed to exclude duplicates, to check for internal consistency, and to add missing but completable information. The Province of Quebec, not having collected information on the nativity of its mental patients, had to be excluded from further consideration but for the remainder of the country birthplace or nativity status was ascertainable in over 99% of cases and it made almost no difference to the rates if one assumed that the remaining 1% of patients were all immigrants or all native-born.

The 1961 rates which resulted from these data and from the population census of that year reproduced the 1958 findings to the effect that immigrants had lower age-specific or age-standardized rates of mental hospitalization than the native-born, but probably not lower rates of admission for psychosis, the age-standardized rates for the latter being 80.2 for the Canadian-born and 80.7 for the foreign-born, a difference of no significance (3). Because Mrs. de Hesse had to complete her work before certain census tabulations were available she could not, for the nine provinces which she was studying, verify her earlier observation that the lower rates derived mainly from post-W.W.II arrivals; and there are other intended refinements in her calculations which she was unable to complete. However, Figure I shows that the excess of hospitalization rates among the native-born is substantially higher in Ontario and British Columbia, the main targets for post-war immigration, than in the Prairie provinces which had attracted proportionately more of the pre-war immigration waves. It seems likely, therefore, that post-war arrivals do have a better mental health picture than either the native-born or the pre-war arrivals, though this is not certain and may differ from province to province. Whether one thinks of the picture as changing with time or as changing with location (U.S.A. versus Canada), however, the question before us is still the same: why should immigrants to Canada nowadays have a better mental hospitalization record than the native-born, when previously the ratio had always been in the opposite direction?

Time and Place

One answer, namely a change in the character of the migration, is suggested by the fact that in Ontario and British Columbia there is a greater gap between the immigrant and the native-born hospitalization rates than in the other three (Prairie) provinces (*Figure I*). Southern Ontario and the Vancouver region of British Columbia are quite industrialized and have acted as a magnet both for the internal Canadian migrant and for the post-war immigrant from Europe. In their urban settings, the new type of immigrant from European cities is likely to feel himself as much at home (apart from the language) as the migrant from the small towns and farming districts of Canada, and he may also be as well educated. Hence the local-born person's advantages of familiarity and schooling are reduced, and on the other hand the immigrant, having had to face medical screening, is less likely than the internal migrant to arrive in an already disturbed state. One would quite expect, therefore, that city-bred immigrants from Europe moving to North American cities would show less mental illness than unscreened migrants from rural Canada, and that this would affect our rates.

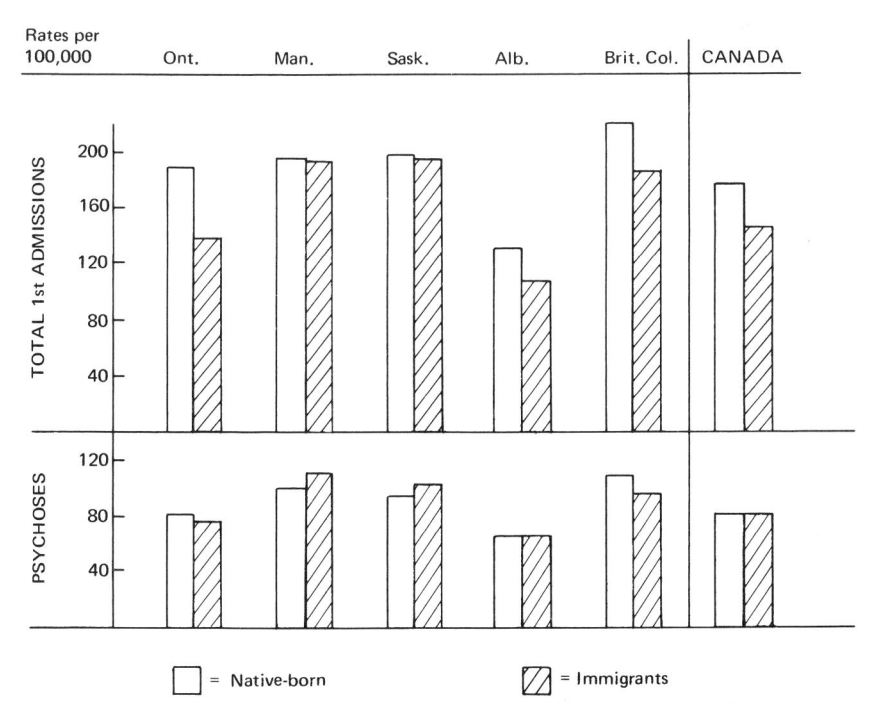

Fig. I. *Age-standardized rates of first admission to mental hospital for immigrants and for Canada-born, by main province of residence.*
(Recalculated from de Hesse (3))

That answer does not explain the whole picture, however, for immigrants have the better rates in the Atlantic and Prairie provinces as well as in the more industrialized ones, and if we are assuming that there is an internal migration of somewhat disturbed individuals from rural to industrial regions, then this should have improved, not worsened, the native-born rates in these regions. Admittedly, the ratios in the psychoses are changed, with the immigrants to the Prairies now having the higher rates, but one must also remember that the latter have on the average less education and that psychosis rates correlate inversely with the amount of schooling. Therefore, before we can say that immigrants to the Prairies are more liable to hospitalization for psychosis than Canadians, we should allow for education and see if the picture still holds.

Table 1 presents the relevant rates for the Atlantic and Prairie provinces only, excluding Quebec, Ontario and British Columbia where larger percentages of the population are involved in industry, and its message is fairly evident. In each of the broad educational strata the immigrants have the lower rates of total first admission to mental hospital, and where they have had at least some high-school education they also have the lower rates for schizophrenia. (Schizophrenia was chosen in preference to the total psychoses for this analysis, since it is the syndrome most often considered to be associated with migration.) Where the immigrants do not have any high-school education, then they are more vulnerable to schizophrenia than the equivalent Canadian-born if they are female, but not significantly different from the Canadian-born if they are male. Even though the industrial regions are excluded, therefore, the immigrants continue to show the better average picture and we are not much closer to an understanding of why the recent Canadian picture should be different from the earlier United States ones.

Minority Status and Subculture

But there are other social factors besides education and age which may need consideration before we obtain a clear picture, and one of these is cultural background. Krupinski and Stoller have shown that although immigrants from Eastern and Southern Europe have higher rates of psychiatric referral and hospitalization than the local-born in the State of Victoria, Australia, those from Britain have lower rates than the latter (6). Therefore, whether immigrants as a whole will have higher or lower rates than the local-born in Australia presumably

Table 1. Combined Rates of Mental Hospital Admission for Seven Provinces of Canada, 1961; by Sex, Immigrant Status, and Broad Educational Level; Standardized for Age and for Provincial Distribution.

		MALES		FEMALES	
		Native-born	Immigrants	Native-born	Immigrants
A. Without high school education	Total 1st admissions	249	180	213	187
	Schizophrenia	58	59	59	57
B. With high school or university education	Total 1st admissions	156	139	137	137
	Schizophrenia	30	26	31	26

depends on what percentage of them come from which background. Possibly the key factor in these Australian rates was education, something which the authors could not allow for, but cultural factors themselves, or a sense of minority status which identification with a small subculture can bring, could also be relevant. For the same Canadian provinces as in Table 1, therefore, let us compare immigrant and non-immigrant rates, with allowance for age and schooling, among populations of different national or cultural origin. This is not something which can easily be worked out in other countries, but in Canada the 'origin' of each individual was enquired into both at census and at admission to a mental hospital, this 'origin' referring to the country or people to whom the subject's first male ancestor to arrive in Canada had belonged, regardless of how many generations back that might have been.

Table 2 presents the results of these calculations, not in terms of actual rates, which vary markedly from one 'origin' group to another even among the Canadian-born, but in terms of the ratios of immigrant to native-born rates, something which enables us to recognize a correlation that might otherwise have escaped us. We see that in the three largest groups the immigrants have lower rates than the local-born for schizophrenia and for total admissions; that in the next three they have, on the average, lower rates of total admission but higher rates for schizophrenia; and that in the three smallest groups their rates are, again on the average, higher than those of the local-born for both schizophrenia and for total admissions. There is thus an apparent association between group size (which can also be

Table 2. Ratios of immigrant to local-born rates of first admission to mental hospital in nine Canadian subcultures; standardized for age, sex, education and provincial distribution; with separate ratios for schizophrenia and correlation coefficients relating ratios to population size. (Ratios were calculated after rates had been adjusted for 4 age groups, 3 educational groups, the 7 provinces and the 2 sexes. All data refer to the Atlantic and Prairie provinces only.)

Cultural 'Origins' in Order of Population Size	Ratios of Immigrant to Native-Born Rates of First Admission	
	Schizophrenia	All Disorders
British	.75	.99
French	.66	.89
German	.86	.76
Russian & Ukrainian	1.51	.78
Scandinavian	1.31	.63
Dutch	2.13	1.31
Polish	1.08	1.26
Italian	1.21	.71
Asian	(1.13)	1.37
r.	0.43	0.41

interpreted conversely as minority status) and the degree to which immigrant mental hospitalization rates exceed those of the local-born of the same 'origin', and this association would have been stronger if some way had been found to allow for factors known to affect the minority or majority status of the different groups. One of these factors is the presence within the largest, British-origin, group of a quite self-conscious Irish Catholic minority whose mental hospitalization patterns are quite different from those of the Anglo-Protestant mass (10) but who could not be distinguished from the latter for this calculation. Another factor is the presence in Ontario of a large Italian-origin population which maintains ties with the small related groups in other provinces and which, if allowed for, would lead to the Italian-origin category in Table 2 being placed higher than it is. A third factor is the tendency of the Dutch-origin to eschew clubs and associations which would provide mutual support and cultural continuity.

Given these facts and the correlation which the table indicates, it seems highly probable that minority status is one important factor underlying differences in immigrant and local-born mental hospitalization rates. However, the correlations themselves are not so high as to exclude the possibility of other explanations for the observed picture, and it behooves us to consider what these might be. Differences in the age and educational structures of the different populations would be a major possibility, but the prior standardization for age is sufficient to exclude this as a serious candidate, and although the standardization for education was more difficult, it has been sufficient to make that explanation highly unlikely. Cultural similarity is another alternative, since life in Canada is likely to be more familiar to an immigrant from West Europe than to an immigrant from Eastern Europe or from Asia. Cultural similarity and ability to identify with the majority, however, are closely linked, and the concept of minority status seems to fit our data on immigrant mental hospitalization rates somewhat better than the concept of cultural distance. For instance, Dutch and Scandinavian cultural traditions are no less distant from Canadian ones than German are, and Malzberg showed long ago (7) that possession of English as a mother tongue did not give immigrants from England or Ireland an advantage over the Germans and Scandinavians in New York State[1]. The case for seeing minority status as the major element, however, rests not so much on these negative arguments as on the fact that one can demonstrate a definite association between minority group membership, the relative strength of that group in a local population, and rates of mental hospitalization, as is done in Figure II.

---

[1] When Malzberg's original data are age-standardized, the ratios of immigrant to native-born-of-immigrant-parentage rates are
        English 1.37   German 1.22
        Irish 1.35   Scandinavian 0.99
The Irish ratio is higher than it should be on the basis of the theory being propounded here, but can probably be accounted for in terms of the way in which they are viewed by the Anglo-Protestant establishment.

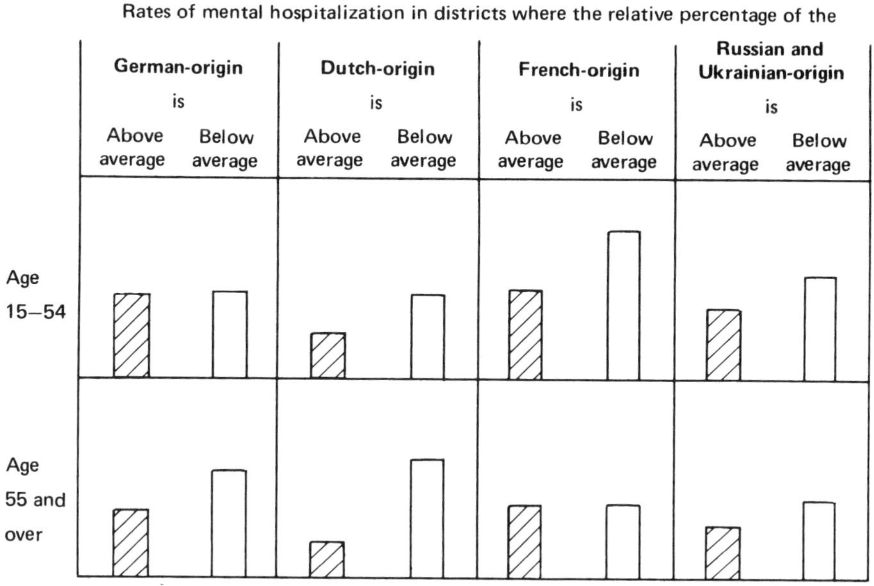

Rates of mental hospitalization in districts where the relative percentage of the

	German-origin is		Dutch-origin is		French-origin is		Russian and Ukrainian-origin is	
	Above average	Below average	Above average	Below average	Above average	Below average	Above average	Below average

Age 15–54

Age 55 and over

Fig. II. *Mental hospitalization rates for four subgroups of the Saskatchewan population in districts where their proportionate strength is above and is below their proportionate strength in the province as a whole.*
(Districts where the proportionate strength is close to the average for the province have been omitted for the group concerned, and an adjustment has been made to allow for differences in the overall rates from each district. Before that adjustment, the differences within most cells of the diagram were greater than is now shown.)

Figure II presents data from a single province, Saskatchewan, where the population is relatively thinly spread. For each of the four subcultures named (the only ones, apart from the British-origin, yielding a sufficient number of cases for this analysis) we calculated their relative strength in the whole province and then their relative strength in each of its eighteen administrative divisions. Excluding those divisions where the subculture being studied had a strength close to the provincial average, we then calculated the hospitalization rate for that subculture from those divisions where it was above average strength and contrasted with the rate from those where it was below average, using two age groups to explore whether the effect was more marked on the older than on the younger people, and making an allowance for each division's overall rate. (As is well known, rates of admission to mental hospital tend to decline in proportion to distance from the hospital, and this needed to be compensated for.) Naturally, if a division had an above-average proportion of one subculture, it was likely to have a below-average proportion of at least one other. The results show that the hospitalization rates when a subculture is below its average strength are almost always higher than the rates when it is above average strength.

I propose, therefore, that an association exists in Canada between relative minority status and mental hospitalization rates and that this association underlies the association between migrant status and mental illness. But how does this help explain the difference between the United States and Canadian findings? The answer, I would suggest, lies in the relative proportions of immigrants and local-born in each country, and the degree to which a single coherent culture has come to dominate the whole society. In Canada in 1961, one adult in five was an immigrant, and the country was still debating the reality of its own culture and nationhood. In the U.S.A., in the same year, only 5% of adults were immigrants and there existed a clear set of national attitudes and values which all immigrants had either to adjust to or oppose. As a result, whereas the immigrant in Canada feels relatively little pressure to mould himself to the majority's demands and can join other immigrants in questioning that pressure, the immigrant to the United States has felt much more pressure, particularly while the 'melting pot' theory was taken as gospel, and will not necessarily have been benefitted by belonging to a large minority rather than a small one. The larger minorities can sometimes become dominant in a community and protect their members, with a concomitant lowering of mental hospitalization rates (2,4), but since they are also conspicuous they tend to be the target of specific pressures to conform to the majority, and their members, if not banded together, can feel such pressures more than if they had belonged to a small and insignificant subculture. I suggest that this sense of minority status vis-a-vis a powerful majority is a key factor affecting the immigrant's mental health, and more important in the United States than in Canada.

Summary

1. Canadian mental hospitalizations in the census year 1961 again show, as in the year 1958, that immigrants have lower rates of mental hospitalization than the local-born, thus reversing the relationship regularly found in U.S.A.

2. Some of this reversal can be attributed to a change in the character of the immigration after W.W.II, with the newer immigrants moving from European cities to Canadian cities, and being in some ways better prepared for modern urban life than Canadian-born migrants moving from rural areas to the cities.

3. When only the less industrialized provinces of Canada are taken and when allowance is made for education, however, the immigrants still have lower rates than the local-born, this difference applying not merely to total first admissions but to admissions for schizophrenia, the condition usually considered to predispose to migration.

4. When cultural background as well as education is taken into consideration, moreover, it is found that excess of local-born rates over immigrant ones apply only to the larger subcultural groups. In the smaller subcultures the local-born still have in these agricultural provinces better rates than the foreign-born.

5. These findings suggest that in Canada the size of the subculture to which the immigrants belong is a major factor in determining whether they will have

higher rates of mental hospitalization than the local-born. This conclusion is supported by data from Australia as well as from a district-by-district study of one province, and is in harmony with the data respecting the Singapore Chinese presented in the previous chapter.

6. To explain the overall difference between Canadian and U.S.A. findings, it is proposed that the relative size of the immigrant population in each country favors the immigrant who comes to Canada, while the greater strength and dominance of U.S. core culture puts greater pressures on the immigrant there than is the case in the newer country.

Concluding Comments[2]

Migration, either within or beyond the bounds of a single country, appears to me to be a special case of social change, and the variations in mental health which accompany it can illustrate the total range of mental reactions to such change. In the past, our attention has been disproportionately focused on only a few of these reactions and to fit this oversimplified picture we have sought oversimplified explanations. Today we are coming to realize that a single migrational situation can yield an improved or worsened picture depending on what indices of mental health we choose to use and what sections of the population we choose to focus on. Conversely, similar improvements in a single indicator of mental health or even over multiple indicators can be traced back to quite different aspects of the migrational process. It is therefore highly doubtful whether the traditional and relatively economical methods of studying the relationship between mental health and migration which are represented in most of the papers of this volume will be able to enlarge much further our present knowledge on either mental health or on migration. Migrants still provide us with better opportunities of studying social change than any other easily available population, but research on them will need to be much more elaborate (and expensive) than has hitherto been considered necessary. The Dutch governmental study published as *De Gaande Man* (12) pointed the way many years ago, but lacked a psychiatric component and ran on too small a budget for the relevant questions to be properly explored.

There are six main elements which one can distinguish in any social change and which may affect mental health in separate and perhaps conflicting fashion.

a) *Origin*. This may be so unfavorable that almost any change will result in improved mental health (consider the Tiv , as described by Bohannan (1)) or so favorable that any change would be felt as a loss. It may be so idiosyncratic as respects living conditions or value orientations that change will demand much adjustment, or so flexible and informed that most new situations can be incorporated into previously acquired models.

b) *Motive*. Change can either be imposed by circumstances or be self-selected,

---

[2] These comments were written for a different purpose and added here for convenience.

and since the former is likely to be accompanied by a reluctance to adapt, it is the more likely to lead to maladaptations and mental disturbance. However, self-selected change implies discontent with one's initial situation (it would save some confusion if it were recognized that immigrants are, almost by definition, the discontented) and the breadth of this discontent is likely to be related to eventual mental health. The person whose dissatisfaction is broad and unspecific is likely to carry the seeds of it with him, whereas the one who seeks to change only a limited, specific aspect of his environment has a good chance of attaining that goal and hence of being more contented.

c) *Target.* A limited or sharply defined target is likely to be associated with less risk of mental disturbance than an extensive or undefined one, in part because the person who defines and limits his objectives is likely to be more capable than one who does not, but also because an ill-defined target is anomic. However, a too-limited target which comes from self-ignorance may induce disturbance when its attainment fails to yield the expected satisfaction, e.g., attaining wealth when more power or more popularity had been the unconscious goal. Pursuing two or more mutually imcompatible targets is a not uncommon cause of mental disturbance.

d) *Means.* Judging from empirical data, variations in the means available for attaining the chosen goals have a greater effect on mental health than any other element in migration, but this may apply to the psychoses rather than the neuroses. These means include information regarding the intended milieu, education and cultural orientations respecting methods of tackling new problems, alliances available in the new milieu, and the person's physical, economic and mental strengths. Thus, acute early psychoses tend to occur only in persons with inadequate education and information. The minority status factor revealed by my Canadian and Singapore data seems mainly to reflect the availability of alliances. Mental defectives tend to become psychotic when there is a marked change in their environment.

e) *Perceived feasibility.* As Kleiner and Parker (5) have demonstrated, the discrepancy between ideal goal and actual state can change from a healthy stimulus to a noxious irritant if the gap is great and perceived as insuperable. However, this element becomes irrelevant if the goal is undefinable due to a lack of models (11) and it may be irrelevant if confrontation of the real and the ideal is evaded.[3]

f) *Extraneous demands.* Mental disturbance is likely to be less if all persons involved in a given change share compatible goals than if they have conflicting ones and make conflicting demands on each other. The goals which a receiving society has when it accepts immigrants may be similar to or very different from the goals which the immigrants possess and the effect of this on mental health is likely to be

---

[3]Some cultures, such as the Filipino, discourage open confrontation of opposing points of view, hoping thus to obtain better social harmony. Where such teaching prevails it seems likely that individuals will tend to avoid serious confrontation of their ideal and actual states.

further influenced by the intensity with which each goal is pursued. But the relationship is probably not rectilinear, since the perception of an out-group as enemies has often the function of simplifying relationships and submerging lesser mental problems.

Though we may make broad statements regarding the effect of each of these elements on mental health, it must still be realized that their effect on the various indicators of mental health which we possess may be considerably different. Change from an intensely interacting to a less intensely interacting milieu, for instance, may increase the risk of reactive depression but decrease the risk of a schizophrenic breakdown. The perceived feasibility of attaining some long-range goal may reduce the risk of sociopathic disorder but increase the risk of an arteriosclerotic one. In the Virgin Isles, the use of the tourist's enjoyment of his wealth as a target by the Carribbean Negro worker probably reduces the risk of certain toxic psychoses and psychosomatic ailments, but increases the risk of alcoholism (9). An increase in the economic possibilities for women may improve the mental health of the family as a whole, but decrease the health of the middle-aged male who thereby loses exclusive rights to the valued role of breadwinner.

It is my opinion that future research into the relationships between migration and mental health should be directed by social scientists rather than by psychiatrists, since it is usually easier for the latter to advise the former respecting the use of psychiatric indicators than for the former to enlighten the latter regarding all the concepts and techniques which have been developed regarding social change. There are necessary exceptions to this, of course, but at the present stage of our knowledge I feel it more important for the researcher to understand the complexity of factors impinging on the migrant than to understand the complexity of mental disorders to which he may succumb.

Origin of Contributions and References: See Page 340

PART IV

Readjustment and New Growth

TRANSITIONAL COMMUNITIES AND SOCIAL RECONNECTION

Adam Curle
U.S.A.

This chapter concerns the problems of readjustment to civilian life of British soldiers who had been captured during the second World War.

The great bulk of these were taken prisoner when France fell in the summer of 1940 and in early 1942 when Malaya was overrun. They were not repatriated until the summer of 1945. However, a few escaped or were exchanged before this time. These men, many of them the "best" soldiers in terms of courage and initiative, proved to be surprisingly restless and ill-disciplined on their return. They were at odds with the army and with their families and their record of delinquency, both civil and military, was serious. Clearly the end of the war would present a major problem of the resettlement of tens of thousands of prisoners of war. The word "resettlement" was used to describe their problem rather than rehabilitation for the precise reason their condition was essentially one of unsettlement. The men were confused and restless. They found it hard to re-establish contact with family and friends from whom they had become estranged by the gulf of the years of unshared experience. Many found it hard to stick at their civilian jobs; many marriages broke up; there was a high incidence of psychosomatic disorders.

Fortunately a number of senior military officers, themselves prisoners during the First World War, took a particular interest in the question and by the time the ex-prisoners started to come back in large numbers from German or Japanese captivity, an army organization, called Civil Resettlement Units (CRU's), had been created. Before describing this, it is necessary to diagnose the syndrome. Essentially what had happened was that they had been removed from their society, and, having made a new adjustment to a new society, had become uprooted from the old one. To begin with they had moved from civilian to military life. This is a dramatic change. The average non-soldier plays many roles in his society; he is husband, a son, a father, a worker, an employer, an employee, a neighbor, a member of various organizations, a citizen who votes and pays taxes. He belongs to a society composed of both sexes, young and old, whose members are engaged in an infinite variety of activities having many different goals. But the soldier, in his one-sex world, abandons most of his civilian roles. Of course, he is still a member of a family, still a citizen and so on, but his military roles are so clustered about the main occupational objective — to destroy the enemy — that all others grow dim. The army provides work, clothing, recreation, food, entertainment, comrades with whom a strong male solidarity is forged, ritual, hierarchy and objectives within the hierarchy, and above all discipline and purpose. The old life becomes slightly unreal by comparison.

When a man's unit goes overseas and particularly when it moves into the front line, where his life depends constantly upon the vigilance and resourcefulness of a small group of companions, his identification and involvement with them becomes amazingly close. His roles are few, but clear cut, forced out of the exigencies of battle. His human relationships are those of the soldierly interdependence of comrades in arms within the structure of rank (a relationship can be thought of a behavior within a role). His values center on loyalty to the men on whom his life depends and for whom he would give his own life. Even when he returns unscathed from the war, it is difficult for him to weaken these roles and relationships as he moves back into civilian life, reassuming his old roles and rebuilding his former relationships. Few men, however unmilitary they might be by inclination, have made the transition smoothly. The former prisoners of war, however, had additional difficulties to contend with. Many labored under painful emotions in which guilt for having been captured and resentment against those who had not suffered as they had were inextricably interwoven. A large number were away from home for five years with very little chance of communicating with their families. They relied, then, all the more closely on their fellow captives for closeness and support. The conditions of a prison camp were such that a man had only two alternatives — either (and rarely) he cut himself off from his fellows, becoming a lonely and usually sick isolate, or he was very strongly united to the group.

Although captives, these men were still at war. Their military duty was to make life as hard for their captors as they could and to escape whenever possible. They also had to preserve their health and morale in circumstances of discomfort and deprivation. This made for a singularly warm and close-knit community which was, moreover, highly democratic. Rank became much less important as it no longer related to the complex divisions of normal military existence (in any case officers and men were separated in the German camps). Instead, the cohesion of the community depended upon freely-given participation. Men learned a new dimension of loyalty which, despite their painful and often appaling circumstances, had great value for them. It was a source, however, of additional emotional strain when they returned, to a society in which these newly-discovered values of human conduct were not recognized and in which relationships followed a norm which is more stereotyped, more lop-sided (or perhaps less egalitarian) and less altruistic. It was bad enough for these men to be unable to convey what they had suffered. For many it was even worse not to be able to describe what they had learned. This combined with their inevitable separation from their society to make them feel utterly estranged. More particularly they felt alienated from those who should have been closest to them, but who — because they could not understand, and because one expects most from those one loves most — now were felt to have failed them utterly. Some men withdrew completely from the society they no longer related to. They left their jobs and their homes. Others remained, but in body rather than spirit. This did not happen at once. There was normally a jubilant reunion, but the excitement wore off after a few weeks, and a gray reaction set in. Some men escaped back to the army, for although this was the organization which — theoretically — almost all wanted to leave, it was also the one which they understood. Its rules were practical and unequivocal. A man knew where he was in the army and many retreated to it from the unexpected emotional hazards of civilian life.

For these reasons it was appropriate that the army, through its Civil Resettlement Units, should take on the task of reconnecting these men to civilian society — it was trusted and it was safe. Nevertheless, the nature of traditional military discipline was even more antithetical to the new "democratic" insights of the prison camp than was society at large. It seemed vital that these insights should be preserved since they apparently constituted the growing edge of what was otherwise an utterly grim experience. Without what has been termed the creative aspect of the casualty there would be much less hope for eventual resettlement. Therefore the part of the army concerned with resettlement must in certain fundamental ways be different from the rest of it.

Of prime importance was the principle of consistency. If what a man had gained was to be retained and strengthened, the whole ambience of the new experience must be directed towards that end. His capacity for freely-chosen participation must be preserved. For this reason there could be no compulsion. This was extended to making entry to the institution entirely voluntary. It was argued by some that men who were disturbed could not tell what sort of treatment they needed, if any, and should be made to attend the CRU's but the prevailing view was that this would constitute an inner contradiction which might vitiate the whole course of resettlement. For similar reasons, within the CRU's there was no formal discipline. This extended, for the sake of consistency, to the clerks, cooks and others on the staff who had not been prisoners of war. All programs and facilities were voluntary; there was no penalty for non-attendance at any activity of the CRU. The aim was to create an environment which provided on the one hand the safety, understanding and stability, and on the other hand, the permissiveness to enable a man to experiment with his capacity for freedom and to extend it from the known atmosphere of the army to the more uncertain environment of civilian life.

At the peak period of need there were twenty CRU's each containing at any one time about 240 men. The average length of stay was four weeks, but if desirable, men stayed longer. Many had some serious practical problems and these were dealt with promptly and efficiently. There were welfare officers who assisted with the uncomprehended problems relating to rationing (which included such things as furniture and clothes as well as food); the spate of post-war regulations; scarce housing; the agonizing issues of broken homes or motherless children. Medical teams dealt with health problems occasioned by privation, by war injuries, or by strain: frequently men who would have feared or scorned to visit a psychiatrist took advantage of an apparently physical condition to seek psychological advice. Employment problems were tackled in several ways. Vocational aptitude tests were given. Ministry of Labor officials provided information on jobs. And finally, local employers were enlisted to give short-term employment, called job rehearsals, to men who were then able to test their aptitudes and inclinations. There were work shops in which men often experienced a sort of occupational therapy; it can be comforting to do something with one's hands when one's mind is troubled. Sometimes an act of material creation restores self-confidence to a man who doubts his ability — since he cannot live happily at home — to do anything.

Men were sent to the unit nearest their homes so that they could visit their families at weekends. This reaching out into the home and indeed into the community as a whole was perhaps one of the most important features of the CRU's. A man might not be able alone and unaided to face the problems of readjustment to his family, but from the safe, secure base of the unit he might be able to transfer his dawning self-awareness to the home scene. Eventually, most men were able to return there and resume happily their familial roles. The job rehearsals constituted, of course, another means of establishing connections with society as well as of trying out different sorts of work.

The community of the unit itself had a therapeutic character. The staff, officers and men, in fact enjoyed their remedial role, perhaps because of the contrast with their prime function of destruction over the previous years. Officers conducted group discussions which, though a crude and early version of group therapy techniques, gave a valuable chance of releasing tension and gaining awareness. Perhaps the most effective agents of therapy, their own and that of others, were the men themselves. As each fresh weekly intake of about sixty came in, a previous intake took care of them, and felt great pride in helping with the process of reconnection.

If a man's view of his own society with its complex of roles, relationships and culture patterns had lost its meaning for him, if its internalized values were seen as relative or worthless, it was reasonable to expect that his uprooting would show itself in his relationship with others. Likewise, if the process of resettlement were to have any real therapeutic effect, these roles and relationships would be restored, and have a richer content. It should be possible to estimate the extent to which a man was resettled by the character of his relationships with family, neighbors, employers and so on. If men were satisfactorily readjusted, then their relationships with their associates might be expected to be less one-sided, less demanding, less dominated by their own driving psychological needs for reassurance, for proving themselves, or whatever it might be. These relationships would be more open, more participant in the sense of the pattern which had been built up in the CRU's, more relaxed, more based on mutual understanding, more based on the attempt to help. During the course of research carried out by the writer he had extensive interviews with 150 former prisoners of war, together with their families, neighbors, and in most cases employers. Several patterns of relationships emerged. The men who, according to a variety of criteria, were apparently most disturbed, who had refused to obtain work, who were anxious, aggressive or depressed, who had separated from their wives, or who were receiving treatment for what had appeared to be psychological symptoms, had relationships with others which were dominated by their own problems. The other people in the relationship had little significance for them except as persons who aggravated or assuaged their pain; if a man is completely dominated by his own difficulties, he has little appreciation of the problems of others. Consequently there was a kind of lonely rigidity about these men which only compounded their basic distress, for what they needed most of all was the closeness which they were unable to accept or to acknowledge. It was possible to identify several stages of the deterioration of the relationships, and it seemed that in many cases they followed right through a man's contact with his immediate family to his attitude towards the community at large.

The local community was included in the study and it was revealing to discover that those modes of behavior which apparently represented the most unsettled condition were also looked upon by the community as being undesirable. It was interesting, however, that the traditional behavior of the community was characterized by convention which severely limited the growth of richly interacting relationships. For example, the idea of co-operation between husband and wife on such homely tasks as house decoration; dishwashing or gardening was despised. Each member of the family had his allotted sphere and to tresspass into another, or to ask for help in his or her particular task, was seldom tolerated. Modes of behavior which once served to organize society along harmonious lines often persist after their usefulness has declined and then serve only to inhibit flexible adjustment to changing circumstances. In the difficult conditions of post-war Europe it seemed fairly clear that many couples were in fact making life much more difficult for themselves by failing to make use of the potentiality of their relationship. For example, if a wife was unable to go out shopping for some good reason, the husband would not go in her place, and thus the whole family would be reduced to eating unappetizing scraps for dinner. Likewise, the household might be upset for days because of some piece of decoration carried out by the husband alone which could have been done in half the time if the wife had agreed to help. Relationships with neighbors and other family members tended to be of a somewhat formal sort based on a set of conventions which were almost stylized in their attention to traditional propriety. By contrast with these ordinary citizens there was a certain group of former prisoners whose behavior showed considerably more adaptability and co-operativeness than was normal for their neighbors who had not suffered captivity. In these families there was an extraordinary degree of vigor and creativity. The men seemed to have discovered how to get the most out of relationships, and had broken the bonds of conventional restriction which keeps many from developing a rich and varied communion with a wife or child. It was significant that these persons were much admired and perhaps even envied by members of a community who, although they did not emulate their behavior, were prepared to accept it, apparently seeing in it a desirable form of adaptation.

Statistical analysis of behavior patterns in fifteen different types of relationships showed that the persons who had the more participant type of relationships were predominantly those who had spent some time in the CRU's, whereas those whose behavior was in varying degrees disturbed tended to be those who had not had this particular form of experience. There was a continuum from those who had been to the CRU's through the control group of community members who had not been prisoners at all, to those former prisoners who had not volunteered to attend the resettlement units, in terms of the degree of flexibility and participation in these relationships.

Some conclusions may perhaps be drawn from this connective process of the CRU's and the subsequent degree of resettlement. The initial trauma caused a painful loss of contact with the home community, but at the same time it laid the broader foundations of adjustment based on an understanding and acceptance of differences rather than on identification with a particular set of norms. Subsequent experiences heightened both tendencies. The shock and separation set men at a great emotional distance from their homes while the participant and democratic culture of the prison camp gave strength to values, which (as shown by the control group) were much less valid at home. Thus when a man returned he was very far from his society. He was often so far that when an occasion of friction arose with his wife, employer or neighbor, he had no means of bridging the gulf. He could no longer handle the tools of his own culture to reach a settlement and would quarrel bitterly and irreparably, leaving home or job, or breaking all communication with his neighbor. In one sense the role of the CRU's was to bring him close enough to his society for inevitable differences and quarrels to be settled peaceably and without rupturing relations completely. As a man became reconnected with his society he was eventually able to drop his protections and to view the world around him objectively, not as a reflection of his own fears or plans. Because the inner hold of the culture upon him had weakened, he was also able to adopt new and more realistic modes of behavior, but this was not possible until the more painful effects of his captivity had been reduced. Before this stage his newly-won awareness did more to exasperate and frustrate than to help him adjust.

Origin of Contributions and References: See Page 341

MENTAL HYGIENE IN REFUGEE CAMPS

Maria Pfister-Ammende
Switzerland

Measures to Remedy the Impact of Camp Life on Refugees

A refugee camp is a place where people are forced to live, often for years. Its effect on mental health is frequently deeply pathological. The only satisfactory measure would be to abolish refugee camps. This goal, however, is theoretical and unattainable and they can be expected to remain for decades. It is therefore necessary to seek a pattern of life for such camps that measures up to basic demands in the field of prevention of mental ill-health.

Taking as a starting point the situation faced by the war-stricken individuals who stayed in Swiss camps, I shall describe the mental health measures that were provided for them, and attempt both to derive basic conclusions on how a camp should be organized, and to point to some tasks which confront mental hygiene on the community level.

Position of Refugees in Swiss Camps

Of the approximately 300,000 refugees and military internees who stayed in Switzerland between 1940 and 1947, 32,000 were civilian refugees who were accomodated in 168 homes and camps of the Federal Administration (Eidgenössische Zentralleitung der Heime und Lager, thereafter called the Hostels Administration). In addition 9,100 repatriates of Swiss nationality were housed in 42 camps and homes in the period from September 1945 to the end of 1947.

Mental Hygiene in Swiss Camps and Homes

An investigation of the psychological aspects of the refugee problem in Switzerland (Pfister-Ammende 1946) provided the basis for mental health measures. The author of this paper who has undertaken the investigation submitted in 1944 a petition to the Swiss authorities. I explained that the psychological situation observed in the camps demanded immediate action: the Hostels Administration had severely harmed and exhausted persons to care for. For all those involved, from the directors down to the most subordinate co-workers, this task placed heavy demands upon tact, human understanding, and the ability to comprehend the particular inner situation of the refugee. If the instituting bodies were not equal to this task, tensions developed between them and the refugees. Such tensions made the work of the authorities more difficult and conveyed to the refugee a feeling of bitterness toward the country of asylum. As a matter of fact, a substantial degree of such bitterness, as well as distrust, was found between the authorities and the inhabitants of the camps. For these reasons I suggested that a Mental Health Service be established at the Hostels Administration to advise the Agency personnel in matters of serious camp conflicts and continuous difficulties with individual refugees or refugee-groups; to deal with overt psychiatric cases; train the personnel in the camps and in the Central Administration in refugee psychology and some general principles of social psychology; finally, to run a permanent discussion group on the refugee problem for camp staff and their supervisors, social workers, psychologists and psychiatrists.

The petition was accompanied by this letter from a group of Swiss psychiatrists[1]:

> "The Board of Supervisors of the Psychotherapeutic Training Institute of the University of Zurich has discussed the attached petition in detail. The entire Board have declared themselves in full agreement with the recommendations. The undersigned are convinced that the creation of a Mental Health Service would assist the Hostels Administration in performing its difficult task and, at the same time, by bringing about in the refugees a more positive attitude to the measures taken by the authorities, contribute favorably to the general psychological situation in Switzerland. Therefore, an alleviation of the difficulties which have arisen in dealing with refugees would be an act that was both humanitarian and in the interests of the country."

The authorities accepted the petition and a Mental Health Service was organized, functioning from 1944 to 1948 as a department of the Hostels Administration. Its main tasks will now be briefly described.

I. Primary Prevention — Mental Health Work on Community Level
Training and education of personnel

The basis and starting point for this work were lectures and courses for the officials of the central administration and for camp personnel. They dealt with the psychology of the refugee, the emotional consequences of internment, relations between administrator and refugee, and with psychological problems in administration. With the help of day-to-day examples from work and life in camps I attempted to present the contrasting approaches to the administration of a camp:

> During lunch in a camp those sitting at the staff table continually talked about the refugees. They complained about "the disorderliness of X" and "the laziness of Z" pointing with their thumbs at these persons and declaring "they are not worth the food they get" or "it's not worth lifting a hand for

---

[1] G. Bally, H. Bänziger, V. Binswanger, M. Boss, H. Brun, C.G. Jung, A. Mäder and H. Trüb.

them". The staff was irritable and felt tired, suffering from the supposed senselessness of their work. Explosions between them and their 'protégés' (Schützlinge) took place daily. The expression "gang" used by the staff corresponded to the invective "scoundrels" applied to them by the refugees. – In another camp small talk and laughter occured frequently at both the table of the staff and of the refugees. Among the staff, reactions of the one individual or the other were discussed and a common attempt was made to explain them. The directress said: "My colleagues often come to see me upstairs. I find mutual contact the most important task of all. Everything depends upon our attitude and our contact." The atmosphere was relaxed. "The scoundrel" of the other camp, a nurse, was referred to here as "an angel".

In a work camp a newly appointed director made the following speech: "I will see to it that order is maintained. At 10 o'clock p.m., you are to be in the barracks; at 10:30 lights are to be out. In the dormitory order is to be maintained and the blankets must be folded all the same way", and he went into the dormitory to demonstrate the new 'order of the blankets'. An atmosphere of distrust spread through the establishment, every measure of this man being negatively received by the refugees. – In another work camp a group of Greeks arrived, coming into this cold, isolated and high-lying area reluctantly and distrustfully. The director greeted them and said: "I know you do not enjoy coming here. This I can understand since I don't like being here, either. The camp is a difficult thing for both of us, particularly here in this lonely area, but we shall get along." Questions concerning a radio, a soccer field and a recreation room were discussed. The director then showed them the camp and introduced them to the other refugees. Relaxed and unconstrained working and living conditions prevailed.

In another camp a woman swept the floor with a broom. Two-and-a-half hours later she was still standing there with her broom. Asked if she had not yet finished, she replied: "Certainly, and a long time ago, but when the control comes, I must be seen with the broom in my hand". The people said: "Nobody enjoys work here; everybody works with the clock in his hand."

I pointed out the specific danger of the job of administering other people, namely that the position contains an inducement to satisfaction of one's own need for power.

In one camp the staff ate alone at a table with white linen, silver and plates, separated from the others by a glass wall. The refugees ate on long tables without linen, food being served in deep trays. A frosty tone reigned, the staff being referred to as "those behind the glass wall". – In another camp the tables were arranged in horseshoe form, the staff sitting right among the refugees. Here the staff was accepted as friends and helpers.

In one camp a theatrical performance took place. The staff entered in formation, accompanied by v.i.p.s from the area. They attended the presentation, applauded, rose and left, again in formation. There was a saying in this camp: "The Court is coming", the director being referred to as "The King", and a compliant refugee with a loud voice as "the master of the ceremony". — In another camp the same event took place, but everyone came individually and freely sat down where he chose to sit, chatting gaily with his neighbors.

These courses of a more general nature concerning administrative problems and refugee psychology were followed by ones with more special themes, such as the war-damaged child, basic aspects of psychopathology, and on vocational teamwork. Refugees were invited to speak to the staff on present and future conditions of refugees. These training courses were supplemented by a document which the authorities accepted and distributed as official directives for the Heads of the refugee camps and homes. It reads as follows:

Directives
for Chiefs of Camps and Homes for Refugees

1. You represent Switzerland to the refugee. He judges the attitude of the Swiss towards the refugee by the way you act towards him.
2. Require your assistants to express themselves with tact and understanding in discussing the refugee.
3. Welcome him cordially. He is a human being like yourself. Treat him as you would wish your mother, father, or brother to be treated.
4. See to it that the newcomer is made to feel at home by his comrades.
5. Take time to show him his work. He will need a few days to learn how your camp is run and become adjusted to it.
6. Camp life is as strange to the refugee as it is to you. Do not compare it with your military service, for at the end of that you return to a home.
7. The only reason for having rules and regulations is to make life in the community easier. To insist on order simply for the sake of order or for the education of the refugee will only irritate him. For you the human being is the first consideration. Ask yourself over and over again: "Is the refugee under my care well treated?"
8. Trust others, then they will trust you. Remember this truth when you are tempted to doubt.
9. Make each refugee feel that you trust him, but do not be too familiar. Make him feel that you are sincerely interested in his fate.
10. Be sure that the refugees who act as spokesmen command the confidence of their comrades.
11. Whenever possible give the refugee responsibility, then he can see for himself what is possible under the existing circumstances. Man needs responsibility.
12. Try to organize the work so that it has a purpose, and make that purpose clear to the refugee. Do not forget that a trained worker accomplishes more in his own field than when he does camp work to which he is not accustomed.
13. Always explain to the refugee the point of each rule and restriction you have

to make. It is a natural human reaction to want to know the reason for orders.
14. Never punish in haste or in anger. Never punish without telling the refugee your reasons. Seek to find a way out of the trouble by talking the matter over with him. If you must punish, try not to injure his self-respect.
15. Keep your sense of humor. Many times it will be more effective than scolding, and help you out of ticklish situations.
16. It is your job to know what goes on in your camp. You will be best informed if your contact with the refugee is natural and unforced. Give the refugee the right to say what he thinks at any and all times. That will form the basis for such contact as well as strengthening your own position.
17. Do not listen to tattle tales. Hate and mistrust rule in a community where there are spies.
18. A final word:
Remember in a camp of refugees there are not only difficulties but great possibilities for psychological development. Your task is hard but it will bring you lasting satisfaction. You are helping your fellow men."
(Eidg. Zentralleitung der Lager und Heime, 1945)

Counseling of Personnel

In this refugee work the staff spent years adjusting day and night to customs and reactions which were strange to them (the refugees in Switzerland came from some 54 nations ...) and which they endeavored to understand. Even those who possessed a strong sense of responsibility underwent severe psychological strain in such a task. They were thus under the pressures of falling victim to the routine or to the danger of losing their own identity (Vermassung), threatened like their charges by uprooting. Here a broad and rewarding area for psychological counseling was to be found. Also, the directors needed advice and supervision in handling individuals of difficult character and borderline psychiatric cases.

Teamwork at the Top Administrative Level

Co-operation and teamwork in dealing with the basic problems of camp administration as a whole constituted the third area of my preventive mental hygiene activity.

The manifold administrative and psychological aspects and the requirements involved were co-ordinated by the ready and open cooperation of all branches of the administration. The account given by the Head of the Hostels Administration, O. Zaugg (1949), scarcely needs to be supplemented. It should only be noted that, as a member of the board of management, the mental health specialist acted not only in an advisory capacity but shared responsibility for all principal questions and decisions.

In 1945 plans and regulations had to be drafted for the administration of 42 new homes for accommodating Swiss repatriates. An outline was made. The mental health specialist was responsible for seeing that form and content of the document fulfilled psychological requirements. The final touch was given to the document at a joint discussion of the board. At a convention of the future directors of these homes the administrative and psychological aspects of the regulations were discussed.

II. Treatment and Rehabilitation

When it was thought that a refugee or a repatriate was severely disturbed or mentally ill, the camp director was obliged to contact the Mental Health Service. If mental illness was later diagnosed, the record which the administration maintained concerning the individual received a special note. Thereafter the opinion of the Mental Health Service was sought in all future measures considered by the administration. This meant that as long as he remained within its jurisdiction, the Hostels Administration's handling of this person was fully oriented to mental hygiene principles. This procedure represents a clear example of secondary prevention. 732 mentally ill refugees and repatriates were cared for in this way. (Pfister-Ammende, UNESCO 1955). Since I was fully occupied by work of a primary preventive nature I only diagnosed these cases and had the severe ones among them referred for treatment to a colleague. Fortunately, 78 psychiatrists, clinical psychologists and special teachers (Heilpädagogen) – 277 of our cases were children and adolescents – were collaborating with us.

Scattered throughout Switzerland our camps and homes were often too isolated, and the professional therapists too few; in these conditions removal from the existing environment was often not therapeutically desirable because of the danger of alienating the patient by a further uprooting. I therefore heavily involved the very willing lay personnel of our camps and homes in the therapeutic process – director or directress, the teacher and the kindergarten instructor, and particularly the nurse as a paramedical collaborator. These collaborators were then afforded a great deal of leeway in their initiative and method for dealing with and caring for the patient; I remained in close consultative contact with them, mostly by telephone.

Most important was the help afforded to certain patients regarding their future life outside the camp (Weichenstellung für das weitere Leben). Our social workers, and particularly the Employment Service for hard-core cases (a service instituted at my request and managed by a psychiatric social worker) were able in most cases to provide these people with opportunities for moulding their own lives and pursuing a productive activity as members of the Swiss community.

> A Polish couple fled to Switzerland with their one year old child, escaping from forced labor in Germany. In a sudden attack of depression a year later, three months after the birth of a second child, the husband committed suicide. The twenty-six year old wife had to be temporarily admitted to a

mental hospital because of the acute danger of suicide. Upon return to the refugee home she was the very picture of desparation, knowing no way out, particularly since she spoke almost no German. She wandered through the home wailing monotonously. Through psychotherapy combined with careful guidance given by the directress of the home she gradually recovered and was able to undergo training as a seamstress. A job was found for her and, finally, she regained her strength and vitality.

III. Summary and Conclusion
I. Organization of Camps for Refugees

Refugees who are uprooted and kept in large numbers and in a schematic manner in camps tend to form aggressive crowds. Their pent-up energies tend to explode in mass-reactions. Or, they become victims of the process of "Vermassung". This is not basically a mass phenomenon, but rather a matter of complete isolation of the individual leading to apathy and resignation.

When circumstances make it necessary to establish camps for refugees, socio-psychological problems of major order are involved. The guiding principles from a mental health point of view for shaping life in a camp must be that the inhabitants should not live in a social and spiritual vacuum. From this point of view the camp structure needs to be carefully studied in all its aspects, kept under continuous examination and if necessary, changed.

Important factors in connection with this are:
(1) the type of dwelling unit;
(2) the number of inhabitants;
(3) the degree of organization of camp life;
(4) the contact with the outside world;
(5) the atmosphere of the camp.

1. *The Type of Dwelling Unit.*

Where the residential unit is very large and gloomy, people are more likely to become buried in the mass and to lose contact with their surroundings inside and outside the camp. The smaller and brighter the camps can be kept, the better. But when a camp houses over 300 people, they can no longer feel an individual human contact with the camp leader. Both from an organizational and from a psychological point of view such camps should be sub-divided into smaller communities capable of being handled separately, somewhat as a large city is sub-divided into districts. And these smaller units should be given attractive names instead of "Block I, Block II," etc.

Where the refugees are obliged to be accomodated in large rooms, light partition walls should be constructed.

Darkness in the dwelling rooms and corridors has a fatal effect on the camp inhabitants, and light should never be economized. The lights should be left on all day wherever the rooms go so far back that insufficient daylight penetrates. The practice of dividing up the rooms with blankets obstructs the passage of light, so that the parts farther from the windows remain in a perpetual airless twilight, where people doze their lives away from morn to night. Light-toned partition walls would also give families some privacy.

In certain camps the corridors remain day and night in semi-darkness. How dreary it is to have to trudge through these dark bare passages month after month or even year after year! Is it not possible to equip them with some form of pleasant, cheerful lighting? A competition among artistically talented refugees, organized for example in youth groups to decorate the walls, might have success. To guard against disappointment, it would be necessary to reckon in advance with greater wear and tear — always a feature in any collectivity. But experience in similar and other collectivities has shown that once a wall is "accepted" it is also respected.

Some camps have their communal and "cultural" rooms; but it is desirable to separate club-room and reading room, and to have both well lit and cheerful. It is useless to try to combat growing lethargy by setting aside a room for "culture" and providing it with tables in long rows and a noisy talkative "librarian". People entering need to see a friendly room, with flowers and pictures and intimately grouped chairs and tables. Furthermore, in the reading room there should be a rule of absolute silence.

2. *Number of Inhabitants.*

Agglomerations of more than 300 can be saved from the blight of anonymity and lethargy if the single immense block is broken up into smaller sub-divisions; but only if the members are in contact with one another and with their leader so that each unit has a life of its own. Monthly discussion evenings might be a valuable device and particularly efforts in the direction of what is known as "neighbor help", for example visits, invitations, excursions, as well as the encouragement of inter-family contact.

3. *Level of Camp Organization.*

In certain camps a gloss of magnificent organization covers appalling mass-treatment, embitterment and isolation of the majority of the inhabitants. The warning cannot be too strongly voiced against regarding the degree of organization of any collectivity such as a camp as an indication of the human quality of its administration. Over and over again the mistake is made of confusing indispensable organization with organization as an end in itself. Organization is only a means; if it operates soullessly the individual has the helpless feeling of being caught up in the cog-wheels of a machine.

4. *Contact with the Outside World.*

The first step has to be made by the local community. Speaking of the inhabitants of a refugee camp, a resident of a nearby village said to me: "To tell the truth, we wish they were all dead." This remark merely gives brutal expression to a fundamental aspect. Frequently brave citizens wish to suppress the fear that they may themselves one day be expelled, persecuted, uprooted ... And this they can do by "eliminating" the homeless wanderers who are before them in the flesh.

Therefore, a more or less unconscious inner resistance in the individual and the local community must often be overcome, once the first enthusiasm of benevolence and the first waves of pity are exhausted. The job has to be done first within community organizations such as parish congregations, youth groups, sport clubs; and the camp leader has an important part to play.

If camp schools cannot be made part of the local schools, the two types of schools should be in friendly and close contact with one another; interchange of pupils and teachers may even be possible. The local teachers should be instructed in refugee and camp psychology. Camp clergy and doctors as well as refugees should furnish the local press with a kind of regular chronicle concerning life and events in the camp. If the press only gets reports of the misdeeds of sporadic asocial elements and if the only contact between local community and camp consists of the local police, it inevitably promotes a false judgement of the camp inhabitants, even without intending to do so.

5. *The Atmosphere of the Camp.*

The factors already discussed have a considerable influence on the atmosphere of a camp. But the moral and mental health of its inhabitants depend on two further factors: first on whether he expects soon to find a way again into active life, and then on the atmosphere generated by the camp leader and his staff. A camp may fall far short of the optimum requirements mentioned in Sections 1-4 above; nevertheless, if a really friendly and human atmosphere prevails in it, the occupants will not sink into bitterness and apathy. There has to be someone there – staff or fellow-refugee – to talk to, someone who cares, who is accessible and who behaves so that the refugees want to turn to him. It means a friendly reception to the newly arriving refugee, and discussion evenings between staff and refugees. A mixed committee might also be set up, but care must be taken that it does not arouse the resentment against committees which is often met with among refugees.

The camp leaders and their colleagues must be:

– carefully selected. Army officers and policemen are certainly not more suitable than members of other professions, and women;

– trained on the job in refugee psychology and in leadership;

– well paid, since they are performing an important function, and the availability of man- and womanpower is governed by remuneration as in other occupations;

– given ample holidays, since the work is arduous;

– carefully supervised. Camp leaders who, even after training, are unsuitable from a psychological point of view, who take a domineering and belittling attitude, must not be allowed to remain, even though they may be organizational geniuses.

6. *The Problem of Difficult Cases*

In every camp, as in every society, there are difficult and also antisocial elements. They may be more conspicuous in a camp than in a community that is well equipped with appropriate facilities; but their number should not be overestimated. In order to prevent a camp from being filled with shirkers, deteriorated and depraved alcoholics, prostitutes and so on, the individual cases must be dealt with on medical, social and mental health levels. Proper measures and socio-medical guidance must be provided.

Such difficult cases are usually a greater burden on camps than they are in permanent settings. In spite of this there is sometimes a tendency of welfare authorities to foist their antisocial elements on the neighboring refugee camp. The tendency must be fought from the outset as a matter of principle. Otherwise a rapid decline in standards (degeneratives Gefälle) will set in. The difficult or antisocial elements, the demoralized family in the community will "temporarily, until a solution has been found" be transferred to a refugee camp, and thereupon the "difficult" refugees, the demoralized refugee family will quietly be put into the backyard – and there be forlorn and forgotten. Such would be the degenerative pattern (Gefälle), if, consciously or unconsciously, three different yardsticks were applied, one for residents, one for the average refugee, and one for hard core and "difficult" camp inhabitants.

7. *Role of Mental Hygiene.*

Socially-oriented mental health specialists should be urged to participate in the care of refugees in camps. If, as was deemed necessary in Switzerland, a mental health service for refugees is organized, this service should, in my opinion, not regard treatment as its first priority. Its therapeutic duty should consist mainly in detecting mental cases and in referring them to psychiatric and mental health facilities in the region, and in watching from the "protective therapy" angle, until such time as a proper solution for the individual and his surroundings has been achieved. However, as I see it, the major task of such a mental health service is in the area of primary prevention of mental ill-health among the refugees, an example which I have tried to give in describing mental health work for refugees in Switzerland.

II. Some Mental Health Tasks on Community Level

Wherever human beings are to be cared for by a public administration the co-operation of mental health specialists is required. This should involve on their part, among other obligations, decision-sharing on top level in respect of the socio-psychological implications of the task in question.

In such community mental health work, teamwork on the part of every member of the responsible body, including the mental health worker, is most important. Narcissism, hypersensitivity, and aggressive tendencies are just as negative here as ambivalence and the shirking of responsibility. Ability in the group can be learned neither at the university nor in the medical consulting room; neither can it be fully acquired in a didactic analysis. Instead, proper training in group work is necessary. However, it should be remembered that the most decisive effect on others within a group comes from the personality of the team member, i.e. from his maturity and ability to take on responsibility.

The viewpoint presented by C.G. Jung in "Psychotherapy of the Present" (1945); "I consider it the most distinguished task of psychotherapy of our times to serve indefatigably the development of the individual, " pertinent as it is for *one* aspect of mental health work, must be expanded in a social direction. Just as somatic medicine during the past decades has gone beyond the sickbed and developed social and preventive medicine, psychiatry and mental health have been faced with socially oriented tasks of a preventive nature. Therefore, medical psychology and mental hygiene are nowadays extending beyond helping the sick individual, and mental health workers are becoming contributing and responsible members of the community as a whole. Alienated, if not uprooted from society, as many among them were, today's psychiatrists are in the process of taking roots again in the very stream of life of this society. (Pfister-Ammende 1971).

Origin of Contributions and References: See Page 341

IMMIGRATION TO AUSTRALIA
Mental Health Aspects

A. Stoller and J. Krupinski
Australia

Post-War Migration

The past 25 years have witnessed an immense change in the growth of the Australian population. Although Australia has been a settlers' country from its very beginning, and the whole non-Aboriginal population consists of migrants or descendants of migrants, the inhabitants of this country were almost entirely of British stock up to World War II. The last pre-war census, carried out in 1933, recorded only 2.6% of the population as being born outside of Australia, British and other white British dominions. These included 18,000 born in non-white British dominions and in the U.S.A., who were most probably also of British stock. The situation did not change until after World War II; for example, during the post-depression decade, 1931-1940, the net gain due to migration was only 30,396.

World War II constituted a landmark in the development of Australia. The danger of a Japanese invasion during that war and the disappearance of the protective British umbrella afterwards brought home the message that Australia had to populate or perish. The first Minister for Immigration of the Commonwealth of Australia, Arthur A. Calwell, formulated the Australian immigration policy in 1945 as follows:

> "We have only the next 25 years to make the best possible use of our second chance to survive . . . Our requirement is additional population. We need it for reasons of defence and for the fullest expansion of our economy" (quoted after Armstrong, 1969).

This policy has been supported by both major Australian political parties, Labor and Liberal, and the then Leader of the Opposition, Sir Robert Menzies, who subsequently became Prime Minister for a prolonged period expressed similar views in 1945:

> "I believe that upon the possibility of our securing a substantial migration to Australia during the next 30 years will depend, not only the preservation of Australian independence, but also the true prospects of advancement of social benefits in Australia" (ibid).

The following 25 years have witnessed a full realization of that immigration policy. The total number of permanent and long-term arrivals during the period

1945-1969 amounted to 3,132,000, of which 1,531,070 were assisted immigrants (Department of Immigration, 1970). Even when the departures of settlers and Australian residents are subtracted, the net gain of Australian population during that period amounted to 1,442,410, constituting 12.0% of the Australian population in 1969. The last national Census, carried out in 1966, recorded 2,130,921, or 18.4% of population born outside of Australia. If the number of 463,250 children born of non-Australian parents are added, the proportion of first and second generation migrants increases to 22.5%. When the number of children with one non-Australian parent is added, the percentage of first and second generation migrants increases to 27.4%.

The rate of migration has not only increased in the post-war period, but has remained steady without the fluctuations previously recorded in Australian history. More importantly the origin of migrants has changed drastically. While immigrants to Australia came along entirely from the British Isles and other English-speaking countries prior to World War II, this was true for only 60.2% of assisted and 50.7% of all permanent and long-term post-war arrivals to Australia; thus the percentage of the non-British-born population increased from 1.5% to 8.5% between the 1947 and 1966 censuses (Rooth 1968). The other important feature of the post-war migration has been the 335,000 refugees, with 170,000 coming directly from Displaced Persons' camps.

Although the initial aim of the post-war migration was to populate Australia, the big influx of immigrants has had nevertheless a great influence on the Australian economy. They have provided and still provide a necessary work-force, without which the development of Australia would have been impossible. Australia is currently the fourth richest country in the world. Between the census years 1947-1966 Australia's workforce increased by 1.7 million, of whom more than one million were post-war migrants (Snedden, 1969).

Rooth (1968) has assessed the influence of migrants on the economic growth of Australia:

"In the manufacturing industries alone, migrants have added 282,000 to the work force and a further 48,000 have joined the building and construction industries. The number of factories has almost doubled in the past twenty years to help accommodate not only migrant men but also their wives, who have joined the work force at a higher rate than Australian women. It is doubtful if places like Woolongong – Port Kembla, Mount Isa and the Pilbara area of the north-west of Western Australia could have developed without migrant labor. More than 20,000 employees of the Australian Iron and Steel Pty. Ltd. at Port Kembla represent approximately forty different nationalities.

Steel production in Australia has more than trebled and migrants have supplied 70% of the extra workers needed in the post-war period. The production of more steel has led to the development of other major industries. The production of motor vehicles has saved millions of dollars in imports and gained approximately $16 million in exports annually."

Zubrzycki (1960 and 1968) has shown how Australia has benefited from upper and lower professional migrants from Britain and other Western European countries, U.S.A., New Zealand and India. Complementary to this is the employment of southern European migrants in unskilled and semi-skilled occupations.

Migrants and their families have increased Australia's internal market substantially, contributing to the booming of the economy. In 1939, ten years after the great depression, 12.6% of the workers were unemployed in Australia; this rate had diminished to 1.1% in 1969, with a constant shortage of labor. Even those who criticize the Australian migration program, claiming it to be responsible for the overheating and inflationary tendencies of the Australian economy, admit that the influx of migrants, especially non-British stock, has added to the colorfulness and richness of Australian life (Hallows, 1970).

It has been stressed already that Australia has admitted over three hundred thousand refugees, the bulk of them coming from Displaced Person's camps in the late forties and early fifties. Displaced persons constituted 58% of all assisted settlers between January 1947 and June 1950. Although migrants were urgently needed because of the extreme shortage of labor, neither their shipping to Australia nor their accommodation after arrival were problems easily solved. There was a politically important and urgent need to repatriate Australian servicemen and provide homes for them and their families. Therefore, as stated by Armstrong (1969):

> "Only one course was open: priority would have to be given in Australia's immigration program to single men and married couples without children who could be used where they would make the greatest contribution to production for the minimum requirements in terms of shipping, accommodation and consumer goods. Workers from the Displaced Persons' camps of Europe were required to sign an undertaking to work anywhere they were sent in Australia for two years. Initially they were housed in former army and air force camps; some were even under canvas."

After the emptying of Displaced Persons' camps in Europe, Australia turned to Britain as her traditional source of migrants. However, Britain alone could not satisfy Australia's burning needs, although the net gain of settlers from that country has exceeded half a million over the past decade. Other western and northern European countries also could not provide sufficient numbers of migrants, especially with the growing prosperity of the European market countries. Southern Europe, especially Italy and Greece, became the main non-British sources of migrants for Australia. In the past decade, 21.8% of the whole, and 39.5% of the non-British, net gain of settlers have been due to migration from southern European countries.

Thus the Australian immigrant population can be divided into four main groups. The most numerous are still the British immigrants who came to an English-speaking country with similar cultural and ethnic features; they remained

British subjects and had the choice of returning home at any time they wished, subject to economic considerations. The second group of immigrants, from western, northern and central Europe came from economically-developed countries with patterns of life similar to Australia; they also could return to their own countries if they did not succeed here; their reasons for migration were similar to those of British migrants; but unlike the latter, they experienced language difficulties. The third group, southern European migrants, came predominantly from peasants of low cultural and educational background; their main reason for emigrating to Australia was the wish to improve their very low standard of living; and although return to southern Europe was theoretically possible, they faced the difficult task of accumulating sufficient funds to pay their return fares to resettle themselves. Migrants from eastern Europe differed from all the others in that those coming to this country, through displaced persons' and refugee camps, could not be regarded as voluntary migrants and had little prospect of return; also, since voluntary migrants from eastern Europe had emigrated chiefly for political reasons, their decision was also irreversible in most cases.

Assimilation and Integration of Migrants

The hope of the first Australian Minister for Immigration, Arthur Calwell "that for every foreign migrant there will be ten people from the United Kingdom" (quoted after Rooth, 1968) has not been fulfilled. The continued influx of non-British migrants has made the 'melting-pot' theory of assimilation of all immigrants to the Australian culture neither practical nor desirable. Instead of forcing migrants to adapt themselves to the Australian way of life without reservation, as was the case prior to the period of post-war migration, the Australian way of life is changing as a consequence of migration. Integration is occurring, involving dynamic interaction and adaptation as between host and migrant populations, and the cultural standards of the former are growing in breadth and variety as a consequence. A pluralistic society exists, with reasonable tolerance of cultural differences. There is no question of forced assimilation, as it is recognized that too rapid assimilation might well result in stresses not only for migrants but also for the Australian population. Economic absorption is occurring smoothly, and social acculturation, in line with the above, is occurring to varying degrees for individuals as well as groups. Changing values are paving the way for physical amalgamation to include ethnic groupings which are becoming well integrated, though final assimilation will not occur until migrant groups become indistinguishable from the host population (Stoller, 1966).

Studies of assimilation have been performed in Australia, especially within the framework of Taft's "shared frame of reference" (1957, 1958, 1959, 1963 and 1966), in terms of an approximation of values, attitudes and behavior between the minority of migrants and the majority of the host population, as an indication of assimilation. Taft and Doczy (1962) compared such different components of the assimilation process as "acculturation", "social interaction" or "identification" among Australians as well as non-British immigrants; while Johnston (1963) has formulated further concepts of "external assimilation" in which the migrant becomes externally less distinguishable from the host society (in terms of such acculturation factors as language, behavior, religious ideas, moral and political values, and so on) as well as from "subjective assimilation" (which involves the inner psychological life of the individual, and implies the development of satisfaction arising from identification with such host phenomena as food habits and leisure activities). Assimilation is only partial where both of these fail to be satisfied. While these sophisticated criteria of assimilation are never met by the first generation of migrants, and rarely even by their children, such criteria as knowledge of English, naturalization and intermarriage are more superficial, but nevertheless valuable, indices of adjustment.

A recent survey carried out in Melbourne (Krupinski and Stoller, 1971) showed that 90% of non-British immigrants who have stayed in this country for at least 10 years have a fair command of English, as compared with 58% of the more recent arrivals. During the post-war period, 608,710 non-British migrants became naturalized. Although these constitute only 36.1% of all non-British permanent and long-term arrivals, one has to remember that, firstly, a proportion have left Australia and, secondly, naturalization is usually granted after at least five years of residence in this country. If the non-British permanent and long-term arrivals during the last five years are subtracted, the percentage of naturalized migrants increases to 65.8%.

Price (1966 and 1968) and Stoller (1968) studied patterns of marriage of different migrant groups and the host population and showed that whereas Britons and western Europeans, and to a lesser degree eastern Europeans, marry predominantly with Australians and other national groups, this is not true for southern Europeans who usually marry within their own national groups, despite the existing imbalance of sexes in the form of an excess of marriageable males (Immigration Advisory Council, 1969).

Discussing the assimilation of immigrants in Australia, one has to realize the different pace of assimilation even within one family. A relatively high proportion of female non-British migrants do not speak English or have only a very poor command of the language, even after a long period of residence in this country. Their husbands learn English at work and their children become assimilated at school. The mother remains the only non-assimilated person and becomes isolated within her own family as her role of mother and wife begins to diminish.

An even bigger discrepancy has been found between the older and younger generations of immigrants. Children and adolescents tend to become assimilated and acculturated rapidly, and this has been shown to be an important cause of intra-familial conflicts. The children want to integrate into the Australian community and the parents want to preserve their own national identity. As Johnston (1968) has stressed:

" ... second generation immigrants are caught, as it were in the cross-current influences of two powerful groups, both inflated with their own cultural superiority. Each group extends rewards for conformity to its own culture and severe punishments for deviation from it. Children studied in the present research are remaining under the pressure of the Australian community to assimilate, and are at the same time held back by some of their parents from doing so."

She added that "the greatest amount of tension occurs in the area of language." Parents speak their native language at home and insist that their children do the same. The usual pattern is that parents use their native language between themselves and in contact with the children. The children use the native language only in contact with parents and use English when communicating with siblings.

These disagreements and conflicts might cover all areas of life, food and clothing included, and result in a higher incidence of behavioral disorders in immigrant adolescents.

" ... rebelling against the imposition of parental values relating to family life and family relations, morals and freedom, brought from their countries of origin and differing from those prevalent in the Australian community" (Krupinski and Stoller, 1966).

Mental Ill Health

In Australia, and especially in Victoria, much work has been done to establish clearly, as a first step, the degree of mental illness in the migrant community (Cade and Krupinski, 1962; Krupinski and Stoller, 1965).

These studies differ in their methodology from others performed in this country (Commonwealth Immigration Advisory Council, 1961). Firstly, an immigrant was accepted as a person born outside Australia; secondly, immigrants were not treated as a homogeneous whole but were analyzed in terms of four geographical areas of origin: Britain, western Europe, eastern Europe and southern Europe; thirdly, the authors did not limit themselves to the evaluation of the overall incidence or prevalence of mental illness, but analyzed the incidence in terms of specific diagnostic categories. Incidence rates of psychiatric disorders were analyzed in terms of first admissions to any Victorian psychiatric facility, whether in-patient or out-patient. Period-prevalence refers to the number of persons under the care of the Victorian Mental Health Department during a given year and point-prevalence rates were computed on the basis of the number of residents in mental institutions on a given date. Whereas the study of Cade and Krupinski (1962) was based only on admissions to the biggest psychiatric hospital in Victoria, Krupinski and Stoller (1963-1970) were able to analyze the total of all first admissions to the various hospitals and out-patient clinics of the Victorian Mental Health Department.

While the distribution of all psychiatric admissions, in terms of country of birth, did not differ significantly from that of the general population, significant differences were found when specific diagnostic categories, which included mental retardation, were analyzed separately.

Some disorders, such as mental retardation and senile brain disorders, occur with less frequency in immigrants than in the Australian-born population. This can easily be explained by the fact that mental retardation, a readily diagnosed disorder, would prevent prospective immigrants and their families from entering this country. Senile brain disorders depend, on the other hand, on the age structure of the population, and there is a much lower proportion of aged persons among immigrants than among the native-born population.

Alcoholism does not appear to depend on immigration. The incidence of this disorder among British and eastern European immigrants roughly equals that of the Australian-born population, while it occurs to a much lower degree among western Europeans, and is almost unknown among those originating from southern Europe. This would indicate that alcoholism depends more on socio-cultural drinking habits of different segments of the Australian population than the mere fact of migration. However, the incidence of alcoholism in Britons in Australia is higher than that in the United Kingdom and therefore, in this group of migrants, it could be associated with migration (Judge and Glatt, 1961). There are, however, disturbances which occur to a much higher degree among the immigrant than in the native-born population, the most important being that major and most chronic psychiatric illness, schizophrenia. The incidence of this disorder, in terms of first admissions per 10,000 of population of each geographical area of origin, are presented in Table 1.

Table 1. Incidence of schizophrenia per 10,000 of population of each geographical area of origin

	1961	1962	1963	1964	1965	1966	1967	1968
				Males				
Eastern Europe	9.3	12.2	14.6	12.9	12.1	11.7	11.9	10.6
Southern Europe	2.7	5.3	5.6	4.9	4.6	6.3	6.4	5.1
Western Europe	4.2	5.6	5.2	4.0	3.9	5.0	5.1	2.7
Britain	3.5	2.5	2.0	1.9	2.1	2.5	2.5	2.5
Australia	2.6	2.1	2.2	2.0	1.7	1.9	1.9	1.4
				Females				
Eastern Europe	11.4	16.0	11.7	8.9	9.0	9.0	9.2	9.4
Southern Europe	5.7	6.7	5.1	4.8	5.9	8.0	8.1	3.8
Western Europe	6.7	2.5	3.0	4.2	5.0	4.6	4.7	5.2
Britain	2.9	2.2	2.5	1.9	2.7	2.3	2.3	2.6
Australia	2.8	2.9	2.4	2.2	2.3	2.2	2.2	1.9

As may be seen, the incidence of schizophrenia is higher for all non-British immigrants than for the British and the Australian-born, eastern European immigrants being affected to the highest degree. This trend has been constant for the last nine years, and is not dependent on the different age structures of the various populations, as will be shown later.

The high incidence of schizophrenia states in eastern Europeans could not but affect the point- and the period-prevalences of these disorders in this group of origin (Tables 2 and 3).

Table 2. Period-Prevalence of schizophrenia per 10,000 of population in terms of geographical area of origin

Schizophrenic	1963	1964	1965	1966	1967
			Males		
Eastern Europe	74.6	69.4	74.0	78.1	79.5
Southern Europe	21.6	21.2	21.1	26.3	26.8
Western Europe	16.9	16.4	15.9	18.0	18.3
Britain	20.5	18.2	16.7	18.6	18.9
Australia	19.4	19.1	18.4	19.5	19.8
			Females		
Eastern Europe	67.4	56.0	58.7	63.7	64.8
Southern Europe	22.0	18.1	22.3	25.4	25.8
Western Europe	21.4	16.4	17.5	19.9	20.2
Britain	24.0	19.6	18.0	18.7	19.0
Australia	25.6	23.5	22.6	22.4	22.8

Table 3. Point-Prevalence of schizophrenia per 10,000 of population in terms of geographical area of origin

Schizophrenic	1961	1964	1965	1966	1967
			Males		
Eastern Europe	41.4	45.3	45.4	49.1	50.0
Southern Europe	12.6	10.7	11.3	14.1	14.3
Western Europe	9.5	8.4	7.8	9.1	9.3
Britain	17.4	13.8	12.6	13.9	14.1
Australia	14.3	13.9	13.6	13.9	14.1
			Females		
Eastern Europe	26.5	28.0	28.8	26.5	27.0
Southern Europe	8.1	8.3	9.4	8.8	9.0
Western Europe	6.2	6.1	7.0	5.5	5.6
Britain	17.1	12.6	11.5	11.1	11.3
Australia	16.6	15.2	14.8	13.8	14.0

Depressive states have been found to be more common in some groups of immigrants, especially among British and eastern European immigrants. Personality and behavior disorders are beginning to emerge to a greater degree in second-generation immigrants as compared with the Australian-born.

Standardization according to age did not change the relationships determined for mental deficiency, schizophrenia, or for alcoholism; however, it diminished the incidence of depressive states and of psychoneuroses in migrants, as compared with the native population. On the other hand, there were higher incidences of personality disorders and situational trait disturbances among eastern European, western European and British migrants as compared with the Australian-born population and, especially, as compared with southern Europeans. The higher incidence of senile brain disorders in British migrants and in the Australian-born depended wholly on the proportion of the ages in both populations.

The question as to which came first, the migration or the psychiatric illness, needs to be considered. In other words, were the higher of mental disturbances in migrants due to the stresses of migration and the difficulties of adjustment in the new country, or were the prospective migrants already psychologically unstable individuals who had been unable to settle even in their own countries?

Schaechter (1965), in the course of obtaining a psychiatric history from both patients and relatives of 100 consecutive admissions of female non-British migrant patients to a Victorian psychiatric hospital, definitely established the presence of psychiatric illness prior to arrival in Australia in 27 cases; of these patients, 19 had been treated in mental hospitals prior to migration. In another 10 cases, there was a strong suspicion of a previous psychiatric illness. The shorter the time interval between the arrival in Australia and admission to a psychiatric hospital, the higher the percentage of patients with previous psychiatric histories. Almost half (45.5%) of those admitted during the first three years of their stay in Australia had what Schaechter regarded as an established mental illness prior to migration. If suspected cases of mental illness prior to migration are added, the percentage of those admitted within three years of arrival to Australia rises to 68.2%. On the other hand, only 17.5% of those admitted to psychiatric care, after eight or more years in Australia, had had an established psychiatric history prior to migration.

Krupinski, Schaechter and Cade (1965), in a further study, analyzed the socio-economic and cultural backgrounds of 755 immigrant patients, admitted to the Royal Park Psychiatric Hospital during one year. Only schizophrenic and depressive states, and alcoholism in males, could be analyzed in greater detail than before, since the number of patients with other diagnoses was too small from which to draw conclusions.

Although the authors were not able to compare their findings with a similar analysis of an appropriately matched sample of migrants who had not suffered from mental illness, their conclusions appear justifiable, even those based on comparisons within their own material.

The incidence of mental disorders was lower in immigrants who had arrived in this country at a later age than in those who came during the prime of life (Figure 1), although it would have been thought that older migrants would have more difficulty in assimilating. Elderly immigrants who came with, or to, their families do not have to work in most cases, and are protected by their families from the ordinary stresses of migration.

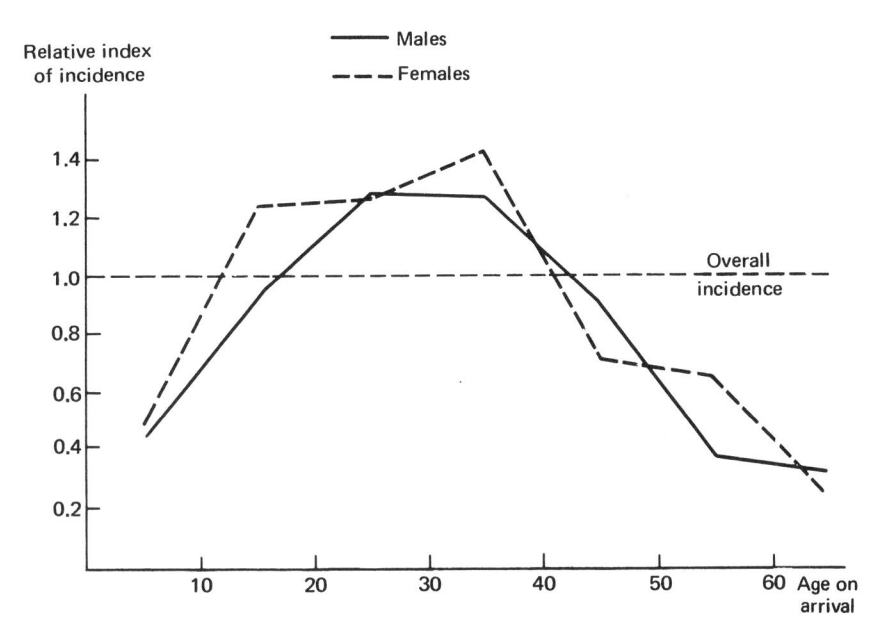

Fig. 1. Relative indices of incidence of psychiatric disorders in male and female migrants according to age on arrival in Australia. (Overall admission rate for males and females = 1).

There was a significant difference between the incidences of schizophrenia in males and in females, in terms of length of stay in this country (Figures 2 and 3). The incidence in males was highest 1-2 years after arrival to Australia, whilst the peak in females occurred after 7-15 years of residence.

The early breakdown in male immigrants can be related to the fact that a proportion migrated because of an already existing mental disorder or mental instability. These were mostly single men, who came here at the age of 20-29 without any family. One cannot, however, discard the possibility that the stresses of the initial struggle during the first years in a new country might also have contributed to the early breakdown of these male immigrants. The late onset cases, in both sexes, could be due to a sudden reduction of tension after a long period of struggle. This thesis may be supported by the fact that the financial situation of most immigrant patients was sound and there were only isolated cases of real financial deprivation in the population studied.

In females, the late onset of mental illness could be precipitated by the onset of the menopause, though it would appear to be predominantly due to the termination of the mother's former role in the family — when the offspring have become adult, independent, assimilated into the community and have left her isolated.

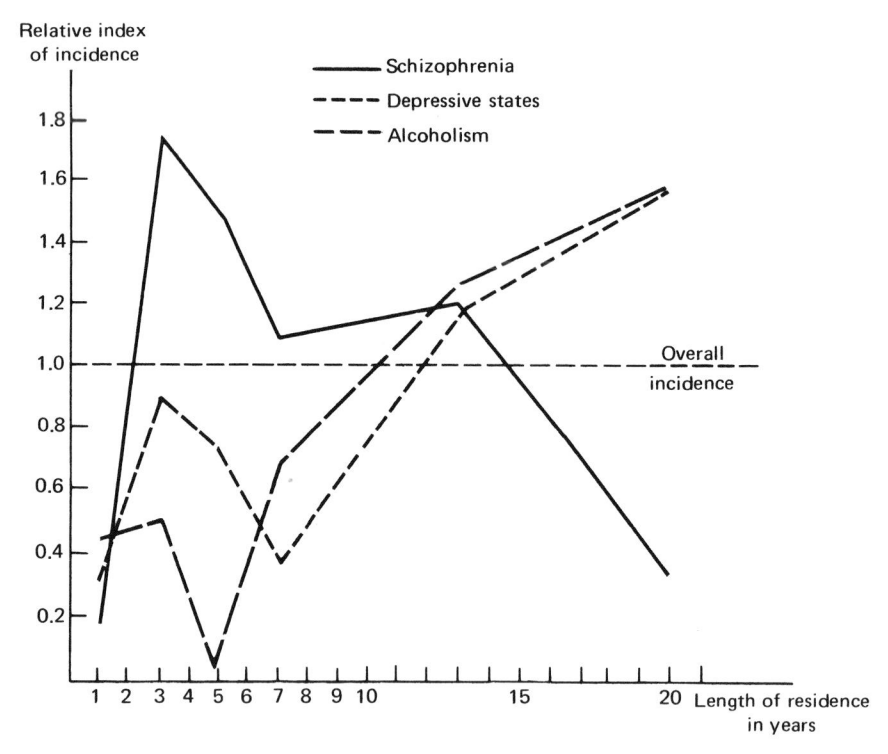

Fig. 2. Relative indices of incidence of schizophrenia, depressive states and alcoholism in male migrants according to duration of residence in Australia. (Overall admission rate for each disorder in males = 1).

One-third of male, but only one-twelfth of the female, migrant patients were without relatives in this country at the time of admission. On the other hand, almost one-third of both male and female patients had their families living in Australia. These figures should be compared with the remaining population. Unfortunately, the only figures available are those concerning the family composition of assisted migrants on arrival in Australia. According to these, two out of every five assisted adult migrants arrived unaccompanied, another two out of five in family groups of three or more, and the rest came in family groups of two. Thus, the proportion of assisted adult immigrants who arrived unaccompanied is higher than that of patients without relatives in Australia. Of course, assisted migrants, who comprise 43% of all arrivals in Australia, cannot be regarded as representative of the whole migrant population. It is very likely that most non-assisted migrants come to their families, who are sponsoring their migration to this country. Even for assisted migrants, these figures have to be accepted with some reservations, as family composition on arrival is not necessarily equivalent to that of immigrants living in Australia generally. For instance, a bride coming to her future husband is recorded as arriving unaccompanied, although she starts a family

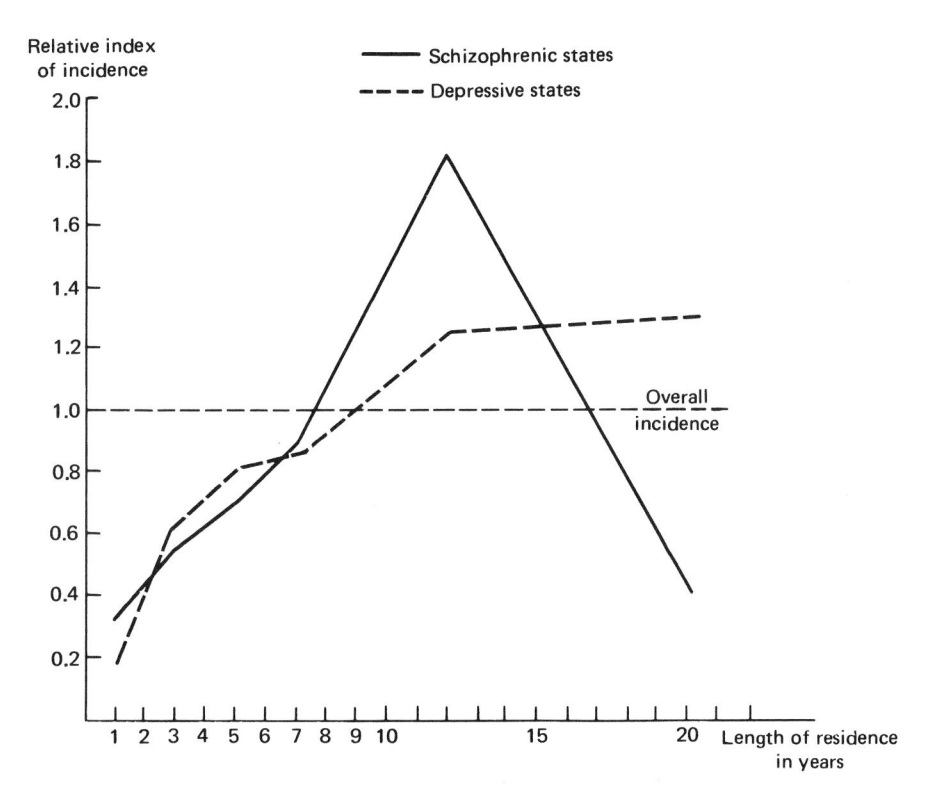

Fig. 3. Relative indices of incidence of schizophrenia and depressive states for female migrants according to duration of residence in Australia. (Overall admission rate for each disorder in females = 1).

life almost immediately after disembarkation. More common perhaps, are the arrivals of "unaccompanied" immigrants who have their families already established in Australia. Thus the proportion of migrants without a family in Australia is probably significantly lower than official reports of the number arriving unaccompanied to this country, but not lower to such a degree that it would indicate a higher incidence of mental disorders in this group of migrants.

While the protective role of family life for male migrants is still disputable, it is quite clear that it does not protect female migrants to the same extent as their Australian-born counterparts. One can still ask whether single male migrants who came here without any family are more prone to mental illness than those married men who came with their entire families, especially as the first group comprises, to a high degree, those unstable young men who could not adjust themselves in their own country and who had succumbed early to mental illness.

There is, however, no doubt that the proportions of single female migrant patients (14.8%), and those who have no relatives in Australia (8.7%), are lower than the corresponding percentages for the entire migrant population. This means that, in contradistinction to the general population, marriage does not protect female migrants from mental breakdown. This could be due, as already mentioned, to the frustration connected with the isolation of the non-assimilated mother within her own family.

Family tensions are probably responsible for the higher incidence of personality and behavioral disorders in adolescent migrants (except southern European), as compared with the Australian-born parents of a similar group of juvenile delinquents. The low incidence of personality disorders in southern European adolescents could be due to the fact that southern European families tend to be integrated to a degree that their children still accept the authority of their parents.

While the protective role of family life is still disputable, the adverse influence of mental illness on family life is directly revealed by the disintegration of immigrant families as a consequence of existing psychiatric disorder in one of its members. It has already been stated that one-third of male patients arrived with no relatives in this country, but almost 60% were living alone when admitted to a psychiatric hospital. This difference is especially striking among alcoholic males, where 72.8% are living away from their families as compared with 41.9% who have no relatives in this country (Table 4).

The difference between the proportion of patients living alone and those who have no relatives in this country is made up by the proportion of those separated and divorced. This indicates the high degree of disintegration of the families of male migrant patients.

In females, this phenomenon is not so marked. The proportion living alone is also higher than that of female patients without families in Australia, but the difference is not so marked as in males (15.8% as against 8.7%). On the other hand, female migrant patients experienced severe difficulties at home to a greater degree than their male counterparts (27.7% for females as compared with 16.5% for males). Thus the male patient, especially the alcoholic, abandons, or is abandoned by, his family while the female patient encounters severe difficulties in her home with less formal disintegration of the family.

The social class status of migrant patients, based on educational, vocational or professional qualifications and on past and present occupations, could not be compared with that of the general migrant population, as no such information was available for the latter. However, the percentage distribution of male patients, according to occupation, could be compared with a corresponding distribution of migrants who arrived in this country from 1947 to 1960 (in 1961 and 1962, a new classification for occupations was adopted by the Commonwealth Bureau of Census and Statistics, not comparable with the previous one). Relative indices of incidence (Figure 4) show that the incidence of all diseases was highest amongst professional and semi-professional migrants, i.e. those who were in higher social classes prior to migration. There is a decreasing incidence through the social scale, but it rises again in unskilled workers as compared to skilled and white-collar workers.

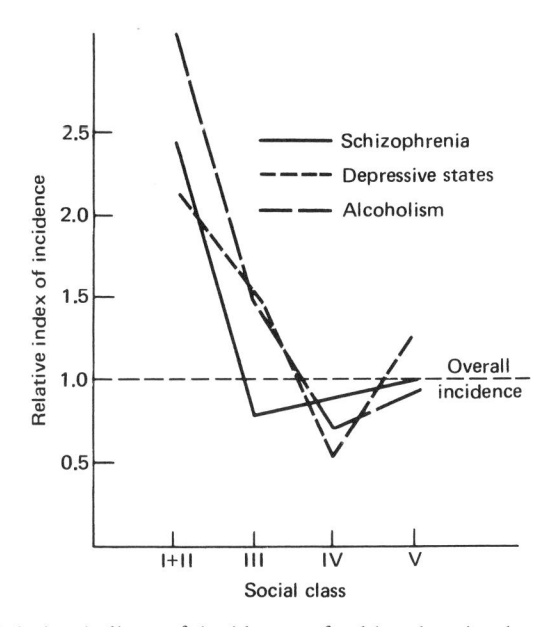

Fig. 4. Relative indices of incidence of schizophrenia, depressive states and alcoholism in male migrants according to occupation prior to migration. (Overall admission rates for each disorder in males = 1).

Table 4. Male migrant patients admitted to the Psychiatric Hospital, Royal Park, in the financial year 1961-1962, in terms of their family structure and psychiatric DIAGNOSIS

Diagnostic category	Percentage without family in this country	Percentage living alone	Percentage separated and divorced
Schizophrenic states	37.4	59.6	12.9
Depressive states	32.4	44.4	19.6
Alcoholism	41.9	72.8	23.5
Total Males	33.9	58.3	15.8

This phenomenon can be explained when present social status is compared with the educational standard achieved. Of all migrant patients with university degrees, 70% had descended to a lower social class. In fact, this loss of status occurred among all eastern European patients in this group, compared with only 20% of British patients. This means that the higher incidences in the professional and semi-professional groups could be a reflection of the difficulties they experienced in working in their own professional fields. Tradesmen and clerical workers experienced less severe difficulties provided they knew English.

The rise in incidence among the unskilled group is not unexpected, since the same phenomenon occurs in the general population. However, one-third of migrant patients, with less than primary education, rose from this lowest grade and became small tradesmen and shopkeepers.

The economic and housing conditions of migrant patients could not be compared with the general population of migrants, as could social class status, since such information was not available. However, it should be stressed that very few patients were in such deprived financial conditions as to contribute to their mental breakdowns. There was a significantly higher proportion of more well-to-do patients among depressive males than among schizophrenic or alcoholic males. Female schizophrenics constituted the only group complaining of difficulties at work, and there were no differences between national groups in this regard. This suggests that the attitude towards migrants, in their work situations, is satisfactory and has not been a significant influence on the incidence of morbidity. In other words, such complaints were a product of the illness, rather than of the work situation. There was a high proportion of patients with difficulties at home, especially among women. Southern European males had practically no difficulties at home, which clearly reflects a cultural pattern.

Eastern Europeans, who showed the highest rates of schizophrenic states (Table 1) and who also scored highly in other disorders, lived through severe war-time experiences to a much higher degree than other groups of origin (Table 5).

Table 5. War-time experiences according to sex and place of birth

Sex	War-time experiences	British migrants	Western Europe	Southern Europe	Eastern Europe	Total
Male	Severe	8.2	20.8	2.4	25.3	14.0
	Moderate	67.2	33.3	30.9	43.9	51.2
	None	24.6	45.9	66.7	30.8	34.8
Total		100.0	100.0	100.0	100.0	100.0
Female	Severe	1.4	—	4.0	62.8	22.0
	Moderate	8.3	63.3	27.6	30.2	27.3
	None	90.3	36.7	68.4	7.0	50.7
Total		100.0	100.0	100.0	100.0	100.0

It should be noted that the decision concerning the category in which a given patient should be included was not made on the basis of the subjective judgement of the patient, but was based on detailed descriptions of war-time experiences. Imprisonment, tortures, concentration and prisoner-of-war camps (the last when connected with special hardships), loss of family, special discrimination, etc., were regarded as severe experiences, while contact with war in the armed forces, in bombed cities, but without special hardship, were regarded as moderate. Patients who positively answered that they did not have any war-time experiences were included in the third category. Almost two-thirds of eastern European female patients went through Nazi concentration camps, lost their families, or suffered other severe hardships.

As immigrants from eastern Europe showed the highest rate of schizophrenia and had had the most severe war experiences, an intensive study of post-war refugees was carried out, dividing them according to their country of birth, with Jewish refugees separated from all others (Krupinski et al., 1971).

It was shown that the refugee groups are not homogeneous in terms of war experiences. As expected, the Jews were the most persecuted during the Nazi occupation and half of them went through concentration and death camps. Refugees from Poland, Russia, Ukraine and Bielorussia also suffered severe hardhsips, mainly in prisoner-of-war and labor camps. In contrast, refugees from Baltic countries, Czechoslovakia, Hungary and Yugoslavia (mainly Croatia) did not report special hardships during the Nazi occupation, essentially escaping from the communist takeover of their countries; they came mainly from middle-class backgrounds and tended to lose social status after coming to Australia.

Jewish refugees showed the lowest rate of schizophrenia and there was no difference between the other two groups in this regard. The Jews however, had the highest rate of severe neurotic symptoms, which was associated significantly with the severity of their war experiences. These symptoms nevertheless did not prevent them from establishing themselves successfully in this country, and as Taft and Goldlust (1970) pointed out, they did even better than Jews who had migrated to Australia from the same countries prior to World War II.

This would indicate that these Jewish survivors were a doubly selected group, firstly, through possession of a degree of toughness which enabled them to survive the Nazi holocaust; and secondly, by virtue of possession of a state of health which enabled them to be accepted for migration to Australia. Nevertheless, they had responded to their severe war experiences by developing neurotic and other psychiatric symptoms which, although not incapacitating them in their social performance, put a great strain on them in their everyday life. Over a quarter of Jewish refugees reported psychological problems in their children. Mental illness in Polish and Russian refugees was clearly associated with war experiences while, in the third group of refugees, it seemed to be related to diminished social status rather than to hardships during the war period.

Discussion

While the immigration program appears to have been largely successful overall, there still exists a constant need to consider the dynamics of migrant adjustment and make efforts to delineate and remedy the problems arising from migration (Stoller, 1968).

Language attainment is a most important aspect of migrant integration. Courses for training migrants in English are begun as early as possible, even in the native country and on ship-board. Although, up to now, this program has worked fairly well (Krupinski and Stoller, 1971), there is beginning to emerge for the first time, large, low socio-economic ethnic groupings with language problems in the centers of large capital cities which tend to be self-perpetuating and affect the upward mobility of both migrant adults and their children. As stated (Stoller, 1968):

"A survey carried out through the Department of Immigration's field officers and the Victorian Migrant Education Section indicated that a high proportion of Southern Europeans were poorly motivated towards language attainment. They were communicating through their native tongue, since over 75% were working predominantly with fellow nationals, 66% did not need to know English for their work, over 80% had no social contacts outside their national group, about 90% were living with relatives, shops where their own language was spoken were patronized, and over 94% used their native tongue exclusively at home."

Although these ethnic accumulations can be protective to the adult, the concentration of children in overcrowded, inner urban schools, could adversely affect the traditional role of the schools in fostering integration. To overcome this, pilot programs of "crash language courses" and language laboratories have been introduced in these areas.

Economic problems arise especially in southern European immigrants who come from low social and economic backgrounds and who are employed mainly as unskilled workers. Nevertheless, they are, from the beginning, mostly better off than in their country of origin and surveys have demonstrated they tend towards considerable upward financial mobility within ten years. Home ownership reaches Australian levels after ten years. However, if their children remain occupationally disadvantaged, this could create problems for the future. To help immigrants cope with early difficulties the Australian Government has recently instituted a plan to insure them against illness for the first two months after arrival, a committee has been set up which is investigating the recognition of migrant qualifications and social workers are being appointed to help ethnic groups develop their own social supports. More, however, needs to be done in regard to the vocational training of immigrant children and adolescents.

Immigration has changed the pattern of the predominantly Australian urban way of life and the Australian himself has become much less isolated and exeurophobic. The traditional "White Australian" policy has given way to a selective policy of admission of Asiatics who have good prospects of integration into Australian society.

It may be anticipated that the rates of mental illness in more recent immigrants will be lower, since there are no refugees and the presence of ethnic groupings will be protective for the adults. However, in these circumstances, may it not be the children who will feel alienated and caught between the two cultures and who will provide the most vulnerable group in the immigrant population? It is for this reason that the authors have undertaken a regular monitoring of patterns of mental illness of immigrants in Victoria, so that remedial measures may be undertaken as soon as maladjustment in any particular group of first or second-generation immigrants appears.

Origin of Contributions and References: See Page 342

MIGRATION AND MENTAL ILL-HEALTH IN INDUSTRY

K. Bhaskaran, R. C. Seth, S. N. Yadav
India

The studies by Ødegaard (1932) and Malzberg (1940) have clearly shown that migration from one country to another is associated with a greater incidence of psychiatric illness in the migrant. Evidence is not so unanimous in favor of a greater incidence of psychiatric illness in populations migrating from one place to another within the same country.

The study of Lazarus, Locke and Thomas (1963) showed that the age-standardized rates of first admission to mental hospitals for major psychiatric ailments in New York, Ohio and California were higher for migrants than for non-migrants. Both in Ohio (Locke et al 1960) and in New York (Malzberg and Lee 1956) migrants living in what are called the "non-metropolitan zones," like migrants living in "metropolitan" areas were found to have higher age-standardized rates than non-migrants.

Everett Lee (1963) has shown that for New York, for the 20-54 age-range, marital status, educational and occupational status has little effect on the picture.

The several studies carried out in U.S.A. established a clear relationship between migration and major mental illness.

As contrasted with these studies, the study by Odegaard (1945) of all first admissions to Norwegian Psychiatric Hospitals during 1926-1939, showed that only in Oslo, did migrants have higher rates than natives. For all other parts of the country, however, people born locally had higher rates than those born elsewhere.

The above-mentioned studies have utilized the first admission-figures of mental hospital and considered the prevalence rates of major psychoses only.

As far as the relationship between the industrial setting and psychiatric disability is concerned, Fraser's study in Birmingham (Fraser 1947) revealed a prevalence rate of 240 per thousand for all types of psychoneuroses. The study by Ganguli and co-workers in a Delhi Textile Factory (Ganguli 1967) revealed a prevalence rate of 128 per thousand for psychoneuroses and psychoses. Caravedo and Valdivia (1961) examining 85 Union Leaders and 33 Managers belonging to 33 industrial corporations showed evidence of "Psychic-Pathology" in the form of mal-adaption in emotional relationships, anguish, tension, susceptibility, irritability, psycho-physiological reactions and conversion symptoms.

There are very few studies, however, dealing with the prevalence of mental morbidity of migrants in an industrial setting as compared to the non-migrants in the same setting, and thus the present study was undertaken.

Material and Method

100 workers in a specific salary-range (Rs. 100-350 P.M.) and a specific occupational-category-range (Turners, Fitters, Crane Operators, Overseers, Foremen and Supervisors) of the Heavy Machine Building Plant of the Heavy Engineering Corporation (H.E.C.), Ranchi, who had migrated from the Southern States of Madras, Andhra Pradesh, Kerala and Mysore, constituted the Migrant Group in this study (Table 14, 15 & 16). Another randomly chosen 100 workers in the same salary and occupational-category-range in the same plant, but who were domiciled citizens of Bihar State constituted the Control Group. Each of the subjects of the Migrant and Control Groups was examined physically and psychiatrically by a Psychiatrist and information obtained through semistructured interviews in the following specific areas:

1. Biographical data.
2. Past history of psychiatric and psychosomatic illness.
3. Family history of psychiatric and psychosomatic illness.
4. Degree of work-satisfaction.
5. Accident record.
6. Leave record.
7. Degree of social inter-action with the local population.
8. Clinical evidence of psychiatric and psychosomatic illness at the time of interview.
9. Data regarding the time of migration, reasons for migration, degree of home sickness, etc., in the case of migrants.
10. Data on the family pattern and functioning of the individual subjects of both groups obtained by a Psychiatric Social Worker through home visits and semi-structured interviews of the family members.

Nearly 20% of the 200 subjects were examined independently by the Senior Psychiatrist and differences in evaluation of psychiatric status, if any, between the two Psychiatrists were reconciled by comparison of case-notes and joint discussion.

Table 1.
Age Distribution

	20-29	30-39	40 & above	Total
Migrant Group	33	59	8	100
Control Group	52	38	10	100

Discussion

Though the two groups were initially matched only for the salary-range and the occupational-category-range, actually, they turned out to be broadly similar in many other respects also, as for example, religious denomination, technical training before joining the H.E.C. and after joining the H.E.C., number of years of service in the H.E.C., number of subjects in the Supervisory and non-supervisory posts, change in the financial status consequent to joining the H.E.C., number for whom the H.E.C. job was the first job ever held, etc. The number of subjects between the ages of 20 and 39 was also similar in the two groups, though, if we consider the number of subjects between 30 and 39, the number in the Migrant Group was higher (59) than the Control Group (38) (Table - 1). The number of married subjects in the Migrant Group was 66 as compared to 82 in the Control Group (Table No. 3).

It may be seen from Table No. 12 that the prevalence rate of psychiatric and psychosomatic illness in both the Control and the Migrant Groups is very much higher than in the general population, as revealed by the studies by Dube (1967) and Sethi et al (1967), though the figures obtained in our study cannot be extrapolated to the whole factory population in view of the relatively small size of our sample. In an earlier study by Thomas, Bhaskaran & Chopra (1966) dealing with psychiatric morbidity survey of a compact village (Boriya) situated about 8 miles from Ranchi, out of 1444 people surveyed, 26 were found to be suffering from psychiatric and psychosomatic illnesses, giving a prevalence rate of 18 per thousand. It may be seen therefore that the prevalence of psychiatric and psychosomatic morbidity in our Control Group is higher than for a select rural population of Ranchi and that for the migrant workers in the same factory is still higher, clearly suggesting that the industrial setting itself poses stresses which increases the mental health hazards of workers and migration constitutes and additional source of stress and further increases the mental health hazard.

While there were 6 cases of paranoid state in the Migrant Group there was no case belonging to this category in the Control Group. Those diagnosed as suffering from Paranoid State showed a clear misinterpretation of reality and a clear delusional system with varying degrees of systematization, this category including both short-lived and persistent paranoid reactions. One subject expressed the strong conviction that he was not promoted because of favoritism and went on complaining to the higher authorities even after the situation was explained to him. His work-record was also unsatisfactory. Another subject felt that the local people were planning to rob his house and was sleepless at nights. He also felt that his life was in danger. A third subject felt that he was being given inferior medicines whenever he was physically ill, as compared to the local employees, and later felt it was even unsafe to take these medicines.

The four subjects in the Migrant Group and one subject in the Control Group who showed clear evidence of Schizophrenia gave a history of similar episodes of illness in the past, so that it is likely that the illness in these subjects was preexistent. It is equally likely, however, that the stresses associated with migration and/or the industrial setting were responsible for the reecrudescence of the illness noticed at the time of interview.

Table No. 10 and Table No. 11 reveal no significant difference between the two groups in the matter of family history of psychiatric and psychosomatic illness and in the past history of such illness in the subjects.

The high figures in the Migrant Group and the Control Group may well be due to the inclusion of milder types of psychiatric illnesses but then, in planning adequately and realistically for the mental health needs of a select population like industrial workers it is important that we take into account all degrees of mal-adjustment including the minor ones.

Regarding the explanation for the higher mental morbidity of migrants as compared to non-migrants, at least three hypotheses have been offered (Murphy 1965). The "drift" hypothesis maintains that migration might be the result rather than the cause of psychiatric illness. In other words, migration may only be a symptom of the underlying illness. In a less radical form, this hypothesis maintains that the mental illness in migrants is pre-existent and has little or nothing to do with migration. Our data do not lend strong support to this hypothesis. It is true that some of the subjects did show evidence of psychiatric disability even before migration, but the history of psychiatric and psychosomatic illness in the pre-migration period in migrants was not more frequent than in the Control Group, while the actual prevalence of morbidity in the Migrant Group at the time of examination was very much higher than in the Control Group.

Secondly, many subjects developed psychiatric and psychosomatic symptoms only after migration.

Thirdly, while six subjects in the Migrant Group showed evidence of Paranoid State, none in the Control Group showed evidence of this illness and the persecutory ideas in these cases concerned the local people.

Fourthly, analyzing the reasons for migration, we find that the most commonly advanced reasons were economic advancement and bettering one's occupational prospects. These, combined with the fact that these migrants got their jobs after very keen competition rules out the possibility that these people were sick before they migrated.

Fifthly, migration was not found to be associated with downward mobility in the occupational status of the migrants, as would be expected if the drift hypothesis was operating.

The second or non-association hypothesis contends that migration is not invariably associated with increased psychiatric morbidity and even if it is, the factors that are responsible for this increased morbidity have nothing to do with migration or migrational stresses per se, the relevant factors being actually concerned with aspiration – achievement discrepancy, frustrations associated with the inability to fulfill conflicting role expectations, etc. The strongest advocates of this point of view are Kleiner and Parker (1965). In an earlier study (Kleiner and

Parker 1959) the authors investigated the differential rates of mental illness for migrant and non-migrant negroes in Pennsylvania, as gauged by first admissions to State Psychiatric Hospitals for the period 1951-1956. They found, contrary to the more widely-held view, lower rates of mental illness for Southern migrants than for native-born Pennsylvanians, particularly for diagnosed Schizophrenia. However, migrants from other Northern States had higher rates than the native-born. They then planned the later study to find out if there were other intervening socio-psychological variables to explain the observed correlations, and concluded that the really important variable was the aspiration-achievement discrepancy. We have unfortunately no data like the verbalized aspirations of the subjects to test this hypothesis directly, but the indirect data available do not seem to support this hypothesis; for example, if we use the data on occupational status and educational status as criteria to infer aspiration-achievement discrepancy, a reference to Table No. 21 reveals that 88% of the migrant subjects stood to gain financially by moving to Ranchi and joining the H.E.C. as compared to 82% of the Control Group. As regards the educational status, a reference to Table No. 4 reveals that while 83% of the Migrant Group had either passed Matriculation or studied up to Matriculation, the corresponding figure for the Control Group is 73%. Considering the educational qualifications of the migrant subjects, the jobs that the majority were engaged in and their income appear to be commensurate with the educational status. If any, the aspiration-achievement discrepancy should be more pronounced in the Control Group than in the Migrant Group; for while there are as many as 21 subjects who had passed I.A. or I. Sc. in the Migrant Group, though the number of supervisory posts held by subjects in the Migrant Group and the Control Group were not widely different, namely 20 and 23, respectively, (Table No. 20).

Again if we analyze the reasons for job-dissatisfaction, while only 45% of the migrant subjects gave "absence of promotion since joining the H.E.C." as a reason for dissatisfaction, 33% of the Control Group also gave the same reason for job-dissatisfaction, and the difference between the two groups in this respect is not significant (between 0.30 and 0.50).

There is, however, some indication that there was a greater preoccupation among the migrant subjects for aspiring to a higher social status, as compared to the Control Group; for while 30% of the migrant subjects claimed friends in a social class higher than their own, only 8% of the Control Group claimed such friends (Table No. 8).

It is possible that this hypothesis has some validity and more adequately planned studies are called for to elucidate the relationships between the sociopsychological variables, like aspiration-achievement discrepancy, conflicts associated with social motility, etc. and psychiatric morbidity.

The third hypothesis which may be termed "migration-as-stress" hypothesis, maintains that there is a clear relationship between migration and the increased mental morbidity and this is held by most investigators. Our data seem to support this hypothesis in view of the following observations:

1. A high prevalence rate of Paranoid State in the Migrant Group, with the local population felt as persecutory agents.
2. A greater degree of job-dissatisfaction among the migrants as compared to the local population (Table 6).
3. Relating the job-dissatisfaction to the "hostile local environment", by as high as 49% of the migrants who were dissatisfied (Table 7).
4. A high prevalence of home-sickness among the migrants (Table 18).
5. Absence of casual contact with the local population in social relationships on the part of majority of the migrants (Table 19).
6. A clearly more marked desire on the part of the migrants to find jobs elsewhere (Table 5).

The study clearly establishes that the migrant subjects are exposed to major difficulties in social adjustment which in turn reflect on their work-satisfaction and mental health. The socio-psychological stresses associated with migration have been well-documented by other investigators and are clearly borne out by this study. They comprise difficulties in communication due to language barrier, home-sickness, social isolation, feeling that the local population is unfriendly, etc.

Summary and Conclusion

The prevalence of psychiatric and psychosomatic illness in 100 migrant subjects from the Southern States of India in a specific salary range and a specific occupational-category-range in the Heavy Machine Building Plant of Heavy Engineering Corporation, Ranchi, is compared with the prevalence of these illnesses in a randomly chosen matched 100 subjects belonging to the local region.

The prevalence of these illnesses was much higher in the migrant group than in the Control Group, the prevalence rate in both the groups seemed to be higher than in the general population.

Socio-psychological stresses associated with migration seem to be significantly related to this increased psychiatric morbidity in the migrants, though one cannot altogether rule out the role of individual-oriented socio-psychological variables like aspiration-achievement discrepancy, conflicts associated with aspirations to upward social mobility and frustrations associated with these and other aspects of goal-striving.

The authors are deeply indebted to the Indian Council of Medical Research for their financial support in the conduct of this study, and to the Chairman, Heavy Engineering-Corporation, Ranchi, General Manager, Heavy Machine Building Plant, and to the subjects themselves for their co-operation in making this study possible.

Recommendations for Action

1. The high prevalence of psychiatric morbidity in the industrial workers needs our immediate attention. Studies should be carried out in different industrial

establishments utilizing a larger number of subjects to —
- a) confirm the high morbidity suggested in this study,
- b) study the types of illness that are most frequent,
- c) study the relevant aetiological factors,
- d) study the relative prevalence of morbidity in the various income groups in the industrial population, and
- e) attempt to identify the "population at risk" among the industrial workers.

2. If the findings in this study are corroborated it will call for the services of a Psychiatrist in industrial establishments, at least on a part-time basis.

3. The problems of "acculturation" of migrants are many and varied and seem to be intimately related to the high prevalence of psychiatric morbidity in this population. The need for increasing their social acceptance by the host-community is obvious.

Establishing Social, Recreational and Athletic Clubs and organizing language-classes for teaching the local language to those lacking fluency will greatly help in facilitating assimilation of the migrants in the host-community.

Appointment of Migrant Welfare Officers to attend to the individual and group problems of migrants will be a great help. These persons should be preferably Social Workers or Welfare Officers with some knowledge and experience of Social Work.

It will be the primary duty of these Officers to interview every migrant employee on first appointment, help him with problems of accommodation and other aspects of living and encourage formation of friendships with members of the host group. He will also concern himself with the problems of the migrants as a group and help in resolving them, or referring them to the administrative authorities concerned.

Further research preferably on a large scale is indicated, to evaluate the relative significance of the various factors outlined in the body of the paper in leading to decompensation in migrant workers. A study of psychiatric morbidity in the relatives of migrants will help us in assessing the relative aetiological relevance of problems of social adjustment of migrants and that of stress associated with work-situation in the industry in connection with psychiatric morbidity among migrants.

Table 2. Religious denomination

	Hindu	Muslim	Christian	Total
Migrant group	75	1	24	100
Control group	79	2	19	100

Table 3. Marital status

	Married	Widowed	Single	Total
Migrant group	66	Nil	34	100
Control group	82	Nil	18	100

Table 4. Educational level

	Illiterate	Primary	Up to matric	Matric passed	I.A. or I.Sc. passed	Graduate	Total
Migrant group	2	8	28	55	6	1	100
Control group	2	4	24	49	20	1	100

Table 5. Number and percentage of subjects who had applied for jobs outside H.E.C. in 2 years preceding the year of interview

	Not recorded	Recorded	Number	Percentage	P.
Migrant group	6	94	28	30	0.01
Control group	3	97	8	8	(X^2 = 14.48 df = 1).

Table 6. Number and percentage of subjects who were dissatisfied with the present job

	Not recorded	Recorded	Number	Percentage	P.
Migrant group	8	92	70	76	0.01
Control group	6	94	40	43	(X^2 = 7.2 df = 1).

Table 9. Membership in clubs, associations, etc.

	Not recorded	Recorded	Ethnic associations	Non-Ethnic associations/ clubs	Both	Nil
Migrant group	4	96	55	3	14	24
Control group	24	76	3	10	1	62

Remarks: Ethnic Associations include Associations like: Kerala Association, Andhra Association, Chotanagpur Association, etc. Non-Ethnic Associations include: Workers' Club, Church Associations, etc.

Table 7. Reasons for job dissatisfaction

REMARKS	Migrant group	Control group
Hostile local environment	49	—
Absence of powers to immediate seniors to reward good work	18	32
Prevalence of favouritism	10	11
Living away from the family	27	12
Aspiration for socially better valued jobs	5	1
Placement in the wrong job	2	1
Absence of satisfying work	10	1
Non-Availability of proper tools	4	1
No incentive bonus for meritorious work	30	36
No properly laid out promotion policy	37	20
No promotion	42	38
Poor pay	54	31
Recorded	94	96
Not recorded	6	4

Many subjects had given more than one reason for job dissatisfaction each of which has been scored.

Table 8. Friendship data

		Migrant group	Control group
Number of friends	Not recorded	8	11
	Recorded	92	89
	No friends	23	22
	1-3 friends	40	48
	More than 3 friends	29	19
Social status of friends	Not recorded	40	50
	Recorded	60	50
	Same status as subjects	42	39
	Higher status	18	4
	Lower status	—	7
Regional distribution of friends	Not recorded	33	37
	Recorded	67	63
	Same region as subjects	62	61
	All regions	5	2

Table 10. Number of subjects with positive family history of psychiatric/psychoanalytic illness in three generations of family including the patients

	Migrant group	Control group
Number	100	100
Number of subjects with positive family history	28	23
Ill-defined	1	2
Excessive drinking	11	1
Immoderate use of drugs like Ganja, Opium	2	3
Psychoses	5	3
Psycho-neuroses	—	4
Sociopathic personality disorder	1	—
Peptic ulcer	3	—
Bronchial asthma	2	2
Hyper tension	2	5
Skin disease like Eczema	1	3

Table 11. Number of subjects with past history of psychiatric/psychosomatic illness

	Not recorded	Recorded	Number with previous history	Ill-defined	Schizophrenia	Depression	Anxiety state	Phobic reaction	Peptic ulcer
Migrant group	6	94	18 (19%)	1	4	7	2	1	3
Control group	10	90	16 (18%)	4	1	7	3	–	1

Table 12. Number of subjects with positive evidence of psychiatric/psychosomatic illness at the time of interview

	Number	Number with + signs	Schizophrenia	Paranoid state	Anxiety state	Reactive depression	Psychogenic impotence	Alcoholism	Sociopathic personality disturbance	Obsessive compulsive neurosis	Compensation neurosis	Peptic ulcer	P.
Migrant group	100	37	4	6	12	6	2	3	2	1	1	3	0.01 ($X^2 = 12.6$ df = 1).
Control group	100	15	1	–	7	5	–	2	–	–	–	–	–

Remarks: 2 subjects of sociopathic personality disturbance (migrant group were also alcoholics and one subject of peptic ulcer was also suffering from psychogenic impotence. Included in "Paranoid State" are psychotic relations with delusion as the predominant feature but with no schizophrenic signs. Both short-lived and prolonged reactions are included in the group.

Table 13. Accident record of the subjects

	Not recorded	Recorded	Major accidents	Minor accidents	Total accidents	P.
Migrant group	12	88	11	6	17 (19%)	Between 0.20 and 0.10 ($X^2 = 2.51$ df = 1).
Control group	8	92	5	5	10(5)	Not significant

Remarks: *Major Accident* refers to an accident with loss of some part of the body or which needed prolonged medical care and/or involved medical leave of more than 7 days.

Table 14. State of domicile of migrants

No.	Kerala	Andhra Pradesh	Mysere	Madras
100	66	26	3	5

Table 15. Migrant's proficiency in speaking Hindi

No.	Not recorded	Recorded	Can understand and speak fluently	Can understand a little but cannot speak	Difficulty in understanding and speaking
100	11	89	10	39	40

Table 16. Period since migration to Ranchi

No.	1-5 Years	6-10 Years	Above 10 years
100	71	29	Nil

Table 17. Occupational status before migration

No.	Not recorded	Recorded	Student	Jobless	In some service
100	9	91	33	23	35

Table 18. Number of subjects suffering from home-sickness

No.	Not recorded	Recorded	Transitory	Moderately frequent	Always	Never
100	12	88	24	43	13	8

Table 19. Relationship with the local population

No.	Not recorded	Recorded	No contact	Casual contact	Intimate contact
100	7	93	80	13	Nil

Table 20. Number and percentage of subjects holding supervisory/non-supervisory posts

	Number	Supervisory posts	Non-Supervisory posts
Migrant group	100	20	80
Control group	100	23	77

Remarks: *Supervisory posts* include – Engineering Assistants, Chargeman, Inspectors, Draughtsmen, Surveyors, Overseers. *Non-supervisory posts* include – Machine Operators of various types, Crane Operators, Furnace-men, Welders, Fitters, Riggers.

Table 21. Change in financial status on joining H.E.C.

	Not recorded	Recorded	Gain	Loss	No change
Migrant group	–	100	88	8	4
Control group	4	96	81	10	5

Remarks: Determination of loss or gain was with reference to the difference in initial pay at H.E.C. and the pay last drawn prior to joining H.E.C.

Origin of Contributions and References: See Page 343

MENTAL HEALTH ASPECTS OF CAMP CLEARANCE

The Activities of the Mental Health
Advisor to the U.N. High Commissioner for Refugees
(1959/1960)

Hans Strotzka[1]
Austria

Introduction

After World War II approximately 8 million former prisoners of war, forced laborers, concentration camp inhabitants, and other displaced persons from the eastern European countries remained in Germany, Austria, Italy and Greece. UNRRA (United Nations Relief and Rehabilitation Administration) repatriated approximately 6½ million of them, IRO (International Refugee Organization) together with other agencies, especially ICEM (International Committee for European Migration), helped with the resettlement of another million. The rest remained under the mandate of the High Commissioner for Refugees of the United Nations, thereafter called UNHCR, in camps and through a slow process different methods, mainly integration into the host countries, were tried. It became a common habit to call the last remnant of displaced persons the "hard core". The meaning of this deplorable expression was that this remaining group did not want to be repatriated mainly for political reasons, was not eligible[2] for further emigration for social and health reasons, and had difficulties with integration partly because of resentments on both sides – foreigners as well as local people. There were some signs of resignation on the part of the national and international authorities: the different welfare agencies were of the general opinion that for this residual group no satisfactory solutions could be found. Pessimism and apathy developed, especially within the camps of the refugees themselves.

---

[1] The author is deeply obliged to Mr. A.R. Lindt, the former United Nations' High Commissioner for Refugees, and to Mr. W. Pinegar of the High Commissioner's Office, without whom this project would not have been possible.

[2] Eligible means that a person is acceptable for a relief- or emigration program according to the conditions of the agency concerned. Eligibility is a special problem for the programs of UNHCR because here these conditions are defined by international laws in a very strict way.

A sudden change in this climate came from two sources. First, through an amazing effort of the international community, it had been possible to solve the problem of some 200,000 Hungarian refugees of 1956 within a relatively short time. Secondly, the call for a World Refugee Year started by three young British journalists had been successful. Thus the United Nations High Commissioner for Refugees could propose a plan for solving the long standing problem of the camp refugees under his mandate in Europe.

In the beginning there existed grave doubts as to whether this would be possible at all. The experience of many able refugee workers mitigated against this. There was the general impression that social disintegration in many of the camps had progressed to such an extent that all efforts at rehabilitation would be hopeless. A psychiatric survey in two camps in Germany recommended that for many cases only admission to psychiatric hospitals could solve the problem. Considerable resistance even against such a step came, however, from many sides and for different, well-founded reasons. Local authorities did not dare to start such action for fear of national and international complications, and international agencies felt that the judgment had been too pessimistic, the possibilities of modern psychiatric casework not having been taken into account.

After consultation with the World Health Organization, and especially with Dr. Maria Pfister-Ammende from their Mental Health Unit, who had the greatest experience in developing psychiatric rehabilitation programs for refugees, the High Commissioner called a Workshop in May 1959 in Geneva, to discuss problems of refugees requiring "special services". During this meeting the representatives of the HC in the countries concerned and of Headquarters presented the problem of those instances where usual integration methods of assistance would probably fail. These methods included finding homes and jobs for immigrants and were carried out by the regular staff of refugee organizations. It was understood that the term "special case" be defined as a family or a household where there was at least one member with a mental or social handicap that could be expected to render integration difficult or even impossible. The participants in the Workshop recommended the appointment of a social psychiatrist experienced in refugee work to act as Mental Health Adviser to the High Commissioner's office. His task would be:

1. To determine the size and nature of the case, the number of those requiring special rehabilitation, treatment, training, or related measures.
2. To prepare recommendations, taking into account the specific needs of the refugees concerned and the availability of funds and facilities in the present country of residence.
3. To employ the methods decided upon by the HC on the basis of his recommendations.

In discharging the duties specified above, the Mental Health Adviser should maintain close liaison and consult with UNHCR Headquarters and branch offices and with competent authorities and institutions in the countries concerned

The author was appointed for this post.

Case Findings and Identification

At the beginning of the operation in October 1959 there were approximately 10,000 refugees and displaced persons in camps in Germany, 5,000 in Austria, 3,000 in Italy and 500 in Greece who were eligible for the camp clearance program. The camp-population was a mixture of many nationalities, of different social and cultural backgrounds, and of different religious and ideological attitudes. There were nomads like Assyrians in Greece, Calmucs, Polish or Baltic city dwellers, Ukrainian farmers, etc. Also there were more than 100 camps which varied from large former military barracks in cities to conglomerations of huts lost in the woods.

Statistical surveys by the counselors[3] working with these groups, with registration of the so-called "special cases", were available at the Headquarters in Geneva. They revealed mainly "psychiatric cases, alcoholics, and characteropaths", which amounted to approximately 20% of the total camp population. It was, however, uncertain whether these judgments had any validity: the professional background of the counselors varied to such an extent that their ability for such difficult judgments of *social prognosis*[4] could not be relied upon. The first task of the Mental Health Adviser was therefore to evaluate the number and the severity of the so-called special cases.

Unfortunately, it was necessary to start this work under pressure of time because the outline of a rehabilitation plan had to be presented at the Third Session of the Executive Committee of the HC's program in March 1960 in order to determine the necessary budget. This demanded a rather speedy survey of the situation. In Germany, where the greatest case-load was located, 10 camps and 14 institutions were selected by the local Branch-Officers (BO) of the HC in cooperation with the Mental-Health-Adviser. The camps were visited and informative discussions with the agencies arranged. One hundred refugees were interviewed. In Austria the same procedure was followed with correspondingly lower figures. Italy and Greece had to be postponed.

To my surprise I found that the original estimate of the counselors was confirmed to a great extent. Many experts had thought special rehabilitation methods would be necessary for at least 50% of the camp population. My final estimate was even lower than that of the counselors, only 10 to 15%. This is the minimum prevalence-figure of mental disorders in a settled population, found in a recent study (Strotzka et al, 1968). In the kind of camp population that we were confronted with, a much higher number might have been expected. But it is neces-

---

[3] The refugee workers of the different local or international welfare agencies, mostly under contract with UNHCR, are called counselors. Some of them were trained social workers, the majority dedicated people with a kind of in-service-training only.

[4] Social prognosis in this respect means the assessment of the chance for integration in normal social life with the help of the specific kinds of assistance, e. g. financial help, social guidance, psychiatric therapy, etc.

sary to stress that it had not been our task to make an epidemiological study on the basis of psychiatric phenomenology, but that we had only to select families where we could not hope for integration with normal methods. Furthermore, the so-called "normal methods" included a remarkable amount of social and millieu therapies. We based our prognosis of additional need for professional care not so much on clinical psychiatric criteria, but mainly on the social history before the displacement and on the general behavior during camp life. The result was therefore not a purely psychiatric study but a social prognostic assessment on social-psychiatric grounds.

Considerable courage was needed to present these surprisingly low figures to the public as the basis for economic planning. P. Berner, my successor as Mental Health Adviser to the HNHCR, however, was able to demonstrate in his final report that our prognosis proved to be right to a high degree.

The following table (UNHCR A/AC/96/206, Annex 1) shows the results of the rehabilitation efforts in 1963 compared with the forecast of 1960. The table on the facing page is self explanatory.

The higher figures for Australia and Greece are mainly due to cases added through changes in eligibility conditions. We asked ourselves if this prognostic exactness could not be explained by the mechanism of the "self-fulfilling prophecy" as described by the American sociologist, R. Merton (1957). It might have been that our rehabilitation procedures admitted only cases designated from the beginning. This cannot be, however, because the work was so decentralized and independent in each region that there was no central control for keeping the numbers of special cases within prescribed limits.

These results are open to speculation. Nor is it possible to enter into the more complicated problems of countries with less favorable economic conditions like Italy and Greece. Berner and I hope that it will be possible to discuss the whole experience in greater detail in a later publication.

Therapeutic Action

Following the general policy in the UN, the programs of UNHCR were based on matched contributions[5] and on the avoidance of *direct* operations. This means that for each program, discussions between the local official and private, national, and international welfare agencies were necessary to determine means of financing and the necessary procedures. The first impression from the diagnostic survey was encouraging. Considerable experience and devotion were invested by these agencies under contract for refugee care. But in line with the general situation of social work and social psychiatry in Central Europe, one could not expect that the necessary level of sophistication, especially in psychiatric casework and modern industrial rehabilitation techniques, had been reached everywhere. For this reason and

---

[5]Under "matched contribution" one has to understand that the programs are financed partly by local authorities and agencies.

Annex I. Progress achieved between June 1961 and June 1963

Category of refugee	Austria June 61	Austria Dec. 61	Austria June 63	Germany June 61	Germany Dec. 61	Germany June 63	Greece June 61	Greece Dec. 61	Greece June 63	Italy June 61	Italy Dec. 61	Italy June 63	Total June 61	Total Dec. 61	Total June 63
1. *Non-settled*															
(a) under treatment	49	11	21	868	674	229	60	38	53	66	37	22	1,043	760	325
(b) still under observation		65	16	34	87	120	20	49	99		64*	32**	54	265	267
2. *Settled but still subject to follow-up*															
(a) under treatment		68		57	94	24	7	21	27				64	183	51
(b) still under observation			49	31	63	245	8	29					39	92	294
3. *Closed cases*	68	91	151	112	265	593	12	27	68		29	79***	192	412	891
Total	117	235	237	1,102	1,183	1,211	107	164	247	66	130	133	1,392	1,712	1,828
Estimated as of Sept. 1960			160			1,200			70			100			1,530

*without hope of emigrating and therefore candidates for admission to protected community
**23 of them are without hope of emigrating and therefore candidates for admission to protected community
***41 of them are without hope of emigrating and therefore candidates for admission to protected community (only physical handicaps or old age)

because of limited time, the principle of non-operation had to be given up to a certain extent, and the Mental Health Adviser operated in part *directly* from the branch offices.

Our concept was the following:

1. Wherever possible, the integration efforts of the counselors and agencies present should be encouraged and their efficiency increased by supervision, in-service training, and support.
2. For this purpose and for direct action in fields where the situation was too difficult to enable the existing personnel to cope with it, trained psychiatric social workers were employed on a full-time basis. Again leaving Italy and Greece aside we succeeded with the assistance of only 8 special counselors, recruited from the host countries and some from Greece, the United Kingdom and the U.S.A.
3. On a regional basis, 8 physicians, mainly from the fields of social psychiatry, social medicine or rehabilitation, were selected for part-time consultation with the special and the regular counselors.
4. Several meetings, informal seminars, and discussions were held on a regional basis, at times including the local authorities. The most ambitious training enterprise was a Groupwork-Seminar without a specialized program based on group-learning principles. It was held in Königstein, Germany, in September 1960. We felt that only in this way real emotional impact could be reached in a short time. The purpose was to change the traditional social work style to a more dynamic casework attitude.
5. By these actions and also through the change of the general climate and the optimism created by the World Refugee Year, and last but not least by the great increase of funds available, the results of counseling improved. Yet, it also became clear that for certain cases outpatient treatment alone was not sufficient to overcome their social withdrawal, apathy and lack of confidence in themselves and in their environment, which is an attitude typical of prolonged camp life. Naturally not all the mental and social handicaps with which we were concerned were results of the refugee situation; many individuals showed psychiatric problems such as we are used to dealing with in all kinds of populations. In such cases the abnormal social conditions were a kind of superimposed stress which led to additional deterioration.
6. In regard to institutional treatment we had in mind mainly two types:
    (a) Rehabilitation workshops in the narrower sense, for retraining and readaption to work in the therapeutic community;
    (b) Sheltered workshops for longer or permanent stay if it was not possible to restore full working capacity.

The institutions were based on the principle of rehabilitation for industrial working conditions, closely resembling the situation in real factories, with pay in accordance with the individual output, but also with the necessary medical, psychological and social care and with great elasticity in work-intensity and hours.

At that time such institutions were rare or non-existent in Germany and Austria. Only in exceptional cases could we run our program in conjunction with existing institutes such as the "Beckhof" at the Bodelschwingschen Anstalten in Bielefeld. The creation of such expensive institutions took time and was not always effective. Therefore it took us longer to set up new facilities than we would have liked. Sometimes we had to compromise with established occupational therapy institutes, of which we were not too much in favor. However, it is a fact that social therapy for a small group cannot be developed much higher than the usual standard of the host country. We also tried to put into effect another principle which turned out to be even more difficult to accomplish: to combine the rehabilitation of all kinds of handicaps – physical, mental and social. While recognizing that this endeavor creates problems such as finding the right combination of different types of those affected and the training of personnel, we tried to enforce this principle for economic reasons since it is expensive to create separate facilities for mental cases only. Also we hoped that the general animosity against psychiatric rehabilitation could be slowly changed by such a combination.

7. Many of these refugees could not fit into the kind of housing arrangement, such as low-rent-houses, institutions or hospitals, that were normally provided by agencies. It therefore became necessary to develop different kinds of homes, such as sheltered homes or "Homes with Care." Ultimately the results of these efforts varied, but the concept was the same in all places; to reach a maximum of independence with only as much assistance as was necessary, to cope with physical handicaps, perceptual defects or deficiencies in the mastering of reality, aggressive or inhibited behavior in social contact, alcoholism, inability to budget, etc. While this may sound a little complex, it was in fact rather simple: a married couple or a single person with training in social work became responsible to the agencies for the inhabitants of a certain number of flats. When problems arose beyond their competence they could call on professional help.

8. In some countries, as in Italy, the last camp for the very small residual group became replaced by a type of home that was called a "protective community". It represented the combination of a sheltered workshop with "housing with care". However, we were not in favor of this arrangement because there remained a stigma of isolation in such communities, even though they functioned more effectively than former camps.

The eight points mentioned summarize our therapeutic activity. Table I shows the size of our case-load and gives an impression of the scope of the work from 1960-1963. It should be remembered that each "case" is not necessarily a single person but frequently a family or household. The principle to involve always the primary group of a handicapped person as a whole in the rehabilitation-procedure proved to be extremely useful.

In order to ensure continuity of care, to control progress and to help with subsequent adaptation crises, an after-care or follow-up Service was arranged, mostly in cooperation with local official or private welfare agencies. We were of course aware that there was a danger of becoming overprotective and to perpetuate social assistance for reasons not so much rooted in the needs of the client but in those of the worker and the agency. However, it could be demonstrated that resettlement without aftercare had a higher number of failures than with such a service. Therefore we tried whenever possible to arrange basic social assistance for approximately 2-3 years after camp clearance.

Discussion of the Program

Concerning a more detailed discussion of manifestations, reference is made to Berner's (1965) description of the different types of reactions to camp life. We felt that only chronic alcoholics (as opposed to a superficial reaction, typical for single men in isolation) needed a specialized and separate type of therapy, such as group-psychotherapy, which was difficult to arrange at that time in the countries where we worked.

Surprisingly, there was not much demand for individual psychotherapy, as there had been for the unaccompanied Hungarian adolescents in Vienna between 1956-1960 (Hoff and Strotzka 1958). Mostly social- and milieu-therapy was sufficient as also found by Pfister-Ammende (1955) in the case of refugees in Switzerland. In such a big operation one needs to resist the temptation to become too perfectionistic and to reach for a higher standard of mental health than is prevalent in the normal population. Even with our modest ambitions we became confronted with the problem that our methods and goals were frequently more developed than the social services of the host countries, a fact which created friction. On the other hand, we were able to initiate some changes in thought and action also in regard to the local population.

Finally, it should be mentioned that in addition to our effort at integration ICEM helped with the emigration for all kinds of handicapped. In this way the well-known injustice, that countries of first asylum were left with the burden of the handicapped refugees, who were not eligible for usual emigration programs, was mitigated.

The operation, which was, we believe, the largest inter-country social psychiatric rehabilitation program ever undertaken, suffered from lack of scientific evaluation and documentation. This is understandable in view of the urgency, the orientation towards action and the lack of specific funds and personnel for scientific work. As far as incomplete reports from follow-up-services have shown, the failure rate of the integration measures has been low: about 10%. To be more exact would require a detailed discussion of what failure means and how it can be measured. Roughly speaking, failure might be assumed because of further deterioration, work-instability, failure to pay rent, etc.

Conclusions

1. Relatively valid predictions with respect to rehabilitation of patients with mental disturbances are possible.
2. The techniques of social and milieu therapy are sufficiently developed to obtain satisfactory results even in deteriorated situations like prolonged camp-life.
3. Positive results are only possible if the responsible authorities support mental health programs by providing the necessary finance and prestige, which was fortunately the case in our undertaking, especially through the interest and help of the HC himself.
4. In general the prognosis of treatment of mental disturbances among those camp refugees we have been confronted with is probably better than among a settled population because external stress factors play a greater role in the behavior disorders of camp groups, and therefore change of the milieu can be more effective.

Origin of Contributions and References: See Page 344

THE ANALYSIS OF A YOUNG CONCENTRATION CAMP VICTIM[1]

Edith Ludowyk Gyomroi
United Kingdom

In her comments on "Grief and Mourning" by John Bowlby, Anna Freud (1960) refers to analyses of young concentration-camp victims who have undergone repeated traumatic separations from birth and infancy onward, and to the expectation that these cases will supply more detailed information concerning the links between early separation and later pathology. The paper which follows is based on the analysis of one of these children and represents an attempt to trace the difficulties of personality development as they occur under the impact of such fateful constellations.

Elizabeth's Prehistory before Arrival in England

Elizabeth's early known history consists of a small number of isolated data pieced together gradually from some information obtained from children in her group or their relatives. She herself had no memory whatsoever of the time before she came to England, with the exception of a very few unconnected images. She and her elder sister, Helen, are presumed to have been born in Czechoslovakia and to have been taken to Auschwitz concentration camp without parents. At least the names of both children were entered in the books of the camp without those of

---

[1] *Editor's note:* The editors differed in agreement about the suitability of this article for this Volume. Ch. Zwingmann rejects it as unscientific. I, M. Pfister-Ammende, take the responsibility for its inclusion.

The paper raises many questions and provokes thoughts such as: It is unknown at which age this child was separated from his parents; it is not excluded that "the protective big brother" and/or some of the women in the concentration camp became mother substitutes; psychoanalysis cannot be regarded as the therapy of choice for this case, so to say the conditio sine qua non for the patient to find roots in humanity and to grow to full maturity. Group psychotherapy in an adolescent group may have brought about the same results. Nevertheless, I decided to include the paper and this for the following reasons:

There are very few published cases which provide the opportunity for gaining deep insight into the psychic processes in a young victim of severe persecution (Grauer, 1969);

There is a paucity of published case histories of detailed psychotherapy of children and adolescents who have survived concentration camp imprisonment.

mother, father, or other relatives. The children had no camp documents, except for the numbers tatooed on their arms.

In Auschwitz they formed part of a group of eight children kept alive for unknown purposes. The eldest among them, Charlie, played the role of protective big brother and – as told by adult supervisors – was instrumental in saving their lives. As part of a constant war waged against the hated guards he had taught the children not to answer at roll call in the morning but to hide under their bunks instead. On the day when the Nazis in the face of the liberating armies swept through the barracks shooting the inmates, the children happened to carry out these instructions and were spared.

On liberation Elizabeth's age was established by medical examination as approximately four years, that of her sister as approximately five. They were fed and nursed somewhere for some subsequent months, but all attempts to trace where they spent the time between liberation and their arrival in England were unsuccessful.

Elizabeth's Early History in England

From her arrival in England until one year before the beginning of treatment Elizabeth and her sister lived in a children's home specially organized for concentration-camp survivors under the devoted and skilled care of Miss Alice Goldberger, who did her utmost to provide these children with natural, homelike surroundings as well as to give them every opportunity for growth, development, and adaptation. Miss Goldberger describes the sisters on arrival as looking like pale little women with puffy old faces, bad skin trouble such as scabies, and short-cropped hair. Their behavior was noisy and exaggeratedly cheerful; new experiences were greeted with delighted shrieks; dancing and singing were their favorite occupations.

While all children of the group showed intense loyalty to each other, Elizabeth and her sister were especially inseparable. Every evening they came to each other's beds, kissed and cuddled, and whispered words in a special baby language reserved for this intimate relationship. Even years after they could often be found in each other's arms, playing mother and child, with Elizabeth in the role of baby, imitating baby talk and behavior. Their excited behavior was noticeable also in the presence of visitors, especially men on whom they wanted to climb, to be taken on their lap and cuddled.

Elizabeth as a Latency Child

According to Miss Goldberger's report, Elizabeth had little difficulty in settling down to her new surroundings. She responded well in her physical development, became proud of her beautiful curly hair, showed lively facial expression appropriate to her age. If anything she appeared too good, as if being good were considered by her the most potent weapon in an incessant fight for special recognition in the group and for being singled out for special attention by the adults, to whom she became deeply and dependently attached. One of her first school reports approximately a year after arrival describes her as "very keen and interested in her work," having made "good progress this term." Although there still were difficulties in some subjects, the teacher had "no doubts that next term will find all problems solved. She shows great promise for the future. Her friendly manner and pleasing personality make her an addition to any class."

However, as Elizabeth grew further into latency, not all this promise of good development was kept. It soon became apparent that her application to schoolwork was dependent on the relationship to the teacher rather than on a genuine interest in the subject matter and her wish to learn. From one term to the next her school reports were apt to change to the opposite extreme whenever there was a change of teacher. Whenever she could not be the ablest and favorite pupil, she was apt to become naughty, disturbing the class and unable to learn. In the home too she changed from being overgood; gentle, an eager participant in occupations and in theatrical performances, to noisy, cheeky, overindulgent behavior whenever she felt not appreciated.

As far as could be ascertained at this period from her behavior and from her confidences, there were various ways for Elizabeth to deal with her missing mother relationship. One was the manifest and constant expectation that the mother might return, a wish kept alive especially by the sudden reappearance of another mother, who had been thought dead. She refused to believe that her mother could be dead since "she was much too young." Opposed to this wishful thinking which was kept alive for years in spite of the disappointing reality, there was also denial of the need for the mother expressed through her deep attachment to Miss Goldberger. She reiterated repeatedly that no one could have been as kind, helpful, and good to her as Miss Goldberger, and praised her luck in living with the latter instead of with her own mother. It was only Miss Goldberger's own efforts which helped her to recognize her dreams and fantasies about the real mother covered by this defense.

That the figures of Miss Goldberger and the absent mother had fused in Elizabeth's mind was borne out by her reaction to the former's hospitalization when Elizabeth was approximately eleven years old. She visited Miss Goldberger in the hospital and wrote her charming, considerate, and loving letters. But simultaneously her appearance and manner changed in a manner frightening to the observer. She looked unkempt and neglected, with her hair – which always reflected her moods – bushy, unattractive, and standing like straw round her head. There were complaints from the school that she had behaved rudely to the teachers and refused to work. The headmistress herself recognized that it was the separation from Miss Goldberger which had brought about the change. How deeply Elizabeth was shaken was proved by one of her letters to Miss Goldberger in which she debated whether she could allow her to go on convalescence and finally found that she could do so, "because you will not goaway for good like other people have done, but will come back like my mother would have done if she had been alive."

There was another, for Elizabeth fateful, way in which her dependent mother relationship found expression. Apart from the attachment to her own sister, she singled out for devotion one after another member of the staff or one of the older girls in the home and offered her friendship to them. Since she especially selected girls with considerable difficulties of their own, she laid herself open in this way to much unhappiness, suffering, and hurt. But instead of giving up she kept clinging to them, made her advances over and over again, did not tire of trying, or performing services unasked, or of offering generously all her possessions and her help, only crying bitterly when she was rejected.

When Elizabeth was eight years old a family made advances to her and her sister, eager to adopt them. In this instance Elizabeth became the rejecting partner, rebuffing all overtures, harshly criticizing the generous couple for being "too rich," and refusing altogether to return to their place, her critical attitude evidently hiding the fear of separation.

Adolescent Changes

With entry into adolescence Elizabeth increasingly became aware of her inability to be a person in her own right, to believe in her own capacities, and to pursue her own wishes. The dependency which in latency could remain hidden behind a facade of a good, conforming, little girl began to assume frightening proportions when measured against the new developmental need for independence. It became obvious to everybody, including herself, how slavishly she had to copy whomever she had singled out for idealization at a given time. Whether this was a simple helper in the kitchen or an ambitious student working for exams, Elizabeth felt forced to copy their movements, behavior, attitudes, irrespective of her own likes, dislikes, or abilities. She was equally unsure of herself with regard to boys; with them she alternated unexpectedly between excited provocation, shyness, and withdrawal.

At the age of seventeen it was Elizabeth herself who expressed the wish for help through analysis, a move which was in part due to her own insight, in part based again on her imitation of and identification with some of the others in the home who had entered analysis before her.

Entry Into Analysis

At the first interview I asked her what help she expected from me. She replied: "I am not a person, I am always like somebody else." And this was the very thing which formed the core of her pathological behavior. Every day her hair was done differently; she moved in a different manner; it was impossible to see a real person behind the various roles she played. No movement of hers was spontaneous and natural, each was deliberately produced. Every step she took was made with the awareness that she was such and such a person walking in such and such a way.

Soon it was possible to link up the changes in her appearance and behavior with the short-lived friendships she entered into which never lasted more than a day or two. Those which did, on account of the partner's persistence, existed for her only during the hours when she was in the company of the friend in question.

She was a heavily built girl with a podgy face and short fat legs. She wore such tight trousers that one wondered how she managed to put herself into them, heavy sweaters; then suddenly some flash jewelry, or a ribbon in her hair. She insisted on lying on the couch like other adults, but she stepped on it with both feet and threw herself down as a toddler might. Her intelligence seemed to be very low, and it was doubtful whether she could understand what the analyst expected of her. Since it was not possible for her to verbalize any of her feelings, I had to put her problems into words step by step when they appeared to come within reach of her understanding. Great skill had to be applied in order to combat the danger of her sinking into absolute and empty silence on the couch.

Instead of reporting this analysis as it proceeded, it seems to be more useful to group the material in a way which will facilitate the understanding of the development of her personality before treatment and during its course. To start with, a special feature of her behavior during the sessions has to be described. This provided insight into the basic problems of her personality and opened up the possibility of handling her difficulties. This was the storytelling which followed the long initial period of silence.

Her stories were of two different kinds. Those which she told the boys she met were relatively easy to understand. She was unable to tell the truth about herself and invented a family living sometimes in Italy, sometimes in another part of the world. The purpose of this was clear. She felt deeply ashamed of being Jewish, of having been in a concentration camp. When she was eight, she and some other children insisted on the number tatooed on their arms being removed surgically. She said once: "It is impossible that so many people were locked in if they did not deserve it." There was a deep conviction of some shameful thing she had to hide, the thing which made her different from the other children at school and which made her mother abandon her because she was not worth caring for. These stories were intended to hide her shame.

The stories told on the couch were of a very different nature and very confusing. Complete silence alternated with elaborate reports of some experience or other. They all sounded unreal, because they did not fit together; they contradicted each other, not only in character but also with regard to details of time and place; if one was true, the other could scarcely have been so. They related most often to some theft, or some other kind of "bad thing" done.

The first explanation of these stories which suggested itself was that she felt she had nothing to offer which would make her interesting and worth while for her analyst. Therefore she had to invent experiences to keep my attention. In addition, it seemed as if she told "bad things" about herself to test me, whether I would give her up if I found out she did something wrong. This explanation, as it was not sufficiently substantiated, was not advanced, and had in fact to be given up very soon.

It was more on the grounds of factual observation and outside information than as a consequence of the possibility of interpreting analytic material that I discovered that the stories she kept telling were not invented. They related to things which really happened, not to her, but to one of the other children. At this point I ventured the interpretation that she borrowed the experiences of others, in order to keep me interested, because she thought she was not good enough for me to bother about her. In the light of the material gained later it became clear that this interpretation was wrong. In spite of this it had a positive result. The storytelling was given up, and for the first time she was able to form a friendship with a girl without trying to be like her. What caused a wrong interpretation to produce this effect will be examined later.

In the third year of her analysis she was able to bring memories. These concerned the first years she spent in England. They were confused, but threw definite light on the storytelling. It was now understood that it was based on a confusion of herself with other children. It was as if for her there did not exist a well-defined "I," but instead there was help derived from the consciousness of "We" – the group of children who shared fate, love of persons, everything. The stories were now recognized as experiences belonging to the "We," which had to take the place of the not-existing "I". In the memories of the first few years in England this confusion of identities was sometimes so impressive that it left the feeling that there was no differentiation at all between self and not-self.

One of the most striking of these was the story of her lovely doll, given to her in Czechoslovakia by a person called Agnes, which she was not allowed to bring to England because it was too dirty. In fact, Agnes is the name of a woman whose memory is cherished by the other children who came from Thereszin, and not from Auschwitz. It is unlikely that she too could have had an Agnes. Similarly she remembered having always wetted the bed as a biggish girl, which, according to Miss Goldberger, is untrue, though some of the other children, notably two boys, did.

I feel that this is a point at which some speculation about Elizabeth's early development is justified.

Object Relations

From the beginning the very primitive nature of her object relations made a strong impression on me. The friendships which lasted only while the partner was present, the imitation of the object, were in some way reminiscent of Helene Deutsch's (1934) "as if" patients. The difference is that the latter went through the motions of emotional reactions without feeling them, displaying feelings and thoughts they believed they ought to have, modeling them on those of the object of identification; but Elizabeth's imitation concerned only features of the object which were within the range of the most primitive perception like modes of dressing, movements, etc. It was fleeting and haphazard, and disclosed more the fantasy of merging with the object than the wish to be like the object (Jacobson, 1954a, 1954b; Reich, 1954). What she longed for in those relationships was not so much the need-satisfying object as need satisfaction itself. So far as the object existed at all it was in the external world, no mental representation of it was established, and it ceased to exist when it was not present. There was no realistic concept of the self "which mirrors correctly the limits of the bodily and mental ego" (Jacobson, 1954a), the boundaries of the self were not firmly outlined, the other children were not separate entities either but were included in it, and separateness itself seemed to be a danger.

Miss Goldberger and Elizabeth's friend Anne (one of the children from Thereszin) belonged to her world from the time she came to England; her sister throughout her life. The characteristic feature of these relationships was a tenacious clinging. This clinging seemed to aim at preventing the threatening separation. Separation anxiety does not seem to be a term exact enough for her state of mind in this respect. It was more a constant expectation of separation, to which when it occurred even for a short period she reacted with a dull and abject resignation. When the first summer holiday brought the first separation from me, I gave her an address where mail would be forwarded, in order to maintain the continuity of a relationship in danger of being severed. Elizabeth, who still at the end of her latency was able to keep contact through letters with Miss Goldberger, now did write several letters which she did not post because she could not imagine that letters would reach a person who was not present and therefore nonexistent. For the same reason making a telephone call was a very difficult task for her.

At times when Miss Goldberger and the other children were experienced as being separate from her, she endeavored to be a good girl to please them. She allowed herself to be exploited by her sister and Anne in every way. Her obedience and compliance, however, were directed not toward any internal agency but toward external objects as a bribe, because if they appeared to be divorced from herself they were potentially lost.

Aggression

Her aggression, so far as aggression occurred, appeared to be objectless too. It was the aggression of an infant, anxious to get rid of, or to destroy, something which is unpleasurable; in fact, it aimed at eliminating the "unpleasurableness" and not the object which caused unpleasure. Time and again she was rude, but the rudeness was not directed against persons but unpleasant situations. "Hatred"was expected from persons who did not supply satisfaction of her emotional needs and therefore had to remain strangers. This expectation of hatred is reminiscent of cases described by Annemarie P. Weil (1953), where "projection of lack of relationship may lead to paranoid trends: 'they don't like me' and then 'they hate me.' "

The differentiation of self and not-self, and the development of self - and object representations, leading to the establishing of the boundaries of the self, are very slow processes indeed. Sandler and Rosenblatt (1962) differentiate between images and representations, the latter gradually developing out of a multitude of images, and they quote Piaget according to whom enduring representation cannot be said to be well established before about the sixteenth month of life. As they put it, self-representation is that organization which represents the person as he consciously or unconsciously perceives himself.

The sum total of self-representations is the foundation of what is usually called identity, which begins to take a final shape in adolescence (Erikson, 1956).

If we try to reconstruct the history of Elizabeth's first years, we may assume that she was separated from her mother very early, probably in her second year, at a time when identification may already have begun to move from being one with to being like the object. The first separation must have reactivated the need of merging with it again. According to Anna Freud (1952), between "five to twenty-four months, separation from the object causes extreme distress, but the infant is so exclusively dominated by his needs that he cannot maintain his attachment to a nonsatisfying object for more than a given period (varying from several hours to several days). After this interval, which is most upsetting for the child, need satisfaction is accepted from and attachment (cathexis) is transferred to a substitute." If in Elizabeth's case separation from the mother had been followed by the possibility of turning to a substitute, her development in respect of establishing object relations proper would have continued. We have to assume that Elizabeth's surroundings and the persons looking after her must have changed constantly so that libido could not have been invested in one and the same person for any length of time.

The concept of the self which gradually develops includes not only self-representations derived from the own experiences centered around need and satisfaction and all that follows the differentiation of inside and outside, but also the ideas the persons in the environment have of the child and which they convey to him. But a child which is moved from one place to another, handed on from one set of relatives living in the greatest insecurity to another, probably transported from camp to camp, does not experience the constantly repeated reaction of a mother or a mother substitute, a reaction which usually reflects the image this mother figure has about the growing infant.

When a wrong interpretation provoked a positive development in Elizabeth's analysis, what took place in fact was the following: granted that secondarily the interpretation had some justification, and the stories aimed at holding the attention of the analyst and testing me, this alone would not have made the storytelling unnecessary. What really happened was that the interpretation conveyed to Elizabeth the analyst's idea that she, Elizabeth, was a separate person who had her own experiences, different from those of others. Elizabeth, identifying with the analyst, accepted the analyst's idea of her as a separate person, added this to her scanty

self-representations, and started to act upon it. This is similar to what happens in the normal development of children: the mother, for instance, regards the infant as being one who can already put food into his own mouth without help, and the infant now includes this in the concept he forms of his own self and acts upon it.

The wrong interpretation produced the first step in Elizabeth's maturation which had to be completed through her analysis.

The Development of Transference

It took a long time before the first transference reactions could be detected and understood. In the beginning I was for Elizabeth predominantly a real person, the first in her life who existed only for her, whom she did not have to share with anyone. I existed for her only in her sessions, not before and not after. She repeatedly expressed the wish to have sessions which would last eight or nine hours — an attempt at clinging. When after a few months it was inevitable for her to realize the existence of other patients, her reluctance to end the session was a mixture of an attempt at warding off separation and at maintaining the situation in which she had the undivided attention of a person, in which she possessed a person without having to share her. The remarkable thing was that Elizabeth did not show, either at that stage of her analysis or later, any jealousy. A careful interpretation was attempted in telling her that she wanted to prolong a pleasure which she did not enjoy before, namely, the feeling that she had a person for herself alone. After this suddenly she was able to verbalize a fear which, as she said, overcame her now very frequently, that I might die. Her long silences now signified a merging with the dead mother, simultaneously they re-established the mother-infant situation in which the mother understands the baby without his having to talk.

After the interpretation of the storytelling, when she started to think of herself as a separate person, I became the fantasy mother who possessed supernatural powers. But I was that mother too who would abandon her at any minute. The silences were interrupted with the repeated: "I am a rotten patient," indicating that a shameful shortcoming of hers was the reason why I would abandon her.

The silences formed a special feature of this analysis, and it was possible to observe subtle changes in them. The first type of silence seemed to be a regression to the preverbal stage as described above. It sometimes alternated with a sulky silence, usually after she had had some unpleasant experience. These silences were repeatedly interrupted by me, because there was a danger of her drifting further and further away.

At a much more advanced stage of her treatment there was a third type of silence. It occurred usually after some disappointment, or something which provoked anxiety in her. She behaved like a person in pain who uses all his available libido to cathect the painful organ. This silence was not interfered with. I permitted the feeling of safety in being able to withdraw, to comfort herself, and find peace again. This wordlessness was very different from the other two, and that she was allowed to remain silent gave her the feeling of security and confidence. She gave the impression of an infant who feels protected on her mother's lap. The danger of severing the tenuous contact between patient and analyst had by this time gone.

She now repeatedly remarked on my silence, "You could be dead behind me." This showed how the ideas "mother" and "dead" belonged together. She had no memory of a living mother — she knew only about a dead one.

After this a further step was made and expressed in the transference. Somebody told her that I too had experienced losses and had had a son who died. Now she was not only silent but lay on the couch completely motionless. This dead rigidity helped me to recognize that in order to re-create the mother-child relationship she now reversed roles: now she was dead and so she became my child. When I interpreted her transference at this point (this was at a time when direct interpretation was already possible and accepted), she replied in a sulky way: "You have your own children to love." This did not express any jealousy. She used what she thought to be reality to disprove with it my transference interpretation; what she proved in this way was her total hopelessness about ever having a mother for herself.

Until the very end her transference showed various aspects of her need for re-creating her mother.

Problems Concerning Her Amnesia

The establishing of a transference relationship and the possibility of interpretation did not introduce the process of lifting the amnesia covering her first five years of life. Even now, after an analysis which justifiably can be called successful, there is no recovery of memory for this period. This raises the question how her particular way of blotting out the past differs from the usual type of infantile amnesia.

We are accustomed to regard an individual's forgetting of his early years as the result of repression set up against retaining in consciousness the primitive infantile drive experiences against which the child has turned. What sets the defense in motion is not only the repudiation of infantile sexuality, aggression, death wishes, etc., but equally the unpleasure, namely, the frustrations, disappointments, and humiliations connected with the events.

But it is also true that the preoedipal and oedipal experiences of an individual do not fall victim to the infantile amnesia without leaving traces in the form of cover memories. While for the purpose of consciousness these phenomena obscure, hide, falsify, and distort the past, for the purpose of analysis they serve as potential entrance doors to the id, i.e., as focal points from which transference manifestations, interpretation of the unconscious, and recovery of past experience can proceed. Such cover memories, and the repressed memories which lie behind them, are organized invariably around the important adult figures in the child's early life and set securely within the framework of his physical environment. Likewise, our analytic interpretations take the path toward re-establishing consecutive stages of past object relationships and use as their clues with regard to time and age whatever changes in the physical surroundings have occurred in an otherwise stable environment due to moving house, traveling, etc.

There seems to be no question that on both counts — quantity of unpleasure and stability of external surroundings — Elizabeth deviates from the norm. The frustrations of her infantile needs and wishes were undoubtedly massive; and while normally the animate and inanimate objects in a child's life are predictable and more or less stable, in her case there must have been a bewildering kaleidoscope of figures, short-lived relationships, passing images, experiences, and even languages. There is no certainty how often the children were passed from one place to another, with complete changes of regime, before as well as after Auschwitz. Adult figures must have changed due to extermination. Nationalities were mixed. The guards and camp staff were German; camp inmates came from a variety of countries; the children's first language and that after liberation may have been Czech, their actual language on arrival was a mixture of Czech and Yiddish. It is no wonder that under such circumstances, memory was clouded and the focal points for its recovery were scarce.

On the other hand, it is of interest to note that even under these adverse conditions Elizabeth was not without a cover memory. This consisted of an image that she had once slept on a table and that she slept together with Charlie (the elder brother figure, himself a child, who had protected the younger ones, stolen bread for them braving punishment, and who, as other sources report, had finally saved their lives). This cover image formed the core of a few fantasies, allowing the conclusion that the wooden bunks without bedding (usual in camps such as Auschwitz) had been her "home" for a significantly longer period than any other place, and that — in the absence of stable adult objects — her fantasies had probably organized themselves around the one available figure of the "elder brother."[2]

Relation to Reality

If we are correct in assuming that, maybe after a very short gratifying period of infancy in which she may have achieved a primitive identification with her

---

[2] The Thereszian children reported on by Anna Freud and Sophie Dann (1951) spent two to three years in the same children's ward there. Though the persons looking after them changed frequently, and being themselves prisoners were anxious and insecure, they were a few who continued there. In addition, the quarters though poor and restricted, the bare yard, remained the same too. This may account for it that though the store of their memories was very poor indeed, they did remember considerably more than Elizabeth. Anna Freud and Sophie Dann mention these in connection with the fears of the children-of dogs, of a van, etc. They mention, too, memories of a little boy, of things he overheard the adults speaking about. It must be that however insecure life in Thereszin was, the fact that the children remained in the same place for years meant a relative, though deficient, stability, as compared with the constant change in Elizabeth's life.

mother, separations from other substitutes and constantly changing environment followed, we may borrow Spitz's (1951) term "emotional deficiency" for Elizabeth's apparent pathology. He used it for psychogenic diseases in infancy caused by the restriction of the mother-child relationship. I take the liberty of extending it to include purely psychic consequences arising from the same cause.

However terrible the objective reality of the concentration camp was, the child was affected not by this but by the fact that her innate needs remained unsatisfied and that there were no lasting objects the relation to which would have made normal ego development possible. The small child was not in a position to compare life in the camp with what we call normal living conditions. We connect the idea of Auschwitz with all we know about its atrocities, and we have to remind ourselves that the interpretation a child puts upon an event may be different from that of an adult.

My impression is that the Thereszin children who lived in cruel conditions, yet conditions less "denaturalized" than those in Auschwitz, were more exposed to traumata than the children in the extermination camps, though living conditions there and the constant danger of torture, humiliation, and extermination were much more extreme. A trauma is an isolated instance in which too much excitation enters the mental apparatus and far too suddenly to be mastered. Even series of traumatic events are isolated occurances. The traumatic conditions in which Elizabeth grew up were, however, her established and persisting reality.

In working with Elizabeth I was often reminded of the little girl whose case was reported by Mary E. Bergen (1958), the girl whose mother was murdered by her father in the child's presence. In the course of the analysis it was established that the outstanding traumatic feature of the event from the point of view of the child was not the murder but that her mother, wishing to save the child the frightening experience, shouted at her: "You get out of here." In Elizabeth's case, too, the pathogenic factor seems to have been not the horror of the camp but the loss of the object before object constancy was achieved; in addition, life among adults who were either hostile or who lived in constant fear and insecurity.

That in spite of this, analysis was able to achieve integration of her personality has to be ascribed to a specially good ego endowment. Freud (1937) states, "We think it credible that even before the ego exists its subsequent lines of development, tendencies and reactions are already determined." We are justified in assuming that a process of maturation does take place even though hindered by events obstructing libido development and that of object relations. Hartmann (1939) distinguishes between three kinds of developmental processes: "those which occur without and essential and specific influence of the external world; those which are co-ordinated to typical experiences (that is, which are triggered off by average expectable environmental situations . . .); and finally, those which depend upon atypical experiences." In the case of Elizabeth the following problem arose: her ego development did achieve a capacity for reality testing to a fair degree. Yet the reality she had to learn to anticipate and to recognize was based on such extreme and atypical experiences as are scarcely met with in analytic practice.

If in London or New York a person were worried that going to the toilet he might meet a leopard, we would think he had no sense of reality at all. But if someone in a remote jungle outpost thinks of this possibility we do not doubt his judgement. If a child after experiencing shorter and longer separation is incapable of learning that after separation the beloved object may reappear, that somebody who is absent still exists, then we have to think at this point his judgment of reality is impaired. But that Elizabeth, who lived in a world where persons who disappeared were gassed, did not learn that a summer holiday does not mean death, does not signify in any way that she did not achieve a degree of reality testing and judgement. In her case it means that she learned to know a special kind of reality and what she failed to achieve was the adaptation to another.

Her ignorance of the significance of money, for instance, and of the fact that it has to be earned by work, was not different from that usual in institutionalized children. This, too, cannot be regarded as a failure in reality testing. It is closely related to the circumstances of her life which was very different from that of an average family, where the children soon learn that the parents have to work in order to earn money for the family's needs.

Libidinal Development

Elizabeth's past is known to us only from the time she was five years old. The clinging, the primitive mode of identification hint at oral fixation, but I could not detect strong pregenital orientation of libido. The libidinal drives appeared to be without great dynamism, in some way her pregenital urges were underdeveloped. Experience of gratification increases the wish for its repetition, its absence also strengthens the need. I asked myself whether a continuous and extraordinary lack of gratification would not result in the stunting of the drive. Anna Freud and Sophie Dann observed that Thereszin children who were fed on dull and starchy food there were uninterested in food and unwilling to try new tastes and dishes.

We know little about the development of Elizabeth's anal drive. Though there was preoccupation with the question of dirtiness (to which I shall have to return later), it is not known what kind of toilet training resulted in the fact that she behaved in an age-adequate way in this respect at the time of her arrival. Toilet training par excellence depends on the relation to the love objects, and we have to ask ourselves what made it possible for Elizabeth to be clean. We remember that the Thereszin children lived in children's wards and were looked after by fellow prisoners who took the trouble to take some of them up two or three times every night. This is unthinkable of Auschwitz. The reports all mention the incontinence of the generally sick adult population and the suffering inflicted on everybody by the dirt and the stench. Lack of anal control is no doubt gratifying to infants, but if the child is not cleaned, drying fecal matter and urine may cause great distress indeed. It is not impossible that what could be extreme gratification in normal circumstances turned into a painful experience which made bowel control preferable.

There is little information about her phallic phase either. Miss Goldberger remembers her passionate riding on a rocking horse, which was no doubt an autoerotic activity on the phallic level. Memories which emerged in a later stage of her analysis showed a preoccupation at that time with the difference between the sexes and penis envy and castration fear which persisted and were greatly reduced in analysis through interpretation and ensuing insight.

With regard to the relationship to persons in her environment, Elizabeth at the time of her arrival was not very different from the Thereszin children. The attachment to the other children was very strong; jealousy and envy were absent; and though she clung very much to some of the adults, the feeling toward the group was very much more positive than to the latter. But in Elizabeth's case even the relationship to the group had the character of clinging, and especially her sister and she were bodily inseparable.

There were no attempts even at substituting oedipal objects or experiencing oedipal relations in fantasy, as it is observed most often in institutionalized children (Anna Freud, 1951). Of her mother she spoke only on rare occasions, but she did have some fantasy image of her. (She had long blonde hair- hair, as will be described later, was the attribute of those who possessed power and importance.) But once when she brought one of the memories shared with the other children, concerning their dolls which were father, mother, and baby dolls, I asked her to describe the father doll to me. At this she volunteered the information with surprise that she never thought of ever having a father. Later she did remember male persons, partly real, partly imaginary, who were important to her and who seemed to be father substitutes but at the preoedipal level. Her fantasies about Charlie belong here but though Charlie was for her a protective male, he was not a figure in an oedipal setting. Throughout her whole analysis no memory of any rivalry of an oedipal nature, either in reality or in fantasy, emerged. Miss Goldberger, to whom she was very attached, was not used either as a figure in any oedipal fantasy.

The Ego Ideal

Though elements which are regarded as the precursors of the superego must have been present in her earliest identifications, neither her libido development nor that of her object relations made the establishing of a superego in the sense in which we use the term possible. She was a good little girl, yet not in obedience to an internal authority, but in order to please and bribe the persons in her environment so that they would not abandon her. As mentioned before, analytic material revealed that she felt she was abandoned because she could not be liked, the reason for this lying in some anal misdeeds. The "memory" of the doll she was given by Agnes, which was taken up in the course of her analysis on various levels, threw light on the connection between these two things. In her memory she had to leave the doll behind because it was dirty. But the doll had long fair plaits, like her fantasy mother, and it was understood that this memory was a reversal of the idea that she was abandoned because she did something bad, something that made her unlovable. This was her dirtiness (the annexation of the bed wetting of the boys must have been connected with this anal- or urethral- anxiety which merged with her later penis envy).

She appeared to have felt much more shame than guilt. Piers and Singer (1953) suggest that guilt is the result of tension between ego and superego, and shame between ego and ego ideal. Elizabeth did not develop a superego, but she very early built up an ego ideal to which more features were added in the course of her later identifications.

This ego ideal was based on the image of a woman with beautiful hair, wonderfully dressed, in every way good-looking, who had, in addition, the power to do as she liked. Where could this ego ideal have originated? If we recall what we know about the concentration camps, the answer to this question is immediately at hand. The prisoners were emaciated, their hair was cropped close, they were dirty, stinking, verminous. (Every drop of water was a treasure and cleanliness was impossible.) In contrast, there were the guards – well dressed, well groomed, and with carefully set hair. In addition, they had power, and they treated the mass of prisoners with contempt and disgust. Elizabeth's preoccupation with her hair, her dejection about her looks, her shame about belonging to the dirty ones is the consequence of her impossibility to live up to her ego ideal. This is the cause of her shame and her lack of self-esteem.

Edith Jacobson (1954a) holds that the degree of self-esteem is rooted in discrepancy or harmony between self-representation and the wishful concept of the self. Elizabeth could never be in harmony with the wishful concept of herself. Even in analysis she had to see herself as a "rotten patient". To the dirtiness of those to whom she belonged, who had no hair and could never be like the one with the beautiful hair-do whom she wanted to imitate, another characteristic was added. The dirty ones were bodily degraded and sick, decrepit – castrated. When she complained about her appearance she always followed this up with the fantasy of plastic surgery. Plastic surgery unconsciously meant the undoing of her castration. Dirtiness and castration were closely linked with each other.

(It is necessary to point out that her equation of dirtiness with castration, her dejection about the impossibility of every being good-looking, with lovely hair, a person of power and importance, were gone into very thoroughly. But as no memory emerged concerning the history and the origin of these feelings, the reconstruction made above was never suggested by the analyst. Her feeling of shame alone could be connected productively with her conviction that having been in a concentration camp was proof of merited disgrace, since this was verbalized by her.)

Anxiety

Yet castration fear was less prominent than penis envy. In fact, Elizabeth did not display strong anxieties (with a single exception — when my foot was bandaged she refused to enter the room). Anna Freud and Sophie Dann (1951) observed the same in connection with Thereszin children and thought that "the fact that they have never known peaceful surroundings rendered them more indifferent to the horrors happening around them." Probably the same indifference protected Elizabeth from great anxieties later too.

Catching Up with Missed Development in Analysis

Elizabeth's analysis had to achieve not so much the solution of unconscious neurotic conflicts as to make it possible for her to reach an age-adequate maturity and to achieve the necessary readaptation to a different reality. It also had the task of helping her to develop an internal authority which regulates gratification not only on the basis of what is "possible" or "dangerous" but on the basis of some criteria of "good" or "bad." I doubt that we are justified in calling this authority the superego which Freud defines as the heir of the oedipus complex, the development of which, though it has its beginnings in preoedipal identifications, is brought to its conclusions through the dissolution of the oedipus complex.

Elizabeth's analysis had to help her to make the step from imitation of external objects to identification proper and to forming internalized object representations. She had to achieve, too, an internal guidance. The fact that she developed into a young woman who can regulate drive satisfaction according to her own views of right and wrong poses the question whether this capacity can be attained without experiencing the drama evolving out of the oedipal relationships. It would be worth while to examine the difference in the behavior of the superego which is a representation of the oedipal parents and that faculty which, as in this case, develops in direct line from the preoedipal identifications up to maturity.

Our material suggests that the agency which now provides Elizabeth with internal guidance is more protective than punitive. This is caused by the fact that due to the difference in the etiology of the two, the quantity of aggression invested in it is negligible as compared with the amount which goes into the superego.

Elizabeth's analysis offered her the possibility of going through the development she missed. I remained to a great extent a real person for her for a long time. I mattered only as a supplier of the comfort of belonging to her alone. She attempted to imitate me, to be the analyst in order to avoid separation, but there was too little material to enable this to be achieved as she had only a minimal possibility for observation. She tried to enact my way of speaking and my intonations; she wanted to arrange her room like mine. When I became in transference the fantasy mother ("You must have had blonde hair when you were young"), this mother figure was really a fusion of the one who abandoned her and the other with the beautiful hair and power — the female guard. In addition, she attributed to this figure all that was demanded of her by Miss Goldberger, teachers, all that the heroes of the many novels she read represented, the whole ideology accepted as proper by the world she lived in now, ultimately achieving an identification with it. This was not imitation any more, it became identification on a higher level. The object was internalized, and slowly she started to behave in the way she thought was demanded of her even when she was unobserved.

Sandler (1960) concludes that when the formation of the superego is achieved "what is introjected is neither the personality nor the behavior of the parents, but their authority." Though the agency responsible for internal guidance in Elizabeth is different in its genesis and its character from that of the superego, yet what went into its formation was, as in the superego, the authority of the object which the analyst became in transference. Needless to say, it took years to achieve this.

Gradually she managed to form new and lasting friendships. Her intelligence became quite keen (though not remarkable), and she was able to train for a craft which now provides her with a living and makes her independent of help and charity. She learned to reassess reality, and with this her fear of separation left her. Her friend Anne went abroad, most of the children are scattered in various countries and she maintains contact with them. To reinforce this attainment she made an important decision — turning passive into active — and on her own initiative made arrangements to go for six months to Israel. She made sure that the analyst would be ready to continue her treatment on her return — demonstrating her new knowledge that separation can be undone.

Relation to the Other Sex

Her relationship with the other sex underwent very definite changes. When she started her analysis she was anxious to have boyfriends, but this was a purely narcissistic need. Other girls had them; if she could not attract anyone, it was proof of her shortcoming. There was no real contact between herself and the boys, she told them lies about herself (the stories), and she did not know anything about them either. There was some passionate sex play without intercourse, of which she was afraid. Fear of penetration played a great part in her reluctance to have intercourse with the boys who demanded it, and this was brought into analysis. She also emphasized always that she was not in love (love was a very great thing), and she would like to sleep only with someone she was really in love with.

After repeated attempts at friendships with boys which brought a great deal of material into her analysis, she met a young man who became slowly a real person to her. She was not "in love," but very attached to him. This was a friendship based on identification with the analyst. The boy was very disturbed, a stammerer, and Elizabeth wanted to help him overcome his difficulties. At this time she sometimes spoke, though very reluctantly, about masturbation and fantasies of sexual intercourse.

In Israel the narcissistic need to be found attractive was reactivated and she fell back into storytelling — probably because the fight to bear up with separation resulted in partial regression. Very soon she understood on her own what had happened to her; she was even able to tell a friend that all she had said to him was lies; and though the hurt of being unable to find a boy to love her was very acute, she felt much better and much more secure. The Israel experience left her somewhat disappointed. She understood in her analysis that she attached to it the unconscious hope of returning a completely changed person, someone who was not castrated, and the wish for plastic surgery which reappeared was now ultimately understood and given up. With this her appearance changed, she dressed with taste and carried herself well, her movements were natural, she was well groomed, and she discovered that with care one can make oneself look quite attractive. The ideal of the woman with the beautiful hair-do lost its phallic character and was not unattainable any more.

That she achieved firm opinions of her own became manifest in connection with a relationship to a young man which ended in a painful disappointment. He was very charming, and it was flattering to her that he showed her persistent attention. She stressed that she was not in love, though she was unable to tell him the complete truth about herself. It was at this time that she first uttered the word "Auschwitz" in her analysis. If ever she referred to the time before she came to England she spoke of Czechoslovakia (it is noteworthy that Thereszin is in Czechoslovakia, Auschwitz in Poland). The shame of being Jewish, having been in a concentration camp, left her completely; she started to think about the events responsible for her early experiences and she joined the Yellow Star movement.

The tie between her and the young man became closer, and she started to wonder whether it was not love after all, had fantasies about giving into his demands and having intercourse with him. She then discovered that he lied and was unreliable. That she found out that he was having sexual relationship with another girl was not the upsetting factor. It did not make her jealous, she found the girl very nice. Here, too it was impressive how different her behavior was from that usually observed. Her relation to this young man did not follow an oedipal pattern, and this may explain the complete lack of feeling of rivalry. What she resented was his untruth, a thing she had managed to give up and judged now very adversely. In spite of all this she continued to be very attracted by him. The break came when on one occasion they had a conversation in which he expressed strong approval of Apartheid and the suppression of the African. Elizabeth was very shocked and immediately gave up meeting him. What cannot be overlooked in this event is that she, the Jewess (who never wanted to admit being one), identified with the Africans on the ground that they were the downtrodden ones, accepting herself in this way as belonging to the dirty prisoners, and this, too, without the slightest feeling of shame.

Another event reflects the stage she reached at the end of her analysis. For the first time in her life she lived in a flat with a normal family consisting of father, mother and child, renting a room there. She felt terribly lonely without knowing why. Then one day it was the child's birthday and she bought a present for him. Returning home after work with her present she found the flat empty, the family having gone out to celebrate. She felt deeply dejected at having been left out. The birthday cake was on the table and she had a strong impulse to steal a piece of it. She had to put up a fight against it, but she was able to restrain herself and she felt greatly ashamed. The significance of this experience is manifold. She now was able to feel envy and sorrow at having been deprived of normal family relations; she was also capable of an aggressive impulse; but more than that, she had the strength to restrain herself from turning impulse into action. This experience was gone into thoroughly and it now made possible the discussion of an episode which took place quite early in her treatment. She was then living in the flat of Miss Goldberger and a young couple came to visit them with their few-weeks-old infant. Elizabeth looked forward to meeting them. But when they arrived and she saw the parents with the child, utter confusion seized her and she ran away. She felt very upset without knowing why, spent the evening in a cinema, and returned home late at night in order to avoid meeting the visitors. It was impossible to help her to understand what made her take flight. Now she herself verbalized the feeling of despair at not belonging to any family, at having been "left out" ever since she existed. She decided that living with a family was too distressing for her, and in order to avoid painful experiences she made up her mind to move into a hostel and share the life of working girls who had to forego the pleasure of a regular home. "I am not running away, but I don't want to be reminded of things that hurt," she said. This shows that her assessment of reality is normal, she is able to anticipate the effects of certain conditions on her emotions, and she can find rational solutions for herself. In the hostel she soon became very popular and the helper and advisor of the girls.

If I may be permitted to make a prediction, I suggest that she will master her dejection about not having had a family in the same way as that over separations: by turning passive into active (as when she went to Israel), creating a family for her future children.

Elizabeth is now twenty-two years old, a pleasant, cheerful working girl. She finds ample opportunity for sublimation in her work which puts her in contact with sick, suffering people. She is especially good in dealing with children. She has a good relation with the people she works with. She does not see Miss Goldberg very often, but when she does she enjoys her company and thinks of her with affection. She is attached to her sister, but is critical of her shortcomings. She keeps in touch with the other children, but regards only a few of them as close friends. Of one girl of the group she said: "She is so different; because we grew up together I need not like her."

And now she confessed to being in love. The object of this feeling is a boy who belonged to the group and who met her after a long absence in another part of the world and was impressed by the change in her. This is a very normal, very romantic, late adolescent love with all the pangs of being unsure of the response to her secret longing. It provokes a very relevant question. We find that this relationship, too, lacks the typical oedipal features normally recognizable in adult sexual relationships. She turns to the sibling and develops heterosexual genital fantasies connected with him and not with a father substitute. Are we justified in assuming that just as there is a constitutionally determined ego potential which does achieve maturation under adverse circumstances too, so a favorable constitution may allow libido development in spite of serious obstructions to proceed from pregenital aims to heterosexual genital ones, even under conditions which do not provide the child with the typical experiences in its relations to objects? Could the relation to male siblings, especially Charlie, have paved the way for this? Of course, whether she will be capable of normal genital gratification will have to be seen. It is likely that the idea she will form of her heterosexual partner will include the image of her pregenital female objects.

The boy returned to the country he came from and Elizabeth, who once could not understand that letters could be read by someone absent, has an intense correspondence with him. That he knows everything about her and shared a lot of her experiences gives her a feeling of security.

The disoriented little girl who started her analysis with "I am not a person," ended it saying: "You know, I like being myself."

Conclusion

The problems brought into focus by Elizabeth's analysis, which were examined in order to attempt a closer understanding of the pathology of motherless children, are as follows: can one reconstruct a person's ego development and libidinal development only through dissecting her present personality and observing its changes in the analytic process, without the emergence of specific early memories; in what way is it possible to adapt the analytic technique to the task of treating a person whose object relations did not proceed beyond the identifications of earliest infancy; and, is it possible to help to build a new concept of reality instead of the first conditioned by artificially cruel circumstances?

The work done with Elizabeth was used to throw light on these problems. I have tried to describe the very atypical evolution of transference and the way she used her analysis to remodel her ego, which was distorted by a normal attempt at adaptation to an abnormal environment and thwarted by the severe blocking of her libidinal development. The agency which now, after concluded treatment, provides her with internal guidance was compared with the superego as defined in analytic theory. It was found that such an agency can be established without being built up on the basis of identification with the oedipal objects and that, on account of the difference in its etiology, this agency is not invested with so much aggressive energy as the superego normally is, and appears therefore to be more protective than punitive.

This paper forms part of a research project entitled "Inquiry into the Development of Motherless Children" which is being financed by a grant from the Psychoanalytic Research and Development Fund, Inc., New York, to the Hampstead Child-Therapy Clinic.

Origin of Contributions and References: See Page 345

UPROOTING AND RESETTLEMENT AS A SOCIOLOGICAL PROBLEM

Maria Pfister-Ammende
Switzerland

On reading the title of this paper one may well ask: a problem for whom? Is it a problem for the person who is changing his home, or a problem for the new environment to which an individual or a group of people are trying to adapt themselves? The duality of the question shows the full range of the problem, which involves the migrant at one extreme, and his new place of abode at the other. Included within its scope are all types of human beings and destinies, and all sorts of sociological situations, ranging from the most deeply disturbed, fleeing individuals and groups of refugees, to well-organized emigrant families and well-provided-for groups of settlers. The problem even includes individuals, families and communities who have had to leave home and go to other towns or parts of a country, in order to look for work and a new home.

I would like to discuss the question of uprooting when it occurs without persecution or expulsion, or is not caused by war. I shall take an example, to illustrate my subject, from the uprooting and structural change that is brought about by technical and industrial development.

My example is taken from the life of an African tribe living among barren hills, scattered over a wide area where there is practically no vegetation. These people are nomads, and for over 4,000 years, as historians have remarked, have been unapproachable and seclusive. They are a martial and well-organized people, who resisted every invasion until towards the end of the 19th century, when they were overcome by modern weapons and had to submit to colonization. From that time on they have paid taxes, but they have not allowed anything to interfere with their tribal life.

In more recent years a port about twenty miles away from the area has developed into an important trading center. As a result of tactful negotiations this mountain tribe was induced to supply the necessary dock-workers, who formed a sort of branch settlement on the border of the town, along the road leading from the mountain to the port. This small settlement grew, as do the outskirts of all harbor-towns, and the present number of its inhabitants amounts to 5,000. The people and their animals live crowded into a narrow space, in barely 2,000 rooms.

These conditions are made even worse by the ceaseless comings and goings of other members of the tribe, who swarm down from their inhospitable mountain-district every time there is a shortage of food, and who are welcomed in the manner customary to such tribes.

The atmosphere there is one of thousands of years ago. The people have retained their characteristic clothing, their hair-style and attitudes, as well as their own language. The dockers work in groups under their own tribal leaders. Though a trade union was formed, it did not last.

In the course of time the authorities decided that this slum could not be tolerated any longer, and it was suggested that a new settlement should be built on the other side of the town, near the docks, which would provide sufficient living-space in solid stone houses for the families and their relatives, and for the tribe's numerous social events.

The new settlement is now ready, but it stands virtually empty. So far the dockers have not moved in, although it has been built specially for them, and the advantages offered, such as hygienic dwellings, absence of overcrowding, prospects of permanent employment in the docks and easy contact between dwellings and working premises, are obvious. These advantages would not only raise living-standards, but would also help the people to settle down permanently, achievements — as it is officially emphasized — that should be aimed at in due course of time, in the interest of the whole country.

It is obvious, at least to outsiders, that the new settlement offers advantages, but how do these appear to the eyes of the people of the tribe? How much or how little do we really know of what they value most — higher earnings and permanent employment, living accommodation near to the place of their work, a higher standard of living, an end to their nomadic way of life? In short, do they value permanent settlement, or are there other things they value more highly?

Many reasons have been given for their reluctance to move into these new premises. They are said to have been poorly built and to be already deteriorating; to be isolated and far distant from the town's shopping center, with bad means of transportation. Some complain that the school is situated three miles away and that there are no transport facilities for the children. On the other hand, had the dockers been willing to move, these matters could have been arranged between the authorities and the tribal leaders before the settlement was built. These people are organized as a tribe, with a strong feeling of community that has enabled them to withstand the hardships of life under a harsh climate, and resist the blows dealt them by history. The tribal chiefs exercise irrefutable authority over the members of the tribe, who accept the opinion and adhere solely to the decisions of their leaders.

Another crucial point concerns the geographical situations of both settlements. The one, bordering the town on the same side as the mountains, gives the docker ample opportunity to take his camel at any time he pleases, and go and see his family if, as is often the case, they are still living in the mountains. It is another question for him to undertake this journey from the new settlement on the other side of town, near the harbor. From there he will first have to cross the bridge and pass through the town, where there is modern traffic; and, although he will cross the same bridge every day on his way to work, it will become a gigantic difficulty and an obstacle cutting off direct access to his mountains, when it is a question of visiting his kin at will. To the mind of the tribes-man, the new settlement with its stone-built houses holds no advantages over the rotting wooden huts on the mountain side of the bridge. Since for many thousands of years these people have been in the habit of working only when they must, they do not see the advantages of regular employment. What they do see is that their work may keep them from returning when they want to, either for family reasons or if called to do so by their clan, to the place where they still have their roots. And to this they attach the utmost importance.

All these facts show that these people cannot be transplanted in this way. Not only is it impossible to transplant them, but — and this is very important for their mental health — it is also impossible to uproot them. To take up regular paid work in the docks was a different question, because they did not have to give up their homes. They have no desire to contact other people or to alter their own way of living so as to adjust it to that of others.

So much for this tribe. Similar types of difference in value systems have been described in relation to the Puerto Ricans, 50,000 of whom moved by commercial air-line to New York within the space of two years. The spirit of enterprise and competition and the commercial instincts of the New Yorker did not appeal to the Puerto Rican, who was still immersed in the traditional manana-culture of his own people. He made little effort to adapt himself to the American ideal of collectivity, in contrast to the middle-class emigrants from Europe who have found it easier to adjust themselves from the start.

Ideological, economical and structural differences can lead to the failure of attempts to resettle migrants. Similar situations may arise if the government of the country through which the migrants are passing negotiates with another country without the participation of the representatives of migrant welfare organizations and the migrants themselves; if warnings of those experienced organizations about economic, climatic and political difficulties in the new, possibly sub-tropic country, are not taken into account; if inadequate and unrealistic information about the new country is given to the migrants while they are in their temporary place of asylum; or if, after immigration, no further advice is available or the religious needs of the immigrants are neglected; or finally, if cooperation between the leaders of such groups and the authorities of the new country is lacking. In such cases it may happen that even as many as 50% of the migrants do not take root and, after urgent requests, have to be brought back to their homeland. In this case the result will have been that of paying their expensive travel fares around the world, only to bring them back to their starting point.

Some Remarks on the Theoretical Aspect of Transplanting

Let us first try to understand the most important factors in transplanting. These are: (i) the reasons for and methods of transplantation; (ii) the time involved; (iii) the sociological structure both of the transplanted and of the new environment.

(1) Reasons and Methods

It goes without saying that a spontaneous change of environment can have an agreeable and stimulating effect. 'Geh' in die Schweiz hinein und mach' dein Glück' ('Go to Switzerland and make your fortune!') was a common saying at the turn of the century around the Bodensee, and countless Germans from Würtemberg and Swabia found their way into Switzerland.

There are always two poles involved in any process of resettlement, and the manner in which they come together will have a decisive effect upon the future relations of the parties concerned. The success of settlement, therefore, will depend on whether the new settlers and the inhabitants of the country clash in a violent impact, embittered, mute and tense, or whether they meet in a spirit of friendliness. At the beginning of the century, the Swiss germans were pro-German and the symbiosis produced no friction; but in later years, Switzerland began to feel threatened by the neighboring country and withdrew into herself, causing a separation in cultural and other relations between the hitherto welcome foreigner and herself. Then the popular Swabian girl became 'that German servant' and a derogatory term appeared, 'the eighth Swiss'. This originated from the Swiss National Exhibition in 1939, at which was shown the figure of a brave Swiss under a cheese bell-glass with the words: 'Every eighth Swiss marries a foreign woman.'

If such changes in mutual relations can happen when immigration has been voluntary, it is only to be expected that they should take a more vigorous form when transplanting occurs under pressure or compulsion. The more compulsory the transplantation, the greater the tendency of the immigrant to develop a regressive attitude, to isolate himself, develop his own false ideas on relationships and misjudge his new surroundings. As for the population of the country of immigration, they often pass through two well-known phases: first they are enthusiastic and then they become gradually less so.

Another essential point is whether an immigrant group is actively engaged in the process of resettlement, or is passively submitting to it. Compulsory, passive submission will delay adjustment. The accumulated negative effect of individuals will become projected into the new environment, which the migrant will not judge with clear insight, but will see through a prism of distrust and negativism. Moreover, resettlement will be impossible if the emigrant remains completely attached to his old home.

I saw, myself, eight people who had been living in a cave for the last nine years, without even the simplest necessities. When asked why they did not leave, the oldest member of the family pointed towards the frontier, a few miles away: 'Our fields are there and unless we can get them back, we shall die here'.

(2) The Time Involved

Another factor is the time available for transplantation. Every period of crisis involves mental strain and may endanger the balance of mind of the person concerned. These dangers are greater when events follow each other rapidly and unexpectedly. The more abrupt the process of transplantation, the greater the risk of uprooting.

(3) The Sociological Structure of the Parties Concerned

With respect to the effect of landscape and climate, a Southern German who merely crosses the border from his own country of Würtemberg, to Switzerland, would find Swiss mountains and climate familiar; whereas the same mountains produced quite a different effect upon people from the Ukranian plains. They could be heard gasping their astonishment at 'those high mountains' as they stood on the terrace of hotels much sought after by visitors from Central Europe because of their marvelous situation.

Landscape and climate greatly influence the economic and social patterns of rural societies, such as the tribe I spoke of, and also help to determine their values. Where the individual alone is too weak for life's struggle, and only a group can survive, we find that strong interpersonal bonds develop, such as we have come to know through wartime and prisoner-of-war comradeships. In group-migration it is always a question of all or none. The contact of the group with the world outside will be channeled through the group's leaders, who represent it as a unit. This is sometimes a sore point, because outsiders often fail to understand this inaccessibility of individuals in the group, and react negatively. The simple fact is that such groups cannot be psychologically uprooted, because they remain centered in themselves. At best they can only be transplanted, together with their roots, like trees. Such very strong bonds within a group make social assimilation most difficult. Here the question will arise, whether it will be more desirable from the point of view of mental health to bring about complete integration or to rest satisfied with peaceful co-existence and mutual contact. Is it better to eliminate all differences, or will variety, in its colorful social aspects, bring fresh life and vigor into a nation? The Canadians, for example, have allowed immigrants groups to follow their own way of life in the belief that in the second and third generations adaptation will follow naturally through increasing contact with the people of the country. These social differences between nations can be considerable. Certain nations seem to have a more standardized social ideal to which all immigrants are subjected.

The real difficulties for an immigrant who travels with a group do not start on arrival, but when he has to face the new environment all by himself. It may be, then, that the strangeness and different nature of the new world will reflect his own image. Having been identified with a group up to this time, he will now begin to see himself as he is – I would not say 'know himself', for the road to this latter point is long and difficult.

In this situation it is not the language which forms the greatest barrier. The newcomer may have learned the language and may understand what words and sentences mean, but their deeper sociological significance will be lost to him. In good Viennese dialect 'Was weiss a' Fremder?' ('How could a stranger know?') is a characteristic expression of this truth. Such failure to understand may arouse strong emotions in an adult and a yearning for something familiar, however simple. There is a great deal in the saying: 'It is easier to change your religion than your favorite cafe.' Nevertheless, to be able to practice his own religion in his customary way is of vital importance to the religiously-minded immigrant. This would mean not just any Protestant Church, for example, but the Lutheran, Calvinistic or Methodist Church, as the case may be. A Yugoslav once said to me that he would not feel lost wherever he might find himself, as long as he could pray and hear Mass in a Roman Catholic Church. But not many peoply have this broadly based religious feeling. Most frequently people feel tied to the local church of their home-land, for example, the Roman Catholic Church of Bavaria, the Lutheran Church of Finland, the Zwinglian Church of German Switzerland or the Roman Catholic Church of Southern Italy — though they may not be aware of how close this tie is. The children of such immigrants may in time turn away from the religion of their parents and then, again, their children or grandchildren may turn back to the original church of their ancestors, thus completing the full circle. The change in the pattern of his social life does not necessarily entail a change in the immigrant's religion. Hence the third generation may revert to its traditional family or group religious heritage, while remaining socially well-adjusted to the new country.

There is a fundamental difference in the situation of an individual immigrant as compared with that of a group. Both individuals and groups have a need to find a new identity. To the individual immigrant, unless he is emotionally shut-in or of a schizoid type, it is almost a question of life or death for him to identify himself with his new environment. Matters are different in the case of the self-contained group, where the individual will be identified with the whole spirit of the group, which accepts the new environment without the same emotional demands being made upon it.

The following question might be asked as a test: When a group moves from one place to another, does it seek human relationship in the new environment? Certainly this was not so in the case of some pioneer groups of the past, who either exterminated or enslaved the people they found in their new environment. On the other hand most of the immigrants in Israel were certainly looking for new human relationships, but even there it may have proved difficult, because of the gulf between utterly different social structures. Out of positive affect and similarity of ideology a common language is born and a desire to serve the country, factors which promote mutual understanding. But it takes more than agreement in theory and a desire for contact to prevent the development of negative emotional attitudes. What is needed, as I have already said, is understanding by the immigrants of the new environment and its mode of life, and this comes only slowly.

These considerations apply equally to the other party, to the country of immigration.

In the process of acculturation, the structure of family life will have an essential part to play on both sides. The question of whether the immigrants originate from a strict patriarchal social structure and whether the new country is organized more loosely or built on a matriarchal social pattern, and so on, must be taken into consideration.

Conclusions

From the preceeding we can now draw certain conclusions with special regard to mental health.

I. Preparatory Phase

1. Planning

If migration occurs in an entirely unexpected and unprepared way, it can cause shock and lead to failure to adjust. It is, therefore, advisable for both parties concerned to allow time, if possible, for a phase of preparation during which the immigrants and the receiving country can enter into direct contact and can settle their problems for themselves. This will give them opportunity to get to know each other and will, furthermore, prevent the bad influence of misleading rumors or inadequate information. Liaison officers should be appointed to act as negotiators, but the choice should be made most carefully, because of their great potential influence. The task of liaison needs more than one person: it requires a team drawn from both sides and should include, if available, social psychologists, social workers and anthropologists of the same or a similar cultural group as the emigrants.

It would be most desirable to study the situation, not only in its sociological and economic aspects and with regard to family structure, but also from the point of view of social psychology and administration. Hopes and fears, expectations and wishes, as well as general conditions of mental health on both sides, should be taken into consideration.

2. Active Preparation

In any transplantation at least the consent, if not the collaboration of the parties concerned, should be asked for, even if this takes time. The social welfare organizations concerned should be co-ordinated and brought under common management.

The liaison teams should be thoroughly briefed on the cultural and psychological difficulties that may arise during periods of transplantation. In cases in which the possibility of unusual psychological reactions can be foreseen, the teams will need clear instructions so as to be able to take action and not be paralyzed by the shock of events.

II. Phase of Action

It is important to bear in mind that mass transportation and crowded camps present great dangers to mental health.

(1) A real menace to mental stability is the breaking up of families. This must be avoided at all costs, and families must not be separated while under movement. They should remain together, each family forming a unit. This means that fathers and husbands are not to be sent alone, in advance, to new districts or countries with the expectation that their families will follow later, or perhaps never, as it may often happen. Children should remain with their parents.

(2) Migrants need time, and they must be given time, for an active and positive response to their new environment to develop. They must also be given time so that they can occasionally retire into themselves, when they feel overcome by the novelty of their surroundings and by phases of uncertainty. One might think that this would apply especially to people coming out of a cultural atmosphere different from that of western Europe, and whose notion of time is different from that of the people of the Western World, who are always in a hurry. This is not so, for a migrating European also needs time for mental adjustment; only he knows it less instinctively than the immigrant from the lands of the manana-culture, or from Islam or the Chinese culture. To his disadvantage, a European often feels driven to 'make haste'.

(3) The first step in any approach must be made by the inhabitants of the new country, but not just as a single gesture, soon forgotten. The approach should be continuous and always ready.

(4) Much can be achieved by using any available administrative organizing bodies within the immigrating groups, such as schools and professional and youth associations. Their co-operation can change the normally aggressive attitude of adolescents into that of constructive activity, instead of leaving it to deteriorate.

(5) Any special requirements of a migrating community should be respected. An example will make this clear: when dams were being built in Switzerland, often whole communities had to be moved as a unit, and not only the living but also the dead, i.e. their cemeteries as well. What the cemetery represents in Switzerland, the tombs and veneration of ancestors may mean to others.

(6) People must be given a warm reception and be made to feel that they are welcome. The new settler will form his judgment of the new country through the first people he meets, and this will leave a lasting impression. The welcome is not enough by itself, but it means a lot.

(7) Customs such as living arrangements and ways of working should be taken into consideration when making arrangements for immigrants.

(8) The education of the children is another problem. If the language is different, should they attend the same school as the local children? School is a natural link and the possibility of using it to help the children to adjust ought not to be neglected, except perhaps when a group has moved as a completely self-contained unit. Results can be obtained only if teachers are willing to act as intermediaries, and it is of vital importance for teachers to have special training for this purpose. For example, the teacher should ensure that a pupil does not get a bad mark and a reprimand for not having anything to say about railways in his essay, when the child has come from a desert and has never even heard of a railway.

(9) If a built-in-evaluation is not possible, a careful check after about two months on how the resettlement is going is necessary, and a thorough follow-up after approximately two years. Here again, the help of teams comprised of public health officers, mental health workers, anthropologists and social workers, should be sought.

So much for our considerations as regards mental hygiene. I feel that we already know something of how to plan migration and resettlement, using both head and heart — as Noah did with his Ark. However, as well as we plan we cannot foresee the future. Who knows? — tomorrow, or even tonight, an invisible force may bring to an end things as we know them. A storm may rage and wipe out our social structure, our administration and even our most careful planning. In this manner thousands of Italians found themselves thrown into the market-place at Locarno in 1944, like other hundreds of thousands who have been tossed about in France, Korea, or other parts of the world. These people were helpless, overwhelmed and stunned by the turbulence of unco-ordinated events, as in a storm. They were truly refugees within the meaning of the Jewish refugee from Hungary who said: 'We do not know where we are going. We are being carried away. We are like trees with roots cut off; like leaves floating on the water. We are waiting for a wind to carry us on, but whether fair or ill, we do not know.' These people have passed through a hurricane and have sought and found refuge. But it is these people who at their work in the new country are liable to misinterpret as ridicule the smile of a co-worker who does not know their language. In such cases, a man may disappear from his work and try to find comfort for the smile he has misunderstood by avoiding strangers and losing himself, unknown, in a crowd. Such are the refugees. Eventually, they will become immigrants, but the shock will still persist as a legacy of mistrust of anyone or anything new, unfamiliar and unknown.

Finally let me revert once more to this great process of change. The mental health problems in this connection may best be illustrated by the words of the religious healer of a desert tribe. He was asked about the tribesmen who were leaving the tribe to move to the growing new city far-away: would they seek advice from a religious healer in that city? 'No, that they cannot do', the healer replied. 'They must go to the healer of their own tribe.' 'And if the distance be too great?' 'Then they cannot go', was the brief reply. 'What then?' A long pause followed, after which the healer finally said: 'They must learn to suffer.' This healer knew his people. He saw no salvation for the uprooted but the way of woe and suffering, in a time of irresistible change and the acute distress in man for footing, strength and nourishment — as of a tree poised on the edge of an abyss pushing its roots into the void.

Let us help these people not to become a prey to despair, but to find a way to overcome and transmute their suffering and thus transform themselves.

Origin of Contributions and References: See Page 346

ANNEX

The Problem of Uprooting
Maria Pfister-Ammende

Interview-schedule[1]

This procedure was used for the interviews investigating the psychological aspects of the refugee problem, sponsored and financed by the Swiss Academy of Medical Sciences in 1944 (Pfister-Ammende 1946). As already mentioned on page 000, the schedule was followed freely by the interviewer according to his own judgement.

A. Material and Method

300 "healthy" adult refugees were examined by means of this procedure, which was known only to the interviewer.

I. Heredity

1. Mental disorders in the family
2. Family history

II. Personal history up to the outbreak of war

3. Family: socio-psychological who preferred?
4. Childhood: earliest memories – feelings of guilt – conflicts
5. Adolescence: friends, pampering
6. Success in school: liked studying?
7. Physical constitution (military service)
8. Type: extrovert, sociable – introvert, dreamer – professional ambition (fulfilled?)
9. General disposition – depressions – inferiority complexes
10. Inner conflicts (moral): illnesses – attitude towards
11. Reading preferences
12. Attitude towards life
13. Goal in life
14. Religious faith and attitude
15. Attitude towards home- (host-) country: vice-versa (antisemitism)
16. Living standard as independent individual
17. Life problems
18. Personality type before war and/or emigration
19. Political orientation
20. Sexual development: autosexual – homosexual – heterosexual
21. Marriage: sex – family – finances – children

---
[1] See Pfister-Ammende, "The Problem of Uprooting", page 7.

III. Personal history as of war's beginning

1. In the home-(host-) country
   22. Consequences: personal – family (who could flee? how? why?)
2. Temporary stay before Switzerland
   23. Evaluation
3. 24. Why to Switzerland?
4. 25. Knowledge, image, expectations and attitude toward Switzerland before arrival?
5. 26. Crossing border and reception in Switzerland – with whom? Reaction: personal – fellow refugees': on crossing the border – immediately afterwards. (Self-centered only? – shock – joy – security – feeling of inferiority as refugee)
   27. Uniform complex: before Switzerland – in Switzerland
6. 28. *Reception camp*
   29. Environment (also landscape)
   30. Head of the camp
   31. Helpers
   32. Food
   33. Leisure
   34. Leave – work? working hours?
   35. Camp community: comradship – morale? – a guiding principle – national frictions? – antisemitism – sexual problems of married couples, the unmarried, teenagers, prostitutes – need for cleanliness – means thereto
   36. How did you feel?
   37. Mood: desire for rest – possibility for it
7. 38. Other transitory stays: camp – homes – private quarters – free room and board – job (why accepted) (why given up?) Evaluation as above.

IV. Present history

Environment

1. Camp
   1. Atmosphere (local-psychological): landscape
   2. Camp leaders
   3. Helpers
   4. Food (hunger?)
   5. Nature of job – working hours
   6. Insurance
   7. Pay
   8. Leisure time
   9. Leave
   10. Camp community: comradship – morale? ties – a guiding principle – national or other frictions? – antisemitism – sexual problems of the married, the unmarried, teenagers, prostitutes.

How do you get along with the camp leader? Does he resemble your father? Do you have a special task in the camp? Health — desire for cleanliness — desire for orderliness — desire for rest — possibility for it.

1a. Other environment: home — private quarters — free room and board — private job etc. Related questions.
   11. Are you relatively satisfied with your life at present?
   12. What do you appreciate?
   13. What do you consider wrong?
   14. What do you consider chicanery?
2. Personal circumstances
   15. Marriage today — present abode?
   16. Children: schooling — language — religion — antisemitism
       attitude towards the child — child's attitude towards the interviewed — child and school — is the child well taken care of? Where and how would you prefer your child to be living?

17. Culture: Cultural needs and hobbies. — Are they fulfilled? — What do you like to do in your free time? — Which books at your disposal? — Reading preferences?
18. Social life: do you prefer to be with people or alone — preferably your countrymen — refugees of other nationality — Swiss
3. Switzerland
   19. Present knowledge of (how acquired): basic concept of the Swiss Federation — economic situation. Officer and soldier, women — attitude toward the refugee. Mentality, average.
   20. Evaluation of: basic concept of the Swiss Federation — economic situation — mentality, average — officer and soldier, women — attitude toward the refugee.
   21. Switzerland's reaction in case of occupation: toward Swiss Jews — toward refugee living in Switzerland.

The individual

1. How is your health (ill?)
2. Sleep
3. Dreams (as a child — adult — emigration — today (make notes)
4. How do you feel mentally and emotionally?
5. What is your mood? compared with former times in your homeland — in transit before Switzerland.
6. Do you feel yourself different today from the person you were before emigration?
7. If so, in which respect?

8. If so, what do you think caused this change (emigration or something else?)
9. Special inner conflicts (of the young — the old: desire for rest?)
10. Sexual relations: heterosexual — masturbation — homosexual — perversions
11. What do you like best here?
12. What do you miss?
13. Is there anything you like or that pleases you (clothes, comfort etc, and the little joys?)
14. How do you feel without a home country? Language? — No rights? — Antisemitism and negation of existence? Do you feel marked? — Do you have an inferiority complex because you are a refugee?
    Degradation (economic — cultural?)
15. What is most difficult for you: your own fate — the fate of your family — present separation from relatives, or else — what do you fear most?
16. How does the war situation affect your mood?
17. Do you keep a diary or make notes?
18. Do you feel the need of a heart to heart talk — is it possible?
19. Whom would you prefer to talk with (priest, psychologist, physician, etc., a refugee or a Swiss?)
20. Does your stay here make sense, and does it have value, mentally and professionally? Or is it merely a passing period of waiting?
21. Did the emigration change or destroy your goal in life?
22. Have you looked for or found a new goal in life?
23. Has life retained its meaning for you after so many misfortunes?
24. Is your attitude towards life positive, or do you consider yourself a victim of fate?
25. What does religion mean to you?
26. What is your interpretation of freedom?
27. Do you feel free here, if not — why not?
28. What are you most preoccupied with? Past — present — future?
29. How do you envision your future in your given state of health?
    Is there anything you can do here for your future?
    What?
30. How do you envisage the post-war period?
31. Would you like to remain here after the war, if you could? If so, which kind of life do you think you would lead?
32. Would you like to return to your home country? (Attitude towards civilians, soldiers)
33. Would you like to return to your first host country?
34. Do you wish to go overseas? Where else?
35. Are you happier knowing that you will be departing? If so, how?
36. Attitude towards home-country (homesick? . . .)

37. Attitude towards Germany: people — Nazi
38. Political orientation
39. Would you rather participate in the war? If so: why and how? If not, why not?
40. Would you prefer another country for refuge if it were not occupied? If so, which one and why?
41. Where would you like to be most?
42. In which life situation would you prefer to be in Switzerland?
43. (If working): Does your present work satisfy you? (Otherwise): What kind of work would you accept? Which would be your conditions?
44. Have you answered the official questionnaire concerning retraining? If not, why not?

V. Miscellaneous Questions

1. How do you judge the Swiss solution of the refugee problem in regard to organization and phychological aspects?
2. What would you suggest?
3. Question of self-administration in the camp
4. Question of camp- (home-) management by a refugee
5. Would you separate camps by nationalities or are you for mixed camps?
6. Would you separate camps by religious creed or not?
7. What would you do if refugees came to your country? Swiss nationals for instance?
8. Separation of families
9. What is your opinion of this investigation?
10. Rorschach-test.

Observations

Constitution
Nervous symptoms, etc.
Nutritional status
Mood
Emotional responsiveness

Impression

In the interrogation of refugees we chose the method of the intimate, individual psychotherapeutic dialogue varying in length from 2 to 22 hours. It is important for the evaluation of the material that the interviewed persons experienced a sense of relief at the end of the questioning.

When I thanked a refugee for his frankness, he said: "Oh no, I am glad to have this load off my chest. Now it is with you and no longer with me" . . . and he went off smiling.

The interviews were supplemented through letters and diaries. In addition I had free access to the files of the Federal Camps and Homes Administration and to the police records at the Federal Department of Justice and Police. I kept in touch with the interviewed as closely and as long as possible in order not to mistake a momentary impulse during the interview for a basic attitude and opinion. My own co-operation later, as the head of a mental health service of the Hostels Administration, however, constituted the best criterion for the validity of my conception of the problem. Rarely did I have to revise my concept.

B. The Sociological Situation of the Interviewed

160 men and 140 women between 15 and 78 years of age and from 17 different nations were interviewed. All social strata, social, and political opinions were represented. Their reasons for emigration and request for asylum in Switzerland were:

Active decision for racial and political reasons;
Single or group flight for the same reasons;
Imprisonment in a concentration camp and transportation to Switzerland close to war's end;
Captivity (PW) or deportation to Germany or Italy for forced labor and subsequent escape to Switzerland.

Most of these people carried a passport. At the time of our interview, 1944, they lived in Switzerland in transit without chance of striking new roots in this country.

Origin of Contributions and References: See Page 329

ORIGIN OF THE CONTRIBUTIONS AND REFERENCES

Zwingmann, Ch., and Pfister-Ammende, M., Uprooting and After . . . . General Review.

A.F.S.C., 1971, (American Friends Service Committee) *Indo-China 1971.* White Paper on Requirements for Peace in Southeast Asia.
Brengelmann, J. and Revenstorff, D., 1970, "Persönlichkeit und Entwurzelung" Max-Planck-Institut für Psychiatrie, Psychologische Abt., München.
Kraepelin, E., 1921, Ueber Entwurzelung. Zeitschr. f.d. ges. Neurolog. & Psychiatrie, 63.
Malzberg, B., 1936, Mental Disease among Foreign-Born and Native Whites in New York State. Amer. J. Psychiat. 93, 127–137.
Malzberg, B., 1956 & Lee, E.S.: Migration and mental disease. New York.
Ødegaard, Ø., 1932, Emigration and Insanity. Acta Psychiatr. et Neurolog. Copenhagen, Levin and Munksgard, Suppl. 4.
WHO, 1970, (World Health Organization) The Adaptation of Migrants to Urban Conditons. WHO/RECS/OSHS/70.11. mimeogr.

Pfister-Ammende, M., The Problem of Uprooting. Condensed and revised from Schweiz. med. Wschr., 6, 1951, 151. Also Zur Psychopathologie der Entwurzelung, in Bull. Schweiz. Akad. Wiss., 8, 4, 1952, 338-345. Translation from German.

Binder, H.: Schweiz, med. Wschr. 1951, 22.
Brun, R.: Allgemeine Neurosenlehre, Basel, 1946.
Hediger, H.: Bemerkungen zum Raumzeitsystem der Tiere, Schweiz. Zeitschr. Psychol. 5, 4, 1946.
Ivanov-Smolensky, J. Nerv. Dis 67, 346, 1928.
Kretschmer, E.: Medizinische Psychologie, Leipzig, 1947.
Pawlow, J.P.: Die höchste Nerventätigkeit von Tieren, München, 1926.
Pfister-Ammende, Maria: Das Problem der Entwurzelung, Schweiz. med. Wschr. 6, 1951, 151.

- Zur Psychopathologie der Entwurzelung, Bull. Schweiz. Akad. Med. Wiss. 8, 1952.
- Die Indikation zur Analyse, Psyche, 1, 1952.
- Psychologie und Psychiatrie der Internierung und des Flüchtlingsdaseins, Psychiatrie der Gegenwart, Bd. III., Springer 1961.

Vischer, A.L.: Die Stacheldrahtkrankheit, Zürich, 1918.

Zwingmann, Ch., The Nostalgic Phenomenon and its Exploitation, in Arch. Psychiatrie und Ztschr. Neurologie, 201, 1961, 445-464. Completely revised 1970.

Bauer, R.A., 1957, "Brainwashing: Psychology or Demonology? The J. of Soc. Issues, 13, 3.

Binswanger, L., 1942, Grundformen und Erkenntnis des Menschlichen Daseins, Zürich, Niehaus.

Binswanger, L., 1944, Der Fall Ellen West. Schweiz. Arch. Neurol. Psychiatr. 54, 69.

Binswanger, L., 1955, Ausgewählte Vortrage und Aufsätze (Bd 2) Francke, Bern.

Fenichel, O., 1945 The Psychoanalytic Theory of Neurosis. New York.

Fischer, F., 1929, Zeitstruktur und Schizophrenie. Zschr. Neurol. 121, 544.

Fodor, N., 1950, Varities of Nostalgia, Psychoanal. Rev. 37, 25-38.

Freud, A. and Burlingham, D., 1943, War and Children, New York, Medic. Warbook

Friedeburg, L. v. und Hübner, P., 1964. "Das Geschichtsbild der Jugend," Inventa Verlag.

Frost, J., 1938, Homesickness and Immigrant Psychoses. J. ment Sci. 84, 801.

GAP, 1956, (Group for the Advancement of Psychiatry) "Factors Used to Increase the Susceptibility of Individuals to Forceful Indoctrination: Observations and Experiments." GAP Symposium Nr. 3, New York.

GAP, 1957, "Methods of Forceful Indoctrination Observations and Interviews. GAP Symposium Nr. 4, New York.

Geisler, E., 1959, Diebstahl und im Traum erlebte Kindestötung als Heimwehreaktion einer 14 jährigen. Z. Kinderpsychiatr. 26, 41-47.

Geyer, H., 1947, Das Flüchtlingsheimweh und seine Behandlung. Nervenzarzt 18, 447.

Gross, F., 1958, The Seizure of Political Power, New York Philosophical.

Haegi, V., 1964, "Bericht über die Diagnostik und Therapie der Lungenerkrankungen, Neue Zürcher Zeitung, 20.6.64.

Hall, G.S., 1920, Adolescence, New York, Appleton, Vol II.

Haspel, A., 1873, De la nostalgie, (Mem. de Medicine) Paris.

Heidegger, M., 1957, Der Satz vom Grunde. Pfullingen.

Helpach, W., 1950, Geopsyche, Encke, Stuttgart.

Hoferus, J., 1678, Dissertatio Medica de Nostalgia oder Heimwehe. Basileae. (Übersetzt von C.K. ANSPACH.)

Homburger, A., 1926, Psychopathologie des Kindesalters. Berlin.

Isaaks, S., 1941, The Cambridge Evacuation Survey, London, Methnen.
Israeli, N., 1936, Abnormal Personality and Time. New York.
Jaspers, K., 1909, Heimweh und Verbrechen. Arch. Kriminal. – Anthrop. 35, 1.
Johnson, W., 1946, People in Quandaries. New York.
Jung, C., 1957, Privatkorrespondenz. 26. Februar.
Jungk, R., 1961, Off Limits für das Gewissen: der Briefwechsel Claude Eatherly – Günther Anders, Hamburg, Rowolt.
Kennedy, F., 1943, In: SLADEN, F.J., Psychiatry and the War. Springfield.
Kinkead, E., 1957, A Reporter at Large: The Study of Something New In History. The New Yorker, 33, 114-169.
Klemm, O., 1911, Geschichte der Psychologie. Leipzig. Teubner.
Kretschmer, E., 1956, Medizinische Psychologie. 11. Aufl. Stuttgart.
Larousse, P., (n.d.) Grand Dictionaire Universel, Tome lle, Paris.
Lavin, R., 1953, "Division Psychiatry," Medical Bulletin, I.
Lifton, R.J., 1957, "Thought Reform of Chinese Intellectuals: A Psychiatric Evaluation," J. of Soc. Issues, 13, 3.
Lemke, R., 1957, Privatkorrespondenz. 27. Marz.
Lenin, V.I., 1965, On Religion, Collection of Articles, Moscow, Progress Publishers.
Linebarger, P. 1948, Psychological Warfare, I.J.P., Washington.
Lippert, E., 1950, "Über Heimweh," Z.f. Kinderpsychiat., 17.
Marx, K., 1927, Zur Kritik der Hegelschen Rechtsphilosophie, Marx-Engels Gesamtausg. Erste Abt., Frankfurt.
McCann, W.H., 1940, Nostalgia: A Descriptive and Comparative Study (Unpublished Doctor's Thesis, Department of Psychology, Indiana University).
Meerlo, J.A.M., 1951, "The Crime of Menticide." Am. J. Psychiat., 197, 594-598.
Meerlo, J.A.M., 1952, "Menticide" in Meerlo, Conversation and Communication, New York, Int. Univ. Press, 149-157.
Meerlo, J.A.M., 1953, Thought Control and Confession Compulsion in R.M. Lindner Explorations in Psychoanalysis.
Meerlo, J.A.M., 1954, "Pavlovian Strategy as a Weapon of Menticide," Amer. J. Psychiat., 110, 173-196.
Meerlo, J.A.M., 1955, "Medication into Submission": The Danger of Therapeutic Coercion," J. Nerv. Ment. Dis, 122, 353-360.
Meerlo, J.A.M., 1956, The Rape of the Mind, Cleveland, World Publishing Co.
Menninger, W.C., 1948, Psychiatry in a Troubled World. New York
Moser, L., 1955, "Analyzing Some of the Transitory Fears of Entering College Freshmen", Coll. and Univ., 30.
Nikolini, W., 1936, Verbrechen aus Heimweh und ihre psychoanalytische Erklärung Imago 22, 91-120.
Nitschke, A., 1955, Das Bild der Heimwehreaktion beim jungen Kind. Dtsch. med. Wschr. 80, 1901-1905.
Nürnberger Nachrichten, 1960, Folge 3. - 7. November.
Peiper, A., 1942, Das Heimweh. Dtsch. med. Wschr. 68, 121.
Percy et Laurent, 1809, Nostalgia: Dict. des Sciences Medicales 36, 265.
Peters, D., 1863, Remarks on the Evils of Youthful Enlistments and Nostalgia. Amer. med. Times 6, 75.
Proust, M., 1919.

Regnier, A., 1955, "A Practical Solution to the 'AWOL' Problem" Mil. Rev. Ft. Leavenworth, 35.
Rose, A., 1948, The Homes of Homesick Girls. J. Child. Psychiatr. 1, 181.
Sartre, J.P., 1938, La Nausee, Paris, Gallimard
Sartre, J.P., 1939, Le Mur, Paris, Gallimard,
Sartre, J.P., 1945, Les Chemins de la Liberté: Paris, Gallimard.
  1. L'age de Raison
  2. Le Sursis
  3. La Mort dans l'âme
Schein, E., 1956, "The Chinese Indoctrination Program for Prisoners of War," Psychiatrie, 19, 149-172.
Schopenhauer, A., 1913, Parerga und Paralipomena, 1. Bd. München.
Schwab, G., 1925, "Über Heimweh beim Kleinkind," Jb. Kinderhk., 108, 15-39.
Schwind, M. 1946, Das Prinzip der Nähe und der geographische Unterricht. Sammlung 2, 105.
Spielrein, S., 1923, Die Zeit im unterschwelligen Seelenleben. Imago, 9, 300-317.
Sterba, E., 1940, Homesickness and the Mother's Breast. 14, 701-707.
Stoessinger, J., 1956, The Refugee and the World Community, Minnesota.
U.S. Congress, Senate. 1956, Committee on Goverment Operations, Permanent Subcommittee on Investigations "Hearings June 26, 1956, Washington D.C. U.S. Gvt. Print. Office.
U.S. Congress, Senate. 1957, Communist Interrogation, Indoctrination and Exploitation of American Military and Civilian Prisoners, 84th Congress, Senate Report Nr. 2832, Washington D.C., U.S. Govt. Print. Office.
U.S. Department of Defense, 1955, POW: "The Fight Continues after the Battle." Report of the Secretary of Defense's Advisors, Committee on Prisoners of War. Washington D.C., U.S. Gvt. Print. Office.
U.S. Department of the Army, 1956, Communist Interrogation, Indoctrination and Exploitation of Prisoners of War. Army Pamphlet Nr. 30-101, Washington D.C., U.S. Gvt. Print. Office.
Varney, A., 1950, The Psychology of Flight. New York
Vernon, M.D., 1940, "A Study of Some Effects of Evacuation on Adolescent Girls," Brit. J. Ed. Psych., 10, 114-134.
Wittson, C.L. Harris I.H., and Hunt, W.A., 1943, "Cryptic Nostalgia" War. Med., 3.
Zwingmann, Ch., 1959, "Heimweh" or "Nostalgic Reaction": A Conceptual Analysis and Interpretation of a Medico-Psychological Phenomenon. Mikrofilm (L.C. Card. No. 59-6908).
Zwingmann, Ch., 1961, Symbolische Rückkehr! Ein psychologisches Problem ausländischer Arbeitskräfte. Psychol. Praxis 5, 97-108.
Zwingmann, Ch., 1961, "Die Heimwehreaction alias 'pathopatridalgia'" Arch. Psychiat. u. Zschr. Neurologie 201, 445-464.
Zwingmann, Ch., 1962, Zur Psychologie der Lebenskrisen, Frankfurt, Akademische Verlagsgesellschaft.
Zwingmann, Ch., 1965, Selbstvernichtung, Frankfurt, Akademische Verlagsgesellschaft.
Zwingmann, Ch., 1971, Katastrophenreaktionen. Frankfurt, Akademische Verlagsgesellschaft.

Allers, R., Psychogenic Disturbances in a Linguistically Strange Environment, in Ztschr. f. d. ges. Neurol. u. Psychiatrie, 60, 1920, 281-289. Translation from German.

Kino, F.F., Aliens' Paranoid Reaction, in J. Ment. Sci., 97, 1951, 589-594.

Allers, R., Z. ges. Neurol. Psychiat., 1920, 60, 281.
Jaspers, K., Allg. Psychopathologie, 1948.
Knigge, F., Z. ges Neurol. Psychiat., 1935, 153, 622.
Schneider, K., ibid., 1930, 127, 725.

Freud, A., and Burlingham, D., Reactions to Evacuation. Excerpt from War and Children, Internat. Universities Press, 1944.

Pfister-Ammende, M., Displaced Soviet Russians in Switzerland, in Die Psychohygiene, M. Pfister-Ammende, ed., Bern 1949, 231-264. Translation from German.

Hediger, H., Bermerkungen zum Raum-Zeitsystem der Tiere, Schweiz. Z. Psychol 4,5 (1946).
Levy-Bruehl, Die geistige Welt der Primitiven, München 1927.
Niederland, W.G., The Problem of the Survivor. y. Hillside Hosp. 10, 233, 1961.
Pfister-Ammende, Maria, Vorläufige Mitteilung über psychologische Untersuchungen an Flüchtlingen, Bullet. Schweiz. Akad. Med. Wissensch. 1, 2, 1946.
    Massenpsychologische und psychohygienische Probleme der Flüchtlingsbetreuung, Schweiz, Mediz. Wochenschr. 31, 1948.
Silone Ignazio, Fontamara, Zurich 1930.

Müller-Hegemann, D., Human Uprooting. Original.

Ruffin, H., Das Altern und die Psychiatrie des Seniums; in H.W. Gruhle et al. (Edit.) Psychiatrie der Gegenwart II Berlin-Göttingen-Heidelberg 1960.
Lange, J., Seelische Störungen im Greisenalter. MMW 93, 1939 (1934).
Hall, P., Some Clinical Aspects of Moving House. Psychosom. Res. 10, 59 (1966) ref. Zbl. Neur. Psych. 188, 63 (1967).
Bovi, A., Wohnungswechsel und Geisteskrankheiten. Nervenarzt, 38, 251 (1967).
Müller-Fahlbusch, H. u. S. IHDA, Endogene Depression bei Wohnungswechsel, Nervenarzt 38, 147 (1967).
Feuerhahn, G., D. Müller-Hegemann et al., Sozialpsychiatrisch-epidemiologische Analyse der in Zweijahresfrist aufgenommenen Psychosen ... Psychiatrie, Neurol., med. Psychol, 21, 91 (1969).
David, H.P. (Edit.), Migration, Mental Health and Community Services. Geneva 1966.
Hollingshead, A.B. and F.C. Redlich, Social class and mental illness. New York 1958.
Pfister-Ammende, M., Migration and Mental Health Services, in David, H.P. (Edit.): Migration, Mental Health and Community Services. Geneva 1966.
Pfister-Ammende, M., Psychologie und Psychiatrie der Internierung und des Flüchtlingsdaseins; in H.W. Gruhle et al. (Edit.) Psychiatrie der Gegenwart III, Berlin-Göttinger-Heidelberg 1961.
Müller-Hegemann, D., Über Schädigungen und Störungen des Nervensystems bei Verfolgten des Naziregimes. Dt. Ges. wesen 21, 561 (1966).

Weinberg, A.A., Mental Health Aspects of Voluntary Migration, in Mental Hygiene, 39, 3, 1955, 450-566.

Girard, Alain & Stoetzel, Jean, 1953. Francais et Immigrees: l'Attitude Francaise, l'Adaptation des Italiens et des Polonais. Travaux et Documents. Cahier No. 19. Presses Universitaires de France.
Guttman, L., 1950. The Principal Components of Scale Analysis. Studies in Soc. Psych. in Wld. War II. Princeton University Press.
Guttman, L., 1954. The Principal Components of Scalable Attitudes. In Mathematical Thinking in the Social Sciences (Lazarsfeld). Free Press. Pages 216-57.
Guttman, L., 1955 (unpublished). Research on Adjustment of New Immigrants in Israel.
Handlin, Oskar, 1953. The Uprooted. The Immigrant in American History, from the Old World to the New. London: Watts & Co.
Hofstee, G.W., 1952. Some Remarks on Selective Migration. The Research Group for European Migration Problems, No. VII. The Hague.
Murphy, H.B.M., 1952. Practical Measures for Refugee Mental Health in Britain Bull. of the Wld. Fed. for Ment. Hlth., Vol. 4 No. 198.
Pfister-Ammende, Maria, 1952. Zur Psychopathologie der Entwurzelung. Bl. der Schweiz Akadamie der Wissenschaften, Fasc. 4, Vol. 8.

Pfister-Ammende, Maria, 1953. Heimatverlust und psychische Erkrankung. Lecture at the Second Meeting of the European League for Mental Hygiene, Vienna.
Saenger, G., 1953. The Social Psychology of Prejudice. New York: Harper & Bros.
Stouffer, S.A., 1950. Measurement and Prediction. Studies in Soc. Psych. in Wld. War II. Princeton University Press.
Taft, Donald R. & Dobbins, Richard, 1955. International Migrations. New York: Ronald Press Co. pages 518-19.
Tyhurst, Libuse, 1951. Displacement and Migration: A Study in Social Psychiatry. Amer. J. of Psychiat., Vol. 107, No. 8, February.
Weinberg, A.A., 1949. Psycho-Sociology of the Immigrant. Jerusalem.
Weinberg, A.A., 1953. Acculturation and Integration of Migrants in Israel. Int. Soc. Sci. Bull., 5 No. 4, pp. 702-10.
Weinberg, A.A., 1953. Problems of Adjustment of New Immigrants to Israel. Wld. Ment. Hlth., 5.
Weinberg, A.A., 1954. Some Aspects of Immigration in Israel. R.E.M.P. Bull., 3, No. 4-6.

Diarra, S., African Workers in France and Problems of Adaptation, in Psychologie Africaine, 2, 1, 1966, 107-126. Translation from French.

Rodriguez, R., Difficulties of Adjustment in Immigrant Children in Geneva, in Médecine et Hygiène, 845, 1968, 1-6. Translation from French.

Zwingmann, Ch., Nostalgic Behavior — A Study of Foreign Workers in West Germany. Revised version of Ausländische Arbeiter im Betrieb, Bartmann Verlag, Köln, 1964.

Carl Duisberg-Gesellschaft, 1956/1957, Ein Jahr in Deutschland, Köln
Chaney, L., und Hanna, H., 1918, Safety Movement in the Iron and Steel Industry, U.S. Bureau of Labor Statist., Series 18, No. 234.

Flicker, J.D., u. Weiss, P., 1943, Nostalgia and its Military Implications, War Med., 4, 380.
Frost, I., 1938, Home-Sickness and Immigrant Psychosis, J. Ment. Sci., 84, 801.
Jaspers, K., 1909, Heimweh und Verbrechen, Arch. Krim. Anthrop., 35, 1.
Lemke, R., 1957, Privatkorrespondenz
Nürnberger Nachrichten, 1960, Eugenio Errico Serie, 3-17.11.,
Schwab, G., 1925, Über Heimweh beim Kleinkind, in: Jb. Kinderheilk., 108, 15.
Zwingmann, Ch., 1959, "Heimweh" or "Nostalgic Reaction": a Conceptual Analysis and Interpretation of a Medico-Psychological Phenomenon, (Mikrofilm, L.C. Card. No. 59-6908), 1959.
Zwingmann, Ch., 1971, "Ausländer in Bahnhöfen", Frankfurter Rundschau, J. 27, 232, 2.

Ødegaard, Ø., Emigration and Mental Health, in Mental Hygiene, 20, 1936, 546-553.

Malzberg, B., 1935, Mental Hygiene, Vol. 19, pp. 635-60.
Ødegaard, Ø., 1932. Emigration and Insanity; A Study of Mental Disease among the Norwegian-born Population of Minnesota. Acta Psychiatrica et Neurologica, supplementum. 4, Copenhagen: Levin and Munksgard.

Ødegaard, Ø., Norwegian Emigration, Re-Emigration and Internal Migration. Original.

Astrup, C. and Noreik, K. (1966): Functional Psychoses. Diagnostic and Prognostic Models. (C.C. Thomas, Springfield, Ill. U.S.A.)
Astrup, C. and Ødegard, Ø. (1960): Internal Migration and Mental Disease in Norway. Psychiat. Quart. Suppl. 34, 116-130.
Dalgard, O.S. (1967): Migration and Functional Psychoses in Oslo. Universitetsforlaget, Oslo.
Eitinger, L. (1959): The Incidence of Mental Disease among Refugees in Norway. J. ment. Sci. 105, 326-328.
Eitinger, L. and B. Grünfeld (1966): Psychoses among Refugees in Norway. Acta psychiat. scand. 42, 315-328.
Halevi, H.S. (1963): Frequency of Mental Illness among Jews in Israel. Int. J. Social Psychiatry, 9, 268-282.
Helgason, T. (1964): Epidemiology of Mental Disorders in Iceland. Acta psychiat. scand. Suppl. 173.

Jaco, E.G. (1960): The Social Epidemiology of Mental Disorders. Russel Sage Foundation, New York.
Karlsson, K.W. (1966): Migration and Mental Illness in Helsinki Excerpt. Med. Internat. Cong. Ser. No. 117, 250.
Lazarus, J., B.Z. Locke and D.S. Thomas (1963): Migration Differentials in Mental Disorders. Milbank Memorial Quart. 41, 25-42.
Malzberg, B. (1962): Migration and Mental Disease among the White Population of New York State, 1949-1951. Human Biology, 34, 89-98.
Malzberg, B., E.S. Lee and D.S. Thomas (1956): Migration and Mental Disease. Social Science Research Council, New York.
Rimon, R.H., A. Stenbäck and K.A. Achte (1965): A Socio-Psychiatric Study of Paranoid Psychoses. Acta psychiat. scand. Suppl. 180, 335-349.
Stenbäck, A. and K.A. Achte (1965): An Epidemiological Study of Psychiatric Morbidity in Helsinki. Acta psychiat. scand. Suppl. 180, 287-309.
Srole, L., T.S. Langner, S.T. Michael, M.K. Opler and T.A.C. Rennie (1962): Mental Health in the Metropolis, McGraw-Hill, New York.
Ødegard, Ø. (1932): Emigration and Insanity. Acta psychiat. (Kbh.), Suppl. 4.
Ødegard, Ø. (1945): The Distribution of Mental Diseases in Norway. Acta psychiat. (Kbh.), 20, 247-284.

Eitinger, L., Concentration Camp Survivors in Norway and Israel, in Israel J. of Med. Sci., 1, 1965, 883-895.

Ström, A., Refsum, S.B., Eitinger, L., Gronvik, O., Lonnum, A., Engeset, A., Osvik, K. and Rogan, B. Examination of Norwegian Ex-Concentration Camp Prisoners. J. Neuropsychiat. 4: 43, 1962.
Hill, R. and Hansen, D.A. Families in Disaster, in: Baker, W. and Chapman, D.W. "Man and Society in Disaster," New York, Basic Books 1962.
Zborowski, M. and Herzog, E. "Life Is with People." New York International Universities Press, Inc., 1952.
Helweg-Larsen, P., Hoffmeyer, H., Kieler, J., Thayssen, E.H., Thayssen, J.H., Thygesen, P. and Wulff, M.H. Famine Disease in German Concentration Camps. Complications and Sequels. Acta psychiat. (Kbh.) Suppl. 83, 1952.
Eitinger, L. Pathology of the Concentration Camp Syndrome. Arch. gen. Psychiat. 5: 371, 1961.
Gronvik, O. and Lonnum, A. Neurological Conditions in Former Concentration Camp Inmates. J. Neuropsychiat. 4: 51, 1962.
Wolff, H.G., Every Man Has His Breaking Point. Milit. Med. 125: 85, 1960.
Schneider, K. Schizophrenie and Dienstbeschädigung. Nervenarzt 21: 481, 1950.
Kolle, K. Psychosen als Schädigungsfolgen. Fortschr. Neurol. Psychiat. 26: 101, 1958.

Venzlaff, U. "Die psychoreaktiven Störungen nach entschädigungs-pflichtigen Ereignissen." Berlin, Springer-Verlag, 1958.
Chapman, L.F., Thetford, W.N., Berlin, L., Guthrie, T.C. and Wolff, H.G. Highest Integrative Functions in Man during Stress. Res. Publ. Ass. nerv. ment. Dis. 36: 491, 1958.
Wwedensky, I.N., Zur Frage der Endzustände nach reaktiven Psychosen. Z. ges. Neurol. Psychiat. 118: 200, 1929.
Strauss, H. Besonderheiten der nichtpsychotischen seelischen Störungen bei Opfern der nationalsozialistischen Verfolgungen und ihre Bedeutung bei der Begutachtung. Nervenarzt 28: 344, 1957.
Nathan, T.S., Eitinger, L. and Winnik, H.Z., The Psychiatric Pathology of Survivors of the Nazi-Holocaust. Israel Ann. Psychiat. 1: 113, 1963.
Eitinger, L. "Concentration Camp Survivors in Norway and Israel." London, Allen & Unwin, 1964.
Jung, C.G. "Über die Psychologie des Unbewussten," 5th ed. Zurich, 1946.
Collis, W.R.F., Belsen Camp. Brit. med. J. 1: 814, 1945.

Eitinger, L., Mental Diseases among Refugees in Norway after World War II, in Psychiatriske Undersokelser Blant Flyktninger I. Norge, Universitetsforlaget Oslo, 1958. Condensed. Translation from Norwegian.

Bakis, Eduard: DP Apathy. In: Flight and Resettlement. Unesco. Paris 1955. Ed. H.B.M. Murphy.
Bernstein, Peretz: Jew-hate as a Sociological Problem. N.Y. 1951.
Bibering, Grete: Psychiatric and Psychosomatic Conditions in Former Concentration Camp Inmates. Bull. World Fed. ment. Hlth. 1951: 3: 229-232.
Cameron, Norman: The Paranoid Pseudo-Community. Amer. J. Sociol. 1943: 49: 32-38.
— The Development of Paranoid Thinking. Psychol. Rev. 1943: 50: 219-233.
Cohen, Elie A.: Human Behavior in Concentration Camp. London 1954.
Hoffmeyer, H., Wulff, M. Hertel: Psychiatric Symptoms on Repatriation. In Helweg-Larsen, P. et al.: Famine Disease in German Concentration Camps.
Hunt. W.A., et al.: Military Performance of a Group of Marginal Neuropsychiatric Cases. Amer. J. Psychiat. 1952: 109: 168-171.
Kahn, Eugen, Richter, Helen, G.: Sensitivity. Amer. J. Psychiat. 1939: 19: 609-622.
Kornrumpf, Martin: Enforced Mass Migration in Europe 1912 - 1954. Integration 1954.
Kraepelin, E.: Psychiatrie. 6. Auflage. Leipzig. 1899.
Langfeldt, G.: Laerebok i klinisk psykiatri 2. oppl. Oslo 1954.
Lilly, John, C.: Effects of Physical Restraint and of Reduction of Ordinary Levels of Physical Stimuli on Intact Healthy Persons Group for the Advancement of Psychiatry, 1955.

Malzberg, Benjamin: Mental Disease among Foreign-Born Whites, with Special Reference to Natives of Russia and Poland. Amer. J. Psychiat., 1935, 92, 627-640.
– Mental Disease among Foreign-Born and Native Whites in New York State. Amer. J. Psychiat. 1936: 93: 127-137.
Murphy, H.B.M.: The Extent of the Problem. In: Flight and Resettlement. Unesco. Paris 1955.
– Refugee Psychoses in Great Britain: Admission to the Mental Hospital. In Flight and Resettlement Unesco. Paris 1955.
Pfister-Ammende, Maria: The Symptomatology, Treatment and Prognosis in Mentally Ill Refugees and Repatriates in Switzerland. In: Flight and Resettlement. Unesco. Paris 1955. Ed. H.B.M. Murphy.
Tyhurst, Libuse: Displacement and Migration. Amer. J. Psychiat. 1951: 107: 561-568.
Ødegard, Ørnulv: Emigration and Insanity. Acta Psychiat. Kbh. 1932. Suppl. 4.
– The Incidence of Psychoses in Various Occupations. Int. J. of soc. Psychiat. 1956: 2: 85-104.

Murphy, H.B.M., Migration and the Major Mental Disorders: A Reappraisal, in Mobility and Mental Health, M.B. Kantor, Springfield, 1965, 5-29. Revised version

Astrup, C. & Ødegaard, Ø.: Internal Migration and Disease in Norway. Psychiatric. Quart., 1960, Suppl. 34, 116.
Cade, J.F.J. & Krupinski, J.: Incidence of Psychiatric Disorders in Victoria in Relation to Country of Birth. Med. J. Austral., 1962, 1, 400.
Clark, R.E.: The Relation of Schizophrenia to Occupational Income and Occupational Prestige. Amer. Sociol. Rev., 1948, 13, 325.
Daumezon, D., Champion, Y. & Champion-Bassett, J.: L'incidence psycho-pathologique sur une population transplantée d'origine Nord-Africaine. Etudes de Socio-Psychiatrie. (Duchêne, Ed.) Ministry of Public Health, Paris, 1955. Monograph No. 7.
Dayton, N.A.: New Facts on Mental Disorders. Springfield, Thomas, 1940.
Eitinger, L.: Psykiatriske Undersøkelser blant Flyktninger i Norge. Universitetsforlaget, Oslo, 1958.
Faris, R.E.L. & Dunham, H.W.: Mental Disorders in Urban Areas. New York. Hafner Publishing Company, 1960.
Halevi, H.S.: Mental illness in Israel: Admissions to Mental Hospitals and Institutions for In-Patients during 1958. Ministry of Health, Jerusalem, 1960. Mimeograph.
Jaco, E.G.: The Social Epidemiology of Mental Disorders. New York, Russell Sage Foundation, 1960.
Kaila, M.: Über die Durchschnittshäufigkeit der Geisteskrankheiten und des Schwachsinns in Finnland. Acta Psychiat. et Neurol., 1942, 17, 47.
Lazarus, J., Locke, B.Z. & Thomas, D.S.: Migration Differentials in Mental Disease. Milbank Mem. Fund Quart., 1963, 41, 25.

Lee, E.S.: Migration and Mental Disease: New York State, 1949-51, Selected Studies of Migration Since World War II. New York, Milbank Memorial Fund, 1958.
Lee, E.S.: Socio-Economic and Migration Differentials in Mental Disease. Milbank Mem. Fund Quart., 1963, 41, 249.
Lemert, E.M.: An Exploratory Study of Mental Disorders in a Rural Problem Area. Rural Sociol., 1948, 13, 48.
Locke, B.Z., Kramer, M. & Pasamanick, B.: Immigration and Insanity. Public Health Reports, 1960, 75, 301.
Malzberg, B.: Social and Biological Aspects of Mental Disease. Utica, N.Y., State Hospitals Press, 1940.
Malzberg, B. & Lee, E.S.: Migration and Mental Disease. New York, Social Science Research Council, 1956.
Malzberg, B.: Migration and Mental Disease among the White Population of New York State, 1949-51. Human Biol., 1962, 34, 89.
Murphy, H.B.M.: Flight and Resettlement. Paris UNESCO, 1955.
Murphy, H.B.M.: Culture and Mental Disorder in Singapore. In (Opler, Ed.): Culture and Mental Health. New York, Macmillan, 1959.
Ødegaard, Ø.: Emigration and Insanity. Acta Psychiat. et Neurol., 1932, Suppl. 4.
Ødegaard, Ø.: Distribution of Mental Diseases in Norway. Acta Psychiat. et Neurol., 1945, 20, 247.
Statistical Bureau, Government of Israel: Statistical Abstract of Israel No. 11, 1960. Jerusalem, 1961.
Sunier, A.: Mental Illness and Psychiatric Care in Israel. Amsterdam, 1956, Mimeograph.
Tietze, C., Lemkau, P. & Cooper, M.: Personality Disorder and Spatial Mobility. Amer. J. Sociol., 1942, 48, 29.

Murphy, H.B.M., The Low Rate of Mental Hospitalization Shown by Immigrants to Canada. Original.

Bohannan, P. (Ed.): African Homicide and Suicide. Evanston, Illinois, Princeton University Press, 1960.
Bruhn, J.G. et al.: Incidence of Treated Mental Illness in Three Pennsylvania Communities. Amer. Public Health, 1966, 56, 880-883.
Canadian Department of Citizenship & Immigration: Report GS-10; Migration and Mental Illness. Mimeogr., 1965, 68 pp. (Principal author: C. de Hesse).
Eaton, J.W. & Weil, R.J.: Culture and Mental Disorders, Glencoe, Illinois, 1955.
Kleiner, R.J. & Parker, S.: Goal Striving and Psychosomatic Symptoms in a Migrant and Non-Migrant Population. In: (Kantor, ed.) Mobility and Mental Health. Springfield, Illinois, Charles C. Thomas, 1965, Chapter 4, 78-85.
Krupinski, J. & Stoller, A.: Incidence of Mental Disorders in Victoria, Australia, According to Country of Birth. Med. J. Australia, 1965, 2, 265-269.
Malzberg, B.: Social and Biological Aspects of Mental Disease. Utica, 1940.

Malzberg, B.: Mental Disease among Native and Foreign-Born in Canada, 1950-1952. Mimeogr., 1963, 36 pp. (This paper also comprises chapter 1 of the author's as yet unpublished collection of studies "Migration in Relation to Mental Disease", Albany, 1968).
Murphy, H.B.M. & Sampath, H.M.: Mental Health in a Caribbean Community. A Mental Health Survey of Saint Thomas, V.I. Mimeogr. 145 pp.
Murphy, H.B.M.: Mental Hospitalization Patterns in Twelve Canadian Subcultures. Mimeogr., 1968, 121 pp.
Murphy, H.B.M.: Psychiatric Concomitants of Fusion in Plural Societies. In (Lebra, W.P., ed.): Mental Health Research in Asia and the Pacific. Vol. II. Honolulu, East-West Center Press. In press.
Regeringscommisaris voor de Emigratie: De Gaande Man. Gravenhage, Holland, Staatsdrukkerij, 1958.

Curle, A., Transitional Communities and Social Reconnection, in Human Relations, 1, 1947, 2-28, and with E.L. Trust in Human Relations, 1, 2, 1947, 240-288. Restatement.

Pfister-Ammende, M., Mental Hygiene in Refugee Camps, from Psychohygiene und Psychotherapie bei der Flüchtlingsbetreuung, in Die Psychohygiene, M. Pfister-Ammende, ed., Huber, Bern 1949, 217-230; and from Gedanken und Anregungen zur Situation in deutschen Flüchtlingslagern, in Jugendaufbauwerk, 5-6, 1955. Completely revised 1970.

Eidgenösische Zentralleitung der Lager und Heime: Richtlinien für unsere Mitarbeiter in Lagern und Heimen für Flüchtlinge Zürich 1945, mimeogr., & as "Help to Refugees" in English, French and German, in World Mental Health, J. World. Fed. Ment. Health. Vol. 10, 1. 1958.
Jung, C.G. Die Psychotherapie der Gegenwart, Schweiz. Zeitschr. f. Psychologie, IV, 1, 1945.
Pfister-Ammende M. Vorläufige Mitteilung über psychologische Untersuchungen an Flüchtlingen. Bull. Schweiz. Akad. Mediz. Wiss. 2, 2, 1946.
Pfister-Ammende M. Psychohygiene und Psychotherapie bei der Flüchtlingsbetreuung. In Die Psychohygiene, ed. Pfister-Ammende, Huber, Bern, 1949.
Pfister-Ammende M. Gedanken und Anregungen zur Situation in deutschen Flüchtlingslagern. Deutsches Jugendaufbauwerk 5, 1955, & Caritas 1955, & in English by the UN High Commissioner for Refugees, HCR/RS/13, 1956, mimeogr.

Pfister-Ammende M. The Symptomatology, Treatment and Prognosis in Mentally Ill Refugees and Repatriates in Switzerland. In Flight and Resettlement, ed. Murphy, Unesco 1955.

Pfister-Ammende M. Psychologie und Psychiatrie der Internierung und des Flüchtlingsdaseins. In Psychiatrie der Gegenwart, Vol. III, Springer 1961.

Pfister-Ammende M. Migration and Mental Health Services. In Migration, Mental Health and Community Services, ed. David, Am. Joint Distr. Comm., Geneva, 1967.

Pfister-Ammende M. The Doctor as a Community Agent. Bull. of the Menninger Clinic, Vol. 5, Nr 5, 1971.

Zaugg, O. Einige Erfahrungen über die Führung von Heimen und Lagern für kriegsbetroffene Menschen. In Die Psychohygiene, ed. Pfister-Ammende, Huber, Bern, 1949.

Stoller, A., and Krupinski, J., Immigration to Australia – Mental Health Aspects. Original.

Armstrong, R.E. (1969). "Migration to Australia, 1945-1969" Wagga Wagga Teachers College, Area of Humanities, Paper No. 4.

Cade, J.F.J. and Krupinski, J. (1962). "Incidence of Psychiatric Disorders in Victoria in Relation to Country of Birth," Med. J. Aust., 1,400.

Department of Immigration (1970). "Australian Immigration – Consolidated Statistics." No. 4., Canberra.

Hallows, J. (1970). "Report on Migration." The Australian, June 8, 9 and 10.

Immigration Advisory Council (1961). "Report on the Incidence of Mental Illness Among Migrants," Canberra, 1961.

Immigration Advisory Council (1969). "Immigration and the Balance of the Sexes in Australia." – A Report to the Minister of State for Immigration.

Johnston, R. (1963). "A New Approach to the Meaning of Assimilation," Hum. Relat., 16, 295.

Johnston, R. (1968). "Culture Conflict and Culture Pension" – Paper Read at Saanz Conference.

Judge, C.G. and Glatt, M.M. (1961). "The Problem of Alcoholism in Australia and England," Med. J. Aust., 1, 596.

Krupinski, J. (1967). "Sociological Aspects of Mental Ill-Health in Migrants." Social Science and Medicine, 267.

Krupinski, J., Schaechter, F, and Cade, J.F.J. (1965). "Factors Influencing the Incidence of Mental Disorders in Migrants," Med. J. Aust., 2,269.

Krupinski, J. and Stoller, A. (1965). "Incidence of Mental Disorders in Victoria, Australia, According to Country of Birth," Med. J. Aust., 2,265.

Krupinski, J. and Stoller, A. (1963-1970). "Statistical Bulletins" No. 1-8, Mental Health Authority, Victoria Melbourne.

Krupinski, J. and Stoller, A. (1971). Ed. "Health of a Metropolis: Results of the Melbourne Metropolitan Health and Social Survey." Melbourne, Heinemann, Educational.

Krupinski, J., Stoller, A. and Wallace, L. (1971). "Psychiatric Disorders in Eastern Europe Refugees now in Australia." In Press.

Price, C. (1966). "Post-war Migration: Demographic Background." In New Faces ed. A Stoller. Cheshire, Melbourne.

Price, C. (1968). "Identification of Ethnic Minorities." In Ethnic Minorities in Australia. ed. H. Throssell, A.C.O. S.S. Brisbane

Rooth, J.S. (1968). "Government Responsibility and the European Migrant." In Ethnic Minorities in Australia, ed. H. Throssel, A.C.O.S.S. Brisbane.

Schaechter, F. (1965). "Previous History of Mental Illness in Female Migrant Patients Admitted to the Psychiatric Hospital, Royal Park." Med. J. Aust., 2, 277.

Snedden, B.M. (1969). "People and Progress." The Australian Quarterly, 12:3

Stoller, A. (1966). "Migration and Mental Health in Australia." Brit. J. Soc. Psychiat., 1:1.

Stoller, A. (1966). "New Faces: Immigrants and Family Life in Australia." F.W. Cheshire, Aust. and Brit., 195 ps.

Stoller, A. (1968). "Stress in Immigrants." in Ethnic Minorities in Australia. ed. H. Throssell, A.C.O.S.S. Brisbane.

Taft, R. (1957). "A Psychological Model for the Study of Social Assimilation." Human Relations, 10, 141-156.

Taft, R. (1958). "Is the Tolerant Personality Type the Opposite of the Intolerant?" J. Soc. Psychol., 47, 397-405.

Taft, R. (1959). "Ethnic Stereotypes, Attitudes and Familiarity: Australia." J. Soc. Psychol., 49, 177-186.

Taft, R. (1963). "The Shared Frame of Reference Concept Applied to Assimilation of Migrants." Human Relations, 6, 45-55.

Taft, R. (1966). "From Stranger to Citizen; a Survey of Studies of Immigrant Assimilation in Western Australia." University of Western Australia Press, Perth.

Taft, R. and Doczy, A.G. (1962). "The Assimilation of Intellectual Refugees in Western Australia." REMP Bulletin, 9-10:1.

Zubrycki, J. (1960). "Immigrants in Australia; a Demographic Survey Based Upon the 1954 Census." Melbourne University Press, Melbourne.

Zubrycki, J. (1968). "Migrants and the Occupational Structure." In Ethnic Minorities in Australia. ed. H. Throssel, A.C.O.S.S. Brisbane.

Bhaskaran, K., Seth, R.C., and Yadav, S.N., Migration and Mental Ill-Health in Industry, in Indian Journal of Psychiatry, 12, 1-2, 1970, 102-116.

Caravedo, B. and Valdivia, O.: A Study on Mental Health of a Cross-Section of Industrial Population. The International Journal of Social Psychiatry, VII, 269-282, 1961.

Dube, K.C.: Pilot Investigation of the Incidence of Mental Diseases in India — An Interim Report to the Indian Council of Medical Research, 1967.

Fraser, R.: The Incidence of Neurosis among Factory Workers – Industrial Health Research Board, Report No. 90. Her Majesty's Stationery Office, London, 1947.
Ganguli, H.C.: Mental Health in Industry. Presidential Address at the Fifty-fourth Indian Science Congress – Section of Psychology and Educational Sciences, 1967.
Kleiner, R.J. and Parker, S.: "Goal Striving and Psychosomatic Symptoms in a Migrant and Non-migrant Population" in 'Mobility and Mental Health', Edited by Mildred B. Kantor, Illinois, U.S.A., Charles, C. Thomas, 1965.
Kleiner, R.J. and Parker, S.: Migration and Mental Illness – A New Look – Amer. Social. Review, 24: 687-690, 1959.
Lazarus, J., Locke, B.Z., and Thomas, D.S.: Migration Differentials in Mental Diease – Milbank, Mem. Fund. – Quart. 41: 25; 1963.
Locke, B.Z., Kramer, M. and Pasamanic B.: Immigration and Insanity – Public Health Reports, 75:301, 1960.
Lee, S.E.: Socio-economic and Migration Differentials in Mental Disease – Milbank Mem. Fund – Quart., 41, 249, 1963.
Malzberg, B.: Social and Biological Aspects of Mental Disease – Utica, N.Y. State Hospitals, Press, 1940.
Malzberg, B. and Lee, E.S.: Migration and Mental Disease – New York – Social Science Research Council, 1956.
Murphy, H.B.M.: Migration and the Major Mental Disorders in "Mobility and Mental Health" – Edited by Mildred B. Kantor – Illinois, U.S.A., Charles C. Thomas, 1965.
Ødegaard, Ø.: Emigration and Insanity – Acta. Psychiat. et. Neurol. Supplement, 4, 1932.
Ødegaard, Ø.: Distribution of Mental Diseases in Norway – Acta. Psychiat. et. Neurol., 20:247, 1945.
Sethi, B.B., Gupta, S.C., Rajkumar: 300 Urban Families – A Psychiatric Study, The Indian Jour. Psychiat. IX, 280-302, 1967.
Thomas, G.E., Bhaskaran, K. and Chopra, H.D.: A Psychiatric Morbidity Survey of a Village in Ranchi (unpublished data), 1966.

Strotzka, H., Mental Health Aspects of Camp Clearance – The Activities of the Mental Health Adviser to the U.N. High Commissioner for Refugees (1959/1960). Original.

Berner, P., 1965, La Psychopathologie sociale des Refugies, L'Evolution Psychiatrique 4, 633-655.
Hoff, H. und H. Strotzka, 1958, Die psychohygienische Betreuung ungarischer Neuflüchtlinge in Österreich 1956-58, Hollinek, Wien.
Merton, R.K., 1957, Social Theory and Social Structure, N.Y. The Free Press of Glencoe, S 421-436.

Pfister-Ammende, M., 1955, The Symptomatology, Treatment, and Prognosis in Mentally Ill Refugees and Repatriates in Switzerland. In Flight and Resettlement (ed. H.B.M. Murphy), UNESCO.
Strotzka, H., I. Leitner, G. Czerwenka-Wenkstetten, S. Graupe und M. Simon, 1968, Kleinburg, eine sozialpsychiatrische Feldstudie, Öst, Bundes Vlg. Wien.
UN General Assembly Documents, A/AC/96/62, A/AC/96/84, A/AC/96/156 (all 1960) A/AC/96/206 (1963) Mental Health Adviser Reports to the Executive Committee UNHCR).

Ludowyk Gyomroi, E., The Analysis of a Young Concentration Camp Victim, in the Psychoanalytic Study of the Child, 18, 1963, 484-510.

Bergen, M.E. (1958), The Effect of Severe Trauma on a Four-Year-Old Child. The Psychoanalytic Study of the Child, XIII.
Deutsch, H. (1934), Über einen Typus der Pseudoaffektivität (Als Ob). Int. Z. Psychoanal., XX.
Freud, A. (1951), Observations on Child Development. The Psychoanalytic Study of the Child, VI.
– (1952), The Mutual Influences of Ego and Id: Earliest Stages. The Psychoanalytic Study of the Child, VII.
– (1960), Discussion of John Bowlby's Paper. The Psychoanalytic Study of the Child, XV.
– & Dann, S. (1951), An Experiment in Group Upbringing. The Psychoanalytic Study of the Child, VI.
Freud, S. (1937), Analysis Terminable and Interminable. Collected Papers, V. London: Hogarth Press, 1950.
Grauer, H. (1969), Psychodynamics of the Survivor Syndrome, Canad. Psychiat. Assn. J. 14: 617-622, December.
Hartmann, H. (1939), Ego Psychology and the Problem of Adaptation. New York: International Universities Press, 1958.
Erikson, E.H. (1956), The Problem of Ego Identity. J. Amer. Psa. Assn., IV.
Jacobson, E. (1954a), The Self and the Object World. The Psychoanalytic Study of the Child, IX.
– (1954b), Psychotic Identification. J. Amer. Psa. Assn., II.
Piers, G. & Singer, M.B. (1953), Shame and Guilt. Springfield: Thomas.
Reich, A. (1954), Early Identifications as Archaic Elements in the Superego. J. Amer. Psa. Assn., II.
Sandler, J. (1960), On the Concept of the Superego. The Psychoanalytic Study of the Child, XV.
– & Rosenblatt, B. (1962), The Concept of the Representational World. The Psychoanalytic Study of the Child, XVII.
Spitz, R.A. (1951), Psychogenic Diseases in Infancy. The Psychoanalytic Study of the Child, VI.
Weil, A.P. (1953), Certain Severe Disturbances of Ego Development in Childhood. The Psychoanalytic Study of the Child, VIII.

Pfister-Ammende, M., Uprooting and Resettlement as a Sociological Problem, in Uprooting and Resettlement, World Fed. of Ment. Health, Geneva, 1960, 18-31.

Gaertner, M. L., (1955), A Comparison of Refugee- and Non-refugee Immigrants to New York City. Flight and Resettlement (ed. Murphy H.B.M.) UNESCO, 1955, 99-113.

Pfister-Ammende, M., (1952), Zur Psychopathologie der Entwurzelung. Bull. Schweiz. Akad. Med. Wiss. 8,4, 338-345.

Pfister-Ammende, M., Psychologie und Psychiatrie des Flüchtlings daseins und der Wiederver-wurzelung. Psychiatrie der Gegenwart, Vol. 3, Springer, 1961.

Weinberg, A. A., (1953), Problems of Adjustment of New Immigrants to Israel. World Mental Health, Vol. 5, Nr. 2, 57-63, and Nr. 3, 129-135.

Author Index

Achte 175
Allers 51, 64, 79
Armstrong 252, 254
Astrup 176, 211, 212, 213

Bakis 198
Bally 32, 242
Balzac 20
Bänziger 242
Bergen 302
Berner 285
Bernstein 198
Bhaskaran 269, 271
Bibering 200
Binder 7
Binswanger 38, 242
Bohannan 229
Boss 242
Bovi 103
Bowlby 291
Brengelmann 3
Brun 8, 242
Burlingham 26, 67

Cade 257, 260
Calwell 252, 255
Cameron 197
Caravedo 269
Chaney 148
Chapman 191
Chopra 271
Ciannanni 36
Clark 209, 210
Cohen 198
Collis 192
Curle 235

Dalgard 175, 176
Dana 301, 303, 306
David 104
Delacroix 32
Deutsch 296
Diarra 121
Dobbins 113

Doczy 255
Dube 271
Dunham 205, 207, 210, 217

Eatherly 35
Eisenhower 39
Eitinger 11, 174, 178, 193, 213
Erikson 298
Errico 42, 149

Faris 205, 207, 210, 217
Fenichel 23
Flicker 148
Fodor 23
Fraser 269
Freud, A. 26, 67, 291, 298, 301, 303, 304, 306
Freud, S. 302
Frost 37, 148

Ganguli 269
Geisler 38
Glatt 258
Goethe 30
Göring 29
Goldlust 267
Grauer 291
Gronvik 185
Gross 32
Grünfeld 174
Guttman 111, 114

Haegi 38
Halevi 174, 215
Hall 26, 103
Haller 20
Hallows 254
Handlin 113
Hanna 148
Hansen 185
Hartmann 302
Haspel 20
Hediger 10, 14, 79
Heideger 29

Helgason 175
Helpach 28
Herzog 185
Hesse 79, 222
Hill 185
Hitler 36
Hoferus 19
Hoff 289
Hoffmeier 198
Hollingshead 104
Homburger 37
Hübner 27
Hunt 203
Hunter 39

Isaaks 26
Ivanow-Smolensky 8

Jaco 175
Jacobson 297, 305
Jaspers 20, 21, 65, 148
Johnson 28, 36
Johnston 256
Judge 258
Jung 21, 79, 192, 242, 251
Jungk 35

Kaila 213
Karlsson 175
Kennedy 27
Kinkead 39
Kino 60
Kleiner 230, 272
Klemm 20
Kolle 187, 189
Kornrumpf 193
Knigge 64
Kraepelin 1, 51, 57, 163, 196
Kretschmer 8, 38, 159
Kristal 19
Krupinski 216, 252, 256, 257, 260, 267

Lange 103
Langfeldt 198
Larouse 20
Laurent 20
Lavin 40
Lazarus 175, 206, 269
Lee 207, 209, 215, 269
Lemert 206, 217
Lemke 33, 38, 149
Levy-Brühl 90
Lifton 39
Lilly 197
Linbarger 37

Lindt 282
Lippert 26
Locke 206, 269
Lonnum 185
Ludowyk-Gyomroi 3, 291

MacCann 26
Mäder 242
Malzberg 2, 104, 155, 174, 175, 204, 209, 210, 215, 221, 222, 226, 269
McCann 29
Meerloo 39
Melsom 169
Menninger 40
Menzies 252
Merton 285
Morgenstern 52
Moser 26
Müller-Fahlbosch 103
Müller-Hegemann 11, 103
Murphy 113, 193, 194, 204, 219, 221, 272

Napoleon 20
Niederland 88
Nikolini 23
Nixon 46

Ødegaard 2, 104, 155, 161, 204, 212, 213, 269

Parker 230, 273
Pavlov 8
Peiper 26, 42
Percy 20
Peters 21
Pfister-Ammende 7, 73, 104, 113, 194, 200, 241, 246, 251, 283, 289, 312
Piers 305
Pinegar 282
Price 256
Proust 32

Redlich 104
Regnier 40
Reich 297
Revenstorff 3
Rodriguez 134
Rooth 253, 255
Rose 26, 29
Rosenblatt 298

Author Index

Rousseau 20
Ruffin 103

Sandler 298, 307
Saenger 114
Sartre 43
Schaechter 260
Schein 39
Scheuchzer 20
Schiller 20
Schneider 64, 187
Schopenhauer 32
Schwab 26, 42, 149
Schwind 27
Seth 269
Sethi 271
Silone 95
Singer 305
Snedden 253
Spielrein 32
Spitz 302
Srole 174
Stenbäck 175
Sterba 23
Stoller 216, 252, 255, 256, 257, 267
Stouffer 115
Strauss 188
Strotzka 282, 284, 289
Sunier 215

Taft 113, 255, 267
Thomas 206, 269, 271
Tolstoi 101
Trüb 242
Tyhurst 113, 200

Valdivia 269
Varney 29
Venzlaff 189
Vernon 26
Vis 115
Vischer 8

Weil 297
Weinberg 110
Weiss 148
Wittson 40
Wolff 186, 191
Wulff 198

Yadav 269

Zaugg 245
Zborowsky 185
Zubrzycki 254
Zwingmann 3, 9, 19, 21, 46, 142, 291

Subject Index

ability to take on responsibility 250
achievement discrepancy 272
accidents 122
accommodation 125
acculturation 256, 275, 318
acculturation factors: language, behavior, religious ideas, moral values, political values 256
adaptation, to an abnormal environment 255, 310
adjustment 14
, difficulties 134
, to change 113
administrative measures 15
admission rates, lowest 174
adolescence 294
, uprooting during 76
adolescent love 310
adolescents, Hungarian 289
advice, psychological 238
advisor 309
affect-constellation, absolutistic and monopolistic 26
affection 309
Africa 213
African countries 2
African tribe 312
African workers South of Sahara 122
Agadir 29
aggression 38, 53
, objectless 297
aggressiveness 8, 12, 250
alcohol 88
alcoholics, chronic 289
alcoholism 91, 209, 258
Algerian workers in France 124
alibi 89
alienating 246
alienation 236
Alsatians 9
ambivalence 250
American Friends Service Committee (A.F.S.C.) 2
American troops in Korea 27

amnesia 300
, infantile 300
anal drive 303
analysis, end of 309
analyst 298
Anglo-Protestant establishment 226
anonymity 248
anthropologists 318
anxiety 299
anxiety phenomena 188
Apartheid 308
apathy 8, 274, 282
aptitude tests, vocational 238
Arabian apprentices 145
Arabs 2
archetop 10, 14, 79, 93
army 235, 237
army officers 249
arrival, pschiatric illness prior to 260
arteriosclerotic psychosis 219
Asia 213
aspiration-achievement discrepancy 273
aspiring to a higher social status 273
assessment, reality 309
assimilation, criteria of 256
, external 256
, forced 255
, migrants 255
, new immigrants 119
, studies of 255
, subjective 256
Assyrians 284
asylum, countries of first 289
atom bomb 29, 35, 47
attitude, domineering 249
, towards immigrants 266
Auschwitz 98, 187, 292
Australia 2, 229, 252
, granted naturalization 256
, immigration policy in 1945 252
, non-British immigrants 216
, origin of immigrant population 254
, origin of migrants 253

350

Subject Index

, priority immigration program   254
Austria   204
authorities, local   283
, national and international   282
authority, internal   304
autoerotic activity   304
avoidance reactions   8

baby language   293
Baltic countries   267
Baltic dwellers   284
Baltimore   205
barbed-wire illness   8
bed wetting   305
behavior patterns, statistical analysis   240
belonging, feeling of   16
Bergen-Belsen Camp   192
Bewegungssturm   8
Bielorussia   267
biotop   10, 14, 79, 93
bitterness   242
blindness   199
Bodelschwingsche Anstalten in Bielefeld, Beckhof   288
borderline cases   163
brain drain   2
brainwashing   39
breakdown, early   261
Britain   213, 254
British soldiers, readjustment   235

California   175, 206
Calmucs   284
Canada   2, 204, 215, 221, 229
, attitude towards ethnic minorities   218
, French-Canadian influence   218
, immigrants to   221
, Italians and Dutch in   216
Canadian Department of Citizenship and Immigration   215
Canadians   316
capitalist class societies   25
cases, difficult   249
case-findings   176, 284
case identification   284
case histories   179
castration   305
cathexis   298
Catholics   198
change   310
, mental health problems   320
changing values   255
character disorders   209
Chicago   207

childhood background   181
children   319
, Italian and Spanish in Switzerland   134
, Russian immigrants of the First World War   95
China, People's Republic of   107
Chinese, importance of group membership   218
Christian-bourgeois manipulators   36
Christian practice, dealing with the enemy   40
Christian Puritan   43
Christianity, homicidal ethics   24
C.T.A.   25
Civil Resettlement Units (C.R.U.)   235
civilian life   237
climate   316
clinging   297
clubs: social, recreational, and athletic   275
cold-war   36
collaborationists attitude in Germany   89
collective reaction   90
colonial repression   26
comfort supplier   306
commitment to an idea   9
communication, difficulties in   274
Communists, hatred of   40
community   238, 250
, international   283
, local   248
, migrating, special requirements of   319
, protective   288
, therapeutic   287
, traditional behavior   239
community organizations: parish congregations, youth groups, sport clubs   249
competition, spirit of   314
compliance   297
complications, national, international   283
comradeship   10, 76
concentration camp survivors in Norway and Israel   178
concentration camp syndrome   185
concentration camp victim, analysis of   291
concentration camps, Nazi   266
concept of the self   297, 298
conditioning, products of   23
confinement   15
consistency   237
constitution, schizothymic   159
consultation   283
consumption, of delusions   35

contact, lack of 76
, with the local population, absence of 274
continuity of care 289
contributions, matched 285
control groups 180
control materials 176
cooperation 314
co-operativeness 239
cosmopolitanism 213
counseling, of personnel 245
counselors 284
cover memory 301
creativity 239
cultural group 29
cultural rooms 248
cultural setting 220
cultural values 218
culture, Filipino 230
culture conflict 207, 217
Cyprus 187
Czechoslovakia 178, 267, 308

Danes 213
darkness 247
dead mother, merging with 299
death wishes 300
decision-sharing on top level 250
decline in standards 250
deep-rooted changes 188
dejection 309
delinquency 235
delusions, acoustic 56
dementia praecox 163
demography 161
denial 294
Denmark 165, 173
dependency 294
, economic 198
dependency feelings 218
dependency upon surroundings 79
depression 8, 31
, reactive 41, 231
, resulting from uprooting 103
, stuporous 15
depression uprooting (Entwurzelungsdepressionen) 188
depressive moodiness 188
development, libido 302, 303
, missed 306
diagnostic category 209
diagnostic survey 285
dialectic-material premises 44
discussion evenings 248
differentiation, of inside and outside 298
, of self and not-self 298

difficulties, language 65, 79, 97
, first starting 202
, in large establishments 97
, psychosomatic 37
, within the person of leadership himself 98
direct operations 285
directives, for camps 244
diseases, infectious 191
, organic, brain 186
, psychosomatic 195
disintegration, community 185
, social 283
disorders, acute confusional 217
, arteriosclerotic 231
, personality and behavior 259
, psychosomatic 235
, senile, brain 258
displaced persons 174, 284
displaced persons' camps, in Australia 253
, in Switzerland 214
distortion, retrospective 33
distrust 242
disturbances, consciousness 200
, situational trait 260
disturbed sleep 188
doctors 249
dreams 11
drift hypothesis 272
drifting individuals 12
drive, infantile 300
drug addicts 44
drug-taking 209

ecology 161
economic problems 268
education 207, 319
efforts, metaphysical revival 46
egocentricity 14, 37
ego development 302
ego endowment 302
ego-gratification 26
ego ideal 304
, incomplete formation 14
, insufficient development 14
ego potential, constitutionally determined 310
electro- and pneumoencephalography 179
eligibility 282
emigrant 14
emigrants, from Europe 314
emigration 195
, age 14
, mental health 155
, overseas 165
, program 282
, selective 168

emotional deficiency 302
emotional ties between parents and children 83
employment problems 238
encephalopathy 186
endeavors, social scientific 47
enterprise, spirit of 314
enthusiasm 249
epidemiological research 162
epidemiology 161
escapists 12
ethnic group 209
Europe 214
evacuation, built-in 320
, children's reaction to 67
evolution, social 46
examination, follow-up 163
excitation-inhibition conflict 8
exiles 29
expectation of hatred 297
expectations, minimal 202
experience, war-time 266
exploitation, political, of the nostalgic disposition 35

facet design 115
factors, language 32
failure, of attempts to resettle migrants 314
families, breaking up of 319
, belonging to 309
family, protective function 185
family cohesion 185
famine edema 191
fantasy mother 299
father, substitutes 304, 310
faulty childhood development 14
fear of time lapse 30
Federal Republic of Germany 36
feeling of belonging 12
, of security 300
feelings of persecution 94
, of solidarity 90
Finland 175, 213
first admissions to mental hospitals 206, 224
first priority 250
flight 7
flight psychosis 10
flight reactions 8
follow-up 320
food, preference for 151
food habits 256
foreign student 41
foreign workers 3

former internalized object representations 306
France 2, 320
freedom, academic, and Christian morality 46
French Canada 218
friendships 307
frustration tolerance 37
functional psychosis 219
funds and facilities, availability 283
futurology 47

Gaustad State Hospital in Norway 155, 162
Geneva, Switzerland 134
German Democratic Republic 36
Germany 142, 178, 284
give-up-itis 39
god-delusions 44
Greece 254, 284
Griesinger Hospital in Berlin 106
group, self-contained 317
group discussions 238
group memberships 210, 218
groups, need of leadership 10
guidance 247
guilt feelings 185, 305
Guttman's scale analysis 115

hallucinations 55
, auditory 63
, visual 63
hard core 282
hard-core cases, employment service for 246
Heimat 14, 17
Heimweh 19
Helsinki 175
Hiroshima 29, 35
homes 288
, with care 288
homesick 78
homesickness 9, 19, 53, 58, 61, 70, 142, 274
homesickness psychosis 37
homesickness ulcer 38
hopelessness 300
, chronic state of 189
hospitalization data 204
hospitals, military 51
Hungary 178, 267
hygiene, mental 101, 241
hypersensitivity 56, 250
hypocrisy 33
hypothesis, environmental 168

ICEM 289
ideal of collectivity, American 314
idealization 294
identification 256, 294
, loss of 13
, with mother 301
, with the analyst 307
identities, confusion of 296
identify 298
image, cover 301
images and representations 298
imitation 294, 296
, of external objects 306
immigrant adolescent, higher incidence of behavior disorders 257
immigrant families, disintegration of 264
immigrants 224
, Australian, Dutch, German, Italian 216
, Canada 221
, discrepancy between the older generation 256
, elderly 260
, from Europe 214
, from Holland 112
, hospitalization rates 223
, Jewish 213
, North Africa 213
, second generation 257, 259
, third generation 317
, United States 228
, voluntary, to Israel 113
immigration, Australia, mental health aspects 252
Canadian 216
Imprisonment psychoses 57, 59
inability, to fulfill conflicting role expectations 272
, to live in a normal way 191
incidence, hospitalized 214
, of mental disorders 260
, relative indices of 264
independence 218, 294
independence training 42
India 269
indication, of assimilation 255
indices, psychiatric disorders in migrants 261
individualism 45
individuality 218
individuals, old 43
, seriously and chronically sick 29
, symptom-free 189
industry, migration 269
inferiority, organic 199
information 238
, inadequate and unrealistic 314

, milieu, education 230
insanity, manic-depressive 159
insecurity, feeling of 118, 197, 199, 200, 302
, projection of 197
in-service training 287
instability, emotional 37
institutionalized children 304
integration, and language attainment 267
, failure rate of 289
, into the host countries 282
, of migrants 255
, peaceful co-existence 316
intelligence 111
interaction 255
, social 256
inter-family contact 248
intermarriage 256
internal guidance 306
internment psychosis 8
interpretating analytic material 296
interpretation, wrong, and positive development 298
interrogations, effect of 191
intimacy 15
introjection 307
investigations, epidemiological 165
, extensive and intensive 176
involution, incipient 107
Iran 3
Irish, ratio of immigrant 210, 226
isolation 78, 196, 207, 247
, linguistic 53, 197
, national 197
, of the non-assimilated mother 264
, social 197
, stigma of 288
Israel 9, 110, 174, 213, 307, 317
, concentration camps survivors 178
, statistical abstract 214
Italians 10, 79, 320
Italy 254, 284

Jerusalem, Talbieh Hospital 189
Jewish citizens of the Soviet Union 36
Jewish people 11
Jewish refugees, schizophrenia 267
Jewish, shame of being 295, 308
Jewry, East European 220
Jews 198
job dissatisfaction, reasons for 277
job rehearsals 238

kibbutzim 180
knowledge of English 256

Subject Index

Korea 320
, U.S. involvement 39

labor-camps, forced 15
, German 63
laborers, forced 179
lack of confidence 287
lack of stimuli 197
landscape 316
language 317
language classes 275
language courses, crash 268
language laboratories 268
Laos, terrorist activities 2
latency 293
legislation, restrictive 177
leisure activities 256
lethargy 248
liaison 283
liaison officers 318
, teams 318
libido 298
living corps stage 184
local-patriotic, ethnocentric training 27
Locarno 320
London, children during World War Two 67
loss of the object 302
loss of weight 184
love, being in 307
, capacity for 16

majority, pressures to conform to the 228
Mali 121
malnutrition 191
Manana-culture 314
marginal cases 203
marital status 207
mass anxiety 8
mass apathy followed by death 39
mass psychosis 8
mass reactions 91, 94, 247
masturbation 308
maturation 302
maturity 250
, reaching 306
Mauritania 121
Mauthausen 187
Max-Planck-Institute for Psychiatric Research in Munich 3
medicine, social and preventive 251
melting pot policy, Australia 218
, theory 228, 255
memories 296
, cover 300
, recovery of 300
, repressed 300

Menschheitsbewusstsein 16
mental defectives 230
mental diseases, refugees 179
mental disorders, minimum prevalence figure of 284
, statistical investigations of 161
mental disturbance, risk of 230
mental disturbances, prognosis and treatment of 290
mental health, chosen goals 230
, emigration 155
, indices of 229
, migration 229
, social changes 229
mental health advisor 283
mental health services 242
mental health specialist 245
mental hospital, admissions 222
mental hospitalization, immigrants 221
, rates of 221, 227
mental hygiene 101, 320
, community level 241
mental ill health, in the immigrant community 257
Michigan, Newberry Hospital 207
, rural 217
microcosmos, American 40
, Christian-bourgeois 24, 142
, idealistic superstitious substratum of the 34
middle-class women 10
Middle East and Asia, refugees and aggression 2
midtown Manhattan study 175
migrant adults and their children, upward mobility of 268
migrant patients, economic conditions 266
, housing conditions 266
, social class status of 264
migrant welfare officers 275
migrant welfare organizations 314
migrants, adolescent 264
, hundred percent 177
, incidence of mental disease 113
, influence on the economic growth 253
, internal 204
, prejudice and superstitions 177
, protective role of family life for 263
, rural Canada 223
, self-selected 174
, unaccompanied 262
, voluntary 255
migration 228
, active preparation 318

, associated with beginning
       industralization and
       urbanization   177
, cities to rural districts   169
, group   316
, internal   210
, inward   213
, major mental disorders   204
, major mental illness   269
, mental ill-health in industry   269
, mental illness prior to   260
, phase of action   318
, planning   318
, post war   252
, selective   111
, short distance   169
, stress hypothesis   273
, voluntary, mental health aspects
       of   110
migrational experience   204
military person, marginal psychiatric
       cases   203
military service   244
Minnesota, Norwegian born   155, 166
, state hospitals   167
minority status   224, 230
, mental hospitalization rates   226
misinterpretation of sensory
       impressions   197
moral behavior   7
morbidity, migrants   171
mother, fantasy   305
, isolated   256
, need for re-creating a   300
mother-infant situation   299
mother relationship, missing   294
mother substitute   298
mothers   261
motivation, positive   195
, towards language attainment   268
motivations   176
, economic, physical, professional,
       psychological, religious, social   1
mourning, a form of nostalgic reaction   27
movement, protest   44
moves, family, to foreign countries   29

Nagasaki   29
narcissism   250
narcissistic need   307
native-born hospitalization rates   223
native language, use of   257
naturalization   256
Near East   213
need for power   243
needs, religious   314

need satisfaction   297
Negro   209, 213
neighbor help   248
Netherlands   2
neurosis   209, 267
neuroses   230
, anxiety   200
, causal factors of   186
, compulsion   200
, conversion   200
New York   175, 205
New Zealand   3
nomads   312
non-association hypothesis   272
Norges offisielle statistikk, mental
       hospitals   162
North Africans   122, 177
Norway   161, 174, 178, 211
, and U.S., difference between   212
, emigration   161
, immigration, internal   161
, mental diseases   168
, mental diseases among
       refugees   179
, receiving situation   213
, re-emigration   161
Norwegian born of Minnesota   155
nostalgia   9, 19, 37
, for war experiences   35
nostalgic activity, an opium for the
       people   45
nostalgic disposition   23, 34
nostalgic fixation   37
nostalgic illusion   32, 147
nostalgic phenomenon, definition of   23
, exploitation   9, 19
, foreign workers in West
       Germany   142
, release factors and manipulation
       of   33
nostalgic wish image   23
nostalgization   25, 34
Nürnberger Nachrichten   42, 149
nurse   246

obedience   297
object of identification   296
object constancy   302
object relations   296
occupation   207
, of subjects   182
occupational therapy   238
oedipal experiences   300
oedipal relationships   306
oedipus complex   306
officers, Soviet liaison   81

Subject Index

Ohio   175, 206
oppression, social   168
oral fixation   303
order of the blankets   243
orderliness   82
organic brain lesion   15
organic brain syndrome   198
organization, as an end in itself   248
organizational geniuses   249
organizations, social welfare   318
Oslo   179, 211
overdependency, affective   38
over-flowing of stimuli   197
overprotective, danger of becoming   289

pacifists, Christian-bourgeois   46
Palestine   2, 111, 187
paradox, nostalgic   33
paranoid affect storm   64
paranoid reaction   59
paranoid state   271
paranoid trends   297
Paris region   213
participation   237
participation mystique   12, 15
pathogenetic factors   200
pathological behavior   294
pathology   37
   , motherless children   310
patients, Polish in Britain   60
Pavlov system   39
penis envy   305
people, old   29
People's Republic of China, U.S. prisoners of War   39
permissiveness   237
persecution, delusions of   55
Persönlichkeitswandel, erlebnisbedingter   189
personal sphere   17
personal value crisis with nostalgic consequence   31
personality, breakdown of the total   197
   , development   295
   , integration of   302
   , irreversible   190
   , schizoid   168
   , syntonic   168
pessimism   282
phallic phase   304
phenomena, anticlimax   32
physicists, nuclear   46
physiological homesickness   20
planning, for mental health needs of a select population   272
pleasure principal   14

Poland   178, 308
Poles   79
policemen   249
Polish army corps   63
Polish dwellers   284
Polish refugees   217
political tutelage   33
politicians, Christian-bourgeois   33
Pope   35
possessiveness of the mother   68
practice, diagnostic, Norway   164
premorbid personality   183
   , significance of   190
preoccupations, suicidal   63
preoedipal experiences   300
press, local   249
prevalence, hospitalized   214
prevalence rate, of psychiatric and psychosomatic illness   271
prevention   42, 119
   , of mental ill-health   241
   , primary   242
   , secondary   246
primary aim, of research   177
prison camp   236
   , American, in China   39
   , democratic culture   240
prisoner-of-war camp   195
prisoners   301
   , escaped war   77
   , for life   29
   , of war   8, 73, 283
   , of war, Russian   54
privacy   248
problem of nature and nurture   177
Problematiker   13
prognosis, attempted   201
projection of lack of relationship   297
projecting, own conflict and faults   98
prophecy, self fulfilling   285
protective big brother   292
protective male   304
protective therapy   250
protest, by young people who rebel against the nostalgic appeal   33
Protestants   198
pseudo-rootedness   12
psychiatric assistance   201
psychiatric casework   283, 285
psychiatric compensation problems   188
psychiatric diagnosis   171
   , uncertainty   163
psychiatric experts   201
psychiatric hospitals, admission   283
   , admission statistics   162
psychiatric interview   180
psychiatric social workers   287

psychiatric survey 283
psychiatrists 231
  , in industrial establishments 275
  , social 283
  , Swiss 242
psychiatry 161
  , American military 40
  , social 177, 285
psychic-pathology 269
psychoanalysis 13, 39
  , concentration camp victim 291
psychoanalytic interpretation 23
psychogenic diseases 302
psychologists, clinical 246
  , social 318
psychoneuroses 260, 269
psycho-neurotics 12
psychopathic grumblers 97
psychopaths 186
psychoses 215, 269
psychoses, arteriosclerotic 167
  , chronic reactive 191
  , in idiots and imbeciles 198
  , of the deaf 196
  , organic 167
  , reactive 196, 198
  , senile 167
  , senile and arteriosclerotic 158
psychosis, manic-depressive 168, 198
psychosyndrome, organic 187, 190
Psychotherapeutic Training Institute of the University of Zurich 242
psychotherapy 188, 247, 251
  , group 289
  , individual 289
public administration 250
public health officers 166
Puerto-Ricans 177, 314
punishment 245

questionnaire 180

race 209
ranz-des-vaches 20
Raron 77
rates of first admission 225
ratios of immigrants to native-born 225
reaction potentials 23
reactions, jealousy 200
  , primitive 200
reactive psychosis 163
readaptation 2, 306
reality, building a new concept of 310
  , relation to 301
reality testing 303
reasons for job-dissatisfaction 273

reasons for migration 272
receiving population 210
reception 244, 249, 319
re-emigration, selective 169
reference, shared frame of 255
refugee, country of asylum 15
refugee camps 241
  , administration 242
  , atmosphere 15
  , clearance 282
  , clergy 249
  , factors in shaping life in a camp 247
  , leaders 16, 244
  , life 11
  , mental hygiene 241
  , personnel 242
  , requirements for leaders 249
  , schools 249
  , staffs 81
refugee organizations 201, 283
refugee policy 15, 16
refugees 36, 282, 320
  , administrative problems 96
  , attitudes toward rules and regulations 88
  , hard-core 179, 201
  , Hungarian 283
  , isolated 197
  , Jewish 112, 267
  , mass behavior 94
  , Middle and Western European 92
  , of the Soviet Union in Switzerland during World War Two 73
  , political 177
  , post-war Norway 178
  , problem of alcohol 87
  , relationship to the staff 99
  , rehabilitation 283
  , sexual drives 85
  , Soviet Union, and local (Swiss) population 90, 100
  , threshold of tolerance 196
regression 308
  , to the preverbal stage 299
regulations 245
rehabilitation 235, 283
  , inter-country 289
  , predictions with respect to 290
rehabilitation workshops 287
rejecting partner 294
relationships, object 301
relationship with internment, causal 186
relief funds, American 69
relief organizations 196
relief program 282
religion 317

religious healer   320
repatriates   2
        , of Swiss nationality   241
repatriation   282
representation, self-   298
repression   33, 44, 300
research, further   275
        , health risks   177
        , interdisciplinary   47
        , large scale, funds allocated for   3
        , psychiatric   164
        , recent   174
resentments   98
resettlement   282
        , as a sociological problem   312
        , prisoners of war   235
resettlers in the German Democratic
    Republic   105
residence   205
resignation   247
resistance, lack of active   185
        , in the local community   249
        , to oppression   185
responsibility   244
        , sense of   16
restlessness   76
retardation, mental   258
revolution, permanent cultural   44
rivalry   308
Rochester, State Hospital at   155
rootlessness, different aspects of   13
root-taking-period   199
Rorschach-test   10
Russia   267
Russian spokesmen   81
Russian women   10, 78

satisfaction of emotional needs   297
schizoid thinking   168
schizophrenia   158, 163, 196, 206, 228,
    231, 258, 271
        , migration   221, 224
        , period-prevalence   259
        , point-prevalence   259
school education   181
schools, local   249
science, definition of   46
scientists, social   231
screening of applicants for emigration   201
search, reckless scientific   47
seasonal workers   3
security, feeling of   16, 310
        , inner   118
Seelengefüge   15
selection   179, 181

self- and object representations,
    development of   298
self-centered   13
self-concept, wishful   305
self-esteem, lack of   305
self-representation   299
Seminar, Groupwork-   287
seminars   287
Senegal   3, 121
sense, of humor   245
        , of reality   303
separation   240, 294
        , expectation   297
        , factors   28, 29
        , fear of change   19
        , spatial   28
        , temporal   30
separation anxiety   297
service, after-care   289
        , follow-up   289
        , mental health   73
settlement policy   15
sex   207
sex play   307
sexuality, infantile   300
shame   305
shirking of responsibility   250
shock   318
Singapore, Chinese   229
        , investigation   216
slavery   190
sleeplessness   76
slogans, military and political   40
slow execution   190
sobranje   93
social acceptance   275
social adaptation of married women   202
social change   231
        , mental reactions to   229
social class   171, 207
social isolation   274
social level, identification with   12
social medicine   287
social prognosis   284
social psychiatry   2
        , preventive   177
social selection   166
social stress   166
social workers   246
socialistic societies   31, 44
society, pluralistic   255
        , receiving   230
sociological problems   312
socio-medical guidance   250
socio-prophylaxis   119
Socio-Psychopathological Research,
    immigrants from Holland to Palestine   115

soldiers, in combat   29
solidarity, among African workers in France   127
somatic disorders   200
somatic illnesses, incidence of   184
somatic preoccupation   200
Soviet citizens, displaced, in Switzerland   73
special cases   284
special teachers   246
Spiegel   19
state, depressive   53
, of elemental panic and confusion   63
states, confusional   187
, depressive   259
, reactive-depressive   78
status, loss of   265
story telling   295, 298
stress, associated with migration   272
, associated with status inconsistencies   176
, influence of mental   185
stress situation, cumulative   185
stresses   204
studies, Finnish   213
subculture   224, 228
, hospitalization rates   227
sublimation   309
submission, compulsory and passive   315
substitute   298
substituting oedipal objects   304
Sudan   177
suicide   219
Sunday neurosis   32
superego   304, 305
super-ego control   7
supervision   287
surveys, mental health   205
Sweden   165, 173
Swedes   213
Swiss Academy of Medical Sciences   74
Swiss disease   20
Swiss Federal Administration   73, 241
Swiss mercenaries   19
Swiss National Exhibition   315
Swiss relationship with Germans   315
Swiss repatriates   241
, returning   9
Switzerland   7, 73, 312, 315
, camps in   241
, cemetary   319
symptoms, conversion   200
, persecutory paranoid   199
, psychotic   107
Szu Hsiang Kai Taso   39

Tartar   55
teams, public health officers, mental health workers, anthropologists, social workers   320
teamwork, at the top administrative level   245
teachers, local   249
tests, psychological   179
Texas   175, 205
themes, administrative   81
, psychological   81
therapeutic action   285
therapies, social and milieu   285
therapy, most effective agents of   238
Thereszin   296
ties, to the native soil   90
time factor   319
toilet training   303
tolerance, of cultural differences   255
, repressive   45
total irritation   10
training   283
, and education of personnel   242
, in group work   250
training courses   244
transference, atypical evolution of   310
traits, personality, pre-psychotic   168
transference   299
transitional communities and social reconnection   235
transplantation   14, 314
trauma   302
, chronic psychic   186
traumatic effects   191
traumatic neurosis   8
traumatization, psychological by internment of young people   191
, schizophrenia by internment of young people   191
treatment   119, 283, 299
, outpatient   287
, and rehabilitation   246
trust   99
, between the authorities and the internees   77
tuberculosis   38

Ukraine   267
Ukrainians   14, 284
Ulpan   115
uncertainty   319
unconscious, interpretation of   300
unconscious hope   308
underpriveledged class   31
unemployment   168

Subject Index

United Kingdom   2, 60, 67, 287, 291
United Nations High Commissioner for
   Refugees   283
United States   2
   , Norwegian immigrants   212
United States Defense Department   39
United States Department of the Army   39
University Psychiatric Clinic   179
unsettlement   235
uprooting   74, 82, 85, 98, 195, 235, 246,
   312, 316
   , as a sociological problem   312
   , by technical and industrial
      development   312
   , problems of   7
   , relationship of one with
      others   238
   , serious mental disturbances   108
U.S.A.   235, 287

value systems, difference in   314
variables   207, 209
   , mental hospitalization rates   205
Verkehrspsychosen   196
Vermassung   247
Vienna   58
Vietnam   2
violation of laws   88
vital statistics   165
vocational training   268

war, significance for children   67
Weichenstellung, für das weitere
   Leben   246

welfare agencies   282
welfare authorities   250
welfare officers   237
welfare services   203
Werner-Reimers Research Foundation   3
white Australian policy   268
widowhood   207
wishful thinking   294
withdrawal   294, 299
   , social   287
women   176, 249
   , married   201
   , Russian   10, 78
   , single, patients   173
work, industrial   121
workers, alien   73
   , foreign   38, 77
   , foreign, in West-Germany   142
   , from Africa in France   121
   , social   196, 318
workshops, sheltered   287
World Health Organization   3, 283
World Refugee Year   283

Yellow Star movement   308
Yemen   174
youth sects, lunatic   44
Yugoslavia   267
Yugoslavians   76, 79

Zionists   9